Clinical Fictions

Clinical Fictions: Psychoanalytic Novelists and Short Story Writers is the first book to explore works of fiction written by prominent psychoanalysts.

Broken down into thematic sections, the book traces the literary output of pioneering psychoanalysts such as Julia Kristeva, Bruce Fink, Thomas Odgen, and Gregorio Kohon, among others. Berman looks at works of historical fiction, detective fiction, and the short story, and shows how recurring themes typical of these genres can be understood both psychoanalytically and through a literary lens. The works included investigate experiences of childhood adversity, life in dystopian societies, experiences of psychosis, bodily autonomy, personal loss and, above all, trauma. Unpacking these themes, and their depiction through fiction, Berman gives the reader the tools to apply psychoanalytic literary theory to further works. Interweaving his personal correspondence with authors, including a heart-warming exchange with Cliff Wilkerson, Berman offers unparalleled access to the inner workings of the writers' minds.

This book will be of interest to students and researchers using psychoanalytic literary theory, as well as mental health practitioners who are interested in the intersections between literature and psychoanalysis and discovering new ways of probing the unspoken and unconscious.

Jeffrey Berman is Distinguished Teaching Professor at the University at Albany, USA. He is the author of over 20 books, including *Death Education in the Writing Classroom* (2012).

Clinical Fictions

Psychoanalytic Novelists and
Short Story Writers

Jeffrey Berman

LONDON AND NEW YORK

Also by Jeffrey Berman

Joseph Conrad: Writing as Rescue

The Talking Cure: Literary Representations of Psychoanalysis

Narcissism and the Novel

Diaries to an English Professor: Pain and Growth in the Classroom

Surviving Literary Suicide

Risky Writing: Self-Disclosure and Self-Transformation in the Classroom

Empathic Teaching: Education for Life

Dying to Teach: A Memoir of Love, Loss, and Learning

Cutting and the Pedagogy of Self-Disclosure (with Patricia Hatch Wallace)

Death in the Classroom: Writing about Love and Loss

Companionship in Grief: Love and Loss in the Memoirs of C.S. Lewis, John Bayley, Donald Hall, Joan Didion, and Calvin Trillin

Death Education in the Writing Classroom

Dying in Character: Memoirs on the End of Life

Confidentiality and Its Discontents: Dilemmas of Privacy in Psychotherapy (with Paul W. Mosher)

Writing Widowhood: The Landscapes of Bereavement

Writing the Talking Cure: Irvin D. Yalom and the Literature of Psychotherapy

Off the Tracks: Cautionary Tales about the Derailing of Mental Health Care (with Paul W. Mosher).

Mad Muse: The Mental Illness Memoir in a Writer's Life and Work

The Art of Caregiving in Fiction, Film, and Memoir

Norman N. Holland: The Dean of American Psychoanalytic Literary Critics

Psychoanalytic Memoirs

Psychoanalysis: An Interdisciplinary Retrospective

Freudians and Schadenfreudians: Loving and Hating Psychoanalysis

Fiction as Resistance: Samuel Shem's Writings

Designed cover image: Getty © SklepSpozywczy

First published 2026
by Routledge
4 Park Square, Milton Park, Abingdon, Oxon OX14 4RN

and by Routledge
605 Third Avenue, New York, NY 10158

Routledge is an imprint of the Taylor & Francis Group, an informa business

© 2026 Jeffrey Berman

The right of Jeffrey Berman to be identified as author of this work has been asserted in accordance with sections 77 and 78 of the Copyright, Designs and Patents Act 1988.

All rights reserved. No part of this book may be reprinted or reproduced or utilized in any form or by any electronic, mechanical, or other means, now known or hereafter invented, including photocopying and recording, or in any information storage or retrieval system, without permission in writing from the publishers.

Trademark notice: Product or corporate names may be trademarks or registered trademarks, and are used only for identification and explanation without intent to infringe.

British Library Cataloguing-in-Publication Data
A catalogue record for this book is available from the British Library

Library of Congress Cataloging-in-Publication Data
Names: Berman, Jeffrey, 1945– author
Title: Clinical fictions : psychoanalytic novelists and short story writers / Jeffrey Berman.
Description: London ; New York : Routledge, 2026. |
Includes bibliographical references and index. |
Identifiers: LCCN 2025005237 (print) | LCCN 2025005238 (ebook) |
ISBN 9781041034629 hardback | ISBN 9781041034513 paperback |
ISBN 9781003623908 ebook
Subjects: LCSH: Fiction–20th century–History and criticism |
Fiction–21st century–History and criticism | Psychoanalysts as authors |
LCGFT: Literary criticism
Classification: LCC PN3503 .B4355 2026 (print) | LCC PN3503 (ebook) |
DDC 809.304–dc23/eng/20250501
LC record available at https://lccn.loc.gov/2025005237
LC ebook record available at https://lccn.loc.gov/2025005238

ISBN: 978-1-041-03462-9 (hbk)
ISBN: 978-1-041-03451-3 (pbk)
ISBN: 978-1-003-62390-8 (ebk)

DOI: 10.4324/9781003623908

Typeset in Times New Roman
by Newgen Publishing UK

For Cliff Wilkerson,
A dear cyberspace friend I met while researching this book

Contents

Acknowledgments   *xi*

Introduction   1

PART I
Historical Fiction   **9**

1 Julia Kristeva: *Teresa, My Love: An Imagined Life of the Saint of Avila*   11

2 James Herman Kleiger: *The 11th Inkblot*   27

PART II
Detective Fiction   **39**

3 Jonathan Kellerman: *The Clinic*   41

4 Alan Krohn: *The Mind's Eye*   50

5 Richard P. Kluft: *A Sinister Subtraction*   58

6 Bruce Fink: *The Inspector Canal Novels*   69

PART III
Privileging Fiction Over Psychoanalysis   **79**

7 Gregorio Kohon: *Red Parrot, Wooden Leg*   81

8 Thomas Ogden's Fiction	91
9 Arlene Heyman: *Scary Old Sex* and *Artifact*	102
10 Austin Ratner: *The Jump Artist* and *In the Land of the Living*	116
11 Joan Wexler: *A Pot from Shards* and *Make Me the Sky*	128
12 Cordelia Schmidt-Hellerau: *Memento*	138
13 Cliff Wilkerson: *The Cotton Flower*	148

PART IV
The Jacobs Brothers — **157**

14 Theodore Jacobs: *The Year of Durocher* and *The Way It Ends*	159
15 Daniel Jacobs: *The Distance from Home*	175

PART V
Short Fiction — **187**

16 Merle Molofsky: *Necessary Voices*	189
17 Richard Reichbart: *Curious Stories of Diverse Places*	200
18 Christopher Gibson: *Tales from the Unconscious*	213
19 Irene Cairo: *Inside Out: Intimate Voices*	218
20 Luke Hadge: *Psychoanalytic Stories*	226
21 Other Psychoanalytic Fiction Worth Reading	234
Conclusion	249
Index	*259*

Acknowledgments

Sections of this book first appeared in shorter and slightly different versions in the following journals:

"Daniel Jacobs, *The Distance from Home*." *American Imago*, vol. 76, 2019, pp. 446–453.
"The Novels of Thomas Ogden." *Journal of the American Psychoanalytic Association*, vol. 70, 2022, pp. 1013–1022.
"Psychoanalytic Fiction Writers." *TAP: The American Psychoanalyst*, June 24, 2024. https://tapmagazine.org/all-articles/psychoanalytic-fiction-writers. Accessed March 9, 2025.

As with my other books, I would not have been able to conduct my research without the invaluable help of the entire Interlibrary Loan staff at the University at Albany, where I have been teaching since 1973. Thanks to Timothy Jackson, Angela Persico, and Glen Benedict for fulfilling scores of Interlibrary Loan requests.

I thank the following members of the American Psychoanalytic Association's listserv for calling to my attention several psychoanalytic fiction writers of whom I was unaware: Aisha Abbasi, Lycia Alexander-Guerra, Brenda Bauer, Tim Brady, Dana Brotman, Irene Cairo, David E. Cooper, Ann Eichen, Harvey Falit, Linda Gold, Steven Gotlieb, Luke Hadge, Elizabeth Hamlin, Ruth Imber, Susan S. Levine, Tarpley Long, Kerry Malawista, Leslie Schweitzer Miller, Mark F. Poster, Daniel W. Prezant, Arnold D. Richards, Michael Robbins, Steven S. Rolfe, Fernanda Sofio, Jennifer Stuart, Jane Tillman, Camilla Van Voorhees, Richard Waugaman, and Cliff Wilkerson. I also thank Irene Cairo, Bruce Fink, Luke Hadge, Arlene Heyman, Theodore Jacobs, James Kleiger, Gregorio Kohon, Alan Krohn, Kerry Malawista, Leslie Schweitzer Miller, Merle Molofsky, Thomas Ogden, Austin Ratner, Richard Reichbart, and Cliff Wilkerson for reading and commenting on the chapters I sent them. Special thanks to Ben Doyle, whose friendship and support I have long appreciated, and whose insights have strengthened this book, including selecting the present title. I'm grateful to the entire staff of Routledge for their help and expertise, particularly Zoe Meyer, commissioning editor for psychoanalysis and mental health, and her editorial assistant Deepika Batra. I'm grateful to Tom

Bedford's superb copyediting of the manuscript. I'm especially grateful to Cliff Wilkerson for allowing me to use his remarks in the Conclusion. One of the joys of writing this book was entering the fictional worlds of so many gifted psychoanalytic novelists and short story writers whose work I had not previously known, and then having lively email conversations with them.

As always, I am grateful to my wife, Julie, for her love, support, and technological savvy.

Introduction

"In my mind," Sigmund Freud confided to Wilhelm Stekel as they hiked through the forests of Berchtesgaden, "I always construct novels, using my experiences as a psychoanalyst; my wish is to become a novelist—but not yet; perhaps in the later years of my life" (Stekel 66). Freud never became a novelist, but he confesses ruefully in *Studies on Hysteria* (with Breuer, 1893–1895) that "it still strikes me myself as strange that the case histories I write should read like short stories and that, as one might say, they lack the serious stamp of science" (*SE*, vol. 2, 160). The only major award Freud received during his lifetime was the Goethe Prize for literature in 1930, recognition that he was one of the century's greatest writers.

In my research, I discovered that no one has written a book on psychoanalytic fiction writers, largely because few analysts pen novels and short stories. Gregory D. Graham made a similar observation in 2015. "In a cursory and informal poll of analysts whom I know, I found that these serious readers and educators could not easily recall even ten novels written by trained analysts that had appeared in English in the last few decades" (521). Graham is right: there are surprisingly few analysts who have written novels—more than ten but probably under 100.

In her 1983 memoir *Code Name "Mary,"* Muriel Gardiner offers an explanation of the scarcity of novels and memoirs written by psychoanalysts: most analysts are "inhibited by feelings of privacy" and by their training (xvi). This inhibition, the fear of disclosing too much of the analyst's private life to patients, much less to the public, has, until recently, stifled psychoanalytic fiction writing. In his 1991 essay "Psychiatry and Literature: A Relational Perspective," Samuel Shem, the pen name of the psychiatrist Stephen Bergman, offers other reasons to explain why those in his profession "may be behind the eight ball" if they want to write creative fiction: "the imprisonment by theory, the separation from identification with others, the fracture of the historical/cultural perspective, the nonimaginative purpose, or the healthy participation in real and not transcribed life" (59). And yet reading fiction, and in some cases writing fiction, are required in some psychoanalytic institutes, as Cordelia Schmidt-Hellerau, herself a novelist, points out in *Driven to Survive* (2018):

> When I trained in the 1980s in Switzerland, psychoanalysts were expected to read fiction. Reading fiction engages our imagination; it touches, stirs and works on our unconscious. In similar ways, writing fiction engages fantasy, part of which is always unconscious. Writing fiction strives to reveal, unfold, and free the core of sentences or images that come to the writer's mind, unbidden, arbitrarily, and on their own. If it's a sentence, it needs to be unfolded in an image, a scene. If it's an image, it needs to be elaborated in words. That's precisely how Freud described the process of making the unconscious conscious… Writing fiction is the elaboration of this intimate encounter between what is known and what is implied or hidden, between what is conscious and what is still unconscious. (452)

The role of storytelling—and listening—is central to both literature and psychoanalysis, as is the role of language: what is said and *not* said. Analysts have highlighted the commonalities between writing fiction (or poetry) and psychoanalysis. Salman Akhtar, one of the most prolific contemporary psychoanalysts, has published seven collections of poems. In his edited volume *Between Hours: A Collection of Poetry and Psychoanalysis* (2012), Akhtar's observation that poetry and psychoanalysis bring together reality and unreality is no less true of fiction and psychoanalysis. "Both poetry and psychotherapy attempt to transform the unfathomable into accessible, tormenting into pleasurable, hideous into elegant, and private into shared" (106).

Psychoanalytic novels and short stories raise fascinating questions about the relationship between life and art. Can one tell, from internal textual evidence alone, that the author of a novel or short story is a psychoanalyst? Nietzsche claimed that every philosophy—and every theory—is the confession of its originator, and thus unconscious autobiography. Is the same true of fiction: unconscious autobiography? In reading an analyst's fictional and nonfictional writings, do we see more continuities or discontinuities? If the latter, why?

For analysts who write about the talking cure, what advantages do they gain by fictionalizing the patient–therapist relationship? Why is it easier for "clinicians of despair," as Allen Wheelis sardonically referred to himself in his 1973 meditation *The Moralist* (14), to speak in a fictional voice? For analysts who do *not* write about the talking cure, how does fiction enable them to reveal aspects of themselves they refuse to discuss in a case study?

Most of the authors in this book are psychoanalysts with three exceptions: Jonathan Kellerman is a clinical psychologist; Austin Ratner is a physician-turned-novelist and editor of *TAP: The American Psychoanalyst*; and David Hellerstein is a psychiatrist. Most of the writers have authored books and articles on the theory and practice of psychoanalysis. Whenever possible, I have tried to connect their fictional and nonfictional publications. I have also sought to make connections between their lives and art. Often, analysts choose to write about a traumatic life event, such as early maternal or paternal loss, or the death of a child, or spousal loss, through the veil of fiction rather than in a professional publication. As Picasso said, art is the lie that reveals the truth.

The present book contains a broad representation of psychoanalytic fiction published in English. In earlier books, I have explored other psychoanalytic fiction writers. Discussions of Allen Wheelis's many novels and Christopher Bollas's three novellas and plays appear in my 2023 book *Psychoanalysis: An Interdisciplinary Retrospective*. Irvin Yalom and Stephen Bergman remain, in my view, America's leading psychiatrist-novelists; readers can learn more about their riveting stories in my books *Writing the Talking Cure: Irvin D. Yalom and the Literature of Psychotherapy* (2019) and *Fiction as Resistance: Samuel Shem's Writings* (2024).

The "literary method is still the soundest technique ever devised for investigating human experience," observes David Hellerstein in "Keeping Secrets, Telling Tales: The Psychiatrist as Writer" (1997). "Instinctively we apprehend that one verse by Emily Dickinson contains more truth than a year of *The New England Journal of Medicine*" (133). Hellerstein argues that the psychiatrist and creative writer are engaged in a "dance between selves, between modes of experiencing and transforming the world" (136)—a dance that may be seen in all of the stories in my book, including Hellerstein's novel *Loving Touches*.

The Plan of This Book

Part I focuses on two novels based on historical fiction. Julia Kristeva's *Teresa, My Love* spotlights one of the world's most influential women, a sixteenth-century Carmelite nun whose ecstatic faith and impassioned religious writings continue to inspire countless Christians and non-Christians alike. Saint Teresa's mysticism remains at the core of her existence, and while Kristeva is, like her narrator, Sylvia Leclercq, a disbeliever, the novel affirms the eponymous heroine's fusion with God. In the chapter I discuss why Kristeva turned to fiction, not biography or psychiatric case study, to bring to life one of the world's most complex historical figures. James Herman Kleiger's *The 11th Inkblot* illuminates a Swiss psychiatrist whose name everyone has heard of but whose life remains unknown to most people: Hermann Rorschach. Kleiger imagines an encounter between Rorschach and a tormented patient, Anton Zellinsky, at times mute and catatonic, shortly after the First World War. Carl Jung makes a cameo appearance in the story, believing, incorrectly, that the patient's psychosis has an organic basis. *The 11th Inkblot* is a novel about traumatic loss and recovery, a story as much about time, the art of clockmaking, as it is about the value of verbal therapy.

Detective fiction holds a special relationship to psychoanalysis, as I discuss in Part II. Freud was a fan of Sherlock Holmes, Peter Brooks points out in both *Psychoanalysis and Storytelling* (1994, 49) and *Reading for the Plot* (1984, 270). Freud realized the close analogies between psychoanalysis and detective work, as the Wolf-Man makes clear in his *Memoirs* (1971):

> Once we happened to speak of Conan Doyle and his creation, Sherlock Holmes. I had thought that Freud would have no use for this type of light reading matter, and was surprised to find that this was not at all the case and that Freud had read this author attentively. The fact that circumstantial evidence is useful in psychoanalysis when reconstructing a childhood history may explain Freud's interest in this type of literature. (*The Wolf-Man by the Wolf-Man* 146)

Freud sometimes makes an appearance in detective fiction, including in Nicholas Meyer's 1974 novel *The Seven-Per-Cent Solution*, later made into a film, where he encounters Sherlock Holmes. Nicholas Meyer is not a psychoanalyst, but his father was, Bernard Meyer, who wrote a psychobiography of Joseph Conrad. Freud does not star in any of the detective novels written by psychoanalytic fiction writers, but they use his understanding of human nature to solve crimes. *The Clinic* investigates the brutal murder of a clinical psychologist, Hope Devane. Abused in early childhood, she restages her trauma, acting it out instead of working through it. To understand the novel's psychological dynamics, I turn to Robert Stoller, the UCLA psychoanalyst who wrote extensively on sexual perversion. Alan Krohn's *The Mind's Eye* casts light on a different form of trauma, a child who grows up without parents, feeling rage that awakens his analyst's unresolved anger toward his own mother, who may have committed suicide. Novelists typically portray psychoanalysts who learn about their patients' lives, but Krohn's analyst must first *unlearn* what he has been taught. Richard P. Kluft's *A Sinister Subtraction* contains a patient suffering from multiple personality disorder who accuses her former psychologist of molestation. One can appreciate *A Sinister Subtraction* without knowing anything about the multiple personality craze that bedeviled psychology near the end of the twentieth century, but the novel takes on greater significance in light of Kluft's scrupulously fair depiction of the vexed history of memory research. *Death by Analysis*, by the Lacanian analyst Bruce Fink, is, arguably, the most sardonic book about psychoanalysis written from an insider's perspective. Readers will appreciate Fink's wordplay and his witty account of the ideological warfare between the "Clanians" and "Calanians."

The Bildungsroman novel, highlighting the growth and education of the writer, or its cousin, the coming-of-age story, holds a special relationship to psychoanalysis, as can be seen in Part III, "Privileging Fiction Over Psychoanalysis." In these novels, the authors do not call attention to themselves as clinicians. Gregorio Kohon's *Red Parrot, Wooden Leg* dramatizes the perils of reading and writing under a brutal dictatorship. The expressive parrot, Joacaría, is a delightful creature who may remind readers of an even more famous parrot in Marion Milner's iconic *On Not Being Able to Paint*, though Milner's parrot cannot speak Yiddish, as Kohon's does. Thomas Ogden is perhaps the best-known contemporary American psychoanalytic fiction writer. The author of three novels, *The Parts Left Out*, *The Hands of Gravity and Chance*, and *This Will Do…*, Ogden demonstrates the role of childhood experience in shaping character development. Like some but not all psychoanalytic fiction writers, Ogden draws a sharp distinction between his two professional identities. Arlene Heyman's short story collection, *Scary Old Sex*, and novel, *Artifact*, hint at the central traumatic loss in her life, the early death of her first husband, the psychiatrist/analyst Shepard Kantor. Spousal loss remains the signature theme in Heyman's writings; paradoxically, the dead not only remain alive in Heyman's fictional world but also become a muse for her creativity. Austin Ratner's *The Jump Artist* and *In the Land of the Living* display a different form of trauma, the early death of his father. *The Jump Artist* and *In the Land of the Living* are narrated by young men who lose their fathers, the former through an unsolved murder, the latter through cancer. "Father hunger" usually refers to women's feelings of emptiness for fathers who were absent presences in their lives, but the expression also applies to Ratner's male narrators, who long for their deceased fathers' approval. Father hunger of a different kind appears in Joan Wexler's memoir, *A Pot from Shards*, and novel, *Make Me the Sky*. Wexler lost her father not through death but through abandonment of his family when she was two, a betrayal that she spent decades trying to understand if not forgive. Cordelia Schmidt-Hellerau's *Memento* shows how fiction writing is both scary and fascinating. The narrator, Sine, yearns to write fiction but, fearing rejection, instead becomes a college teacher of creative writing. Her life is upended when her star student commits suicide because his novel, more than 1000 pages long, has been rejected by four publishers. Suicide also appears prominently in Schmidt-Hellerau's earlier novel, *Memory's Eyes*. Cliff Wilkerson's *The Cotton Flower* is the story of five people, a mother, her parents, her son living in rural Oklahoma during the Second World War, and a fifth, the father, overseas fighting. Wilkerson initially wrote the novel from the point of view of a nine-year-old boy, but he later revised it to include the viewpoints of the four adults, giving the story a broader focus. Many of the events in the novel reflect his own experiences at the time. Wilkerson's two memoirs, *Moving On* and *Still Moving On*, chronicle the many challenges he had to face on the journey from his birthplace on an Oklahoma farm to the office in Chicago where he practiced psychoanalysis.

Part IV looks at Theodore Jacobs and Daniel Jacobs, the only two American brothers who are both acclaimed psychoanalysts and novelists. The two brothers have strikingly different personalities, prose styles, and literary interests. Tellingly, Theodore Jacobs's *The Year of Durocher* and *The Way It Ends* and Daniel Jacobs's *The Distance from Home* show how early traumatic experience influences later life. Unsurprisingly, the theme of fraternal twinship appears in both brothers' writings.

Other psychoanalysts write short fiction, as I discuss in Part V. One recalls Julio Cortázar's pugilistic quip that the novel wins by points, the short story by knockout. Many of the short stories interrogate traumatic loss. Merle Molofsky's *Necessary Voices* contains a story, "Miriam 1960," about a bungled abortion that almost results in death. The story takes place before the Supreme Court legalized abortion in the 1973 landmark case of Roe v. Wade, but the tale becomes more distressing to read in light of the overturning of Roe in 2022. Richard Reichbart's *Curious Stories of Diverse Places* presents a different trauma, one that every parent fears: the death of a child. The event casts a shadow over several stories in the volume. Reichbart was a lawyer before becoming a psychoanalyst, and some of the tales in *Curious Stories of Diverse Places* highlight his lifelong passion for social justice, including working on behalf of civil rights for African-Americans and Native Americans in the 1960s. Christopher Gibson's *Tales from the Unconscious* illuminates different aspects of psychoanalysis for beginning students and clinicians. The most haunting stories for me involve a fellow therapist's suicide, along with the culture of silence that surrounds the event. Many of the stories in Irene Cairo's *Inside Out: Intimate Voices* emphasize the trauma of early maternal loss. Cairo has never written about this subject in her professional articles, but she uses the veil of fiction to write authentically about it in her short stories. Luke Hadge's *Psychoanalytic Stories* records the young practitioner's experiences, including treating a world-famous analyst who, not many years earlier, was one of Hadge's professors. In the last chapter, I comment briefly on other psychoanalytic fiction writers whose stories merit attention.

In the Conclusion, I discuss the many surprises I encountered while researching this book. Many authors shared with me their impressions of reading my discussions of their stories. The authors gave me permission to include their responses to my discussions. I end the book by noting a valuable epistolary friendship I made with one psychoanalyst, Cliff Wilkerson, a nonagenarian whose life and work I've found inspirational. In seeking to glimpse the writer's life behind the writer's art, I am mindful of two paradoxical pronouncements about biography: George Gissing's observation that the "only true biography is to be found in novels" (quoted by Shengold 6), and Oscar Wilde's remark that literary criticism is the only civilized form of autobiography. Additionally, just as the biographer is always there in some major way in the biography, so is the literary critic always there in his or her interpretations. Or as Spinoza said, "What Paul says about Peter tells us more about Paul than about Peter."

Throughout the book I offer brief biographical sketches of the authors, showing the interconnections between their lives and their fictional stories. I'm particularly interested in the extent to which their clinical insights endorse or challenge contemporary psychoanalytic thinking. With the exception of Julia Kristeva, before beginning this book, I was unfamiliar with nearly all of these psychoanalytic fiction writers. After reading an early draft of this book, an anonymous literary scholar asked whether any of the writers in this study "compare with, say, Philip Roth?" No, is my answer: there is only one Philip Roth. But the scholar's larger question is whether any of these writers are "great" authors. My answer is still in the negative; but I believe that most readers will find these novels and short stories lively and worth reading. Regardless of whether the authors in my study seek to integrate or separate their identities as psychoanalysts and fiction writers, they bring clinical insights into their novels and short stories. In writing a book about psychoanalytic fiction writers, I don't claim that I have discovered the "Key to All Mythologies," the title of the grandiose book that the dry-as-dust pedant Edward Casaubon fails to complete in George Eliot's novel *Middlemarch*. My primary goal is to introduce these psychoanalytic fiction writers to readers who are interested in the many intersections between literature and psychology. *Clinical Fictions* is the first book-length study of psychoanalytic fiction writers, but it will not be the last. It is appropriate for Freud to have the last word in this Introduction. As Joan Riviere reports, he once exclaimed to her: "Write it, write it, put it down in black and white; that's the way to deal with it; you get it out of your system" (167)—advice that psychoanalytic fiction writers are belatedly following.

Works Cited

Akhtar, Salman, editor. *Between Hours: A Collection of Poems by Psychoanalysts*. Karnac, 2012.
Berman, Jeffrey. *Fiction as Resistance: Samuel Shem's Writings*. Ethics Press, 2024.
Berman, Jeffrey. *Psychoanalysis: An Interdisciplinary Retrospective*. State U of New York P, 2023.
Berman, Jeffrey. *Writing the Talking Cure: Irvin D. Yalom and the Literature of Psychotherapy*. State U of New York P, 2019.
Breuer, Josef and Sigmund Freud. *Studies on Hysteria*. 1893–1895. *The Standard Edition of the Complete Psychological Works of Sigmund Freud*, translated and edited by James Strachey. vol. 2. The Hogarth Press, 1955.
Brooks, Peter. *Psychoanalysis and Storytelling*. Blackwell, 1994.
Brooks, Peter. *Reading for the Plot: Design and Intention in Narrative*. Knopf, 1984.
Gardiner, Muriel. *Code Name "Mary": Memoirs of an American Woman in the Austrian Underground*. Yale UP, 1983.
Graham, Gregory D. "Review of *The Parts Left Out*." *Psychoanalytic Quarterly*, vol. 84, 2015, pp. 517–523.
Hellerstein, David. "Keeping Secrets, Telling Tales: The Psychiatrist as Writer." *Journal of Medical Humanities*, vol. 18, 1997, pp. 127–139.
Meyer, Nicholas. *The Seven-Per-Cent Solution*. Dutton, 1974.
Riviere, Joan. "A Character Trait of Freud's." *Psycho-Analysis and Contemporary Thought*, edited by John D. Sutherland, introduction by Sylvia Payne. The Hogarth Press, 1953, pp. 145–149.
Schmidt-Hellerau, Cordelia. *Driven to Survive: Selected Papers on Psychoanalysis*. IP Books, 2018.
Shem, Samuel. "Psychiatry and Literature: A Relational Perspective." *Literature and Medicine*, vol. 10, 1991, pp. 42–65.
Shengold, Leonard. *Is There Life Without Mother? Psychoanalysis, Biography, Creativity*. The Analytic Press, 2000.
Stekel, Wilhelm. *The Autobiography of Wilhelm Stekel*, edited by Emil A. Gutheil, introduction by Hilda Stekel. Liveright, 1950.
Wheelis, Allen. *The Moralist*. Basic Books, 1973.
Wolf-Man, The. *The Wolf-Man by the Wolf-Man*, edited, with notes, an introduction, and chapters by Muriel Gardiner. Basic Books, 1971.

Part I

Historical Fiction

Chapter 1

Julia Kristeva
Teresa, My Love: An Imagined Life of the Saint of Avila

"Why is there such a female infatuation with mysticism?" (45). Sylvia Leclercq raises this provocative question in Julia Kristeva's novel *Teresa, My Love: An Imagined Life of the Saint of Avila* (2008). Sylvia, a psychoanalyst and academic, like Kristeva herself, ponders the question throughout the 631-page historical novel. She knows that Freud was dismissive of mysticism, which he called the "oceanic" feeling. "To me mysticism is just as closed a book as music," the musically challenged Freud confessed to Romain Rolland in 1929. "I cannot imagine reading all the literature which, according to your letter, you have studied" (*Letters of Sigmund Freud* 389). Freud admitted in *Civilization and Its Discontents* (1930) that he could find no trace of the oceanic feeling within himself, and while granting that it might exist in other people, he was content to attribute it to the primary narcissistic union of the mother–infant relationship. The rational Freud equated mysticism with the mystification with which he associated religion. "What Jung contributed to psychoanalysis was mysticism," Freud complained to his analysand Joseph Wortis in 1935, "which we can well dispense with" (Wortis 146). Most psychoanalysts have followed Freud's lead in dispensing with both mysticism and the religious impulse. Not Kristeva. Mysticism animates her story, and she offers a complex answer to Sylvia's question that might have forced Freud to rethink the psychology of women had he read the novel carefully.

Saint Teresa has long beguiled novelists, musicians, painters, sculptors, and philosophers. She served as a source of inspiration for two of the greatest female protagonists in British fiction. George Eliot modeled Dorothea Brooke after her in *Middlemarch* (1871), as did Thomas Hardy in his masterpiece *Tess of the d'Urbervilles* (1891). Tess apprehends her soul ecstatically, a mystical union that unites her with Teresa, after whom she is named. The "ecstasy of faith," Hardy remarks, "almost apotheosized her" (107). Despite Tess's violation by the predatory Alec d'Urberville and her eventual murder of him and execution, she remains a "pure woman," as the novel's subtitle implies.

Teresa, My Love is also about a pure woman, albeit tormented by dark desire. Kristeva offers us a love story about the Counter-Reformation's greatest and most enigmatic woman. Josef Breuer wryly called Teresa, in *Studies on Hysteria* (1893–1895), coauthored with Freud, the "patron saint of hysteria," a "woman of genius with great practical capacity" (*SE*, vol. 2, 232). The sixteenth-century Catholic mystic became a Carmelite nun, the founder of 17 monasteries in 20 years, and an indefatigable religious reformer who miraculously survived the Spanish Inquisition. *Teresa, My Love* is a self-reflexive novel that repeatedly calls attention to the relationship between reality and fiction. Part of the novel reads like a postmodern Freudian case study. Sylvia is the novel's first-person narrator, and her prose style and vision of the world resemble her creator's. Indeed, there are few if any differences between the French novelist and her alter ego. Moreover, Sylvia recalls taking one of Kristeva's seminars at Columbia University—where Kristeva taught in the early 1970s—and often references her publications and those of her husband, Philippe Sollers, the French novelist who founded the avant garde literary journal *Tel Quel*. Translated into English in 2015 by Lorna Scott Fox, *Teresa, My Love* is not for the faint-hearted nor for those uninitiated in French poststructuralist theory and Lacanian psychoanalysis. While reading this densely written novel, in which plot, setting, and dramatic suspense are largely absent despite Sylvia's pilgrimage to Spain to document Teresa's life, one wonders why Kristeva chose to write fiction instead of biography.

Born in Bulgaria in 1941, Kristeva has lived in France since the mid-1960s, where until her retirement she was a professor of linguistics at the Université de Paris VII. Kristeva remains, along with Hèlene Cixous and Luce Irigaray, France's best known contemporary feminist thinker, and her controversial ideas about female identity may be seen in her fictions. A public intellectual, Kristeva has garnered many prestigious prizes and awards. She was the first recipient of Norway's Holberg Prize in 2004 for her exceptional work and its significance to the human and social sciences. Alice Jardine, Kristeva's biographer, has called the Holberg Prize the "equivalent of the Nobel Prize for the Human Sciences" (244). Kristeva is the author of more than 30 books, many of which have been translated into English and published by Columbia University Press, including *Powers of Horror: An Essay on Abjection* (1982), *Black Sun: Depression and Melancholia* (1989), *New Maladies of the Soul* (1995), and the trilogy *Female Genius* (2001–2004), consisting of biographies of Hannah Arendt, Melanie Klein, and Colette. Kristeva's novels include *The Samurai* (1992), *The Old Man and the Wolves* (1994), *Possessions* (1998), *Murder in Byzantium* (2015), and *The Enchanted Clock* (2017). Kristeva had written briefly about Saint Teresa of Avila in *Hatred and Forgiveness* (2010), describing her, as the Carmelite referred to herself, as managing to "checkmate" God by absorbing Him in herself (123), but Kristeva must have felt that a terse comment could not do her biographical subject justice. Hence, *Teresa, My Love*, an experimental novel that combines a close psychoanalytic reading of Teresa's often recondite writings; musical scores; images of paintings and sculptures; a four-act play that imagines Teresa lying on her deathbed, conversing with luminaries who came after her; and a letter to the eighteenth-century French philosopher Denis Diderot. Writing before the publication of *Teresa, My Love*, Carol Mastrangelo Bovè remarks that Kristeva uses psychoanalysis in her novels and recent theory in which "formidable female figures spring to life" (146), one of whom is Teresa, another female genius.

In her 1987 book *In the Beginning Was Love: Psychoanalysis and Faith*, Kristeva writes about her loss of faith despite being raised as a Catholic. Nonetheless, as an adolescent she was moved by the tragic mysticism of Dostoevsky's characters. "I knelt before the icon of the Virgin that sat enthroned above my bed and attempted to gain access to a faith that my secular education did not so much combat as treat ironically or simply ignore" (23). Kristeva remained a disbeliever but began using psychoanalytic theory to understand religious mysticism as a fusion with the divine Other. She credits Saint Augustine for comparing the Christian's faith in God with the infant's connection to its mother's breast, a comparison developed in *Teresa, My Love*.

Defender of the Faith

An analyst since the mid-1970s, Kristeva has always been a fierce defender of psychoanalysis, as can be seen in *Hatred and Forgiveness*, a collection of nearly 40 articles, lectures, and interviews written between 1998 and 2005. Psychoanalytic listening, Kristeva asserts, reminds us of our vulnerability. Rather than being concerned with the "normative thinking that marred its fundamental notions," contemporary psychoanalysis considers a number of "perverse" behaviors that mark the complexity of personality (167). Like most French analysts, Kristeva privileges early Freudian thinking, drive theory—in a word, desire—over Freud's later ego psychology, the study of defense mechanisms. She sees her role as an analyst in helping patients question themselves rather than providing them with answers. "Psychoanalysis teaches me everyday that one can offer tranquillity [sic] without offering a positive answer" (305). Psychoanalysis accentuates and preserves inner space, psychic space, something Kristeva fears is being lost in a highly technological age. Though not entirely rejecting psychopharmacology, she maintains that psychoanalysis is an "unbeatable antidepressant" (277).

Kristeva acknowledges in *Intimate Revolt: The Powers and Limits of Psychoanalysis* (2002) the striking differences between French and American psychoanalysis. Collaboration with American psychoanalysts, she observes ruefully, has not been fruitful. "Aside from a few recitations of Lacanian discourse, more frequently encountered in literature departments than in clinical circles, psychoanalysts in the United States are scarcely interested in Freudian psychoanalytical research in France." She offers a French explanation for the absence of collaboration with American colleagues. "They tend to succumb to a sort of anti-Freudian revisionism, when not to a prickly retreat to Freudian tradition, understood moreover and paradoxically as a prescriptive psychology more than as a careful reading of Freudian texts" (vol. 2, 259). American psychoanalysts, by contrast, would offer a different explanation: their greater interest in ego psychology as well as in relational and intersubjective approaches. Of the two models of freedom Kristeva discusses in *Intimate Revolt*, "freedom-adaptation and freedom-revelation" (236), she favors the latter over the former.

Kristeva distinguishes between semiotic language, connected to the early mother–child relationship, and symbolic language, associated with the grammar and structure of signification. She identifies the semiotic as the "translinguistic logic of the unconscious self" (*Hatred and Forgiveness* 11); the semiotic is often the language of literature, painting, and music. Kristeva implies that semiotic language, which involves the infant's identification with the mother as the origin of pleasure, is characteristic of femininity while symbolic language is characteristic of masculinity. Given Kristeva's interest in female genius, it's not surprising that she focuses on semiotic language. In positing two types of language based on sexual difference, Kristeva has been criticized for essentialist thinking. Scholars continue to debate her theorizings on phallocentrism and gynocentrism.

Another key Kristevan idea is *abjection*, an early form of development in which the "distinction between 'subject' and 'object' is not clear, and in which these two pseudo-entities exhaust themselves in a dialectic of attraction and repulsion" (*Hatred and Forgiveness* 12). Abjection is the tortuous process in which the child separates and rejects the mother. Jardine reports that while Kristeva was in analysis, the word *abjection* came to her in a dream, perhaps expressive of her anxiety over her disabled son. "I awoke with this word: *abjection*," Kristeva told her analyst, who replied, "It is what you are living as well, in a way" (Jardine 196). According to Anna Smith (150), Kristeva derived the idea of abjection from Freud's concept of the superego, which he believed appears, developmentally, at the same time as the castration complex.

Kristeva's Fictional Characters

Kristeva tries to give Sylvia Leclercq an independent existence. We learn that her father was a physician (like Kristeva's father), her mother a literature teacher; the two professions help to explain her interest in healing and appreciation of the arts. Born in 1953, Sylvia had a relationship with a man for about a decade, an affair she now explains as a symptom of masochism. The affair with her partner was so meaningless that she cannot remember his name. Sylvia became depressed, for which she was hospitalized, and then underwent a lengthy analysis and psychoanalytic training. Sylvia later wrote about the French author and experimental filmmaker Marguerite Duras, as did Kristeva, who discussed her in *Black Sun*. Sylvia has a temperamental and intellectual affinity to Teresa, about whom she is now writing a book—like Kristeva herself. The authorial Sylvia is a reliable narrator, reflecting the novelist's point of view.

The minor characters are Sylvia's colleagues. Marianne Baruch, the psychiatrist at the Medical-Psychological House, appears in the novel mainly because she "loathes all that Freudian-Lacanian mumbo-jumbo" (*Teresa* 14). Jérôme Tristan, a Lacanian analyst married to an analyst, reduces mystics to hysterics, a crude generalization Sylvia finds unsatisfactory. Tristan comes across as glib, superficial, and cynical, using Lacanian puns that Kristeva's translator must explain to her readers. The French word *père-vers*, "toward the father," means *perverse* in English, a pun English readers would miss. The translator must explain not only puns but also the play of homophony, in which words of different origins become identical, such as *penser*, "to think," and *panser*, "to bandage or heal" (403). Then there's Sylvia's on-again-off-again relationship with her boyfriend, Andrew Garnett. The minor characters are never developed and are easily forgettable or mistakeable; Jardine refers to Paul as Sylvia's son (278) when, in fact, he is her autistic patient.

Teresa dominates the novel, and the story's power lies in the complexity of her character. Kristeva's interdisciplinary research in multiple languages is formidable; she has read not only all her biographical subject's writings but also the extensive commentary, past and present, on her life and work. Kristeva offers us nothing less than a history of mysticism in the world's three great monotheistic religions: Judaism, Christianity, and Islam. The mystics "are merely the vestiges of a vanished humanity" (48), Sylvia bemoans, but Kristeva's Teresa is far from vanished. Moments occur when Sylvia strikes us as too certain about her knowledge of Teresa. "How well I understand you!" (235), she enthuses, a claim that implies a psychobiographer can have complete knowledge of a subject. Notwithstanding this overconfidence in knowability, the novelist convinces us that she grasps Teresa's character, and unlike Tristan, Sylvia does not overwhelm us in the "diagnostics" of her biographical subject's personality.

Teresa remains a round rather than flat character, capable of growth—personal, psychological, and theological. I found myself caring for Teresa regardless of the novel's aesthetic problems. To her credit, Kristeva never pathologizes Teresa's life story, never reduces her to a two-dimensional caricature. Teresa lies on Sylvia's couch, but the analyst avoids the pitfalls of psychobiography. Teresa gains rather than loses complexity when placed under the novelist's magnifying glass. Teresa idealizes her love for God—Sylvia calls her the "high priestess of the continent of idealization" (561)—but Kristeva, while herself in love with her heroine, acknowledges her darker side. Teresa could be hard-hearted toward the weak, the infirm, the mad; perfectionism compelled her to be severe toward those who did not have her implacable will. She was not a proto-feminist: she had little sympathy for weak women, exhorting them to be like strong men. Forgiveness may have been her religion, but she disliked mothers and sometimes behaved heartlessly toward women who lost young children.

Sylvia is, like Kristeva, a "disbeliever," meaning that she is interested in "miracles"—such as Teresa's body not rotting after it was disinterred long after her death—for their psychological, not supernatural, meaning. Kristeva's examination of Teresa's devout faith will not please those who maintain that sainthood proves the existence of God, but it will prove satisfying to readers who search for rational explanations of divinity. The secular Sylvia does not speak much about her own religious upbringing, presumably Catholic, but she rejects Lacan's belief that Catholics are incapable of being psychoanalyzed. Unlike Lacan, who privileges the "law of the father," the phallocentric world, Kristeva emphasizes the mother's role and the mother–infant relationship.

Sylvia views Teresa as embodying female *jouissance*, a term popularized by Lacan meaning joy or pleasure, often of a sexually orgasmic nature. But the term cannot easily be grasped, and its meaning is lost in translation. Lacan originally used the term to signify phallic pleasure but then began speaking about female *jouissance*. Insisting that *jouissance* is not equivalent to Freud's pleasure principle, Lacan linked the word to Freud's death drive—an aspect of late Freudian theory that appeals to French but not to most American analysts. Experiencing *jouissance* for Lacan implies loss, hence, suffering, because the pleasure is fleeting. *Jouissance* has been appropriated by mainly French analysts, literary critics, and philosophers, and, like the death drive, American psychoanalysts largely disregard the concept. Kristeva used *jouissance* in *Desire in Language* (1980), and it appears repeatedly in *Teresa, My Love*. The Lacanian Tristan uses *jouissance* early in the novel, explaining that he learned about the word in a Lacan seminar he took with Sylvia. Speaking directly to Teresa, Sylvia offers her own explanation of the word.

> Indeed it was Jacques Lacan, himself born into the Roman and Apostolic Church, who first extolled the *jouissance* he thought he detected in you and defined it as *other*. For it twines around the paternal phallic axis a novel way of being aroused: sensory, forever unsatisfied, and for that very reason outside time, on a cosmic scale. (69)

Kristeva's portrait of Teresa abides by the known facts of her life. Born of Spanish-Jewish parentage in Ávila, Spain in 1515, she experienced strange raptures as a youth. Her mother's early death left her bereft, and the search for a mother surrogate led her to a lifelong identification with both the Virgin Mary and Jesus. Teresa found her calling in the Catholic Church, and after becoming a Carmelite nun, she used her passion, dedication, and organizational abilities to reform the religious order. She and the mystic friar John of the Cross established in 1568 the Decalced (barefooted or sandaled) Carmelites, who committed themselves to a life of prayer. She died at age 67 in 1582. Pope Gregory XV canonized her in 1622, and Pope Paul VI proclaimed her in 1970 the first female "Doctor of the Universal Church."

Sylvia has little doubt that Teresa's self-flagellation and mortification of the flesh revealed sadomasochistic desire. Teresa's many illnesses throughout her life, beginning in childhood, were punishments she inflicted upon herself out of the fear she was unworthy of love. The future saint discovers, Sylvia observes, what the superego enjoins: "Delight in suffering" (11). There are other explanations of Teresa's strange fits and paroxysms of passion. Sylvia cites the possibility, reported by the French neurologist Pierre Vercelletto in 2000, that Teresa's raptures may have been caused by temporal epilepsy, which might explain her four-day unconsciousness in 1539. Dostoevsky also suffered from epilepsy, as Kristeva remarks in *Black Sun*: "Epileptic fits and writing are in the same way the high points of a paroxysmal sadness that reverses into a mystical jubilation outside time" (176). Kristeva leaves open the possibility of Teresa's epilepsy and offers other explanations as well, such as the possibility that Teresa suffered from alexithymia, the inability to express and interpret one's own emotions.

Why does Sylvia identify so closely with Teresa? To begin with, Sylvia contends that the Other dwells within her, not in the beyond. Like Teresa, Sylvia believes in the "you in me" and the "me in you" (23), a mystical unity that overcomes the split between self and other. The soul can thus incorporate the absent beloved, enabling one to be alone with God. In Sufi thought, Sylvia explains early in the story, immanence and transcendence are not mutually exclusive, an insight that Teresa grasped in the sixteenth century and that Sylvia believes continues to be true in the twenty-first century. Sylvia may have lost her faith in human relationships, but Teresa becomes a role model for her in pursuing a fulfilling life. "Your work seems deathless to me in the here and now" (62), Sylvia exclaims, reflecting Kristeva's belief that Teresa's mystical faith continues to be inspirational to those who study her life. Sylvia never experiences Teresa's mystical states nor shares her religious faith, but she has learned much from understanding her life. In the beginning of the story, Teresa's interiority feels like a closed book to Sylvia, but by the end she has opened and read the mystic's book and completed her own study as well.

Kristeva is not the first to point out the resonances between Freud's discovery of the unconscious and Jewish mysticism: she cites David Bakan's 2005 book *Sigmund Freud and the Jewish Mystical Tradition*. But she goes beyond Bakan and later scholars by suggesting that psychoanalysis is a "metapsychology of mysticism" by linking unconscious desire to the ego. She is careful to point out, however, a crucial difference. Psychoanalysis seeks to strengthen human agency—she quotes Freud's famous formulation, "where id was, there ego shall be." By contrast, the mystical path plunges the ego into the id, leading to the ego, in Kristeva's words, "in thrall to the darkness of the realm of the id: revelation and absence, *jouissance* and Nothingness" (60).

In analyzing her tormenting, ecstatic passion, her body "sick with desire and exultant in its affliction" (18), Teresa becomes for Kristeva a precursor of Freud. Kristeva portrays Teresa as a spiritual conquistador, the counterpart to Freud, an intellectual conquistador. Sylvia admires Teresa for her unsurpassed ability to feel and think: her extravagant visions fused ecstasy and rationality. Sylvia also admires Teresa for her "acute lucidity, rhetorical exuberance, and staggering levels of social activity" (47). Later in the story Sylvia admits being astonished by the power of Teresa's self-destructiveness and the resurgence of her rebirths. Kristeva captures Teresa's humility and ambition, a paradoxical fusion of opposites that reminds me of Walter Kaufmann's statement in *The Faith of a Heretic* (1961) that ambition is the best teacher of humility. In Kaufmann's view, humility and ambition are not admirable by themselves, but fused they represent a cardinal virtue. Kaufmann then coins the felicitous neologism "humbition" (318). Teresa's humbition is palpable, and it's likely that without it, she would not have been able to pursue her euphoric visions and document her extraordinary life.

Beating Fantasies

The novel's key psychoanalytic chapter, "A Father Is Beaten to Death," offers a Kristevan reinterpretation of Freud's 1919 essay "A Child Is Being Beaten," part of his contribution to the study of sexual perversions. Freud admits his case study is based on only six cases, four women and two men. A girl's beating-fantasy passes through three phases, Freud conjectures; the first and third are consciously remembered while the middle phase remains unconscious:

> The two conscious phases appear to be sadistic, whereas the middle and unconscious one is undoubtedly of a masochistic nature; its content consists in the child's being beaten by her father, and it carries with it the libidinal charge and the sense of guilt. In the first and third phantasies the child who is being beaten is always someone other than the subject; in the middle phase it is always the child herself. (*SE*, vol. 17, 195–196)

"A Child Is Being Beaten" is less concerned with the process than with the motivation behind repression. Freud suggests in the case study that masochism is not, like sadism, a primary instinct (though he later changed his mind about this in *Beyond the Pleasure Principle*); rather, sadism is transformed into masochism under the influence of guilt. Beating fantasies represent to Freud the various transformations of incestuous love toward the father. "A Child Is Being Beaten" is noteworthy not only because it casts light on Freud's vision of how children express and repress sexuality but also because of the singular autobiographical origins of the case study. Only in the 1960s, Louis Breger reports in his 2000 biography, did it become public knowledge that Freud based "A Child Is Being Beaten" on his analysis of his own daughter, Anna (302). She, in turn, wrote about herself in disguise in a companion essay, "Beating Fantasies and Daydreams" (1922); she used the essay to enter the Vienna Psychoanalytic Society "though she presented the material as if it were a patient that she was treating" (303). Kristeva undoubtedly was aware of the autobiographical nature of "A Child Is Being Beaten," but curiously, Sylvia never mentions this in the novel.

Sylvia maintains that Teresa's implicit credo, "I love because I am loved, therefore I am" (387), which possibly influenced Descartes's "I think, therefore I am," is a precursor to psychoanalytic theory. Sylvia's first-person dialogue with Teresa is also a dialogue with Freud. Unlike the founder of psychoanalysis, who assumed that a girl's beating fantasies are similar to a boy's, Sylvia argues, based on her (and Kristeva's) female analysands, that a girl's first love object is the mother. This pre-Oedipal relationship, which Freud ignored because of his belief that the Oedipal relationship constitutes psychological bedrock, characterizes, in Kristeva's view, Teresa's foreshadowing of psychoanalytic thinking. Sylvia calls the search for forbidden love the "sublimatory *jouissance* of my own power to speak and think *for and with* the beloved/lover" (394), a sublimation revealed throughout Teresa's writings. Teresa is a precursor to Freud in other ways, according to Sylvia. The future saint explored the world of interiority as a psychoanalyst does, and her works amount to an extended case study of masochism and sadism. Anticipating that the chapter "A Father Is Beaten to Death" will be difficult to grasp by non-Lacanians, Sylvia uses a lecturer's rhetorical devices, such as "Let us recapitulate," "Let us recap," and "Let us pause." Elsewhere, Sylvia expresses insights in the form of questions, as when she muses, "Could Teresa's rapture be a way to *lift* depression?" (220).

For those who, like Teresa, experience mystical unity with God, there is neither simile nor metaphor but "both at once" (98). Citing Baudelaire, who compared himself to a tree, Sylvia argues that he *was* the tree. Teresa experienced this oneness in her transference relationship with the Christian trinity or, as Sylvia puts it, in one of her most theoretical pronouncements, "A lethal, blissful metamorphosis, this writing heals the melancholy of separation by appropriating the Other-Being in an infracognitive and psychosomatic yet infinitely nameable encounter" (98). Sylvia characterizes Teresa's writing as a "cascade of metaphors-metamorphoses" (352), a style of writing that, in its fluidity and expansiveness, may be more characteristic of female than male writers. By the end of the novel, Teresa has sublimated her sadomasochistic desire into a creative life, anticipating the comment expressed wryly by Adam Phillips and Barbara Taylor in their 2009 book *On Kindness*: "Sadomasochism is the religion for those who believe you have to be cruel to be kind" (65).

Kristeva offers an intriguing contrast between Freud's creativity and Teresa's. Freud writes "like a sculptor using the chisel of free association to chip away the patient's defenses and uncover the infantile impasses of the capacity for loving and thinking." By contrast, Teresa proceeds like a painter of a baroque cupola, "applying layer upon layer" of paint and "adding twist upon high-wire twist to her tale" (559). And Kristeva's creativity? Her writing styles combine an analyst's close reading of Teresa's language with a poet's lyricism and a novelist's preoccupation with the inner world of character. Kristeva's impassioned prose captures Teresa's ecstatic language.

Graphomania

Sylvia refers to Teresa's years of "graphomania" (497), also called hypergraphia, a condition in which one feels an oppressive impulse or compulsion to write. Kristeva does not discuss Alice W. Flaherty's *The Midnight Disease: The Drive to Write, Writer's Block, and the Creative Brain*, published in 2005, three years before the French edition of *Teresa, My Love*, but the study highlights the complex relationship between writing and emotion. Flaherty quotes from *Black Sun*, expressing Kristeva's insight that for "those who are racked by melancholia, writing about it would have meaning only if it sprang out of that very melancholia" (*Black Sun* 3; Flaherty 119). Interestingly, Flaherty, a neurologist who teaches at Harvard Medical School and who herself grappled with episodes of compulsive writing and writer's block following the postpartum mood disorder caused by the premature births and deaths of twin boys, observes that hypergraphia is often a symptom associated with the temporal lobe changes found in epilepsy. According to Flaherty, some patients with temporal lobe epilepsy exhibit a cluster of five personality traits (called the Geschwind syndrome), most of which Saint Teresa also demonstrated in her writing. These traits include:

> hypergraphia; a deepened emotional life sometimes described as hyperphilosophical or hyperreligious (a squishy category ranging from attending mass twice a day to believing oneself to be the Buddha); emotional volatility, including aggressive outbursts; altered sexuality (usually decreased sexual activity); and overinclusiveness, an extreme talkativeness caused by excessive attention to detail. (Flaherty 24)

Religious and creative inspiration have much in common, Flaherty contends. She mentions Saint Teresa, one of many religious leaders whose mystical experience compelled them to express the inexpressible. Flaherty then seeks to understand the similarity between mystical and creative states. One explanation proposes that the two activities may come from similar brain regions. "The temporal lobe's roles in hypergraphia and the inner voice point to its importance in the drive to write. There is evidence that the temporal lobe underlies mystical experience as well" (257). People with epilepsy, Flaherty adds, have a much higher interest in religion and philosophy than the general population. During her postpartum depression and experience with hypergraphia and writer's block, Flaherty began looking at herself differently. As a neurologist, she had been trained to regard psychoanalytic therapy as unscientific, but she started to admit, begrudgingly, her growing fascination with fantasies and unconscious motives. "Although drugs could dull what was happening to me, psychodynamic explanations seemed more likely to give the events meaning" (90–91).

Kristeva would likely be sympathetic to much if not most of Flaherty's discussion of the drive to write. In a sentence with which Kristeva would entirely agree, Flaherty remarks that "Suffering has driven great writing, and problems with writing, notably writer's block, have caused great suffering" (6). Kristeva would also agree with the following assertion by Leon Wieseltier, whom Flaherty quotes: "If you can write about the wreckage the wreckage is not complete. You are intact. Here is a rule: the despairing writer is never the most despairing person in the world" (Flaherty 119). Or as Edgar says in *King Lear*, "The worst is not / So long as we can say, 'This is the worst.'"

Sometimes graphomania degenerates into "graphorrhea," incoherent rambling or "word diarrhea." But there is no reason to pathologize hypergraphia, a state common to many authors, prolific or otherwise: the conviction that they are most fully alive, and joyful, during the act of composition. Writing is, for both Teresa and Kristeva—and Flaherty—as necessary as breathing. According to Jardine, Kristeva regularly wakes up at 3:00 am and immediately begins writing.

A Celebration of Writing

Sylvia is mainly interested in Teresa as a writer. She was prolific, writing about herself in the autobiographical *The Life of Teresa of Jesus* and in other works, including *The Interior Castle* and *The Way of Perfection*. Teresa's *Collected Works* run to nine volumes in the Spanish critical edition. Her writings, according to Sylvia, are an early foreshadowing of Freudian self-analysis. "This scriptorial therapy deepened the confessional analysis of raptures and agonies—sensations that were appeased, if not effaced, beneath the torrent of texts and monastic foundations" (19). A few pages later Sylvia declares, speaking directly to Teresa, "By writing, you hold psychosis in suspense" (69). In arguing that Teresa came into full existence only through her writing, birthing herself through literary texts, Sylvia speaks both for herself and Kristeva. Teresa writes in order to be, to exist, and her passion for writing is nothing less than a passion for life itself. The historical Teresa wrote in a number of genres, including what Sylvia calls "ungenred" genres—much like Kristeva's novel—but the one that mattered the most to Teresa was fiction, which presumably is also true of Kristeva. Sylvia later adds that Teresa experienced *jouissance* only in writing. Teresa becomes Sylvia's literary muse, and when she observes that she will deliver to her colleague Tristan "my novel interpretation of Teresa's raptures" (224), we appreciate the double meaning of the word *novel* in English, both as a noun, an invented prose narrative, and as an adjective, something new, original, fresh.

Teresa, My Love remains a paean to writing, Teresa's, other authors', and Kristeva's own writings. "Hail Teresa, borderless woman, physical hysterical erotic epileptic, made word," Sylvia intones at the beginning of the novel (26). The rhapsodic sentence, evoking a breathless and almost punctuation-less flow of emotive words suggestive of semiotic language, recalls Joyce's stream of consciousness prose in *Ulysses*. Echoing Molly Bloom's soliloquy at the end of Joyce's 1922 novel, Sylvia conveys Teresa's rhapsodic affirmation of the soul's existence: "*Yes* to requited desires and reconciled alterities. *Yes* to the affirmation of co-presence, to the acceptance of otherness that founds the subject of desire, *yes to the infinity of being*" (448–449). Here and elsewhere Kristeva pays tribute to her literary forbears, and lest we miss some of the allusions, she identifies them for us, as she does in the chapter "How to Write Sensible Experience, or, Water as the Fiction of Touch," where she displays her fondness for intertextuality, locating her own literary text as an intersection of other texts:

> Gardens. The Paradise of Dreamers, of Persian astronomers, of lovelorn poets, of seekers of the Grail, of Beatrice, of Molly Bloom, of flowers... and yours, too, Teresa? "And all my spring-time blossoms rent and torn" (Omar

Khayyam); "O perpetual flowers / Of the eternal joy, that only one / Make me perceive your odors manifold" (Dante); "Sweetheart, let's see if the rose..." (Ronsard); "I pray thee, give it to me. / I know a bank where the wild thyme blows, / Where oxlips and the nodding violet grows" (Shakespeare); "I have punished a flower for the insolence of Nature" (Baudelaire); "Oh, rose, pure puzzlement in your desire to not be anyone's sleep beneath so many eyelids" (Rilke); "Though haunted by telephones, newspapers, computers, radios, televisions, I can watch right here, right away, dozens of white butterflies visiting roses against a backdrop of sea. The Work alone triumphs, that great Flower" (Sollers). (*Teresa* 102–103)

The novel's lyricism, in the service of the pleasure principle, remains its greatest strength. The imagination serves the eternal, Teresa reminds us on her deathbed, adding that the great enemy is "nothing other than the deficiency of imagination and desire" (555).

"Religion is always a mystery for you psychologists" (20), Sylvia's publisher tells her, and by the end of the novel the mystery has been illuminated psychologically. Sylvia remains, like Kristeva, an atheist, but they both appreciate the role of faith in life. Kristeva maintained that her discovery of psychoanalysis helped her understand the interdependence of faith and religion. Jardine cites Thomas Altizer's observation that Kristeva is a "*great* theologian second only to Karl Barth, the Swiss Reformer reputed to have been the greatest Protestant theologian of the twentieth century" (Jardine 273). We don't often think of psychoanalysts as theologians, and for this reason alone, *Teresa, My Love* is remarkable.

Religion continues to pose a challenge to psychologists, and it remains to be seen whether Kristeva's embrace of mysticism will influence psychoanalysis. Freud had the first though not the last psychoanalytic word on the subject. In *The Enigma of the Oceanic Feeling: Revisioning the Psychoanalytic Theory of Mysticism* (1999), William B. Parsons, a professor of religious studies at Rice University, argues that Freud's attitude toward mysticism was richer and less negative than has been acknowledged. Nevertheless, Parsons cites a little-known comment Freud expressed to the young Swiss poet Bruno Goetz around 1904–1905, warning of the danger of immersing himself in the *Bhagavad Gita*:

Do you know what it means to be confronted by nothingness? Do you know what that means? And yet this very nothingness is simply a European misconception: The Hindu Nirvana is not nothingess, it is that which transcends all contradictions. It is not, as Europeans commonly take it to be, a sensual enjoyment, but the ultimate in superhuman understanding, an ice-cold, all-comprehending yet scarcely comprehensible insight. Or, if misunderstood, it is madness. What do these European would-be mystics know about the profundity of the East? They rave on, but they know nothing. And then they are surprised when they lose their heads and are not infrequently driven mad by it—literally driven out of their minds. (Parsons 48)

The above passage suggests that Freud was not only wary of mysticism but also frightened by it. Yet Parsons cites other psychoanalysts who viewed mysticism positively, including Heinz Kohut, the founder of self psychology. Kohut believed that mysticism, or "cosmic narcissism," is, in Parsons's words, the "religio-ethical goal" of psychology (Parsons 163), a dictum that Kristeva would likely endorse.

Kristeva and Erikson

Kristeva often mentions Martin Luther in *Teresa, My Love*, the leader of the Reformation, but she never refers to Erik H. Erikson's influential 1958 psychobiography *Young Man Luther*. There are noteworthy similarities and differences between the two psychobiographical studies. Both Kristeva and Erikson use psychoanalysis to understand history, biography, and theology. Both explore religious leaders who, wracked by psychopathology, underwent spiritual crises in adolescence and early adulthood. Erikson spotlights young Luther's "fit in the choir" when he suddenly fell to the ground in the monastery at Erfurt, Germany, and raved like a lunatic. Teresa and Luther had mystical experiences, though Luther's German mysticism appeared to be more passive than Teresa's ecstatic union with God. Both Teresa and Luther were prolific authors, each speaking directly to God, meeting face to face, dissolving boundaries between self and other. Both reported on the transformation of their identities. Both embraced monastic penitence for the sake of eternal afterlife. Both Kristeva and Erikson show their subjects emerging from illness to health, curing themselves through new visions of faith. Both Kristeva and Erikson affirm their subjects' transference relationship to God. Both see their subjects as having timely interest to contemporary life. There are, however, theoretical and methodological differences between *Young Man Luther* and *Teresa, My Love*. Erikson relies on American ego psychology to understand Luther; Kristeva, by contrast, focuses on the vicissitudes of desire. And whereas Erikson remains coolly analytical and detached, albeit empathic, Kristeva is enraptured with her heroine, identifying passionately with her.

To return to the question I raised earlier, there are at least four reasons Kristeva chose fiction over biography to write about Teresa's life. First, penning fiction may have given her greater access to her character's inner life than writing biography. Freud believed that creative writers had a more intuitive understanding of the unconscious than psychologists such as himself. The novelist is best suited to imagine the life of interiority. Second, fiction allows Kristeva to use her own unique cascade of metaphors-metamorphoses to bring Teresa to life. Kristeva's incantatory prose is performative art, reproducing and recreating Teresa's own language, achieving a sensory immediacy that creates emotional impact. Third, fiction enables Kristeva to express her profound love for Teresa, whom she rhapsodizes and apostrophizes throughout the story, often using second-person soliloquies to convey the intimacy of their relationship. "Teresa, *my* love" expresses the depth of Kristeva's passion for the Saint of Avila, a historical figure who is now inscribed in the writer's—and reader's—heart. And finally, fiction permits Kristeva to comment on the violence and nihilistic despair of contemporary life, filled with the murderous violence of suicidal terrorists and religious bigotry. Trapped between secularism and fundamentalism, Sylvia searches for spiritual guidance and finds it in a woman who lived half a millennium ago.

This does not imply that *Teresa, My Love* succeeds entirely as a novel. The sheer length of the tome is daunting. In *The Incredible Need to Believe* (2009) Kristeva admitted that when she looked at the nearly thousand-page manuscript on her computer, she feared the novel would not be published. A good editor would have been able to trim the manuscript without sacrificing salient ideas. For example, the long discussions of Miguel de Cervantes, the author of *Don Quixote*, and the French-American artist Louise Bourgeois could be sharply curtailed. The lengthy commentary on the Christian concept of kenosis, the emptying of Jesus's will to facilitate God's divine will, could also be reduced. (Kenosis is one of the six revisionary ratios in Harold Bloom's *The Anxiety of Influence*.) There are other problems with the novel. Greater narrative distance could have been achieved if Sylvia admitted that she did not entirely grasp the Kristeva texts to which she enthusiastically refers. Instead of proclaiming how well Sylvia understands Teresa, Kristeva could have used Joseph Conrad's narrative technique in his impressionistic novel *Lord Jim* (1900), where the authorial Marlow is always changing his mind about the eponymous hero, who remains, finally, a mystery, confirming the unknowability of character. Or Kristeva could have shown that Sylvia is markedly different at the end, changed by the story she narrates. At the end of the novel, Marianne, the biologically oriented psychiatrist, unexpectedly decides to become a psychoanalyst, despite Sylvia's bemused observation, "nobody wants to be a psychiatrist anymore" (591). Marianne's decision undoubtedly suggests Kristeva's faith in the revitalization of dynamic psychotherapy. "The new Marianne," Sylvia informs us, "is unrecognizable, energetic, outspoken, confident, briskly efficient" (592). Marianne's unlikely transformation of character and conversion to psychoanalysis is told to us rather than shown, and thus not fully convincing.

As Benigno Trigo points out in his edited volume *Kristeva's Fiction* (2013), her novels have received a poor reception in the popular media, largely but not entirely because of the highly theoretical and psychoanalytic content of her stories. In a review published in the *New York Times*, Carlene Bauer praises Kristeva's affection for Teresa but complains, as nearly all reviewers do, about the novel's extreme length. "Ms. Kristeva's excess doesn't lead to illuminating insight." Bauer makes one factual error, referring to the novel's three-act play near the end. (Jardine makes the same error in her biography.) The anonymous reviewer in *Publishers Weekly* describes the novel as "impenetrable," an ambitious literary experiment that is finally disappointing. Abby Kluchin lauds the novel for setting Teresa into conversation with a variety of interlocutors but finds Kristeva's language overwrought and didactic. Anikó Szilágyi concludes her review in *Translation and Literature* by declaring that despite the novel's erudition, *Teresa, My Love* is "too analytical to be sexy, too informative to be entertaining, and too distracting to be treated as non-fiction" (273). The harshest review appears in *Prabuddha Bharata* ("Awakened India"), the English-language monthly journal of the *Ramakrisha Order*, where the anonymous editor challenges Kristeva's authority as an interpreter of sacred texts. "Psychoanalysts self-appointing themselves to 'investigate' saints' lives forget that there is a sublime 'desireless' passion, just as there is an 'asexual' orientation" (722). From this point of view, *any* psychoanalytic approach to a religious mystic would be offensive.

"I'm not one of those who bemoan the extinction of Literature with a capital L," Sylvia declares, "plaintive aesthetes left high and dry by the tsunami of the spectacle" (*Teresa* 270). Kristeva rolls with the breakers in *Teresa, My Love*, offering us a novel that is not a bestseller but that nonetheless brings to life a female character who loses and finds herself through the love of God and the act of writing. Unlike Freud's dismissive comments about religion in *The Future of an Illusion* (1927), Kristeva imagines religion as an illusion with a future. Kristeva's prose, like Teresa's, reveals that a woman's dwelling place is not a "fortified castle," as the novelist observes in *Hatred and Forgiveness*, "but an aquatic construction with fluid contours" (289). Fiction and psychoanalysis enable Kristeva to explore this flowing interior world, showing how it can survive in a world antithetical to serenity.

Works Cited

Bakan, David. *Sigmund Freud and the Jewish Mystical Tradition*. Van Nostrand, 1958.
Bauer, Carlene. "Imagining a Saintly Life, Some of It Not So Holy." *New York Times*, December 14, 2014.
Bloom, Harold. *The Anxiety of Influence*. Oxford UP, 1973.
Bovè, Carol Mastrangelo. *Language and Politics in Julia Kristeva*. State U of New York P, 2006.
Breger, Louis. *Freud: Darkness in the Midst of Vision*. Wiley & Sons, 2000.
Breuer, Josef and Sigmund Freud. *Studies on Hysteria*. 1893–1895. *The Standard Edition of the Complete Psychological Works of Sigmund Freud*, translated and edited by James Strachey, vol. 2. The Hogarth Press, 1955.
Erikson, Erik H. *Young Man Luther*. Norton, 1958.
Flaherty, Alice W. *The Midnight Disease: The Drive to Write, Writer's Block, and the Creative Brain*. Houghton Mifflin, 2005.
Freud, Sigmund. "'A Child Is Being Beaten': A Contribution to the Study of the Origin of Sexual Perversions." 1919. *The Standard Edition of the Complete Psychological Works of Sigmund Freud*, translated and edited by James Strachey, vol. 17. The Hogarth Press, 1955.
Freud, Sigmund. *Letters of Sigmund Freud*, selected and edited by Ernst L. Freud, translated by Tania & James Stern. Basic Books, 1960.
Hardy, Thomas. *Tess of the d'Urbervilles*. 1891. Oxford UP, 2005.
Jardine, Alice. *At the Risk of Thinking: An Intellectual Biography of Julia Kristeva*, edited by Mari Ruti. Bloomsbury Academic, 2020.
Kaufmann, Walter. *The Faith of a Heretic*. Doubleday, 1961.

Kluchin, Abby. "Review of *Teresa, My Love*." *The Revealer: A Review of Religion & Media*, August 26, 2015. therevealer.org/review-teresa-my-love. Accessed September 17, 2022.

Kristeva, Julia. *Black Sun: Depression and Melancholia*, translated by Leon S. Roudiez. Columbia UP, 1989.

Kristeva, Julia. *Desire in Language: A Semiotic Approach to Literature and Art*, edited by Leon S. Roudiez, translated by Thomas Gora and Alice Jardine. Columbia UP, 1980.

Kristeva, Julia. *Hatred and Forgiveness*, translated by Jeanine Herman. Columbia UP, 2010.

Kristeva, Julia. *In the Beginning Was Love: Psychoanalysis and Faith*, translated by Arthur Goldhammer. Columbia UP, 1987.

Kristeva, Julia. *The Incredible Need to Believe*, translated by Beverly Bie Brahic. Columbia UP, 2009.

Kristeva, Julia. *Intimate Revolt: The Powers and Limits of Psychoanalysis*, vol. 2, translated by Jeanine Herman. Columbia UP, 2002.

Kristeva, Julia. *Powers of Horror: An Essay on Abjection*, translated by Leon S. Roudiez. Columbia UP, 1982.

Kristeva, Julia. *Teresa, My Love: An Imagined Life of the Saint of Avila*, translated by Lorna Scott Fox. Columbia UP, 2015.

Parsons, William B. *The Enigma of the Oceanic Feeling: Revisioning the Psychoanalytic Theory of Mysticism*. Oxford UP, 1999.

Phillips, Adam and Barbara Taylor. *On Kindness*. Farrar, Straus and Giroux, 2009.

"Review of *Teresa, My Love*." *Prabuddha Bharata*, October 2017, pp. 53–54.

"Review of *Teresa, My Love*." *Publishers Weekly*, November 2014.

Smith, Anna. *Julia Kristeva: Readings of Exile and Estrangement*. St. Martin's Press, 1996.

Szilágyi, Anikó. "Review of *Teresa, My Love*." *Translation and Literature*, vol. 25, 2016, pp. 269–273.

Trigo, Benigno. *Kristeva's Fiction*. State U of New York P, 2013.

Wortis, Joseph. *Fragments of an Analysis with Freud*. McGraw-Hill, 1975.

Chapter 2

James Herman Kleiger
The 11th Inkblot

Authors seldom pen imaginary letters to deceased historical figures who have inspired their scholarship, but this did not prevent James Herman Kleiger from writing an open letter to Hermann Rorschach, the creator of the iconic projective psychological test. "The theory underlying the nature of your experiment has remained elusive," Kleiger admits in an article published in *Rorschachiana* in 2015. "Much like the veil that has kept us from knowing more about who you were, the essence of your Rorschach test or method, itself, has remained elusive, the proverbial 11th inkblot" (228). Kleiger wrote the fictional letter on November 8, 2013, the 129th anniversary of the Swiss psychiatrist's birth. Kleiger notes that the "Google doodle" for the day featured a cartoon image of the Rorschach test, signifying, in Kleiger's words, the universal meaning and importance of that date" (221). Kleiger has devoted his career to testing the limits of thought-disordered responses, and he is an expert on the Rorschach test, with its ten evocative inkblots. Researchers and clinicians continue to offer their own commentary on the inkblot's meaning and validity—hence, the reference to the 11th inkblot, the serendipitous title of Kleiger's 2019 novel.

Nearly everyone has heard of the Rorschach test, but few know anything about its creator's life. Born in Zurich, Switzerland, in 1884, Rorschach was affectionately known as *Klex*, or "inkblot," because of his delight in klecksography, the art of making images from inkblots. His father, Ulrich Rorschach, was an art teacher who encouraged his son's creativity through painting and drawing, but his death in 1903, at age 50, compelled Hermann to give up his plans to become an artist. Instead, he attended medical school at the University of Zurich, from which he graduated in 1909, the year he met his future wife, Olga Stempelin, from the present-day Republic of Tatarstan, Russia, whom he married in 1913. Rorschach completed his doctoral dissertation, which was at the time required for a medical degree, in 1912 under his mentor, Eugen Bleuler, one of the world's most renowned psychiatrists. Carl Jung's teacher, Bleuler named "schizophrenia" and coined the indispensable neologism "ambivalence" as well as "autism" and "depth psychology." Both Bleuler and Jung had a complicated relationship with psychoanalysis. The former was equivocal about psychoanalysis while the latter was a Freudian for only a few years, breaking with Freud, who had chosen him as his heir and successor, in 1913, and founding his own movement, analytic psychology. Rorschach, by contrast, was no rebel, serving as Vice President of the Swiss Psychoanalytic Society, though his major interest lay in inkblots, believing they could identify the disordered thinking that appeared to be symptomatic of schizophrenia. In 1915 Rorschach was appointed Assistant Director of the psychiatric hospital at Herisau, Switzerland, where he continued to work on inkblots. He published the diagnostic book that would forever link inkblots to his own name, *Psychodiagnostik*, in 1921, a year before his premature death at age 37 from peritonitis, likely caused by a ruptured appendix.

Few books have had a greater impact on psychological testing than *Psychodiagnostik*. According to Damion Searls, Rorschach's biographer, the ten inkblots "are probably the ten most interpreted and analyzed paintings of the twentieth century" (ix). In the 1950s and 1960s, Searls adds, the Rorschach test was the most popular in the world. The Rorschach test is still used, in a revised form, but its popularity has been eclipsed by newer personality tests, such as the Minnesota Multiphasic Personality Inventory (MMPI). Nevertheless, the word *Rorschach* has entered popular culture, inspiring films, cartoons, and now a novel. From its inception, researchers wondered whether the Rorschach inkblots—some of which were black and white while others were colored or shaded—were scientific or merely pseudoscience, a controversy that continues to this day. There is no doubt, however, that Rorschach was a man of many talents and sensibilities, as his colleagues and early disciples realized. "In their tributes," Kleiger remarks in his letter, "they noted that you had the mind of a scientist, the heart of a healer, and the soul of an artist" (224). These qualities appear in *The 11th Inkblot*.

One could not have predicted that Kleiger would write a novel about Rorschach. Born in Denver, Colorado, in 1952, Kleiger majored in anthropology at Harvard and received his PsyD in clinical psychology at the University of Denver in 1980. A graduate of the Topeka Institute for Psychoanalysis, he was on the faculty at the Karl Menninger School of Psychiatry and Mental Health Sciences, Menninger Foundation, from 1992–2000. He is now in private practice in Bethesda, Maryland. Written mainly for clinicians, his books—*Disordered Thinking and the Rorschach* (1999), *Assessing Psychosis: A Clinician's Guide* (with Ali Khadivi, 2015), and *Rorschach Assessment of Psychotic Phenomena* (2017)—are meticulously researched, highly technical and statistical, and well written, but they are not page turners. *The 11th Inkblot* is.

The 11th Inkblot

Countless books exist on Freud and Jung, both of whom have become household names, but far fewer studies appear on Rorschach, and none, as far as I know, that involves a fictional encounter between a patient and the creator of the Rorschach test. Kleiger may have been inspired by Irvin Yalom's 1992 historical novel *When Nietzsche Wept*, a story about a fictional encounter between Freud's older collaborator, Josef Breuer, and the great philosopher. The breadth and depth of

The 11th Inkblot are impressive for a debut novel. Kleiger has done his homework in researching the crude state of psychiatry at the turn of the twentieth century. The story opens in a small Russian village, Zastavia, shortly before the First World War and proceeds chronologically. The novel abounds in secrets, psychological, familial, and spiritual mysteries that engage the reader's attention from beginning to end. *The 11th Inkblot* also contains treacherous betrayals, some of them real, others imagined. Anton Zellinsky's father, Herman, is a master horologist—watchmaker—but as a father and husband he leaves much to be desired. He favors his older son, Chaim, his pride and joy, whom he regards as his immortality project, his successor in the family business. Chaim can do no wrong in his father's eyes—except when he tells his father that he wants to become a soldier in the Tsar's army. The father regards his young son with scarcely concealed contempt, the same way he treats his young Hungarian wife, Marina Vodomer. Anton idealizes his four-year-older sibling, whom he calls "my golden brother," his beloved protector, but how can he not feel envy and resentment of the favored son?

Anton is ten when his mother permanently disappears, but she remains the key figure in his world, the person for whom he searches the rest of his life. The villagers refer suspiciously to Marina as "gypsy-witch," partly because of her dark hair, skin, and eyes, and partly because she is the "village dancer." Everyone except for Herman's older sister, Nadya, acts like Marina is invisible. Soon she becomes fascinated with dark smudges of ink which, she is convinced, can reveal the secrets of a person's soul, a window "for seeing into the eye of God" (24). Though Marina is not Jewish, as her husband is, she believes with the Jewish mystics that numbers and symbols, including, in her own case, inkblots, can interpret the unknown. She is not only a fortune teller but also a healer, convinced that helping others see into their own minds and hearts will make them better people. She knows what to say and not to say. "I see you hide behind smiles," she says to one woman, "but with such great sorrow" (14). Marina's obsession with inkblots thus parallels Rorschach's; one is a therapist by intuition, the other by training. Both are drawn to psychology and art.

Resembling Marina in his expressive gifts, Anton loves drawing horses, a talent only his mother appreciates. In a fit of rage, Herman hurls his wife's inkblots into a fire, destroying all but one, which Anton rescues from the flames and gives to his mother—the 11th inkblot. "You will be a great man one day," she predicts, gratefully. "You can become an artist! I will teach you *kleckographia*" (29). After his mother's disappearance, which he experiences as an abandonment, Anton feels "encased in stone, unreachable and inconsolable" (31). He stops drawing horses and begins instead drawing inkblots in an effort to hold onto her. He smears himself in mud, evoking taunting cries of "*Schmutzie*" (Yiddish for "the dirty one") from the village children, the same epithet Herman used when he incinerated his wife's drawings. To win his father's love, Anton begins making watches, but Herman remains unmoved, referring to his son's hands as "like rocks," an insult Anton never forgets.

Stuck in Time

The metaphor of clockmaking is as noteworthy in the novel as the construction of inkblots. Time is singular in historical fiction, where a story takes place in a time and a place that appear to be historically accurate but are not. Time can be linear or circular; many of the plot events in *The 11th Inkblot* are repetitive, as when Anton states that his father became like his own father, Anton's grandfather, "making time for strangers but leaving little time for his son" (10). Time is the inescapable antagonist in life, an enemy that can never be defeated except through the illusion, or delusion, of an afterlife, eternity, for all time. Kleiger captures our love–hate ambivalence toward time, as in the expressions *precious time* and *killing time*. Anton can never decide whether he wishes to move forward in time, stop time, or reverse time. He is often lost in time, or biding time, or fearing he has run out of time. His mother teaches him her favorite song—*Idövel Jobban Leszeck*, which means "I will be better with time" (6)—but her absence means that he is stuck in time, marking time, remaining in the shadow of time. Only near the end of the novel, when Anton finds himself working around the clock, does he have the time to change his life.

Anton is literally and metaphorically "The Madman in the Clock," the title of chapter 7. *The 11th Inkblot* is not exactly a how-to book about clockmaking, but it describes in intricate detail the mechanisms of timepieces. Anton is fascinated with the myriad complications of watchmaking, "*le grandes complications*, as the Swiss called them" (39), the inner working of a watch's movements. The first horologists discovered a method in which wheels and gears could transmit energy, using a crown wheel in which tiny teeth, attached to a stem, could turn in one direction and then in another. "This backward-forward movement, which turned linear into circular motion, seemed somewhat mad to the early horologists." Adds Anton, "When my mother disappeared, my *foliot* became stuck in a backward direction, moving the wheel of my life toward darkness" (92). Kleiger conveys the commonalities between human life and timepieces. "Like a parent hearing for the first time the beating heart of his baby, I was mesmerized when the escapement [the mechanism that controls the transfer of energy] brought a soft pulsing life to the watch" (40). Anton steals his father's rare watches as an act of revenge for the stabbing words that have pierced his heart. But on another level of meaning, the stolen watches symbolize his paternal legacy that he later puts to good use. Watchmaking is central to Anton's history and identity, affecting every aspect of his conscious and unconscious life. Later in the story, when he slowly descends into madness, he tries to maintain his tenuous grip on reality by picturing and inventorying each part of a watch he had memorized years earlier. He develops acute catatonia, mute and frozen like a stopped watch. "Stillness would now be my refuge. No movement" (179). He physically resembles a clock with its hands stuck at the 3:00 position.

After Chaim enlists in the army, Anton is conscripted against his will, forced to dig latrines and burn human excrement. Amidst the war's killing fields, he is given a rusty rifle and, in a moment that remains frozen in time, fires a single shot, fatally shooting a man who calls out his name in battle—his brother. "I saw his face and recognized his dead blue eyes, with the fixed expression, 'why?'" A fellow soldier notices a gaping hole in Chaim's chest, mouthing the words, "*Pucano u leda. Ne front.* Shot back. Not front" (90), the meaning of which Anton and the reader do not discover until the end of the story.

Anton suffers other losses, including two friends, a corpulent storyteller whom he dubs Rheshevsky, "Shev," who has the sharp ribald wit of a jester, and Vasily Steponovich, whose stuttering prevents him from completing a sentence. Unlike Vasily's family, who ridicule his stumbling speech, Anton listens carefully and empathically, a gift that will help him later in life. "I listened to Vasily with a third ear," Anton states (108), anticipating Theodor Reik's 1948 book *Listening with the Third Ear*, describing a type of listening that goes beyond what a patient is consciously saying. Both friends are killed in war, but they continue to speak to him in death, haunting voices that become part of his inner trialogue. Anton appears to others as a ranting madman. Sometimes the inner voices, phantoms of the imagination, betray an accusatory tone, whispering that he must kill himself, but other times the voices serve as allies and guides, helping him survive.

Thought Disorder and Psychosis

The 11th Inkblot succeeds in showing Anton's disordered thinking. Even during his darkest moments, when he is catatonic, he is not, strictly speaking, psychotic. What is the distinction between disordered thinking and psychosis? Kleiger answers this question in *Rorschach Assessment of Psychotic Phenomena*:

> One's experience of reality may be impaired while one's reality testing remains intact. For example, one may hear voices or see other figures in a room when no one else is present yet judge correctly that this experience of reality is inaccurate, that these are hallucinatory experiences. Conversely, one may perceive reality correctly but interpret its source or meaning incorrectly. An example would be an individual who accurately perceives people whispering in the hallway and concludes that they must be conspiring against him. (10)

This distinction is not always clear in the novel. "I do not believe either of you is real," Anton tells his inner voices, "but I fear even more that you might be" (116). He begins walking backwards, with vines wrapped around his head, so that he can keep the revenants who are raging in his head in front of him. Determined to kill himself, he instead falls into a 30-hour sleep, after which the inner voices are temporarily silent. The voices reemerge, warning him of danger when he meets a young Hungarian woman, Katarina, "Kata," who speaks in her native Romani tongue. She explains to him the meaning of his mother's affectionate word for him, her *kicsi*, "small love." Anton's inner voices order him to kill Kata, forcing him to cover his head with a pillow to drown out the sounds. Kata brings him to an older woman, Baba Zsófia, his mother's aunt, who, like Sheherazade, narrates to him three stories over the next three days about Marina's history. "She told me," Baba Zsófia informs Anton, "about a great Professor Freud who had written that the blots were tangled webs that might reveal stains and secrets inside a person's mind. This is what she wanted to know" (148). These fictional details are within the realm of possibility, although Freud never wrote about inkblots or Rorschach's psychological test. Nevertheless, it's plausible that someone in Marina's situation could believe that the creator of psychoanalysis might regard inkblots as the royal road to the unconscious. Ernest Jones reports in his biography that Freud rated Rorschach's intelligence highly but did not believe he had a "deep knowledge of psychoanalysis" (Jones, vol. 3, 84).

Marina never has the opportunity to visit Freud nor the other eminent doctor she has heard about, Carl Jung, to whom she wishes to convey a message, presumably about the psychological mysteries of inkblots, but this becomes Anton's mission. After witnessing members of his mother's family brutally murdered by a man whose son, Tamás, married Marina but soon died after the birth of his son, Anton arrives at the Burghölzli, the legendary Swiss psychiatric hospital, founded in 1870, where Bleuler and Jung worked. Kleiger acknowledges that some of the material he used to describe the tensions between Bleuler and Jung came from reading John Kerr's 1993 book *A Most Dangerous Method: The Story of Jung, Freud, and Sabina Spielrein*. Many of the physicians who worked with Bleuler admired him, Kerr points out, but others, like Jung, "chafed under his rule and found him insufferable" (Kerr 43).

Anton spends nearly a year in the hospital as a psychiatric patient, most of the time mute and catatonic, albeit in a moment of clarity he utters the words, "My Mama has a message for Jung." Jung, who no longer works at the Burghölzli, is brought in to examine Anton, and his diagnosis has the ring of authenticity: it's likely that the historical Jung would have reacted in the same way as his fictional counterpart. In the seven-page description of Jung's interview with Anton, the Swiss doctor comes across as thoughtful but overly self-assured, courteous but abrupt. To his credit, Kleiger never caricatures Jung. The Swiss doctor observes, accurately, that Anton's nose indicates he is "outside the Aryan race" (191). Throughout his life, the historical Jung believed in racial stereotypes. He insisted that "Aryan psychology" was different from "Jewish psychology," not realizing that "race" is a poisoned concept. There is an element of condescension in the fictional Jung's voice as he describes the readiness of non-Aryans to believe in "magical and spiritual forces" to explain mental illness. He uses the word association diagnostic test he had pioneered to suggest that Anton is fixated on his mother, in accordance with the Oedipus complex; Jung also believes that Anton regards him as a rival, a " 'rock-hard' father substitute" (195). Additionally, Jung remarks that Anton speaks in a "word salad" suggestive of schizophrenia. There is no doubt in Jung's mind that Anton's psychosis has an organic basis: "He is not an appropriate candidate for psychoanalytical treatment, much less analysis.

Sadly, gentleman and ladies, the prognosis is rather grim" (196). But Bleuler respectfully disagrees, telling Anton that his symptoms suggest the result of massive trauma rather than an organic collapse, a more hopeful diagnosis because of the possibility of effective treatment. Bleuler recommends that Anton visit a brilliant young psychiatrist who works in the modest canonical asylum in Herisau. At last, after 200 pages, Kleiger is ready for his protagonist to meet Dr. Rorschach.

Kleiger chronicles in the remaining 50 pages of the story Rorschach's kindness in his treatment of Anton and the value of expressive therapy. The novelist distills without distorting the essence of Rorschach's personality that appears in Searls's biography. A Brad Pitt lookalike, Rorschach was as gifted as he was modest, a character filled with, to use Walter Kaufmann's word, humbition. According to Searls, Rorschach "had a wonderful ability to connect with his patients, helping them by whatever means to re-emerge from their shells of paranoia or catatonic madness" (71–72). Kleiger takes poetic or novelistic license by having Rorschach meet with Anton in daily therapy sessions. "He had about a hundred male patients and did his twice-daily rounds quickly to keep time for his other interests," Searls reports, making it improbable that he could spend so much time with a single patient. Nevertheless, the historical Rorschach "spent more time on patients who interested him" (Searls 347)—like the fictional Anton.

Kleiger brings Rorschach to life in the story, offering us a highly sympathetic portrait of a man who sees his patients not primarily as psychopathological case studies to be analyzed, like Jung, but as fellow human beings. Unlike Jung, Rorschach is never authoritarian. Whereas the fictional Jung attributes magical thinking to non-Aryans, Rorschach, like Freud, regards it as universal. Rorschach's passion for work is infectious. "We find that drawing frees the mind to express itself unencumbered by words," he says reassuringly. "We encourage art as a creative activity here at our small hospital" (203). Anton begins drawing dark horses again, which represent, as Rorschach surmises, his childhood terrors, and during his year at Herisau he has morning therapy sessions with Rorschach, afternoon treatments at the baths, and evening drawing sessions. Slowly he narrates the horrific events of his life before, during, and after the Great War. In the novel's epiphanic moment, Rorschach points out that Anton could not have killed his brother because Chaim was shot in the back: a bullet's exit wound is much larger than at the point of entry. Hence, the meaning of a fellow soldier's words at the time of the shooting: "*Pucano u leda. Ne front.*" Rereading the novel, one sees how skillfully Kleiger has shown that Anton is *not* a brother murderer. The novelist also shows, in Rorschach's words, that Anton's inner prosecutor is a persecutor. Why do you need to punish yourself for a crime you were not guilty of, Rorschach gently asks his patient. Without citing Freud's theory of the "omnipotence of thoughts," which he advanced in *Totem and Taboo* (1913), Rorschach explains to Anton that in the unconscious mind there is no distinction between thought and deed. For years Anton had been punishing himself for being in the shadow of his brother, seething with resentment and envy associated with sibling rivalry. It is time, the therapist adds, for Anton to forgive himself for being human.

The Dodo Bird Effect

Kleiger attributes Anton's recovery to expressive and verbal therapy, but another explanation, only hinted at, is the therapeutic value of a strong patient–analyst relationship. Kleiger's Rorschach anticipates the counterintuitive conclusion reached by Saul Rosenzweig in 1936 that all forms of psychotherapy can lead to beneficial outcomes. The "Dodo Bird effect," a reference to Lewis Carroll's novel *Alice's Adventures in Wonderland*, in which all contestants who run around a lake are judged to be winners, has been confirmed many times. As Bruce E. Wampold and Zac E. Imel note in *The Great Psychotherapy Debate* (2015), common factors— "hope, expectation, relationship with the therapist, and corrective experience" (33)—are far more important in therapy than a particular therapeutic approach. Kay Redfield Jamison, in her many groundbreaking books, including her most recent one, *Fires in the Dark: Healing the Unquiet Mind* (2023), notes that the therapeutic alliance, "based on trust, expectation, competence, and collaborative purpose" (150), is a consistent indicator of outcome.

Kleiger's Rorschach knows this. His voice is never coldly clinical, as is Jung's. Kleiger's portrait of Rorschach bears the influence of Heinz Kohut, the creator of self psychology, which affirms the role of empathy in therapy. Rorschach's empathy for Anton never wavers. Upon learning Anton is Russian, Rorschach confides that he is married to a Russian woman, also a physician. Rorschach respects professional boundaries, but he is warm, reassuring, and understanding. Anton always feels calm in his doctor's presence. Rorschach knows when to raise questions about Anton's troubled past and when to remain silent. He is never critical or judgmental. When, near the end of treatment, Anton shows his mother's inkblot to Rorschach, he looks amazed, explaining his own research, and adding that Marina was an early pioneer. Rorschach achieves many therapeutic goals by giving credit to Anton's mother: he validates Anton's reality; strengthens what later will be called the therapeutic alliance; encourages the patient's feelings of equality; and becomes a positive father figure, fulfilling Anton's father hunger. Rorschach knows instinctively how to remain empathically attuned to his patient's needs, healing his narcissistic wounds.

Curiously, Kleiger does not have Rorschach use his experimental inkblot technique to help diagnose and treat Anton's illness. Given Anton's rescue of one of his mother's inkblots, it's likely that he would have been a willing patient. Anton would have eagerly assisted Rorschach in refining the inkblot technique, perhaps being Rorschach's first inkblot patient. Was this a missed opportunity for the novelist? One can imagine Kleiger's response to the suggestion of a literary critic like me who has never written a novel: "If you think you're so smart, why don't you write your own damned novel about inkblots!" Fortunately for me, Kleiger's response to reading my discussion of his work was much less sarcastic than I anticipated. The reason Rorschach did not administer the inkblot test to Anton, the novelist told me, was because he wanted the story to be more about the metaphor of inkblots than the actual test. "I also think," Kleiger added, "writing about Anton's Rorschach responses would have felt uncomfortable since I'm always mindful of the need not to publish too much about how the test is supposed to work and what constitutes 'good' and 'not so good' responses."

Anton's nightmares gradually end after being in Herisau for about a year, but Shev's voice emerges one more time, reminding him of the importance of storytelling, quoting the words from *The Rubaiyat of Omar Khayyam*: "The moving finger writes and continues to write or, should I say, 'right,' your story" (217). One wonders whether Kleiger has read Sandra M. Gilbert's spousal loss memoir *Wrongful Death* (1995), in which she talks about "writing/righting wrong," "writing (recording) as well as seeking to right (rectify) wrong" (86). Shev then tells him that he is the incarnation of Nicolai Keloskovich, or "Nike," as in Nike of Samothrace, a votive monument, according to *Wikipedia*, originally found on an island north of the Aegean Sea. Kleiger uses quotes that he ascribes to Nicolai Keloskovich but that the novelist himself created as apt epigraphs to the four parts of *The 11th Inkblot*:

He who closes his mind to mysteries of beauty and sorrow is but a machine with moveable precision gears cased inside a cold metal hull.

It takes only but a handful of madmen to unleash madness in all men.

A solitary journey with one's ghosts makes for a crowed and noisy road.

In the circle of life, mysteries abound and then confound, but alas, most journeys end with not all answers to be found.

Anton's journey is now all but complete. Restored to health, he meets a "Russian beauty," whom he eventually marries, serves as Rorschach's research assistant, rejoices over the publication of *Psychodiagnostik*, and temporarily relapses into a catatonic paralysis when his esteemed mentor suddenly dies. In the epilogue, which takes place more than three decades later, Kleiger updates his protagonist's fate, summarizing a life well-lived. In the last sentence, Anton is informed that a white-haired woman from afar asks to see him, saying that she brings a "song for *kicsi*"—either his long-awaited reunion with his mother, or, in a deliberate ambiguity I had not seen until the novelist pointed it out to me, the other Romani woman who loved him, Kata, aged by the passage of time, who might have followed him into the forest as his protector, as she once had been.

Anton takes special pride not only in his wife and four children but also in his major psychiatric publications, *Beyond Madness: Mystery and Meaning in Reflex Hallucinations* (a title close to Rorschach's doctoral dissertation, *On Reflex Hallucinations and Related Phenomena*), and *Rorschach's Inkblot Experiment and the Disturbances of the Mind*. The latter is well received, the former is not.

Tellingly, Anton writes similar books as his creator, though there is no biographical evidence that Anton is a portrait of the psychoanalytic fiction writer as a young man. Nevertheless, aspects of *The 11th Inkblot* are based on Kleiger's family history, as he acknowledges in the author's notes. "My father, Pvt. Ralph Richard Kleiger, served in the 36th Infantry Division in WWII. Several of the events depicted in Chapters 5 and 6 were adapted from stories that continued to haunt him until the day he died" (260). Kleiger's father died in 2018 at the age of 96; his obituary hints at this trauma: "His years of service to our country were a deep source of pride but sadly left scars that haunted him through the years." Kleiger's pride in his children is also evident: he uses their names in *The 11th Inkblot*, Nike and Katie ("Kata" in the story). The song lyrics Marina teaches Anton, *Idövel Jobban Leszeck*, come from Katie Kleiger's song *Adaptations*. Kleiger acknowledges the help of his wife, Nanette, "Noni," the nickname of Anton's wife.

The 11th Inkblot is a novel about trauma, grief, and recovery, dramatizing a scarred protagonist who is now, in Nietzschean and Hemingwayesque words, strong in his broken places. Kleiger's language is richly metaphorical throughout the story, particularly when describing psychological conflicts. "Sometimes, there is an earthquake inside the mind," Rorschach explains to Anton, "with subterranean fault lines that badly damage the psychic apparatus" (210). Kleiger's colorful Yiddishisms, such as words like "nudnik" (a pest or nag), "mishegass" (craziness), and "fercockt" (messed up), along with Russian, Hungarian, and Romani expressions, capture Anton's Eastern European world. The novel earned an enthusiastic endorsement from *Kirkus Reviews*, which called it a "spellbindingly measured narrative that entertains and enthralls." Every story is, intentionally or not, a projection screen of its author, a verbal inkblot. *The 11th Inkblot* reveals an author who is passionate about the complications of the mind, heart, and spirit, the movements and countermovements of life. One can say about Kleiger what Rorschach's disciples said about him: he has the mind of a scientist, the heart of a healer, and the soul of an artist.

Works Cited

Freud, Sigmund. *Totem and Taboo*. 1913. *The Standard Edition of the Complete Psychological Works of Sigmund Freud*, translated and edited by James Strachey, vol. 13. The Hogarth Press, 1953.
Gilbert, Sandra M. *Wrongful Death: A Memoir*. Norton, 1995.
Jamison, Kay Redfield. *Fires in the Dark: Healing the Unquiet Mind*. Knopf, 2023.
Jones, Ernest. *The Life and Work of Sigmund Freud*. 3 vols. Basic Books, 1953–1957.
Kaufmann, Walter. *The Faith of a Heretic*. Doubleday, 1961.
Kerr, John. *A Most Dangerous Method: The Story of Jung, Freud, and Sabina Spielrein*. Knopf, 1993.
Kleiger, James Herman. *The 11th Inkblot*. International Psychoanalytic Books, 2019.
Kleiger, James Herman. *Disordered Thinking and the Rorschach: Theory, Research, and Differential Diagnosis*. The Analytic Press, 1999.

Kleiger, James Herman. "Emerging from the 'Dark Night of the Soul': Healing the False Self in a Narcissistically Vulnerable Minister." *Psychoanalytic Psychology*, vol. 7, 1990, pp. 211–224.

Kleiger, James Herman. "An Open Letter to Hermann Rorschach: What Has Become of Your Experiment?" *Rorschachiana*, vol. 36, 2015, pp. 221–241.

Kleiger, James Herman. *Rorschach Assessment of Psychotic Phenomena: Clinical, Conceptual, and Empirical Developments*. Routledge, 2017.

Kleiger, James Herman and Ali Khadivi. *Assessing Psychosis: A Clinician's Guide*. Routledge, 2015.

Reik, Theodor. *Listening with the Third Ear: The Inner Experience of a Psychoanalyst*. Farrar, Straus and Giroux, 1948.

"Review of *The 11th Inkblot*." *Kirkus Reviews*, February 15, 2020.

Rosenzweig, Saul. "Some Implicit Common Factors in Diverse Methods of Psychotherapy: 'At Last the Dodo Bird Said, Everybody Has Won and All Must Have Prizes.'" *American Journal of Orthopsychiatry*, vol. 6, 1936, pp. 412–415.

Searls, Damion. *The Inkblots: Hermann Rorschach, His Iconic Test, and the Power of Seeing*. Broadway Books, 2017.

Wampold, Bruce E. and Zac E. Imel. *The Great Psychotherapy Debate: The Evidence for What Makes Psychotherapy Work*. 2nd ed. Routledge, 2015.

Yalom, Irvin D. *When Nietzsche Wept*. Harper Perennial, 1992.

Part II

Detective Fiction

Chapter 3

Jonathan Kellerman
The Clinic

Outspoken feminist psychology professor brutally stabbed to death. In heart, groin, back. Did research on self-control. Murdered by a psychotic? Or a psychopath? Three months ago. Hated by many. Others slain in the same way. Serial killer. Kinky sex, bondage. Cold case. Whodunit? Whydunit? This is the plot of Jonathan Kellerman's 1997 novel *The Clinic*, abounding in staccato dialogue and percussive rhythms that mess with the reader's (and literary critic's) language!

Kellerman is the bestselling author of more than three dozen crime novels, including the Alex Delaware series, of which *The Clinic* is a part. In his earlier life, Kellerman was a clinical psychologist, earning a PhD from the University of Southern California in 1974. He served as a staff psychologist at the USC School of Medicine, rising to the rank of full clinical professor of pediatrics. As a result of his work with pediatric cancer patients at the Children's Hospital of Los Angeles, the hospital established the Psychosocial Program, Division of Hematology-Oncology, under his leadership, the first such program in the country. Before turning to full-time fiction writing, Kellerman edited or authored three books on psychology: *Psychological Aspects of Childhood Cancer* (1980), *Helping the Fearful Child* (1981), and *Savage Spawn: Reflections on Violent Children* (1999). As he notes in *Savage Spawn*, while working days at Children's Hospital, conducting research on catastrophic childhood illness and setting up support systems for children with cancer and their families, he found himself "learning more about human misery and resilience than I'd ever imagined possible" (6).

"I would never have been a novelist without working as a psychologist," Kellerman told Kristin Masters in a 2014 interview; "it was a great education in human nature." As Masters reports, Kellerman credited his career as a psychologist with improving his writing: "adhering to [doctor–patient] confidentiality made me a better writer because it forced me to invent, but it gave me a sense of authenticity." In a 2016 interview in the *New York Times*, Kellerman explained what most moves him in a work of literature: "Depth of characterization and, when the subject is dark, an empathic, compassionate authorial voice" ("By the Book"), qualities seen in his best novels. An authority on child psychology, Kellerman served as an expert witness and consultant during many court trials. He uses his clinical and legal experience in his murder mystery novels, which explore violent crime, childhood abuse, sexual trauma, psychopathology, and the nature of evil.

Dr. Alex Delaware, the psychologist in *The Clinic* who consults with the LAPD, is well aware of evil, announcing Hope Devane's horrific murder on the opening page of the story. Alex serves as both a reliable narrator and an astute judge of character, probing every aspect of Hope's contradictory character. Kellerman does not expect readers of *The Clinic* to know many of the details of Alex's life, but we learn he has killed a man, in self-defense, and that he has recurrent nightmares. In his 2007 novel *Obsession*, Kellerman offers an insight into Alex's childhood, describing his perfectionism and rage over his mistakes. As one of his teachers wrote, "Alexander needs to understand that not everyone in 3rd grade learns as quickly as he does and that making mistakes is acceptable." Alex's three-year experience of being in psychotherapy during his doctoral program in clinical psychology proved invaluable. "By my final year of grad school, the cognitive starbursts and compulsive corrections were gone. Farewell, also, to rituals, invisible or otherwise" (*Obsession* 61–62).

Kellerman is sympathetic to a variety of psychological approaches, including psychoanalysis. "I consider psychoanalysis a fine way for a generally well-adjusted adult to learn about himself," he writes in *Helping the Fearful Child*, and although he maintains there is no convincing evidence that psychoanalysis can cure childhood anxieties, children may benefit from the "tangential aspects of analysis," including the "warmth and support offered by the analyst" (*Helping the Fearful Child* 259). He is also supportive of cognitive behavioral therapy and hypnosis. Without mentioning that Anna Freud named the defense mechanism, Kellerman singles out *identification with the aggressor* to explain how, in a child's mind, "one good way to deal with something frightful is to *become* that thing" (60), a phenomenon that appears in *The Clinic*. In *Savage Spawn*, Kellerman discusses a triad of factors that strongly predict child criminality: psychopathy, low IQ, and love deprivation, factors present in his novels.

In *The Clinic*, Alex has a close relationship with his wife, who loves to restore old guitars—much as Kellerman does. (The future psychologist/novelist supported himself throughout college at UCLA by giving guitar lessons and has written a book about restoring vintage guitars). Alex also has a close relationship with the only acknowledged gay detective in the LAPD, Lieutenant Milo Sturges, who reappears in the Alex Delaware novels. The two team together to search for Hope Devane's killer, and the reader follows along, analyzing innumerable clues, many of which lead back to her traumatic past. Kellerman credits Joseph Wambaugh, the LAPD detective turned crime-solving novelist, as one of the inspirations behind his own murder-mystery stories; another inspiration is Robert J. Stoller, whose psychoanalytic insights illuminate Kellerman's tormented characters.

Kellerman thrusts his readers into the position of being both a psychologist and a detective, searching for one or more characters who might have committed heinous crimes. Every detail must be evaluated, no matter how trivial or irrelevant; many of these details are red herrings, false information designed to mislead readers. Rereading the novel heightens one's understanding and appreciation of Kellerman's craft, for we see the subtle patterns not apparent on a first reading.

Our knowledge of Hope Devane's life and death is constantly changing, depending on those who knew her. She is a contradictory character, and one of the strengths of the novel is that we see her many conflicting sides. Like one of the great impressionistic novels in English, Joseph Conrad's *Lord Jim* (1900), in which the narrator, Marlow, can never reach an unambiguous conclusion about the eponymous hero's moral and psychological identity, *The Clinic* seeks to uncover the motivation behind Hope's murder. Everyone has a different theory of her death. Motive is double-headed in the detective novel, as Marie Rodell observes in *Mystery Fiction* (1954): "it implies *motive to kill a specific person*, and *temperamental ability to kill*" (18). According to Rodell, detective fiction is more intellectual than emotional, but *The Clinic* is gut-wrenching from beginning to end. Despite the generic constraints of detective fiction, we learn enough about Hope to understand how she is implicated in her own death. "Sometimes we do fall into dangerous patterns," she admits on a television show promoting her self-help book, *Wolves and Sheep*, with its alarming subtitle, *Why Men Inevitably Hurt Women and What Women Can Do to Avoid It*. "The crux, I believe, is in the lessons we learn as children" (11). The insight contains more truth than she realizes.

A brilliant student, Hope was the class valedictorian in Bakersfield high school and went to UC Berkeley, where she graduated summa cum laude, then received a PhD at the same institution. She became a university professor, teaching in the psychology department, writing professional papers on how sex roles and child-rearing methods affect self-control. Her career took off with *Wolves and Sheep*, earning six-figure royalties that are a rarity among academic authors. In the classroom and on the lecture circuit, she was a wolf, ferocious in her defense of women's rights. Hope tries to "psych out" everyone, students, colleagues, and acquaintances, partly because, as one person suggests, she always needed to feel in control. It's understandable that her notoriety was somehow responsible for her murder. But what's probable in real life may be deceptive in a murder mystery, where readers look elsewhere for solutions to a crime. The wolf in the classroom turns out to be a sheep in the bedroom or, to change metaphors, a sacrificial lamb.

The prime suspect is Hope's husband of ten years, Philip Seacrest, a man 15 years her senior and a fellow academic, a history professor, well versed in medieval torture. "More women are killed by so-called loved ones than by all the scumbags combined" (30), Milo informs Alex. Was Seacrest jealous that she made more money than he did? Did he fear she would leave him for a younger man? Seacrest is evasive when questioned; he and his wife had little in common with each other, and he claims to have no knowledge of her work. Another suspect is the Beverly Hills physician Milan (Mike) Cruvic, an OB/GYN and "fertility" specialist who has paid Hope a hefty consulting fee for reasons unknown, as did a prominent "porn" lawyer.

Did Hope's role on her department's Interpersonal Conduct Committee, which she created and chaired, without administrative approval, have something to do with her death? Much of the novel focuses on the three cases brought to the committee involving male students allegedly abusing female undergraduate students. Deborah Brittain accused Patrick Allan Huang, an engineering major, of stalking her; Cindy Vespucci maintained that Kenneth Storm Jr., a business major, attacked her when she refused to have sex with him; and Tessa Ann Bowlby accused Reed Muscadine, a theater arts major, of date rape. Another suspect on the committee is Casey Locking, a graduate student in psychology chosen by Hope, his dissertation director, to investigate student misconduct. The committee's existence and function are controversial; the dean warns Hope that she is putting herself in danger, legally, since she appears to function on the committee more as an independent psychologist, giving therapy to female students she believes have been sexually abused by male classmates, than as a disinterested faculty member.

Kellerman understands the ambiguities of sexual misconduct cases when there are no witnesses in "he said, she-said" cases. He also understands how victims of sexual crimes may be revictimized by defendants' lawyers. Kellerman never trivializes any of the cases brought before the Interpersonal Conduct Committee, but he calls into question Hope's motives not only in creating the committee but also in refusing to allow one of the alleged victims, Cindy Vespucci, from withdrawing her complaint because of what she calls a misunderstanding. In her interview with Alex and Milo, Cindy complains that Hope's attitude toward the accused students was "inquisitional"; the professor viewed the Interpersonal Conduct Committee as countering women's helplessness.

Tellingly, both Seacrest and Cruvic speculate that Hope's killer was likely a "schizophrenic fiend" or a "psychotic who hates women." In *Savage Spawn*, however, Kellerman states that psychotics should not be equated with psychopathic killers, who are "anything *but* crazy": "Psychopaths know exactly what they're doing" (23), unlike those who suffer from hallucinations or delusional thinking. Kellerman doubts that psychopaths are capable of rehabilitation through either insight or behavioral therapy. His advice is simple. "Lock up the psychopaths for as long as possible, and the streets will be safer. Keep the psychopaths away from the rest of us as completely as possible, and quality of life will soar" (34). The psychologically astute reader of Kellerman's novels is thus wary of Seacrest and Cruvic's speculations; the killer is likely to know exactly what he is doing, though we still don't know until the story's end the motivation behind the murder. Kellerman complicates the plot when three more people are murdered: a call girl, Mandy Wright, also stabbed in the heart, groin, and back; a waitress, strangled; and Locking, shot to death.

The only other faculty member on the Interpersonal Conduct Committee, Professor Julia Steinberger, muses, during Alex's first interview of her, that Hope might have had a personal history of abuse, one that explains the fact that although she was generally cool and composed in the classroom, she had a certain look in her eyes when it came to female victimization. In a second interview, Steinberger elaborates. Walking into the faculty club ladies' room, she sees Hope peering at her upper arm. "There was a strange look in her eyes—almost hypnotized—and her expression was blank. And on the arm was a bruise. A large one. Black-and-blue" (184).

Restaging Early Trauma

Not until Alex interviews Hope's sixth grade teacher, Elsa Campos, two-thirds of the way into the story, do we learn that the future professor was tied to her bed by a dog leash with a bicycle lock, by her mother, Lottie, a sex worker who sometimes disappeared for hours. At other times, Hope was bound by the men whom her mother brought home. The young Hope confided this information to her teacher but insisted she wasn't hurt by the ordeal. Hope presumably *never* talked about this experience to anyone other than Mrs. Campos, neither her husband, colleagues, nor a therapist. Hope later convinced herself that self-control was a function of gender identity, *female* gender identity, and that what her mother had done to her was not only justified but had also strengthened her. Later we discover that Hope became involved in dangerous bondage-and-domination games with men, including with her graduate student Locking and then with her husband. "*She* made the rules," Seacrest ruefully admits to Alex, "*she* was the one in control. Being able to surrender herself without fear thrilled her, and her pleasure thrilled *me*. I admit that at first I was repelled, but one learns. I learned. Hope taught me" (302). Hope was so controlled as a child, Alex explains to Milo, that she craved someone willing to subjugate himself entirely to her—her husband. "She kept trying to work it through. And Seacrest's passivity made him a perfect mate for her" (303). Restaging the trauma of being tied up and bound, Hope suffers bruises on her body. Because she feels the need to view the bondage-and-domination rituals, she documents the spectacle with hundreds of Polaroids.

Kellerman shows how Hope's early childhood trauma shapes her adult life, including her teaching and scholarship, but to understand her character in more depth, we may turn to Robert Stoller's work. A professor of psychiatry at the UCLA Medical School, Stoller (1924–1991) was a leading psychoanalytic theorist on sexual perversions. Unlike Freud, who regarded perversion as a sign of fixation on an early stage of psychosexual development, Stoller viewed perversion as a way to heal childhood traumas. Stoller wrote several books on gender identity, a term he coined in 1964. Stoller's research has been criticized for pathologizing transgender identity; like many psychiatrists and psychoanalysts of the late-twentieth century, he was opposed to gender confirming surgery, but his insights into the psychological dynamics of sexuality are still valuable. In his 1975 book *Perversion: The Erotic Form of Hatred*, Stoller offers a definition of perversion that casts light on Hope's situation:

> *Perversion*, the erotic form of hatred, is a fantasy, usually acted out but occasionally restricted to a daydream (either self-produced or packaged by others, that is, pornography). It is a habitual, preferred aberration necessary for one's full satisfaction, primarily motivated by hostility. By "hostility" I mean a state in which one wishes to harm an object; that differentiates it from "aggression," which often implies only forcefulness. The hostility in perversion takes form in a fantasy of revenge hidden in the actions that make up the perversion and serves to convert childhood trauma to adult triumph. To create the greatest excitement, the perversion must also portray itself as an act of risk-taking. (4)

Every aspect of Stoller's definition of perversion applies to Hope Devane. By binding herself during the bondage-and-domination games, she enacts the childhood experience of being tied to her bed. Throughout her life she remains "tied" to her mother, reexperiencing childhood humiliation and transforming herself from victim to victor. She never seeks revenge on her mother, whom she defends, but she projects her hostility onto men in general, including the male students brought up before the Interpersonal Conduct Board. Yet no matter how often Hope repeats and replays these rituals, in the hope of clinically working through traumatic experiences, she remains stuck in the past. In Stoller's words, "the need to do it again—unendingly, eternally again in the same manner—comes from one's inability to get completely rid of the danger, the trauma" (6). Hope's subjugation during the bondage-and-domination rituals preserves the trauma in its original structure. Stoller's statement in his 1985 book *Observing the Erotic Imagination* also applies to Hope's situation: perversion "*seems* to be audacious. One seems to take a risk in approaching the old danger" (29). Additionally, Hope's Polaroids confirm Stoller's characterization of perversion as "theater, the production of a scenario, for which characters—in the form of people, parts of people, and nonhuman (including inanimate) objects—are cast" (*Observing the Erotic Imagination* 31). Discussing the "aesthetics of excitement," Stoller notes how Janet Daily, the author of romance novels that have sold 100 million copies, used sexual innuendo without being specific. Kellerman similarly uses innuendo to convey Hope's erotic imagination: "The open mouth expressing fear or arousal. Or both. The brown eyes wide, bright, focused and distant at the same time" (*The Clinic* 291).

Hope's emphasis on personal and professional self-control, and her transformation from prisoner to guardian of women's rights, suggest counterphobic motivation: the need to master fear. Counterphobic motivation recalls Freud's repetition-compulsion principle, the need to convert a passive experience, in this case, childhood trauma, into active triumph. Although Stoller rejected the repetition-compulsion principle, mainly because Freud associated it with the biological "death instinct," one can view the former as a psychological phenomenon. Ironically, Hope's empathy for women fails to defuse her hostility toward men, a form of splitting that leads to unanticipated consequences.

Revenge

In the second major plot of the convoluted novel, Kellerman links Hope's death to those of three other characters. At the center of the mystery lies the tangled relationship between Hope and Cruvic, childhood friends who bond together through dark family ties. Cruvic has a shady past. Thrown out of a surgical residency program for removing a heart from a terminal patient, he trains himself to steal a kidney for his ailing father, a sex impresario and gangster who has undergone two failed kidney transplants and is ineligible for a third. Hope and Cruvic conspire to harvest a kidney from an unsuspecting donor, Reed Muscadine, who vows revenge on those complicit in the crime: Hope; the two women who have set him up; and Locking, who humiliated him on the Interpersonal Conduct Committee. Muscadine chooses a symbolic form of retaliation: stabbing two of the women to death, including Mandy Wright. "First in the heart, because they'd broken my heart by looting my body, robbing me of my entire future. Then in her cunt because she'd used her cunt to trap me. Then I put her on the ground and turned her over and stabbed her in the back. Just like she'd done to me. Right over her kidney" (367). Stoller's 1986 book *Sexual Excitement* enables us understand the erotic motivation behind Muscadine's revenge. "What purer form can it take than to inflict on one's attacker the same trauma or frustration one has been forced to suffer? The torture of one's object in fantasy becomes even more exquisite if one degrades him or her into nonhumanness or to the status of part-object" (8).

In light of Lottie's tying up of her daughter throughout her childhood, the reader may find unintended double entendres, as when Alex reflects on "Tying up loose ends" (150). Are we reading more into the novel than we should when a receptionist tells Alex, "I'm tied up, gimme a minute" (122)? *The Clinic* emphasizes, literally and metaphorically, the ties that bind children to unnurturing parents. Muscadine knows nothing about Hope's past when he ties up Tessa Bowlby, shortly before raping her; her disclosure of this detail to Hope seals his fate as well as hers, each the victim and victimizer of the other.

The meaning of the novel's title becomes apparent at the end of the story when we learn that Cruvic has used his home as a clinic to treat his father. Kellerman uses his own clinical skills to highlight certain details that do not appear in other detective mysteries. For example, during Alex's interview of Tessa Bowlby's father, Walt, he learns that she had a "wild" imagination; taken to a psychiatrist because of anorexia, the 14-year-old suddenly accused her father of having molested her when she was two or three years old. "It's not true, sir" (163) the father poignantly tells Alex, and indeed the accusation is a fabrication, an example of a false memory, perhaps implanted, consciously or not, by her therapist. The false memory movement was at its height in the 1990s, when *The Clinic* was published. Near the end of the story, Alex learns that Tessa has attempted suicide, and when he tells her that he believes her accusation against Muscadine is true, she responds in character: "'So I'm a martyr,' she said. 'Finally'" (353). Kellerman's compassion for Tessa reminds us of his background as a child psychologist; her surname is perhaps an allusion to John Bowlby, the distinguished attachment theorist who was never accepted by the psychoanalytic community.

Muscadine also sees himself as a victim. Because there is no evidence he was responsible for the murders—no weapon, no witnesses, no incriminating information—Alex fears that the district attorney will release him from jail or allow him to enter into a plea bargain on the grounds of diminished capacity or mental anguish. Without conclusive evidence, a jury is unlikely to convict a defendant victimized by a cruel violation of his body. In a shrewd legal move, Alex agrees to serve as an expert witness for the *defense*, for once deposed by the inexperienced public defender, Alex can then reveal the truth under cross-examination by the district attorney during trial. By concluding the novel in this way, Kellerman allows Muscadine to have the last words, showing how a psychopathic killer feels no guilt or regret for his barbaric actions.

"I want to know as much as I can about you, Reed" (357), Alex says disingenuously. His professional training has taught him how to establish rapport with patients, and he uses this skill, including active listening, to elicit Muscadine's full confession. He knows how to stroke the killer's ego. The psychologist uses silence effectively as a therapeutic and narrative device. He often repeats Muscadine's last words, coaxing him to continue his self-incriminating confession. Kellerman deploys the rhetoric of aggrievement to convey Muscadine's point of view. Muscadine regards himself as being "set up" by the Interpersonal Conduct Committee, a "prey," violated and degraded. "I wouldn't treat a *dog* that way" (361), he sobs. An aspiring actor whose career was cut short by the nasty scar on his back, Muscadine speaks the truth, *his* truth, when he relates how, after his kidney was cut from his body, "they *dumped* me like garbage!" (362). The entire experience strikes him as Kafkaesque; it felt like watching a Fritz Lang or Hitchcock film. Alex uses the passive voice, which denies agency, when asking Muscadine about the "night Professor Devane was killed" (360). He also questions Muscadine about the "script" for revenge, a word popularized by Stoller to describe the fantasies people create to trigger sexual excitement. We regard empathy as always positive, but Alex uses it to circumvent the psychopath's defenses. Muscadine never realizes that the psychologist to whom he unburdens his heart is the superior actor. After admitting that being the hunter is better than being the prey—"They cut me, I cut them" (366)—he then exclaims to the attentive psychologist, a proponent of the talking cure, "Tell the truth, it feels good to finally unload" (369).

Murder mystery fans, more than devotees to any other form of fiction, are *reading for the plot*, the title of Peter Brooks's 1984 book. Brooks points out that in all classical detective fiction, the detective must "repeat, go over again, the ground that has been covered by his predecessor, the criminal" (24). This is also true of contemporary detective fiction. Agreeing with the Bulgarian-born literary theorist Tzvetan Todorov, Brooks regards the detective story as the "narrative of narratives, its classical structure a laying-bare of the structure of all narratives" (25). No one would argue that Kellerman's novel approaches the greatness of the other texts in Brooks's study, but *The Clinic* demonstrates the power of repetition in Hope Devane's life, the compulsion to repeat a childhood trauma that cannot exhaust the demand for revenge.

Critics have offered qualified praise for *The Clinic*. "Kellerman may not be a great stylist," the reviewer in *Publishers Weekly* concludes, "but his serpentine plot and cast of mysterious characters grip the reader to the final page." In his *New York Times* review, Mark Lindquist faults the novelist for trying too hard to be "hard-boiled or hip," but he acknowledges that Kellerman's "creeping revelation of the professor's secret story is sordid and perverse—and it rings unsettlingly true." Kellerman's use of psychoanalytic theory also rings true. The language may sometimes be overwrought, but the novel's exposure of dark secrets highlights the ambiguities of acting out and working through childhood trauma. In the final analysis, Hope Devane is both a wolf and a sheep, and one can only imagine how her life might have been different had she grasped the hidden agenda behind her work.

Works Cited

Brooks, Peter. *Reading for the Plot: Design and Intention in Narrative*. Knopf, 1984.
Kellerman, Jonathan. *The Clinic*. Bantam, 1997.
Kellerman, Jonathan. *Helping the Fearful Child: Coping with Nightmares and Insomnia, School Avoidance, Toilet Problems, and Other Childhood Anxieties*. Contemporary Books, 1981.
Kellerman, Jonathan. "Jonathan Kellerman: By the Book." *New York Times*, March 3, 2016. www.nytimes.com/2016/03/06/review/Jonathan-kellerman-by-the-book.html. Accessed March 1, 2023.
Kellerman, Jonathan. *Obsession*. Ballantine, 2007.
Kellerman, Jonathan, editor. *Psychological Aspects of Childhood Cancer*. Charles C. Thomas, 1980.
Kellerman, Jonathan. *Savage Spawn: Reflections on Violent Children*. Ballantine, 1999.
Lindquist, Mark. "Review of *The Clinic*." *New York Times*, February 23, 1997.
Masters, Kristin. "Jonathan Kellerman's Journey from Psychologist to Bestselling Author." blog.bookstellyouwhy.com/jonathan-kellerman-journey-from-psychologist-to-bestselling-author. Accessed February 27, 2023.
"Review of *The Clinic*." *Publishers Weekly*, December 30, 1996.
Rodell, Marie F. *Mystery Fiction: Theory and Technique*, introduction by Maurice Richardson. Hammond & Company, 1954.
Stoller, Robert. *Observing the Erotic Imagination*. Yale UP, 1985.
Stoller, Robert. *Perversion: The Erotic Form of Hatred*. Pantheon, 1975.
Stoller, Robert. *Sexual Excitement: Dynamics of Erotic Life*. Karnac, 1986.

Chapter 4

Alan Krohn
The Mind's Eye

Alan Krohn's cliff-hanging 2008 novel *The Mind's Eye* contains an analyst, Ivan Weiss, who was told by his psychoanalytic supervisor years earlier that he has "a lot to unlearn" (40). The comment was understandable at the time, for Ivan's clinical doctoral program was entirely behavioral, and his internship was at a hospital that was still preoccupied with nineteenth-century descriptive psychiatry. But then Ivan chose a psychoanalytic direction, convinced by his supervisor that he needed to find, within himself and his patients, the "inner story, which like a psychological genetic code, determines everything the patient needs" (40). Having spent many years in psychoanalytic training, including a training analysis, Ivan still has a lot to unlearn when he confronts a mysterious patient, or pseudopatient, who proceeds to kidnap his daughter, Sonya, and threatens to kill her.

Unlike Dr. Alex Delaware in Jonathan Kellerman's *The Clinic*, whose self-knowledge allows him to solve a series of murder mysteries, everything Ivan Weiss thought he knew about himself and his wife is called into question in *The Mind's Eye*. Fictional psychoanalysts, whether created by psychoanalytic or nonpsychoanalytic novelists, are sometimes riven with inner conflicts, but rarely do they struggle with severe paranoid thoughts, as does Krohn's analyst. *The Mind's Eye* provides insight not only into the theory and practice of psychoanalysis but also into the analyst's troubled interior consciousness, where he begins to doubt the fidelity of his wife, Dana, and his best friend and professional colleague, Jake Hanson. To grasp the core story of his daughter's kidnapper and the location of her whereabouts, Ivan must first recognize his own core story, something he had not entirely learned even after a long analysis.

Surface similarities exist between the novelist and his fictional psychoanalyst. Krohn received his PhD in clinical psychology from the University of Michigan (in 1972), as did Ivan Weiss, and since then, Krohn has been on the faculty of the department of psychiatry at the University of Michigan, on the senior staff of the University of Michigan psychological clinic, and in private practice in Ann Arbor, again like his protagonist. Both then became members of the Michigan Psychoanalytic Society. Krohn's writings include articles on dreams and object relations, borderline psychopathology and adolescence, and a 1978 book, *Hysteria: The Elusive Neurosis*. Reading his scholarly publications, one would not conclude that he writes primarily to understand his own conflicts. By contrast, Ivan's publication, *Early Childhood Loss and the Adult Criminal Mind*, foreshadows the unresolved themes in his life story and in Krohn's whodunit.

Indeed, at the center of *The Mind's Eye*, as in *The Clinic*, lies the restaging of childhood trauma, acting it out instead of working through it. Both novels show how early childhood trauma, if neither mastered nor assimilated, dominates an adult's later life. Additionally, both novels reveal revenge scripts that enact Freud's repetition-compulsion principle, converting a passive experience, victimization, into an active one, victimizing others. The trauma in *The Mind's Eye*, however, is not sexual perversion, as in Kellerman's story, but early maternal loss. A patient who calls himself Adam Stone shows up in Ivan's office. Claiming he has a PhD in anthropology with an expertise in Native American archeology, the patient, who is in his late 20s, presents what appear to be classic Oedipal conflicts, trouble with male authority figures and the pursuit of unobtainable women. Stone is, from the start, unusually aware of his stormy transference relationship with the analyst. Ivan is delighted to have what seems to be a perfectly straightforward case. Yet the case may be misleadingly simple, as Jake cautions Ivan, a warning Ivan dismisses as an example of his friend's jealousy over his superior analytic skills. At around the same time, a man who calls himself Nick Streeter, trained as a historian whose field is the history of child abuse, enlists the help of Sonya, an interior decorator who has recently returned to Ann Arbor after having been raped in New York City. Though wary of men, Sonya visits Streeter's home and sees a complete set of the *Standard Edition* of Freud's writings. "My father is a psychoanalyst, and the Standard Edition was like the Bible in our house," she tells Streeter. "When I was little I saw more of these books than I did of my dad" (22). Despite having a boyfriend, Sonya is oddly drawn toward Streeter, perhaps because of his haunting eyes, which look strangely familiar. Meanwhile, a third man, who calls himself Joseph Benedict, an assistant professor in the University of Michigan psychology department, with an interest in criminal personality, meets with detective John Farley to lodge a complaint against Ivan for harassment.

The three men turn out to be elaborate disguises engineered by Paul Matin, the novel's antagonist. Matin vows to revenge himself on Ivan and his family. Matin knows how to toy with Ivan's mind, opening a Pandora's box that releases the analyst's old demons. But why does Matin single out Ivan and his family? What is the origin of Matin's rage? Ivan's rage? What is it about Matin's dark eyes that seem uncanny to Ivan and his daughter? In a novel in which nearly every detail has meaning, why has Dana advocated for adopted children? These questions drive the story.

In the Analyst's Office

The Mind's Eye is psychoanalytically authentic. Ivan reflects his creator's belief that reliving the past, however painful, is part of every analysis, and that the unconscious always finds a way to express itself. Ivan is a classically trained analyst who knows what to say and not to say to his analysands. We have access to his thoughts, and we can witness what he chooses to reveal to and conceal from his patients. Though he has much to unlearn about himself as an analyst, in most cases he is a reliable narrator with respect to psychoanalysis, reflecting the authorial viewpoint. Ivan offers us a vivid difference, for example, between a neurotic and borderline patient. Treating a neurotic patient, he says, is like peeling an onion, peeling away layer after layer until the patient cries and reveals the source of pain. Treating a borderline patient, on the other hand, is like seeing a cobra egg: the shell is transparent, and moving in with an interpretation causes the snake to spring to life, wild and deadly.

Following Freud's recommendation to remain a blank screen, Ivan is opaque to his patients, concealing every aspect of his personal life. One patient, Jennifer Andrews, a victim of childhood sexual abuse, dresses provocatively and tries to seduce him, demanding to know the attractive young woman with whom she had seen him. Ivan's refusal to disclose that the woman was his daughter infuriates Andrews, who becomes more sexually aggressive. He remains analytically neutral, asking, "You're looking to me for something right now. What is it?" (109). By refusing to succumb to her sexual advances, which would unquestionably sabotage therapy, Ivan remains available to help her identify the pattern of her self-defeating behavior. Later, when another patient, who is remarkably attuned to the feelings of others, senses that something is distressing him, he reassures her that she is not the source of his anxiety. Ivan refuses to explain to another patient, whose analytic hour he has abruptly rescheduled, the reason for the cancellation. Krohn succeeds in showing Ivan's clinical expertise in psychoanalysis, which he regards not simply as a career but as a calling.

Ivan maintains appropriate boundaries with all of his patients except Paul Matin, who knows how to get under his skin. In one early session, Matin claims to report a dream that he hopes will incense Ivan, but he disingenuously holds back the details, as if he must overcome intense clinical resistance. Ivan forges ahead, oblivious to his patient's deception. Krohn's dialogue captures the drama of the moment, especially when Matin says that because of Ivan's "background," he is reluctant to disclose his dream. "My background?" queries Ivan, to which the patient replies, "I gather from your name that you're Jewish. Are you?" (56). Ivan is immediately thrown off balance, suddenly thrust back into time when his father was in the Nazi death camp at Treblinka. Seymour Weiss, we learn, tortures himself not only for being a survivor but for having served as a barber for his fellow Jews who, he knew, would soon be gassed to death and then incinerated in the crematorium. Feeling complicit with the Nazis, he spends the rest of his life overcome by guilt. The father's horror is part of the son's dark past. "Memories of the hours spent listening to his father talk about being in the camp surged through him" (57). Ivan's body continues to clench when Matin admits his fascination with Nazi memorabilia. Matin has discovered Ivan's "Achilles heel," a metaphor he exploits when, in an earlier session, he told Ivan that as a boy, his father made him lie on the floor, face down, and put his heel on his son's neck. Krohn extends the metaphor of Ivan's Achilles heel by disclosing his tendency of "running ahead" of his patients, now allowing them to convey their feelings in their own words. It's unclear how Matin suspected Ivan's Achilles heel: a lucky guess? Regaining his balance, Ivan recognizes that the patient has, through transference, rendered him into a hated father figure, an interpretation that, while accurate, fails to capture the complexity of the analytic situation.

Why weren't Ivan's conflicts resolved in his training analysis? No analysis is complete, and sometimes life intervenes to create new blind spots and vulnerabilities, raising unforeseen countertransference issues. As a fictional character, Ivan is compelling *because* of his vulnerability. Krohn does not use the expression, but Ivan is a wounded healer, a term first formulated by Carl Jung and then developed by the sociologist Arthur W. Frank in *The Wounded Storyteller* (1995). Wounded healers and wounded storytellers must use their own vulnerability to comprehend their patients' stories. To do this, however, Ivan must first learn—or unlearn—his analytic style. Ivan's style, as Jake reminds him, has its advantages and disadvantages. Dreams are Ivan's forte, and they hold the same fascination for him as discovering the richness of a poem by tracing its pattern of images and symbols. Dreams are also, we should add, *Krohn's* forte, and his literary gift extends to weaving into his rich novel a pattern of images and symbols that expertly unite eye, tower bells, stone, and ice imagery. Ivan's wish to be a "perfect" analyst, rescuing others from distress, compels him to privilege knowing over feeling. "When this fantasy takes over," he realizes late in the story, "I lead with my mind and what I say to patients comes out dry and intellectual" (*The Mind's Eye* 200). This is the main difference between the two analysts' styles. Unlike Ivan, Jake has a "no nonsense directness": "This bluntness gets him in trouble with the administration," Ivan concedes, "but it's damn effective with students and probably, when timed right, very powerful with patients he's treating" (30).

Krohn grasps that both analytic styles are complementary and that, to craft a forceful detective novel, he must use both. *The Mind's Eye* is intellectually powerful because of Ivan's gift for insight, and it's emotionally powerful because of Jake's affective openness. Without Jake's presence, the novel would be cerebral; without Ivan's presence, the novel would be melodramatic. The two analysts recognize the limitations of the other's analytic style, but they have difficulty understanding the conflicts in their own lives, conflicts that are played out in their relationships with each other and with the other characters in the novel. These conflicts are the stuff of Krohn's art. Krohn's writing never falters, and he puts into practice the advice that Ivan's supervisor has given him: "If it cannot be said in plain English, it's rubbish" (38).

Interestingly, there are no theoretical differences between Ivan and Jake, only stylistic ones. Both believe fully in the truth of psychoanalysis. Ivan recalls a young psychiatrist who began psychoanalytic training at the same time he did but who could not accept his analyst's conviction that all people are bisexual, an idea Freud took from Wilhelm Fliess. The psychiatrist abruptly ended training and became a "lifelong critic of psychoanalysis" (112), a statement that may imply homophobia is a defense against repressed homosexuality. But if pressed by a skeptical reader, it's likely Ivan would agree that not all criticism of psychoanalysis reflects clinical resistance.

Ivan's Cuban-born analyst, Dr. Ernesto Sanchez, first pointed out his desire for perfection. "So, why do you need to be such a rare bird, Dr. Perfect?" Sanchez sarcastically asks him (36). Ivan's need to be perfect, he admits, was the most painful part of his analysis. Was this also true of Krohn? The novelist based the fictional Sanchez on his own analyst, the Cuban-born Humberto Nagera (1927–2016), whose help he acknowledges in *The Mind's Eye*. The author of many psychoanalytic books, Nagera studied at the Hampstead Clinic in London with Anna Freud. He was a professor of psychiatry and chief of the Youth Service at the University of Michigan and a training analyst at the Michigan Psychoanalytic Institute.

The central catastrophe in Ivan's past, one that continues to affect his life and work, was his mother's death when he was in the fourth grade. The event was so terrifying that he fainted when he heard the news. The circumstances surrounding her death continue to puzzle him: there were no skid marks when her car crashed into a bridge support, suggesting a disguised suicide. "Everyone knows your mother offed herself" (138), an anti-Semitic high school classmate cruelly told him. The novelist may have derived the idea of a single car accident suggestive of suicide from Arthur Miller's *Death of a Salesman*, a play which Krohn wrote about in a 1988 article: "There are really two types of suicide, one planned, the other repeatedly attempted and finally carried out. The latter is suicide by a single car accident" ("The Source of Manhood" 457). Like many suicide survivors, Ivan came to believe he was responsible for the death. "You imagined she collapsed under the weight of your badness," his analyst explained to him. "In your mind, you murdered her. You are still trying to figure out the evil inside you, the evil that made her die" (127). The revelation does much to explain Ivan's inner life, his core story, but it doesn't defuse his paranoid fear that the women he loves, including his wife, will one day abandon him. Ivan has acquired a national reputation for his clinical research on the role of early childhood loss on the formation of the criminal mind, research that is deeply personal, suggesting the ongoing counterphobic motivation behind his scholarship.

Paul Matin

Enter Paul Matin. An expert in manipulation and impersonation, his main reason for entering analysis is to inflict the same pain onto Ivan that he has lived with his entire grief-stricken life. Matin turns the table on his perceived tormentor, using two closely linked defense mechanisms, identification with the aggressor, popularized by Anna Freud, and projective identification, formulated by Melanie Klein, in which one projects unacceptable elements of the self onto others, with whom one then identifies. Dying of AIDS, which was a death sentence for most people before 1996, when the first combination drug therapy became available, Matin believes he has nothing to lose in setting up a suicide that will appear to be a homicide, with the analyst as murderer. Alternately moody, melancholy, mocking, and meditative, Matin is a formidable actor and director. He opens the novel, which is set around 1997, with a recurrent dream of mystical union with his mother: "There is no boundary, no inner me or outer you" (9). There is little that is ecstatic or rhapsodic about Matin's mystical dreams, as we find in Kristeva's *Teresa, My Love*; unlike Teresa, Matin derives no delight in suffering. Moreover, Matin's mystical dreams are only momentary escapes from his life's deadness.

Krohn conveys Matin's past through a series of five letters penned by his unwed mother. The letters span the years 1970, a few months after his birth in a French orphanage, St. Boniface, run by nuns and monks, through 1976, when she breaks off all communication. The epistolary technique is particularly effective in presenting Matin's traumatic history, supplemented by information he later acquires on his own. Beginning with "Dear Son," to whom she never gave a name, and ending with "Mom" or "Your Mother," the letters describe the American teenager accidentally becoming pregnant, considering and then rejecting an abortion, traveling to France to give birth, and then breaking her promise to see him, mainly because, she guiltily confesses, she has met a kind and loving man who would never accept the fact that she has abandoned a child. Krohn slowly fills in the rest of the salient details of Matin's story: being raised by grim foster parents and then returned to St. Boniface, after his foster mother's death, where a pedophilic monk, Brother Anthony, infects him with the AIDS virus. Unresolved mourning characterizes Matin's life. He has buried his mother, alive to others but dead to him, in a crypt, the metaphor Abraham and Torok use in *The Shell and the Kernel* (1994) to describe an isolated region in the psyche in which the lost object resides. The crypt remains locked even when Matin reintroduces himself to his mother in the story.

The attentive reader will figure out, two-thirds through the novel, that Dana, the advocate for adopted children, is, ironically, Matin's mother. And the target of Matin's rage, the man responsible for Dana's final abandonment of him, is Ivan, who has similarly lost his mother at an early age. Ivan realizes that the reason he feels a kinship to Matin, along with a desire to protect him, is because of Matin's eyes, which are identical to those of his half-sister's almond-shaped eyes. Or as Matin ambiguously tells Ivan's daughter, in one of several sentences with a hidden meaning, "We came through the same door, Sonya, you and I, and then we went down different roads" (187).

Eye imagery constitutes the novel's main image pattern. Krohn has chosen a title with a richly literal and metaphoric meaning. Eye imagery pervades Matin's "real" and contrived dreams. Obsessed with seeing and being seen, after Matin kidnaps Sonya, he tries to rape her, but she weaponizes her eyes, piercing and paralyzing him, and he cannot complete the incestuous act. Matin flees, leaving Sonya, without food or water, handcuffed to a heavy pipe that ran along the wall in a small room located in an abandoned building in another city. Unless she is soon discovered, she will perish from cold or starvation. Matin kidnaps the Weiss's daughter mainly to hurt the three of them, but his entry into their lives is also, paradoxically, a desperate way, however self-destructive, to create an attachment with them, a form of behavior that sometimes explains brutality, as Krohn observes in a 2000 article, "The Anatomy of Adolescent Violence." Ivan must infer Sonya's location from the process notes he wrote following each session with Matin. Using his own mind's eye, Ivan enlists Jake's help for a marathon analysis that will allow him to discern Matin's frozen state of mind. Jake initially refuses but then agrees, stating, "what you want me to do is probably the greatest testament I've ever heard of a person's respect for psychoanalysis" (189), an assertion that likely reflects one of Krohn's motivations in writing the novel.

Ivan's relationship to Matin conjures up the theme of the double, two motherless sons, still filled with rage, whose lives are inextricably related. Otto Rank was the first psychoanalyst to point out the persecutory symbolism of the double in literature and mythology. In his pioneering 1914 essay, later published in book form, Rank argues that the double personifies narcissistic self-love. The pursuit and slaying of the double frequently result in suicide, as in Oscar Wilde's *The Picture of Dorian Gray*, but sometimes it ends in liberation. "You made me your mirror," Ivan declares near the end of the novel. "I have the feelings you banished a long time ago. But you know what, Paul? You are my mirror, too" (231). Like other stories that dramatize the theme of the double, such as Mary Shelley's *Frankenstein*, Ivan and Matin haunt and hunt each other in a frantic need for love and acceptance. In a different universe, they could have been loving stepfather and stepson, but now they are implacable enemies. Matin manages to infect Ivan's life, not with the AIDS virus, but with equally virulent rage. Seeing the world through Matin's eyes, Ivan must own his own rage before he can help his dark double.

As an example of their doppelganger relationship, Ivan considers throwing himself in front of an approaching train, passing into a "simple, free nothingness" (157). He then dreams of sitting in a director's chair, auditioning actors for roles in a play. Matin, too, is a theater director, drawing others into his revenge tale. Ivan's dream proves prophetic; in their next meeting, he confesses to being an imposter, impersonating the role of pseudopatient to gain control over Ivan. Both Ivan and Matin read everything they can about psychoanalysis, the former to heal himself and others, the latter to get into the minds of his victims. One is a Freudian, the other, a Fraudian.

The Mind's Eye inexorably leads to Burton Tower, housing the huge carillon on the main campus of the University of Michigan, where Ivan tries to coax Matin from the ledge. In the novel's climactic scene, Matin tentatively extends his hand to Ivan for help, but events conspire against him, and a sudden surge of wind, along with the explosive chiming of the massive bell, culminates in the latter's plunging to his death. Matin's suicide is, as we shall see, the first of many imagined by psychoanalytic fiction writers that represents internalized violence directed against another person.

Ivan's greatest challenge is to discover, from Matin's "real" and contrived dreams, where he has taken Sonya. Ivan recalls, early in his psychoanalytic training, asking a senior psychologist if it is possible to fake a response on projective tests like the Thematic Apperception Test or the Rorschach. The "fake" responses, he learns, are still the patient's productions. "They are by him, they are of him" (180). In both James Herman Kleiger's *The 11th Inkblot* and *The Mind's Eye*, two characters remain frozen in time, the former temporarily, the latter permanently. Ivan's extended analysis of Matin's dreams, symptomatic of the bleak topography of his mind, enables him to rescue his daughter, where they are reunited in the novel's deeply satisfying ending. Ivan has succeeded in unlearning his previous assumptions, and he no longer feels the need to punish neglectful mothers. *The Mind's Eye* is an entertaining work of fiction, but it is also an eloquent commentary on the potentially catastrophic implications of disruptions in the mother–child relationship. Additionally, the novel affirms the rights of adopted children, a subject that is close to home for Krohn, as can be seen in his 2015 article "Psychological Struggles of Children in Alternate Care Setting," based on what he learned as a Red Cross disaster mental health worker in the United States, Sri Lanka, and Ethiopia. In the novel's epilogue, a retired Harvard professor calls Ivan a "scientist of the mind," an appellation he happily accepts (263). Whether psychoanalysis, like other forms of psychotherapy, is scientific remains a controversial question, but one can say about *The Mind's Eye* what Ivan says to Matin: "You gave me a story rich with imagery, colorful characters, and a suspenseful plot" (214).

Works Cited

Abraham, Nicolas and Maria Torok. *The Shell and the Kernel: Renewals of Psychoanalysis*, edited, translated, and with an introduction by Nicholas T. Rand. U of Chicago P, 1994.
Frank, Arthur W. *The Wounded Storyteller: Body, Illness, and Ethics*. U of Chicago P, 1995.
Kellerman, Jonathan. *The Clinic*. Bantam, 1997.
Kleiger, James Herman. *The 11th Inkblot*. International Psychoanalytic Books, 2019.
Kristeva, Julia. *Teresa, My Love: An Imagined Life of the Saint of Avila*, translated by Lorna Scott Fox. Columbia UP, 2015.
Krohn, Alan. "The Anatomy of Adolescent Violence." *JPCS: Journal for the Psychoanalysis of Culture & Society*, vol. 5, 2000, pp. 212–216.
Krohn, Alan. *Hysteria: The Elusive Neurosis*. International Universities Press, 1978.
Krohn, Alan. *The Mind's Eye*. Xlibris, 2008.
Krohn, Alan. "Psychological Struggles of Children in Alternate Care Setting." *Psychoanalytic Inquiry*, vol. 35, 2015, pp. 668–681.
Krohn, Alan. "The Source of Manhood in *Death of a Salesman*." *International Review of Psycho-Analysis*, vol. 15, 1988, pp. 455–463.
Rank, Otto. *The Double*, 1914. Harry Tucker, Jr., translator and editor. University of North Carolina Press, 1971.

Chapter 5

Richard P. Kluft
A Sinister Subtraction

Not often do I begin reading a novel with intense skepticism, but that's how I felt at the beginning of *A Sinister Subtraction*, Richard P. Kluft's 2019 story about a patient suffering from multiple personality disorder who accuses her psychologist of molestation. The little I knew about the author was that he was an expert on the subject, one that I had written about, to my chagrin, decades earlier. Allow me to explain.

The Multiple Personality Craze

Few subjects are more fascinating, from a literary and psychological perspective, than multiple personality. I recall being dazzled when I read Flora Rheta Schreiber's *Sybil*, published in 1973, the "true and extraordinary story of a woman possessed by sixteen separate personalities," to cite the words on the paperback cover. *Sybil* compelled me to write one of my earliest articles, published in 1978, in which I discussed the psychiatric case study as literary art, focusing on *Sybil* and its predecessor, *The Three Faces of Eve* (1957), written by the two psychiatrists who treated her, Corbett H. Thigpen and Hervey M. Cleckley. *Sybil* was on the bestseller lists for six months, selling 7 million copies, distributed by two major book clubs, *The Psychology Today Book Club* and the *Literary Guild*, further proof, I wrote at the time, of the story's interdisciplinary appeal. *Sybil* was made into two acclaimed films for television, the first, in 1976, starring Sally Field, who played Sybil Dorsett, and Joanne Woodward, who played her psychoanalyst, Cornelia B. Wilbur (Woodward received an Academy Award for Best Actress in the film version of *The Three Faces of Eve*), and the second version, in 2007, starring Tammy Blanchard as Sybil and Jessica Lange as Dr. Wilbur. Despite a few early skeptics who challenged Wilbur's diagnosis of Sybil, many mental health professionals believed in the story's medical authenticity. "This book is destined to stand as a significant landmark both in psychiatry and in literature," Dominick A. Barbara proclaimed authoritatively in the *American Journal of Psychiatry*, words cited in the paperback edition. I also believed in the book. "Sybil deals with perhaps the most rare and mysterious of all psychological illnesses" (1), I gushed. I was not entirely laudatory, however, and after surveying the published reviews of the book, I pointed out an irony that has bedeviled many medical writers, including Freud: "whereas some reviewers sympathetic to the medical importance of the story nevertheless object to its literary style, other reviewers apparently sympathetic to its literary value nevertheless question its medical importance" (5). Schreiber read my article and sent me an appreciative letter, and when a friend held a party for me to celebrate the publication of my first book, on Joseph Conrad, in 1977, she attended. Schreiber graciously wrote a blurb for my second book, *The Talking Cure*, published in 1985.

As my scholarly interests turned elsewhere in the following decades, I was dimly aware of the increasingly hostile reaction to *Sybil*, but it was not until Paul Mosher and I began writing *Off the Tracks: The Derailing of Mental Health Care* (2019), that I looked closely at the growing research on the "memory wars," in general, and Sybil, in particular. As we observed, the memory wars of the 1980s and 1990s played a significant role in the development of four fads that dominated psychotherapy in the last quarter of the twentieth century: the recovered memory movement, the proliferation of the psychiatric diagnosis of multiple personality disorder, past lives regression therapy, and the satanic ritual abuse phenomenon. In all four examples of rogue therapy,

> psychotherapists were seriously misled by their "discovery" of memories in their patients, presumably "recovered" during sessions, which then led to a series of epidemics in the general public and a series of crazes indulged in by therapists. Some of these memories were inadvertently implanted in the patients' minds by the therapy itself. (*Off the Tracks*, vol. 2, 642)

Often it is impossible to know, definitively, whether a repressed memory of childhood sexual abuse is accurate. Pamela and Peter Freyd created the False Memory Syndrome Foundation (FMSF) in 1992 in response to their adult daughter Jennifer Freyd's claim that her father had sexually abused her throughout childhood, a memory that emerged in psychotherapy. The parents' portrait of their daughter is stunningly different from her portrait of them, which appears in her 1996 book *Betrayal Trauma*, published by Harvard University Press. Kluft favorably reviewed the book in the *Journal of the American Medical Association*, and his endorsement appears on the book cover. One cannot determine who has betrayed whom in this Rashomon-like family tragedy.

The public began to learn about the real Sybil, Shirley Ardell Mason, shortly after her death in 1998 at age 75. Wilbur initially treated her for depression and anorexia before concluding she was suffering from multiple personality, which at the time was a rare diagnosis. After the 11-year treatment ended, Mason followed Wilbur first to West Virginia and then to Kentucky, where she taught art at a community college and cared for the ailing analyst, who died in 1992. One of the first critics of the story was psychiatrist Herbert Spiegel (1914–2009), who hypnotized Mason and found she was highly suggestible. Spiegel never saw any of Mason's "alters," or alternate selves. He did not accuse Wilbur of deliberately implanting false memories in Mason, but he concluded that she told Wilbur what the psychoanalyst wanted to hear.

By contrast, the investigative reporter Debbie Nathan argues in *Sybil Exposed* (2011) that Wilbur, Mason, and Schreiber perpetrated a fraud. After examining thousands of pages of Wilbur's clinical notes and tape recordings of therapy sessions, housed at John Jay College of Criminal Justice in New York City, where Schreiber taught, Nathan concluded that Wilbur deliberately implanted memories of childhood sexual abuse and torture. None of the extensive biographical evidence, which consisted of interviews with people who knew Mason and her family, corroborated any of these Gothic horrors. Nevertheless, despite its many falsehoods, *Sybil* remains a cultural icon, as the title of Alexandra Jacobs's article published in the *New York Times* on May 28, 2023 reveals: "Even After Debunking, *Sybil* Hasn't Gone Away."

As a result of the popularity of *Sybil*, arguably the most famous psychiatric case study of the age, there was an astonishing increase in the diagnosis of multiple personality disorder. Nathan reports that one leader of the International Society for the Study of Multiple Personality and Dissociative Disorders estimated that 3 percent of the population, over 7 million people, suffered from the psychiatric disorder (218). These "latter-day multiples," Joan Acocella writes sardonically in her 1999 book *Creating Hysteria*, "looked a lot like Sybil" (4). Other researchers, including the highly respected psychiatrist Paul R. McHugh, a member of the FMSF, agreed that the diagnosis was not only overprescribed but largely fictitious. McHugh's 2008 book *Try to Remember* charts the rise and fall of multiple personality disorder in the *Diagnostic and Statistical Manual of Mental Disorders* (*DSM*), the official "bible" of the American Psychiatric Association. Multiple personality disorder first appeared in the third edition of the *DSM*, published in 1980, but in later editions it was changed to a less polarizing term, dissociative identity disorder, its current designation. The name change reflects that of the professional organization of health professionals who study trauma-based disorders, including posttraumatic stress disorder. In an example of a wry identity crisis, the International Society for the Study of Multiple Personality and Dissociative Disorders changed its name in 1994 and then again in 2006. Now it is called the International Society for the Study of Trauma and Dissociation.

Of the many academic researchers who have cast doubt on the accuracy of recalled or "false" memories, none has been more influential than Elizabeth Loftus. She has received many awards and honors during her career, including the Distinguished Scientific Award for the Applications of Psychology from the American Psychological Association. In *The Myth of Repressed Memory*, coauthored with Katherine Ketcham (1994), Loftus devised a series of classic experiments in which children were told by a parent that a few years earlier they were briefly lost in a shopping mall before being reunited with their parents. Loftus was stunned not only by how easy it was to create false memories but also by the extent to which children embellished these memories, called confabulations, false memories created to fill in gaps in memory. Loftus's research showed, additionally, that adults sometimes recalled memories of experiences that never happened. As many as a third of the people in Loftus's experiments recalled childhood events that never occurred.

Dissociative identity disorder has not disappeared as a clinical diagnosis. In a review of the documentary *Busy Inside* published in the *New York Times* in 2021, Jane Brody interviewed Stanford University Psychiatrist David Spiegel (the son of Herbert Siegel), who gave dissociative identity disorder its current name. Spiegel estimates that 1 percent of the population suffers from the condition. Spiegel believes, as Loftus reports, that patients suffering from dissociative identity disorder "really have less than one personality rather than more than one personality" (Brody 85), suggesting that the disorder is, psychologically, a sinister subtraction.

A Sinister Subtraction

In light of what I learned about memory's unreliability and the notoriety of multiple personality as a clinical diagnosis, I was skeptical before I started reading *A Sinister Subtraction*. Kluft is a psychoanalyst, a clinical professor of psychiatry at Temple University School of Medicine, director of the Dissociative Disorders Program at the Institute of Pennsylvania Hospital, and a past president of the International Society for the Study of Trauma and Dissociation. He is the author and co-editor of several books, one of which, *Clinical Perspectives on Multiple Personality Disorder* (1993), was dedicated to the memory of Wilbur.

A Sinister Subtraction focuses on 34-year-old Melody Jarrett, an art teacher—shades of *Sybil!*—who claims she was molested by her former psychologist, Gordon Travers, and turns to the psychiatrist Joan Underwood for help. In the course of her treatment with Underwood, Melody suddenly dissociates into a helpless little girl, "Cindy," and then, once again, flees therapy. When Travers learns about Underwood's treatment of Melody, including the accusation of sexual abuse, the politically connected therapist files a multimillion-dollar lawsuit against Underwood, alleging that she had created an iatrogenic condition, through leading questions and the implanting of false memories, that led to the inaccurate diagnosis of dissociative identity disorder and to the damaging of his reputation and practice. The novel's title alludes to the office, Suite 312, in HighPoint Centre, a boxy apartment building in which Melody claims the abuse occurred. But the office apparently does not exist, thus undermining her credibility. The sensationalistic lawsuit makes the headlines, characterized on CNN and NPR as a "holy war against bad therapy." Expert witnesses are brought in by the plaintiff and defendant to speak about the controversial diagnosis.

A Sinister Subtraction replays the controversies and ambiguities surrounding the memory wars. *Sybil* is never mentioned in the novel, but like Mason, Melody draws sketches that offer an insight into her state of mind. In what may be a coincidence, the surname of a minor character is "Mason." It is certainly not a coincidence that Joan Underwood follows the guidelines of the International Society for the Study of Multiple Personality and Dissociation, an organization identical to Kluft's own professional society. Moreover, the novel contains a character, an expert academic researcher of false memory, who is modeled on Elizabeth Loftus. The surname of the Loftus character, Diane Bublekopf, conjures up the pejorative term "bubble head" ("kopf" means "head" in German and Yiddish). All the more reason to be cynical of the novel, I fumed silently, unwilling to be a bubble head again. No one wishes to be gullible a *second* time, forced to offer another *mea culpa*. In the acknowledgments at the end of the novel, Kluft admits that, as an expert on trauma and dissociation, he was "thrown into the cauldron of the memory wars" and ultimately became the defendant in a false memory case (426). Does this admission imply the novelist's self-justification? Prepared to dislike the novel, I was in for a shock.

Surprises

My first surprise was that Kluft conveys through the novel's engaging heroine, the young and inexperienced lawyer Linda Gilchrist, a brief albeit accurate history of the memory wars. Asked where she stands on this vexing issue, she responds, "With the folks in the middle," and then explains: "There's enough information out there to challenge both extremes. Go skeptical, and it becomes impossible to confront possible perpetrators. Go credulous, and 'innocent until proven guilty' gets turned into 'guilty until proven innocent'" (10). Linda knows, however, that the safe middle ground is not always possible—and sometimes the most dangerous place to reside. She attends a workshop for legal professionals called "Confronting the Consequences of Voodoo Science," an advocacy group that defends people from false accusations—a thinly veiled reference to the FMSF. Linda speaks for Kluft when she tells her law firm's managing partner, Bill Mackey, that in both law and science she prefers "honest confusion over arrogant certainty, congenial or not" (11). Linda also points out that the memory wars—the term originated with Frederick Crews (who started his career as a Freudian and then became a Schadenfreudian)—began with Freud's momentous decision in 1897 to abandon the seduction theory, the conviction that many of his female patients were sexually molested in early childhood, some before the age of four, in favor of psychic reality, the role of unconscious fantasies, fears, and desires. Freud's rejection of the seduction theory continues to draw furious criticism, but it affirmed the importance of psychic reality, which does not always coincide with "real" or external reality.

Kluft is scrupulously fair in his depiction of Diane Bublekopf. The plaintiff's attorney recites Bublekopf's "illustrious career and numerous honors"; more importantly, she handled every question "with becoming modesty" (204). As an expert witness, she concedes under cross-examination that false memories may nevertheless contain a degree of truth. The novel reports that about one fourth of Bublekopf's subjects accepted suggestions to endorse a false memory, a percentage only slightly less than the figure reported by Loftus. Kluft accurately points out the limitations of Bublekopf's research; a witness for the defense, the psychiatrist Benjamin Jordan, observes that although research shows it is possible to create false memories over mundane issues, it is harder to induce false memories of a traumatic event. Kluft never discredits Bublekopf's credibility by suggesting anything odd about her personality. That does not mean, however, that Kluft fails to undermine other characters who deserve criticism, such as the psychiatrist Joseph Chaudvent, an expert witness for the plaintiff and the author of a book with the tabloid title *America's Most Dangerous Psychiatrists and Psychologists*. Chaudvent is ignominiously dismissed as an expert witness when he admits he has not read the publications of the researchers he condemns. In Kluft's world (and mine), the supreme vice is *hubris*, and those who embody this quality ultimately fall from grace, to the reader's satisfaction.

In learning about the history of memory research, we never believe we are reading a dry textbook. Reading a clinical case is largely a cerebral activity, but reading a fictional story is both an intellectual and affective experience; we remember stories longer than textbook cases. Kluft juxtaposes factual material with often sparkling dialogue. "[I]f you want to bet on something that may occur less than a quarter of the time, and forget about failures to follow the misleading suggestions, something that occurs over three quarters of the time," Jordan asks the plaintiff's counsel, "I would like to play poker with all of you" (322–323).

A second surprise is that the novel's accurate account of the memory wars is matched by its compelling description of vulnerable characters. *A Sinister Subtraction* is a novel of ideas, dramatizing one of the most vexing questions in contemporary psychological research, but it also contains flawed, believable characters, human, all too human, who struggle with problems of living. Kluft gives each of the sympathetic characters one or more failings. The cast of characters is huge, but the major figures struggle, emotionally, in ways with which most readers can identify. We learn little about Melody Jarrett, mainly because in the middle of deposition she bolts from the room, muttering in child-like terror, "Bad men! Bad men!" (80). She doesn't return until the end of the story, after her accusations have been confirmed. Although the novel revolves around Melody, Kluft keeps her in the background, forcing us to imagine the process of dissociation. Linda is the main character, and we have access to her inner thoughts. She is a "demon researcher," but her lack of courtroom experience and insecurity lead to a near-disastrous rookie error, when she raises an open-ended question (which experienced lawyers are taught never to do) that enables the plaintiff's attorney to introduce newly discovered information about Joan Underwood's dark past. Appalled by her blunder, Linda is filled with shame. Linda is close to her sister, Eve, a psychiatrist who has both a career and a family, awakening Linda's envy because for a decade she has been unable to become pregnant.

In a novel filled with mysteries, none is greater than Joan Underwood's identity. She is not a multiple personality, but she has attempted to run away from her lurid past. Early in the novel she describes herself as one of the shrinks who understands everyone but herself, and soon we know why. The beautiful Veronica Fairbanks dropped out of Bryn Mawr College in her sophomore year to pursue an acting career in Hollywood, but her life spiraled out of control. After experiencing two breakdowns, a suicide attempt, and prolonged episodes of mental illness, she returned to college with a new name, Joan Underwood. Kluft has chosen his character's current name carefully, as she explains. "I picked Underwood because that's where I wanted my past to be. Under the wood of a coffin, the coffin of a past I wanted to kill" (328). Joan finally regains control of her life and makes the fateful decision to become a psychiatrist, wishing to help those as she herself has been helped. But when the revelations of her past come out during the trial, she once again breaks down, becoming catatonic, and she is hospitalized. Returning 100 pages later, she acknowledges that living with dark secrets is intolerable, one of the themes of the novel. Although the plaintiff's lawyers argue, predictably, that in overidentifying with the fragile Melody Jarrett, Underwood reached an incorrect diagnosis, the defense is able to refute this claim. What is perhaps most noteworthy about Joan Underwood is that, as with many people who become mental health professionals, she entered the field because of counterphobic motivation. "I wanted to be able to help other people the way I'd been helped," she admits in court. "Sounds corny, but that's why I decided to become a psychiatrist" (328). This is also true of Eve Gilchrist, who, raised by two alcoholic parents, resolves to become a psychiatrist to help those with similar or related problems. Linda's Aunt Kate also has a drinking problem, and the novel offers high praise for Alcoholics Anonymous.

Of all the characters, Jay Phillips changes the most. A short, fat, balding man with a stammer, Philips is a pioneer in the area of dissociative disorders, but he has lost his academic position, cannot publish his clinical articles in the best psychiatric journals, struggles with depression, and, shortly before the trial begins, learns that his wife has abandoned him. "Jay Philips is damaged goods" (26), Eve warns Linda, but when all the other potential experts drop out, Linda has no choice but to hire him, albeit reluctantly. Kluft rehabilitates Philips by showing his solution to Suite 312's disappearance: Travers had covered his tracks by getting the building's owner to tape over the doorway that originally appeared in Suite 312. Philips's ingenious solution leads to the discovery of a conspiracy between Travers and the governor of the state, both of whom were, unbeknownst to anyone, related, and both of whom were guilty of multiple sexual crimes. Philips's discoveries enable his psychological redemption at the end of the story. Philips's oft-rejected manuscript is accepted for publication, and he is appointed an adjunct professor in the English department of an Ivy League university. Who cannot be happy about that!

Ben Jordan deserves special attention, if only because he has appeared in Kluft's earlier novels, *Good Shrink/Bad Shrink* (2014) and *An Obituary to Die For* (2016). We learn in *Good Shrink/Bad Shrink* that Jordan served as a counterterrorism expert in the Israeli Defense Forces, was captured, tortured, and broke down under interrogation. But Jordan is now battle hardened, and he embodies the Nietzschean idea that whatever doesn't kill me makes me stronger. In the tradition of the 1962 American film *The Manchurian Candidate*, based on the 1959 novel of the same title, *Good Shrink/Bad Shrink* is a cloak and dagger thriller about brainwashing, the dark side of psychiatry, the misuse of hypnosis, and the vagaries of memory, but it also shows how characters like Jordan can survive overwhelming trauma. Like Joan Underwood, Jordan does not want to talk about his past, but when he is forced to do so—savvy about courtroom proceedings, he sets a trap that ensnares a plaintiff attorney—he reveals how he was hospitalized for 14 months with post-traumatic stress disorder. "I'm told Dr. Underwood wanted to be a movie star, and it didn't work out. It blew up in her face. Well, I wanted to be some James Bond kind of guy, and that blew up in mine" (*A Sinister Subtraction* 325). Kluft and Jordan are alike in several ways: both have earned an MD and PhD; both rely on their extensive knowledge of medical hypnosis, psychiatry, and psychoanalysis; and both live in the same Philadelphia suburb with a Welsh-sounding name: Bala Cynwyd. Is Jordan Kluft's alter ego? I don't know whether Kluft has flown a jet plane in the Israeli Army, a C-141 Starlifter for the New Jersey Air National Guard, killed innumerable villains while saving damsels in distress, or worked in a psychiatry department in which rogue colleagues were engaged in brutal brainwashing, as his fictional character did, but he obviously relishes Ben Jordan, as do readers.

At least two characters in *A Sinister Subtraction* are based on real figures. Miles Ernest, "psychoanalyst to the stars," evokes Ralph Greenson, the Hollywood analyst of Marilyn Monroe, Frank Sinatra, Tony Curtis, and Vivien Leigh. The psychoanalyst Nate Donaldson is based on one of the novel's dedicatees, Donald Nathanson (1936–2017), whom Kluft describes as "Polymath and Friend." Nathanson edited *The Many Faces of Shame* (1987) and authored *Shame and Pride: Affect, Sex, and the Birth of the Self* (1994). Donaldson's book, *Understanding the Bully and Bullying: A Study of Narcissistic/Sadistic Compensation for Personal Inadequacy*, affectionately referred to by Jordan as *Down with Bullies*, conveys Kluft's attitude toward those who humiliate others. One cannot equate Jay Philips with Kluft, but one aspect of the former's life is true of the latter's. George B. Greaves points out in "A History of Multiple Personality Disorder" (1993) that the Harvard-trained Kluft "watched his practice almost wither and die" when he started writing about the disorder, and he was "also refused publication of his findings in mainstream psychiatric journals" (365). In a 2018 interview with Warwick Middleton, Kluft admits that he had become a target of the FMSF when he was a psychiatric resident. The stigmatization ironically led to his specialization in multiple personality disorder. Kluft's fall from grace enables him to understand how his most complex characters, including Philips and Joan Underwood, experienced breakdowns followed by recoveries.

"I love mysteries" (112), Linda exclaims, as does Kluft. He had Nancy Drew in mind when he created Linda Gilchrist—she drives the same blue roadster as the teenage amateur sleuth. Kluft also had Agatha Christie in mind, offering a lively account of her history. I hadn't known that in 1926 the creator of the Hercule Poirot detective novels disappeared for 11 days, claiming, in Philips's words, that she had been in an alternate personality when she anonymously checked into a hotel in response to her husband's infidelities. Philips is a perceptive literary scholar. "Her books contain dozens of references to amnesia, to one person passing for another, disguises, and all sorts of trickery, and you can see how the poor woman keeps looking for a happy ending" (155). After reading *A Sinister Subtraction*, I turned to Agatha Christie's 1966 novel *Third Girl*, a story Philips urges Linda to read, in which the eponymous character, Norma Restarick, described as "Ophelia devoid of physical attraction" (10), believes she has committed a murder, although she cannot remember it. A psychiatrist offers several possible explanations. "There can be confusion, loss of memory, aggression, bewilderment, or sheer fuzzleheadedness!" (96). The reader wonders throughout the novel whether Norma is mad or a murderess. She is neither, as Hercule Poirot discovers; rather, Norma has been gaslighted by two criminals. I next turned to Janet Morgan's 1984 biography of Agatha Christie, where she accepts the likelihood of amnesia as an explanation of the 11-day disappearance.

A third and final surprise is that contrary to my expectations, it was a pleasure to read *A Sinister Subtraction*. Kluft's psychiatric expertise is evident throughout the novel, as is his literary talent. He doesn't shrink from exposing the egregious sexual boundary violations that have sabotaged psychotherapy. Almost one in ten male therapists have exploited at least one patient, Joan correctly informs Linda. Kluft's legal expertise is equally impressive. He has created a page-turning suspense story about medical malpractice, usually a dry subject. Reading the novel is a delightful way of taking "Lawyering 101." We learn as much about the four D's of medical malpractice—dereliction of duty directly leading to damages—as we do about the ambiguities of memory. *A Sinister Subtraction* is especially interesting to readers like me who, despite having a daughter and son-in-law who are both attorneys, do not know what it means to think like a lawyer. Lawyers are trained to be adversarial, but the novel insists that psychiatry and the law must be based on respect. The novel contains sly humor, sometimes of an ethnic nature, as when the pompous Chaudvent is introduced to his invited lecture at the American Psychiatric Association by Harvard Medical School Professor Tzimmis, a word that means "big fuss" in Yiddish. Kluft consistently roots for the underdogs, people who regard themselves, or who are regarded by others, as losers, lost souls. The good are rewarded, the evil punished. Bullies receive comeuppance in Kluft's world. The novelist's politics are never in doubt, as when a CNN commentator refers to Trump's book *The Art of the Deal*, which is called by another character the "art of war" (408)—or, we might add, the "art of the steal."

A Sinister Subtraction is a more accomplished novel than *Good Shrink/Bad Shrink* or *An Obituary to Die For*, both of which abound in gratuitous violence and suffer from a convoluted plot. "While the large cast slows its momentum," *Kirkus Reviews* concludes about *A Sinister Seduction*, "this courtroom tale should appeal to readers who enjoy legal and psychological maneuvers." There are a few aesthetic problems not always associated with mystery novels. The story could have ended with Joan Underwood's legal victory and a speedy resolution of the plot, but instead we learn about a character, outraged by Travers's rape of his wife, bizarrely beheading him and stuffing the headless corpse into a trash can. Justice is doubtlessly achieved in different ways. Kluft resolves the loose ends in the final pages of the novel. The governor has been arrested for murder and rape; Linda has given birth to twins; the forlorn Philips has found a new love interest in Linda's aunt Kate; and Melody Jarrett is doing well, partly because of her strong religious faith.

Freud urged his readers to be benevolent skeptics, and while the history of psychoanalysis sadly demonstrates that this has not always been the case with Freud himself or his followers (or detractors), the advice remains sound. Those who study dissociative identity disorder must carefully weigh the evidence in every case. In a posting to the American Psychoanalytic Association listserv on June 4, 2023, Kluft pointed out that dissociative disorders are commonplace rather than rare. "*Sybil* may be imperfect, but it brought hope to many victims of childhood mistreatment," adding, "Efforts to correct our profession's longstanding misunderstandings and mistreatments of any group of patients (or colleagues) are always in order." In the 2023 case study "Encountering the Singularities of Multiplicity: Meeting and Treating the Unique Person," Kluft demonstrates how he seeks to address a person's alters through what he calls "invitational inclusionism" (797). The seven-and-a-half year case study of a woman who was repeatedly sexually abused as a child and then sexually exploited, years later, by a therapist, is as moving as *Sybil* but far more convincing.

In the acknowledgments of *A Sinister Subtraction*, Kluft pays tribute to one of the major inspirations behind his novel, an adroit lawyer named Phyllis Lile-King who uncovered a plaintiff's deceptive effort to conceal the existence of the office in which evil events took place. By the time Kluft appeared in court as a witness for the defense, his testimony was "mere window-dressing" (426). Lile-King gave Kluft permission to write a novel based on her sleuthing, and he generously credits her influence. Kluft's dual career as a psychoanalyst and fiction writer has served him well—a multiple identity that does not strain the reader's belief.

Works Cited

Acocella, Joan. *Creating Hysteria: Women and Multiple Personality Disorder*. Jossey-Bass, 1999.
Berman, Jeffrey. "The Multiple Faces of Eve and Sybil: *E Pluribus Unum*." *Psychocultural Review*, vol. 2, 1978, pp. 1–25.
Berman, Jeffrey and Paul W. Mosher. *Off the Tracks: Cautionary Tales About the Derailing of Mental Health Care*. 2 vols. International Psychoanalytic Books, 2019.
Brody, Jane. "A Documentary Explores Dissociative Identity Disorder." *New York Times*, March 22, 2021.
Christie, Agatha. *Third Girl*. Pocket Books, 1966.
Diagnostic and Statistical Manual of Mental Disorders. 3rd ed. American Psychiatric Association, 1980.
Freyd, Jennifer J. *Betrayal Trauma: The Logic of Forgetting Childhood Abuse*. Harvard UP, 1996.
Greaves, George B. "A History of Multiple Personality Disorder." *Clinical Perspectives on Multiple Personality Disorder*, edited by Richard P. Kluft and Catherine G. Fine. American Psychiatric Association, 1993, pp. 355–380.

Jacobs, Alexandra. "Even After Debunking, *Sybil* Hasn't Gone Away." *New York Times*, May 28, 2023.

Kluft, Richard P. "Encountering the Singularities of Multiplicity: Meeting and Treating the Real Person." *Dissociation and the Dissociative Disorders: Past, Present, Future*, edited by Martin J. Dorahy, Steven N. Gold, and John A. O'Neil. 2nd ed. Routledge, 2023, pp. 687–712.

Kluft, Richard P. *Good Shrink/Bad Shrink*. Karnac, 2014.

Kluft, Richard P. *An Obituary to Die For*. Karnac, 2016.

Kluft, Richard P. *A Sinister Subtraction*. International Psychoanalytic Books, 2019.

Kluft, Richard P. and Catherine G. Fine, editors. *Clinical Perspectives on Multiple Personality Disorder*. Washington, DC: American Psychiatric Association, 1993.

Loftus, Elizabeth and Katherine Ketcham. *The Myth of Repressed Memory: False Memories and Allegations of Sexual Abuse*. St. Martin's Press, 1994.

McHugh, Paul R. *Try to Remember: Psychiatry's Clash Over Meaning, Memory, and Mind*. Dana Press, 2008.

Middleton, Warwick. "An Interview with Richard Kluft, MD." *ISSTD News*, December 13, 2017. https://news.isst-d.org/an-interview-with-richard-kluft-md/. Accessed January 14, 2023.

Morgan, Janet. *Agatha Christie: A Biography*. Collins, 1984.

Nathan, Debbie. *Sybil Exposed: The Extraordinary Story Behind the Famous Multiple Personality Case*. Free Press, 2011.

Nathanson, Donald L., editor. *The Many Faces of Shame*. Guilford, 1987.

Nathanson, Donald L. *Shame and Pride: Affect, Sex, and the Birth of the Self*. Norton, 1994.

"Review of *A Sinister Seduction*." *Kirkus Reviews*, July 15, 2019.

Schreiber, Flora Rheta. *Sybil*. Warner Books, 1973.

Thigpen, Corbett H. and Hervey M. Cleckley. *The Three Faces of Eve*. Popular Library, 1957.

Chapter 6

Bruce Fink

The Inspector Canal Novels

Bruce Fink begins *Death by Analysis* with an epigraph by a "certain French psychoanalyst": "Symptoms speak even to those who do not know how to hear them. Nor do they tell the whole story even to those who do" (1). Fink was so enamored of the quote that he cited it in his 2017 book *A Clinical Introduction to Freud* (1). The French analyst is, of course, Jacques Lacan, the notoriously inscrutable, iconoclastic thinker who founded his own school of psychoanalysis. Lacan was the inspiration behind Fink's fictional protagonist Quesjac Canal, a retired French Secret Service inspector who appears in all five detective novels: *The Adventures of Inspector Canal* (2010), *Death by Analysis* (2013), *The Purloined Love* (2014), *Odor di Murderer, Scent of a Killer* (2014), and *The da Vinci Staircase: Love and Turbulence in the Loire Valley* (2022). But an even more striking observation appears on the second page of *Death by Analysis* when New York Police Department inspector Peter Ponlevek seeks Canal's counsel about a recent death at a psychoanalytic institute. Entering Canal's consciousness, the narrator remarks ruefully that "yet another aged analyst had died in the saddle—of boredom, no doubt." Fink's aesthetic challenge is to convey this boredom in a lively manner to his readers.

Fink is a practicing Lacanian psychoanalyst and a prolific scholar. After graduating from Cornell University in 1976, he traveled to France to train at the University of Paris, VIII, where he worked with Jacques-Alain Miller, Lacan's son-in-law, and the Lacanian philosopher Alain Badiou. Fink received a PhD from the Department of Psychoanalysis and then became a member of the École de la Cause freudienne, a French psychoanalytic institute. Returning to the United States in 1989, he served as a professor of psychology at Duquesne University in Pittsburgh from 1993 to 2013; he is currently on the Board of Directors of the Pittsburgh Psychoanalytic Center. Fink is the author of many books on Lacanian psychoanalysis, including translations of several of Lacan's seminars. Fink remains one of Lacan's most ardent supporters, a defender of the faith, and he has never lost confidence in his muse.

Through the fictional Canal, Fink presents us with a sophisticated and engaging detective who uses his formidable linguistic skills, literary erudition, and shrewd intelligence to solve crimes that baffle police: he is a detective in the tradition of

Sherlock Holmes, Hercule Poirot, Lord Peter Wimsey, and Auguste Dupin. Canal relies not on intuition, as he remarks in *The da Vinci Staircase*, but on the ability to "generate multiple hypotheses and the cooperation of my unconscious that assembles incongruous things and silently works on them while I sleep—yes, sleep" (154–155). Fink reserves his most withering criticisms for non-Lacanians, especially American analysts, who have long been wary of French psychoanalysis.

It is not easy, even for a scholar who has spent many years reading Lacan's writings and translating them into English, to understand the French psychoanalyst who aimed for maximum ambiguity and opacity in his language. The most intriguing section of Fink's first book, *The Lacanian Subject* (1995), is the afterword, where he admits that the readers of the manuscript, selected by Princeton University Press to evaluate whether the study was worth publishing, concluded he was not critical enough of Lacan. But an even more singular admission follows: "Reading Lacan is an infuriating experience!" (149). Having translated five of his books, Fink confesses that he finds Lacan an "unbearable writer to translate, but a pleasure to read in French" (150). Those who cannot read Lacan in French are sadly denied this pleasure. Reading Fink's novels, on the other hand, is fun, mainly because Canal, while inspired by Lacan, never embodies the more exasperating qualities of his muse.

The portrait of Canal does not change much in the five novels. Canal reveals almost nothing about his personal life. "In the Secret Services, it was usually best not to talk about one's private life" (*Death by Analysis* 78). This is also true of French psychoanalysts, who, unlike many of their American counterparts, are not self-disclosing to their patients. In *The Purloined Love* Canal admits that he enjoys "delving into people's psyches and into the mysteries they stumble upon in life, whether personal or historical" (215), but he doesn't explain the reasons for this enjoyment. We never learn why Canal is an "amateur analyst" nor anything about his involvement with psychoanalysis. In *The Adventures of Inspector Canal*, Jack Lovett, one of New York's leading analysts—he reappears in later novels—declares that Canal is "practically a bona fide member" (275) of the New York Psychoanalytic Institute, a comment Canal does not welcome. Nor do we know why Canal has decided to live in New York rather than in France, where he worked until his retirement.

Canal is a far more genial character than the psychoanalyst on whom he is modeled. Canal "generally found something to like in most people," the narrator observes in *Odor di Murderer, Scent of a Killer* (50), suggesting that he is a more benevolent figure than Freud or Lacan. Playful, mischievous, unflappable, Canal is seldom at a loss for words. Thankfully, Canal never engages in linguistic mystification while solving mystifying crimes. Hospitality takes precedence over business, and he embodies *joie de vivre*, indulging every pleasure in life. Unlike Arsène Lupin, who pockets valuable jewels as his reward for solving crimes, Canal's only remuneration for assisting the police is a sumptuous dinner. Fink is deliberately vague about specific details of his hero's life, telling us only that he is a man of "average build and indefinable years" (*The Adventures of Inspector Canal* 195), but he is as well-read as his creator, revealing a deep and wide understanding of literature, linguistics, history, music, mathematics, art history, philosophy, and theology, not to mention psychology. As an accomplished translator, Fink endows Canal with a thick French accent. He pronounces *th* like *z*, *is* like *ease*, and sometimes drops his *h*'s. Fink is not always consistent about these mispronunciations, and Canal often speaks the King's English—largely because, as the novelist explained to me, his publisher asked him to omit the thick accent, which he did so "begrudgingly."

Canal is never a "split subject," as Lacan claimed about human subjectivity: we see no gap between what Canal thinks he knows about himself and what is hidden from view. He is always stable, sure of himself without being cocky, deeply fulfilled in his work. He rarely speaks about having a love relationship with another person, either in the past or present, but this has not been a problem for him—although at the end of *The da Vinci Staircase*, he is prepared to begin a romantic relationship. We don't know why he first became a Secret Service inspector and then an amateur psychoanalyst, but it was not for a counterphobic reason, that is, a need to come to terms with a traumatic experience. The *bon vivant* loves life: he is not only a wine aficionado but can also draw conclusions about a person's character based on the drinks he or she orders. Canal has no regrets about life, and he never regards himself as superior or inferior to another person. In short, a delightful character!

There is little narrative distance between Fink and his fictional sleuth; the former nearly always endorses the latter's psychological musings, however improbable. "There are no accidents," Canal proclaims in *The Adventures of Inspector Canal* (25), and he ingeniously tracks down Freudian slips, including his own. Like Freud and Lacan, Canal believes that the Oedipus complex is psychological bedrock. In speaking to Saalem about Mozart's devastation over his mother's death, Canal remarks, "Most of us spend much of our lives mourning the loss of our mothers, long before she dies" (35). The symphony conductor agrees, adding that the son's love of the mother is never exclusive because of the father's presence. Using Lacanian language, Canal expresses amazement to Lovett over the number of men "looking for a woman to be the phallus for them" (280), a remark with which the analyst readily agrees. Some of Canal's pronouncements strike the other characters (and perhaps readers) as dubious, as when he maintains that many men and women in their 20s and 30s delay marriage because of the unconscious hope that someday they can marry their sisters and brothers, respectively, a claim Fink appears to endorse. Sometimes Canal is startled to hear another character express one of his own maxims on love, as when Errand paradoxically declares that the "essence of love is giving what you don't have" (168), similar to Lacan's declaration that "love is giving something you don't have to someone who doesn't want it." Canal is a prescient social critic, lamenting that human relations have become "epistolary" as a result of social media. Another character immediately concurs: "the ever more glaring lack of face-to-face verbal intercourse leaves people poorly equipped to negotiate the inevitable gulf between fantasized and actual relationships" (105).

Canal spends most of his spare time, when he is not helping the police, reading psychoanalytic literature, and he sounds like an analyst when he maintains that solutions to interpersonal conflicts cannot be remedied without in-depth therapy. Curiously, despite the lack of narrative distance between the novelist and his hero, three times Canal makes insightful cultural observations followed by the narrator telling us that Canal "pontificated," suggesting perhaps Fink's fear that his detective speaks in platitudes. Fink uses third-person narration throughout the story, but on one occasion he refers to "Our three investigators" (262). On another occasion, the narrator speaks directly to the "faithful reader" who understands that Canal is experienced enough to know when delicate raillery is required or when a confidence should be forced.

Fink's language combines sophisticated if not arcane diction with New York ethnic expressions. In *The Adventures of Inspector Canal*, he refers to an "autochthonous [indigenous] waitress" (75) and a New Yorker's "unusual catachresis [semantic error]" (200), words with which most readers will be unfamiliar. At one point, Canal wets his lips in anticipation of a "stesichorean [Stesichorus was an ancient Greek lyric poet] palinode" (240); at another point, he delights in the neologism "superfetatory" (244). Fink is fond of the unusual word "tardive," which means "late," as in "tardive hour" or "tardive arrival." (The term "tardive dyskinesia" is a neurological condition characterized by repetitive movements.) Fink relishes Yiddishisms, as when Canal refers to Errant's "OY-VEY boardroom" (87). Another Yiddishism occurs when the narrator refers to Trickler's tarnished reputation even though he had admitted "bupkis" (275)—meaning, "nothing." Referring to the proverbial health benefits of champagne, Errand mutters, "yadda yadda yadda!"—an expression first identified with the comedian Lenny Bruce and popularized on the television show *Seinfeld*. Then there are sexual puns, as when Canal ponders what a "certain group of boisterous women," under the influence of alcohol, once told him: "A hard man is good to find!" (254), a joke attributed to Mae West. (One of Fink's analysands in *Against Understanding* [2014] sees this sentence on a poster in a female college dorm [vol. 2, 31].) Jokester, punster, and wordsmith, Canal displays his creator's linguistic talents, including speaking in tangled riddles. Musing on the entangled plots of the various characters in the story, Canal considers drawing on a blackboard a Borromean knot, reflecting Lacan's obsession with the image, which he believed depicted the interrelationship among the symbolic, the imaginary, and the real, his tripartite system of psychology.

Canal knows how to gain the trust of his acquaintances, including victims of crimes and victimizers. He does not hesitate to dispense advice to the lovelorn. He explains to Errand, for example, who has been wounded (and wounding) in love, the difference between desire and enjoyment. "Love," he tells her, sounding like Ann Landers or Dr. Ruth, "can help desire and enjoyment overcome their differences—not definitively, I suspect, for they are situated in fundamentally different realms, but at least long enough for sexual satisfaction to supervene" (172). Errant is so impressed with his advice that she calls him "doctor," a verbal slip he does not call to her attention. Indeed, he often sounds like a therapist, and Fink ends the novel with Canal recommending (in fact, blackmailing) some of the more conflicted characters, such as Ponlevek, to enter into analysis with Jack Lovett, a recommendation that comes true in Fink's next novel.

Death by Analysis

Death by Analysis is the most darkly satirical novel about psychoanalysis written by one of its own practitioners. Of the five novels, *Death by Analysis* is the most entertaining, especially for readers interested in learning about the development of psychoanalysis, including its troubled history of internecine warfare. For this reason, it is the novel on which I will focus, using the other novels as a gloss. The plot of *Death by Analysis* is simple. An attractive 29-year-old woman, in her fourth year of study at a psychoanalytic institute in New York City, suddenly collapses and dies at a conference dinner attended by 300 guests. She had no known medical condition. The coroner finds a prick mark on her arm, and a toxicological analysis indicates death from the rare poison curare. But who would want to murder the young woman, Doreen Sheehy, who was about to receive the student-of-the-year award? It turns out that there are many suspects who wanted the manipulative and unscrupulous Doreen dead, including her teachers, fellow students, and her own analysands. There's even the possibility that she pricked herself to disguise a suicide. During the investigation, another person, Sam Sorrel, an analyst dressed as a general, drops dead during a Halloween party, apparently murdered by the same person. Inspector Canal's task is to solve the mysterious crimes.

The last character Fink introduces in the novel, Loral Lamour, commits the murders. Miffed upon being turned down for three consecutive years for psychoanalytic training, she blames the rejections on her analyst, Doreen, who had entered the institute with false credentials and, in doing so, prevented Loral from being accepted into the same program. "Doreen got my spot" (171), she matter-of-factly informs Canal, who diagnoses her as a paranoic and realizes that she, rather than her fiancé, the police's leading suspect, was the murderer. But as her surname suggests, there is another reason Loral Lamour murders Doreen: she is in love with the analyst. She begins wearing her hair like Doreen, buying the same clothes, speaking like her, imitating her in every way, becoming, in effect, her double. Loral murders Sam Sorrel (who was her second analyst) because she regards him, too, as responsible for her failure to be accepted into psychoanalytic training.

An early discussion in *Death by Analysis* about the nature of psychosis presages the appearance of Loral Lamour. Clinicians see "tons of psychotics in outpatient settings," Lovett explains to Canal; the problem is that "most practitioners can't tell psychotics from neurotics—unless their patients report hallucinations and delusions that can't be overlooked" (31). Although Canal sees a "gleam of pure murderous rage in her eyes" when he interviews her about Doreen, he is most struck by her abrupt shifts of mood and the changes in her body language. Loral's lack of guilt or remorse over her actions confirms that she is psychotic rather than neurotic. Fink shows rather than merely tells us how a psychotic murderer looks and speaks.

"Clanians" and "Calanians"

Death by Analysis satirizes every aspect of the New York psychoanalytic community from an insider's perspective. The institution at which Doreen studied—the tautological-sounding New Institute for Psychoanalytic Psychoanalysis on the Lower East Side—is abbreviated NIPPLES, an anagram that recalls Trickler's portfolio in *The Adventures of Inspector Canal*: TITs. Another anagram, APE, refers to the American Psychoanalytic Establishment. (In one of the few factual errors in the novel, Lovett cites the abbreviation of the American Psychoanalytic Association as APsaE when it was APsaA, and now APsA.) Fink describes the bitter clashes between two extreme ideological factions, the traditional "Clanians" and the new "Calanians," both of whom Canal believes should be called the "Clownians," along with a "middle group" that is no less dogmatic. As in his earlier novel, Fink revels in wordplay. One character, "L. Thario," is truly a lothario, an unscrupulous seducer of women. Canal chooses as an alias "Jean-Pierre Kappferrant," the surname of which evokes errant head. The story abounds in sexual puns, albeit one character, addressing Canal as a "private dick," forgoes pointing out the phallic symbolism. Fink recognizes that double entendres and repartee can sometimes become tedious. In *The Purloined Love* Canal admits to having had the experience more than once that the "primitive puns and other wordplay I was able to invent in only partially acquired foreign tongues were either boring or incomprehensible to my interlocutors, even when they amused me thoroughly" (237). Most readers will appreciate Canal's delight in wordplay, which remains one of the strengths of Fink's fictional stories. Canal is usually a reliable narrator, but sometimes he errs in insignificant ways, as when he refers to Freud's expression the "narcissism of small differences" instead of, as an analyst gently corrects him, the "narcissism of minor differences" (92); Freud uses the expression in *Civilization and Its Discontents* to describe the constant feuds among people who are closely related to each other in communities with adjoining territories (*SE*, vol. 21, 114). On one occasion, the analyst Jack Lovett appears to be wrong: "Was it not Freud who said that even when two partners are making love, there are already six people involved?" (214). The same remark appears in *The da Vinci Staircase* when Canal claims that Freud believed there are six people whenever two make love: "two partners and all four of their parents!" (314). I can't find this assertion in any of Freud's writings, although writing to his confidant Wilhelm Fliess in 1899 about bisexuality, he observed: "I am accustoming myself to regarding every sexual act as a process in which four individuals are involved" (*Complete Letters of Sigmund Freud to Wilhelm Fliess* 364).

Most of Fink's satire is directed against institutional psychoanalysis. Paraphrasing the opening of *Anna Karenina*, Canal observes: "Every institute is unhappy in its own way." Many of Fink's criticisms of institutional psychoanalysis are, alas, accurate. Dr. Wilma Watkins, an anthropologist who teaches at

City University, laments the intellectual narrowness of psychoanalytic instruction. Unlike in the past, she confides to Canal, when there was a rich cross-fertilization among psychoanalysis, the humanities, and the social sciences, now psychoanalytic candidates learn nothing about literature, linguistics, anthropology, or sociology. Nor can her criticisms be dismissed as cynicism arising from the sudden end of her 30-year marriage to an analyst who teaches at NIPPLES. Fink is also correct about the loss of prestige in psychoanalysis and the difficulty of finding new students to enter psychoanalytic training. The "patient pool was drying up" (27), Jack Lovett complains to Canal. Lovett might have added that there are few clinical psychology doctoral programs that have a psychoanalytic or psychodynamic orientation. "In most psychology doctoral programs," I heard a psychoanalyst recently say, "psychoanalysis is brought up only as an object of derision and ridicule, if it is brought up at all." Further complicating the situation, another analyst responded, is the "diminishing number of internships and postdoctoral fellowships that provide good psychoanalytic psychotherapy training for young analysts." Or as Fink bluntly states in *Lacan to the Letter* (2004), "Virtually all of the classical analytic institutes in the United States are dying, training very few new analysts per year" (46).

Death by Analysis offers several recommendations to reinvigorate psychoanalysis. Fink suggests, as do many contemporary analysts, that the hierarchical structure of psychoanalytic institutes, where all the power resides in training and supervising analysts, often the most resistant to change, should be eliminated. The ideological differences between the Clanians and Calanians seem absurd to Canal, who, musing aloud, concludes that the only difference between the warring factions lies in a single letter, *a*, which reminds him of "aporia," a word signifying an irresolvable, internal contradiction. (Both Jacques Derrida and Paul de Man popularized the term to describe how a text's internal contradictions lead to a logical impasse.) Jack Lovett tells Canal that psychoanalysts must learn to distinguish between neurotics and psychotics.

> Treating psychotics as if they were neurotics makes them incredibly anxious or angry, in the *best* of cases. In the worst of cases it can even trigger a psychotic break, leading to a fundamental change in people who had managed to live their whole lives without any hallucinations or delusions at all. (31–32)

This is precisely what happens with Loral Lamour, whose psychotic break was triggered by Doreen's analytic incompetence. Doreen's sodden analyst, George Peterson, believes that analysis is a "lifetime endeavor"; he keeps his analysands in treatment for decades. Peterson proclaims that analytic neutrality is the most sacred virtue in psychoanalysis: "Every topic the patient discusses is treated with equal interest," but when Canal, playing devil's advocate, responds—"Even if the patient recites the phone book to you, or every film he has ever watched?"—the analyst mindlessly agrees, all the time becoming more inebriated. Canal's question remains valid, however. Peterson has spent nearly three years analyzing two of

Doreen's bogus dreams, both of which she plagiarized from Freud's 1905 classic study *Fragment of an Analysis of a Case of Hysteria*, the story of Dora—a case study the venerable analyst has not read. This leads to another Fink recommendation: Read Freud.

One senses, however, that these institutional reforms will not be easy, especially when Canal remarks, upon hearing Jack Lovett recite the history of breakaway psychoanalytic institutes, "Pluralism is the new fascism" (194). Fink is not sanguine about the possibility of psychoanalysts agreeing to disagree with each other in an intellectually healthy way. Canal sees no real theoretical differences among the Clanians, Calanians, and the middle group, yet these warring factions call to mind the "controversial discussions" in the British Psychoanalytic Society in the early 1940s among the supporters of Melanie Klein (the Clanians), Anna Freud (the Calanians), and the middle (or later independent) group. The history of psychoanalytic warfare becomes more complicated when we realize that "Calanian" is a perfect anagram for Lacanian, Fink's own psychoanalytic affiliation. One of the analytic students in *Death by Analysis* travels to Paris to study "French innovations in psychoanalysis" (52), but Fink never reveals precisely what he learns about psychoanalysis, perhaps because the novelist does not wish to satirize his own theoretical beliefs. Nor does *Death by Analysis* comment on the dramatic changes in psychoanalytic theory and practice in recent decades, including the rise of intersubjective and relational analysis, where meaning is co-created by analyst and analysand. Fink implies in *The Lacanian Subject* that there is nothing inherent in psychoanalytic discourse that must necessarily lead to power struggles among different institutes, but he recognizes, accurately, that this claim "will no doubt be disputed by many, given psychoanalysis' long history of schisms and infighting" (137).

While reading *Death by Analysis*, I recalled Norman N. Holland's only novel, *Death in a Delphi Seminar: A Postmodern Thriller* (1995). Like Fink, Holland turns to detective fiction to satirize psychoanalysis, in Holland's case, what he irreverently calls the "New Cryptics," the excesses associated with French poststructuralism, particularly Lacanian and Derridean theory, the latter of which he calls "Decockstruction" (38). Like Fink, Holland believes that "Inside every critic is a frustrated writer" (48). Like Fink, Holland creates an obnoxious female student, Patricia Hassler, who appears to be murdered, though no one knows how or why, in Holland's graduate reader-response seminar at the University of Buffalo, where the novelist, who was the chair of the English department, taught for many years. Each of the members of the graduate seminar in *Death in a Delphi Seminar*, including Holland himself, is a suspect. As in *Death by Analysis*, a second death takes place in *Death in a Delphi Seminar* during the police investigation. Both Fink and Holland use the Freudian technique of free association and slips of the tongue to track down the murderers. Additionally, the two novelists rely on twinning: the appearance of a dark double. Both Fink and Holland use Poe's method in "The Purloined Letter" of hiding in plain sight. And both use the same method of murder: envenomation. Hassler's murder turns out to be a suicide: she sits on a chair in the seminar room on which she had placed a thumbtack containing a deadly nerve toxin. Hassler's suicide, Holland implies, following Freud, represents the internalization of aggression symbolically directed against another person. The second murder in Holland's novel is that of an interloper who had been disrupting the graduate seminar. The interloper's name, Felix Kulper ("*felix culpa*," or "happy fault" in Latin), reveals Holland's fondness for wordplay, particularly when he mocks, as I remark in my book on Holland, "French fried Freud." Kulper's murder was caused by a French student, Christian Aval, who had plagiarized an essay by Hassler when they were both studying at Yale. Aval readily admits that he is not a unitary person but deeply divided. Aval's intellectual theft, which he claims, paradoxically, is his only "authentic act," is not unlike Doreen's theft of two dreams from Freud's case study of Dora. In short, I was convinced that there are too many similarities between *Death by Analysis* and *Death in a Delphi Seminar* to be accidental—until Fink told me that he had never heard of Holland's novel and that, strangely, he never reads detective fiction.

Fink ends *Death by Analysis* in the same way he begins it: with an allusion to Lacan. Jack Lovett cites a pronouncement by Rimbaud, "I really is an other," which he had come across while reading a book by a "Parisian psychoanalyst" recommended by Canal. Ironically, one can praise Canal for *not* being like Lacan; the novelist has made Canal more of a bon vivant than the French analyst and a much more likable character—or, as he said to me, "more American, certain of my French colleagues might say." *Death by Analysis* is stimulating, and although it does not contain any psychologically complex characters, this is partly due to the genre of detective fiction, which is more concerned with the solving of a crime than with uncovering the mysteries of identity. "Truth is often far stranger than fiction" (200), an analyst tells Canal, but in the case of *Death by Analysis*, fiction reveals a softening of Lacanian truth, for which Fink's readers remain grateful.

Works Cited

Berman, Jeffrey. *Norman N. Holland: The Dean of American Psychoanalytic Literary Critics*. Bloomsbury, 2021.

Fink, Bruce. *The Adventures of Inspector Canal*. Karnac, 2010.

Fink, Bruce. *Against Understanding*. 2 vols. Routledge, 2014.

Fink, Bruce. *A Clinical Introduction to Freud: Techniques for Everyday Practice*. Norton, 2017.

Fink, Bruce. *The da Vinci Staircase: Love and Turbulence in the Loire Valley*. (In collaboration with Héloïse Fink.) Sphinx, 2022.

Fink, Bruce. *Death by Analysis: Another Adventure from Inspector Canal's New York Agency*. Karnac, 2013.

Fink, Bruce. *Lacan to the Letter: Reading Écrits Closely*. U of Minnesota P, 2004.

Fink, Bruce. *The Lacanian Subject: Between Language and Jouissance*. Princeton UP, 1995.

Fink, Bruce. *Odor di Murderer, Scent of a Killer: An Adventure from Inspector Canal's New York Agency*. Karnac, 2014.

Fink, Bruce. *The Purloined Love: An Inspector Canal Mystery.* Karnac, 2014.
Freud, Sigmund. *Civilization and Its Discontents.* 1930. *The Standard Edition of the Complete Psychological Works of Sigmund Freud,* translated and edited by James Strachey, vol. 21. The Hogarth Press, 1961.
Freud, Sigmund. *The Complete Letters of Sigmund Freud to Wilhelm Fliess, 1887–1904,* translated and edited by Jeffrey Moussaieff Masson. Belknap Press of Harvard UP, 1985.
Holland, Norman N. *Death in a Delphi Seminar: A Postmodern Mystery.* State U of New York P, 1995.

Part III
Privileging Fiction Over Psychoanalysis

Chapter 7

Gregorio Kohon
Red Parrot, Wooden Leg

"Why do you write?" Daniel Goldstein, the protagonist in Gregorio Kohon's 2007 novel *Red Parrot, Wooden Leg*, asks his friend Luigi Marino this question, which is central to the story. Daniel is a poet, Luigi a novelist, and each offers different answers to the question. *Red Parrot, Wooden Leg* highlights the political violence and chaos in Latin America during the 1960s through the 1980s, but the story also shows how reading and writing are essential survival strategies during a frightening age.

Born in Buenos Aires, Argentina, in 1943, Kohon was himself a survivor of a brutal military dictatorship, from 1976 to 1983, where thousands of people "disappeared," most of whom were civilians. He spent the first 27 years of his life, as he reports in *Reflections on the Aesthetic Experience* (2016), growing up with institutionalized violence:

> I was lucky enough to have moved from Buenos Aires to London in 1970, unwittingly escaping the junta's particularly vicious persecution of the 1970s: the relentless harassment of students, workers and professionals, the systematic disappearances and the murders. It is estimated that the junta did away with some 15,000 to 30,000 people—a whole generation. Some of the victims were my friends and colleagues; some of them had been particularly close. (135, n.2)

Before leaving Argentina, Kohon studied law, literature, and philosophy, and trained as a clinical psychologist at the Universidad de La Plata. In London he worked with the famed psychiatrist R.D. Laing, whose 1960 book *The Divided Self*—which helped initiate the anti-psychiatry movement—insists that "madness" is a sane response to an absurd world. "Laing restored a sense of respect for all psychotic phenomena as something strange, alien, perhaps beyond interpretation," Kohon observes in his 2019 book *Concerning the Nature of Psychoanalysis* (57), qualities he tries to capture in his own writings. After studying psychoanalysis and becoming a member of the British Psychoanalytic Society, Kohon and his family moved to Australia in 1988 where he and his psychoanalyst wife, Valli Shaio Kohon, founded the Brisbane Centre for Psychoanalytic Studies. Kohon returned to London in 1995 and became a training analyst in the British Psychoanalytic

Society. He is now Distinguished Fellow of the Society. He also has a private practice in London. Kohon has written or edited eight books on psychoanalysis, along with coauthoring two books, one with the French analyst André Green, whose writings he has championed, the other with Rosine J. Perelberg. In addition, Kohon has written four books of poetry in Spanish. One of them, *Odetta in Babylon and the Canada Express*, was translated into English in 2021.

First published in Spanish, *Red Parrot, Wooden Leg* was a finalist in 2003 for the Fernando Lara Novel Award, established in 1996, given annually to a novel published in Spanish. Once translated into English, the novel quickly caught the attention of the psychoanalytic community. Two leading analysts, Adam Phillips and Thomas Ogden, wrote blurbs, the former praising the novel's "creation of atmosphere," the latter (also an acclaimed novelist) lauding the "sparing and highly nuanced" dialogue.

Combining fiction, poetry, and autobiography, *Red Parrot, Wooden Leg* is both a Bildungsroman and a coming-of-age story about the growth and development of a writer. Chapter 1 takes place in 1966, a time of growing horror and political repression in Argentina and Brazil, the two settings of the story. Shortly before leaving Buenos Aires, Daniel had published his first book of poems that had been celebrated by a raucous party filled with local rock bands, but the joyful event quickly darkened by the presence of two drunken policemen. The morning newspaper headlines screamed: "COMMUNIST WRITER'S PARTY ENDS IN SHOOT-OUT" (7). Unsure what to do with his life but unable to remain in his birth country, Daniel leaves his family and travels with Luigi to Rio de Janeiro, Brazil, where they encounter an army of cockroaches, indestructible creatures that turn out to be the least of their worries.

Daniel seldom thinks about his family until the end of the novel. "I wish you could change your life and work" (25), his mother laments in an early letter from home. Kohon conveys the news from Argentina through letters, an epistolary technique he adroitly uses throughout the story. Daniel does not have much contact with his sisters, Miriam and Shoshana, and he broods over his failed relationship with Lola, whom we never see. For reasons that are never entirely clear, Daniel remains estranged from his father, who was severely injured years earlier in a tram accident. "He loved his father, but the accident changed their relationship" (185). Daniel soon found himself despising his father, and his visits to the hospital to see him became shorter and shorter. Part of Daniel's resentment arises when his father unexpectedly sold his son's typewriter because the family desperately needed money—and perhaps because, more significantly, of the father's disapproval over his son's efforts to earn a living through writing.

Nor can another noteworthy character, Damián, support himself, however much he would like to, through his writing. He now teaches history at a secondary school in Lomas de Zamora. Through Damián's letters we learn about the history of repression in Latin America, including the rise of fascism in Argentina during the Perón regime. Damián's brutal murder near the end of the story is a grim reminder of the price paid by intellectuals for speaking out against tyranny.

The other colorful character is Wanda Ribeiro, Daniel's "black goddess" Brazilian lover and *inspiratrice*, a "woman who inspires poets to write the best love poems" (106). Wanda is the most gifted storyteller in the novel. Pregnant at 15, Wanda is thrown out of her home by her father who, following the family's adopted Jewish customs, declared her dead. After the pregnancy was terminated by an illegal abortion, Wanda traveled to Lapa, Rio de Janeiro, where she was picked up and seduced by a pimp who forced her to work as a prostitute. Wanda and Daniel, a "whore and a poet," in the former's stark words, seek comfort from the other. Wanda becomes pregnant with Daniel's child and begins to experience vivid dreams and nightmares that portend another pregnancy—and abortion. Based on the sentence, "Daniel needed a wet-nurse, not a whore" (21), Francesca Segal opined in a review published in *The Guardian* that "It is impossible to forget that the author is a psychoanalyst," but I would not have reached this conclusion from the novel alone. *Red Parrot, Wooden Leg* is about the vicissitudes of writing, and there is little if anything in the story that reveals the novelist's psychoanalytic identity. It is true that a minor character crows, "I'm a bit of a psychologist" (70), a pompous statement that arouses Daniel's amused sarcasm. No other character pretends to understand the inner workings of the mind. To his credit, Kohon never "psychoanalyzes" his characters' motivations; rather, he allows us to infer their thoughts and feelings through dialogue.

Kohon's Jewish background is evident. He conveys through summary rather than scenic narration—telling, not showing—that Daniel's large, extroverted family "barked and grumbled at each other" through Yiddish, which in their conversations sounded "contentious" (11). As in Kluft's *A Sinister Subtraction*, *Red Parrot, Wooden Leg* abounds in Yiddish expressions. Waking up in the home of Olinda Morais, a Brazilian painter and member of the Communist party, Daniel hears an expression vaguely familiar: "*Shlof gikher, me darf di kishn*" (64): "sleep faster, I need the pillow." One page later, he repeats his grandmother's expression: "*Got heyst oykh keyn nar nit zayn!*" (65)—"God never asked anybody to be stupid." Shortly before he dies, Daniel's father is asked, by the hospital chaplain, whether he wishes to make a confession. "I'm a Jew of the Diaspora," he responds indignantly, "and as such, God should ask *me* for forgiveness, *He* is the one who's sinned against us" (188), a remark with which his secular son silently agrees. Daniel promises to honor his father's dying request not to be buried in a Jewish cemetery, but he breaks his word, a betrayal that later haunts him.

The Write Stuff

For Kohon and other authors, writing fiction is an act of resistance, especially in a politically repressive society. Not that Kohon is naïve enough to believe the pen is mightier than the sword. Daniel grasps that given the dictatorial government in which he lived, "poetry was no longer enough to confront the brutality of the police and the military" (208). He also knows that "No one earned a living writing poetry, or even writing novels" (190). Daniel's favorite poets and novelists form a list of the twentieth century's greatest Latin American and European writers. Inside his suitcases are books by Salvatore Quasimodo, Jorge Amado, Raúl González Tuñón, Roberto Arlt, and Cesare Pavese. The suitcases are later stolen, but Daniel will never forget these writers. He quotes poems by Pedros Salinas, Paul Eluard, Yevgeny Yevtushenko, Dylan Thomas, and Robert Desnos. He cites the famous lines by the Spanish poet Antonio Machado: "Walker, there are no roads / Roads are made by walking" (151); Kohon cites the same lines in *Reflections on the Aesthetic Experience*, pointing out that art is created only by taking risks.

"Analysts write at the expense of their patients, of their families, of their friends," Kohon reminds us in his 1999 book *No Lost Certainties to Be Recovered* (89), and this is also true of the three writers in *Red Parrot, Wooden Leg*. Unlike analysts, who must not betray their patients' confidentiality, poets, novelists, and memoirists are under no such constraints, yet writing about others always poses ethical questions, especially when writing about living people. Writing also involves struggling with language. True writers keep on writing despite the impossibility of writing. Daniel is in love with language, but he realizes that words both reveal and conceal. "*The very impossibility of a metaphor*," he declares in his notebook, underscoring the importance of his insight, "*confronts you with the strange passion present in the desire to write*" (54). He imagines the act of writing as a physical struggle. "As much as he loved words," the narrator tells us about Daniel, "he also wanted to destroy them, spoil them, force them to reveal their falsehood" (54).

Luigi, Daniel, and Damián offer their own reasons to write, some better than others. "First, it helps me to seduce more women," Luigi boasts exuberantly. "Secondly, I can discover what I feel. I don't know which is more important" (25). Far from repudiating Luigi's first explanation, Kohon playfully suggests that writing is allied with the pleasure principle—pleasure for the writer and reader alike. Kohon excels as a Rabelaisian storyteller. The pleasure principle involves, for Kohon's characters, zany sexual descriptions, as when, during a university conference focusing on "The Engagement of the Poet in Modern Society," the poet Hildon Medeiros walks up to the podium and offers his reason for the purpose of art. "'This is the only thing I have to say about poetry.' He proceeded to undo his trousers, pulled out his dark, long, truly enormous penis, and urinated on the microphone" (31). The audience, astonished at first, begins wildly applauding before he is taken away for indecent exposure. Luigi, four years older than Daniel, recalls his obsession with masturbation and wet dreams; once he tried to have sex with his sister. Fearful of losing his mind, he decides to become a priest and enters a seminary. Life inside the seminary provides no relief, however: the students and priests are as tormented by sex as Luigi is. Convinced that he could smell the semen of those masturbating in the seminary, a mad priest suggested that the liquid should be collected in a container and added to the fertilizer for the vegetable garden. "The problem was, of course, how to collect it without the procedure giving too much pleasure" (164). Luigi leaves the seminary after two years.

Writing is also connected to the reality principle, including the mind's ability to make sense of the external world. Writing is a choice that the three characters consciously make, an act of volition, yet at the same time, writing is instinctual, as necessary for life as breathing. "The truth was that they both knew that they wrote because they couldn't do otherwise. They wouldn't know what else to do with their lives" (25). A passage from *No Lost Certainties to Be Recovered* emphasizes the compulsory and addictive nature of writing. Musing on the distinct reasons for writing, Kohon invokes André Green's words in *On Private Madness* (1986): "I write because I cannot do otherwise"; Green adds that writing is "imposed upon me rather than freely chosen" (Green 3; *No Lost Certainties to Be Recovered* 89). Kohon cites Maurice Blanchot's observation in *The Gaze of Orpheus and Other Literary Essays* (1981) about the paradox of writing: "The writer finds himself in this more and more comical condition—of having nothing to write, of having no means of writing it, and of being forced by an extreme necessity to keep writing it" (Blanchot, 5, *No Lost Certainties to Be Recovered* 90). Noting that Blanchot's remark echoes Flaubert's similar belief in the impossibility of writing, Kohon offers a useful explanation: "The writer suffers the fragmentation in language; the reader creates a 'unity' where there is none" (90). And in *Reflections on the Aesthetic Experience* Kohon cites Marguerite Duras's belief that writers who find themselves at the bottom of a hole, isolated and helpless, can be saved only by writing (38).

Daniel also finds himself at the bottom of a hole; suffering from writer's block caused by the fear, he has nothing to say. Then, one day, he locked himself in his bedroom and wrote for three consecutive days and nights. "He did it with rage, with nostalgia, as if this were his last creative gesture." During this time he felt "possessed, mad, but happy" (101). What allowed Daniel to overcome writer's block? In a word, *ruthlessness*, an idea Kohon expands upon in *No Lost Certainties to Be Recovered*: "This cannot be done without ruthlessness, without a measure of wickedness and obstinacy. It requires a hardness of heart and a considerable amount of egoism; without selfishness, an artist cannot achieve many of his artistic goals" (89).

The idea of ruthlessness comes from D.W. Winnicott, who argued that the child uses the mother "ruthlessly" to survive. "The normal child," Winnicott suggests in *Collected Papers: Through Paediatrics to Psycho-Analysis* (1958), "enjoys a ruthless relation to the mother, mostly showing in play, and he needs his mother because only she can be expected to tolerate his ruthless relation to her even in play, because this really hurts her and wears her out" (154). In *Playing and Reality* (1971), Winnicott asserts that ruthlessness is involved in both object-relating and object-usage, where the former implies the child's subjective reality, including the sense of isolation, and the latter implies shared reality.

Ruthlessness may be necessary for the creation of art, but Kohon rejects art motivated solely by the desire for social change. Daniel hears a literature professor, an "imposing woman of forceful convictions," argue that poetry requires social justification, a Sartrean view that art must destroy the status quo. "No literature! Only praxis!" the professor shouts. Daniel condemns her "misdirected brilliance" (31). Social justice is fundamental in Kohon's world, but Daniel is always aware, like his creator, of the aesthetic dimension of art, the beauty of language and the difficulty of creating something new and original. He carries his notebook with him wherever he goes to record ideas or phrases that may be transformed into poems. He pens the words "*to be developed*" but then reproaches himself: "Such grandiosity" (55), the only remotely psychoanalytic word that appears in the novel. But here the reader disagrees with Daniel, for there is nothing egotistical about the ambition to become a good poet, especially if one has the talent, determination, and grit to succeed. Why should the desire to become a good poet be more grandiose than the wish to become, for example, a good teacher or a good analyst?

And yet Daniel remains conflicted about his identity as a poet, for although he knows that literature is necessary for his survival, he also fears that this makes him, for most people, an elitist. There is nothing dilettantish about his love for poetry. Nevertheless, he realizes that he was not a great poet like the many poets he cites. He might have consoled himself with the knowledge that he was a "good enough" poet, as Winnicott talked about good enough mothers, but Kohon does not want to diminish this protagonist's anxiety over his present and future identity. Daniel can imagine himself writing poetry for his creative survival while supporting himself as a merchant or taxi driver. "Other poets had done it," he muses (89). Kohon leaves the question of Daniel's future in doubt.

The fate of writing is always uncertain, as can be seen with another writer, Eugenio Paredes, who had arrived in Buenos Aires with 1500 poems and four novels in his satchel. He invited friends to a party where, ritualistically, he created a bonfire and burned one of his manuscripts. Does this suggest that the process of writing was more important to him than the publications of his works? Eugenio suffers a gruesome ending, decapitated by thieves. The writers in *Red Parrot, Wooden Leg* live with the constant dread that their writings will lead to arrest, imprisonment, or death. Literature is, as Franz Kafka wrote, the axe for the frozen sea within us, but the axe highlights the potential violence surrounding the creation and reception of art.

As Daniel's life becomes more disoriented, symptomatic of the larger chaos in Argentina and Brazil, he begins to experience a feeling best described by the title of Freud's 1919 essay "The Uncanny." The word conjures up the simultaneous familiar and disturbingly unfamiliar. For Kohon, as for Freud, the uncanny is a foundational aspect of the aesthetic experience. The uncanny emerges "when something is present but has not yet become explicit," Kohon writes in *Reflections on the Aesthetic Experience*; "it might refer to a feeling of anxiety that something is pending, is about to be revealed" (13). Just as the uncanny lurks throughout Alan Krohn's *The Mind's Eye*, so does it appear throughout *Red Parrot, Wooden Leg*, which is filled with uncertainty, anxiety, aloneness, and silence. The novelist succeeds in capturing the uncanny in Daniel's and Wanda's dreams, a netherworld abounding in strangely familiar fears. One can convey, intellectually, the experience of the uncanny in a nonfictional text, but a poet or novelist seeks to reproduce the uncanny, emotionally, in readers.

The Parrot

"In Kafka's writings," Kohon avers in *Reflections on the Aesthetic Experience*, "animals relate to the human world in strange ways: dragons, snakes, storks, dogs, and 'unearthly horses' appear in a variety of bizarre circumstances" (39). A parrot plays the same role in Kohon's novel. The eponymous character in the story is Joacaría, the red-fan parrot owned by Olinda's mother-in-law. Ironically, Joacaría is the most Jewish figure in the novel. His favorite expression voices Jewish resistance amidst persecution: "*Kish me in tochis! Kish me in tochis!*—Kiss my ass!" (85). Joacaría's vocabulary may be limited, but his humor enlivens the story, and his presence is an inspired touch. Artists recreate rather than reproduce reality; they are not parrots. And yet Kohon's parrot does more than merely mimic the human characters: he shows the value of connection, a quality crucial for survival in the human and animal worlds.

The parrot has a surprisingly long history in psychoanalysis. Freud referred twice in his letters to the tropical talking bird. In an 1895 letter to his future wife, Freud writes about seeing his dying friend Ernst von Fleischl-Marxow. "He keeps a parrot in his room, a bird which means more to him than many a human being. It is a creature with plumage of outrageous colors to which he attributes all manner of subtleties, whereas I maintain that it is very stupid" (*The Letters of Sigmund Freud* 141). In a 1900 letter to his confidant Wilhelm Fliess, Freud resigns himself to "living like someone who speaks a foreign language or like Humboldt's parrot. Being the last of one's tribe—or the first and perhaps the only one—these are quite similar situations" (*The Complete Letters of Sigmund Freud to Wilhelm Fliess* 430). Like the German naturalist and explorer Alexander von Humboldt (1769–1859), who encountered parrots while exploring the Orinoco and Amazon rivers, and who brought them to Europe, where he transcribed their words, Kohon's parrot reveals clues into Daniel's world, including the need for friendship and concern for others.

The best-known talking bird in psychoanalysis is the "Angry Parrot" in Marion Milner's iconic *On Not Being Able to Paint*, first published under the pseudonym Joanna Field in 1950 and then under the author's own name in 1957. Of the 49 figures that appear in the book, the central image is the "Angry Parrot," which shows a furious bird, sitting on a large fiery red egg, amidst tempestuous water. Milner offers several interpretations of the Angry Parrot, which represents Milner herself, fearful of expressing her own dark emotions. Milner develops the meaning of the Angry Parrot's egg in *Eternity's Sunrise* (1987), where she remarks that it represents the "theme of the cocoon, safe place in which change can take place" (102). As I observe in *Psychoanalytic Memoirs* (2023), one of the meanings of the egg in the Angry Parrot drawing is the work of art itself, *On Not Being Able to Paint*, which Milner jealously guards. "She solves the classic dilemma for women, 'brains versus babies,' by giving birth to a new creation, her book, which springs from the lovingly nurtured egg."

The most striking physical detail about Kohon's parrot is his wooden leg, the result of an accident when it became entangled amongst the keys of Luigi's typewriter; the broken leg was amputated. Is it fanciful to see the injury as one more example of the perilous nature of writing, or typing, in Kohon's world? Joacaría soon drops his Yiddish expressions and learns a few French expressions, which prompts Luigi to observe to Daniel that the parrot has become a "living symbol of the destiny of your race." Joacaría dies near the end of the novel—of sorrow, Luigi speculates, when he was forced to leave the parrot with his mother—but then Daniel recognizes the embalmed parrot while walking past a store. "Even in death, Joacaría looked alive and seemed to be enjoying himself," Daniel thinks to himself, "some things will never die" (210). The stuffed parrot in Kohon's novel resembles the golden bird in Yeats's 1926 poem "Sailing to Byzantium," a symbol of art that survives the onslaught of time.

Daniel's Future

Freud believed that a father's death is the "most important event, the most poignant loss, of a man's life," as he wrote in *The Interpretation of Dreams* (1900; *SE*, vol. 4, xxvi), an event that inspired Freud's self-analysis and the creation of his most revolutionary book. Daniel appears to hold the same view, for after his father's death, which follows the parrot's death, he pens a 45-line poem that he reads aloud to Luigi. The elegiac poem, addressed to his father in second person, evokes Daniel's last sight of him in the hospital, with the "oxygen cylinder and the rubber tube insolently up your nose." Daniel refuses to sentimentalize the father–son relationship. The poem recalls the dying man's last request that the son cannot fulfill. Will his father's death, which he describes ambiguously as a "suicide," allow Daniel to attain peace? The poem ends with the poet's uncertain future.

Kohon concludes *Red Parrot, Wooden Leg* with two chapters, each only a couple of pages long. Five years later, in chapter 2, we learn that Allen Ginsberg read Daniel's poem, published in Spanish, in New York. The novel includes this detail, I suspect, to validate the autobiographical nature of Daniel's—and Kohon's— poem. Crafting the poem was, in the narrator's words, the "single moment [that] marked the end of his youth" (214). The novel ends in 1986, in chapter 3, in which Daniel writes to the deceased Damián, meditating on their many friends who perished during the horrific 1970s: "I wish that you could have been with us, walking in Lapa, ignorant of dangers, discovering that wonderful music, writing these lines" (218). The sentence echoes Olinda's earlier wish to "leave a mark in the world" (194). Daniel's poem and Kohon's novel represent this mark.

As the novel ends, Daniel has completed one chapter of his life and awaits the next. He will, almost certainly, continue with his writing: he has always been more interested in poetic rather than political revolutions. There is no indication he will become a psychoanalyst, like his creator. One can imagine Daniel becoming a psychoanalyst, though curiously, in his interview with André Green, Kohon contends that based on the creative artists and writers he has analyzed, he was struck by the contrast between their capacity to create and their incapacity to love (*The Dead Mother* 53).

The reviews of *Red Parrot, Wooden Leg* are brief but enthusiastic. In a review published in the *Financial Times*, Lottie Moggach refers to the coming-of-age tale as "lusty and spirited as it is thoughtful." Writing in *The Independent*, Amanda Hopkinson notes that the "encounter between the bourgeois porteños of Buenos Aires and the alternative lifestyle cariocas of Rio lends the book a character as original as that of the lame parrot." The reviewer in *Goodreads* states that Kohon's text "might be deceptively read as personal reminiscences. In fact, this is one of the many achievements of this wonderful piece of fiction."

Readers who follow Kohon's career may be disappointed that he has not continued to write fiction, but he has made notable contributions to psychoanalysis. In the final analysis, literature and psychoanalysis are intimately interconnected, parallel efforts to explore the sorrow and nobility of life. To return to Daniel's question that I raised at the beginning, there are many reasons Kohon's characters write, including the need to bear witness to persecution, memorialize loss, and honor the memories of those no longer alive. *Red Parrot, Wooden Leg* shows how grief and trauma can be transmuted into deeply moving art, enabling the bereft to continue moving forward with their lives.

Works Cited

Berman, Jeffrey. *Psychoanalytic Memoirs*. Bloomsbury Academic, 2023.
Blanchot, Maurice. *The Gaze of Orpheus and Other Literary Essays*. Station Hill, 1981.
Freud, Sigmund. *The Interpretation of Dreams*. 1900. *The Standard Edition of the Complete Psychological Works of Sigmund Freud*, translated and edited by James Strachey, vol. 4. The Hogarth Press, 1953.
Freud, Sigmund. *Letters of Sigmund Freud*, selected and edited by Ernst L. Freud, translated by Tania & James Stern. Basic Books, 1960.
Freud, Sigmund. "The Uncanny." 1919. *The Standard Edition of the Complete Psychological Works of Sigmund Freud*, translated and edited by James Strachey, vol. 17. The Hogarth Press, 1955.
Green, André. *On Private Madness*. The Hogarth Press, 1986; rpt. Karnac, 1997.
Hopkinson, Amanda. "Review of *Red Parrot, Wooden Leg*." *The Independent*, November 1, 2007. www.independent.co.uk/arts-entertainment/books/reviews/red-parrot-wooden-leg-by-gregorio-kohon-398526.html. Accessed May 31, 2023.
Kluft, Richard P. *A Sinister Subtraction*. International Psychoanalytic Books, 2019.
Milner, Marion. *Eternity's Sunrise: A Way of Keeping a Diary*. London: Virago, 1987; rpt. with a new introduction by Hugh Haughton. Routledge, 2011.
Milner, Marion. *On Not Being Able to Paint* [Joanna Field]. Heinemann, 1950; 2nd ed. 1957. Foreword by Anna Freud; rpt. 1981.
Moggach, Lottie. "Review of Red Parrot, Wooden Leg." *Financial Times*, September 21, 2007. www.ft.com/content/61383f34-665e-11dc-9fbb-0000779fd2ac. Accessed May 31, 2023.

"Review of *Red Parrot, Wooden Leg.*" *Goodreads*, August 1, 2007. www.goodreads.com/book/show/969290.Red_Parrot_Wooden_Leg. Accessed May 31, 2023.

Segal, Francesca. "Review of *Red Parrot, Wooden Leg.*" *The Guardian*, October 6, 2007.

Winnicott, D.W. *Collected Papers: Through Pediatrics to Psycho-Analysis*. Tavistock, 1958.

Winnicott, D.W. *Playing and Reality*. Basic Books, 1971.

Chapter 8

Thomas Ogden's Fiction

Thomas Ogden is one of the world's most acclaimed psychoanalysts. A graduate of the San Francisco Psychoanalytic Institute, where he serves on the faculty, he is the Director of the Center for the Advanced Study of the Psychoses. He served as an Associate Psychiatrist for a year (1975–1976) at the Tavistock Clinic in London where, he told me, he learned

> what it means to live British object relations theory. The people I worked with there showed me far more than one can learn by reading texts. One of the more useful things I have done in my career is help bring Klein, Fairbairn, and Winnicott to this country at a time they were hardly read, much less understood.

A prolific author of more than a dozen clinical books, Ogden has garnered many honors, including the 2004 *International Journal of Psychoanalysis* Award for the most important paper of the year; the 2010 Haskell Norman Prize for outstanding achievement as a psychoanalytic clinician, teacher, and theoretician; the 2012 Sigourney Award; and the 2014 Hans Loewald Award for Psychoanalytic Education. These awards become more impressive because of Ogden's challenge to psychoanalytic orthodoxy; for example, he does not believe in Freud's "fundamental rule," arguing that patients have the right to privacy and therefore should not be instructed to say everything that comes to mind. Ogden's writings have been translated into 19 languages. In addition to practicing psychoanalysis, he teaches creative writing in San Francisco. Ogden told Noya Kohavi in a 2017 interview that he was seven the first time he saw his mother cry, when her psychoanalyst died. In a 2021 interview with Nicolas Gougoulis and Katryn Driffield, Ogden elaborated on the significance of his early introduction to psychoanalysis:

> My mother began analysis when I was aged three (this was in 1949). Although she never spoke to me using psychoanalytic terms or concepts, I believe, in retrospect, that she developed in analysis a greater capacity for self-reflection, which had an influence on the sort of person she was to me. And again, in retrospect, her analyst was an additional presence at our dinner table each evening, along with my mother, father, and younger brother. (223–224)

Ogden began psychoanalytic child therapy when he was six, and it lasted for three years. Without being specific about the nature of his childhood conflicts, he remarks that therapy helped him greatly.

As a literature and premed student at Amherst College, Ogden never doubted he would become a psychoanalyst. He didn't begin to write fiction, however, until he was in his 60s. Despite the many interconnections between literature and psychoanalysis, he seeks to keep the two disciplines separate. "When I write novels," he told Kohavi, "I'm a novelist, and when I'm with patients, I'm an analyst." Ogden made a similar observation in his interview with Nicolas Gougoulis and Katryn Driffield. "Depending on the kind of writing I am doing, I think of myself as a psychoanalyst who is also a writer, or a writer who is also a psychoanalyst" (225). Ironically, despite Ogden's attempts to keep his two identities separate, he argues in "Analytic Writing as a Form of Fiction" (2021) that the two are inseparable. Fiction for him refers to writing that "attempts to convey what is real and alive, or unreal and dead"; in this sense, "the fiction that an analytic writer writes is *more true* to the analytic experience than a transcript of the session" (222). He privileges storytelling over theory even in his clinical writings. "During the case presentation," Ogden told me, "I present nothing of theory: the analytic experience itself is where I create the life of the presentation."

Ordinarily, it would be irrelevant to point out that none of Ogden's characters in his three novels is Jewish, but after reading Kleiger's *The 11th Inkblot*, Kluft's *A Sinister Subtraction*, and Kohon's *Red Parrot, Wooden Leg*, in addition to, as we shall see, Theodore Jacobs's *The Year of Durocher* and *The Way It Ends*, and Daniel Jacob's *The Distance from Home*, all of which are filled with Jewish characters and often laced with Yiddishisms, one is surprised that this is not true with Ogden. Responding to Noya Kohavi's statement that his professional books have been published in Israel, including his novels, which have been translated into Hebrew, Ogden has a ready explanation: "I think that Jewish people—I'm Jewish—value introspection in a way that mainstream America does not," adding, "Jews have been interpreting texts forever, and language is text. It's just part of the genes of the people." Ogden's parents were, culturally, "thickly Jewish," from New York, and it's likely that one reason he has avoided writing about New York Jews is to tap into the heartland of America.

The Parts Left Out

Ogden has written three novels: *The Parts Left Out* (2014), *The Hands of Gravity and Chance* (2014), and *This Will Do...* (2021). His debut novel is based partly on a story told to him by a friend about a homeless member of his family.

> I asked him [Ogden told Kohavi] if, growing up with her, he had any sort of clue that she was in very severe psychological difficulty. He said no, the only thing that came to mind is that she sucked her thumb into adolescence and her parents had her wear a glove to bed to help her break the habit.

The comment inspired a central event in the novel.

The Parts Left Out raises questions that every novelist and psychoanalyst must consider. What are the human truths that are inevitably left out of fictional and real characters' stories? Can we know the full complexity of human motivation? Are we responsible for others' lives and deaths? To probe these questions, Ogden focuses on Earl Bromfman who, while studying to become an engineer at a Kansas State University, finds himself irresistibly drawn to a fellow student, Marta, afflicted with mental health challenges that only worsen when she gives birth to two children whom she neither wants nor loves. Tragedy strikes when Marta, unable to accept her 11-year-old son Warren's thumb-sucking, becomes unhinged. To cure the problem, Marta first applies a foul-tasting ointment to Warren's thumb, and when that fails to have the desired effect, she forces him to wear leather working gloves when he sleeps. Unable to watch her brother's silent humiliation, Warren's older sister, Melody, who has herself suffered her mother's wrath, intervenes by taking off his gloves at night. Enraged by her thwarted plans, Marta grabs a knife, determined to punish her son. Horrified, Earl, a football star in high school, explosively drives his shoulder into Marta's neck, killing her instantly. As Aparna Mishra Tarc (2019) remarks about Marta's maternal breakdown, readers struggle between condemning and trying to understand the desperate act. A police investigation ensues, and Earl, contrary to what Warren and Melody have seen, informs the deputy sheriff Randy Larsen that Marta had been trying to stab him rather than Warren. Why does Earl leave out the crucial information that will exonerate his behavior? Earl's refusal to tell the truth mystifies his children, the deputy sheriff, and the reader. "People don't do what Marta did for no reason," Randy tells Earl. "Even crazy people have their reasons for doing what they do, otherwise they wouldn't be doing them" (25).

Because Ogden never diagnoses or clinically explains his characters' conflicts, we are left to fathom them as best we can. The novelist shows us, in convincing detail, the subtle changes in Marta as she loses her mind. From the beginning of their relationship, Earl has found Marta unreachable, unknowable, unreadable. Is her fury toward her son a product of her hatred of her father, whom she has wanted to kill? Marta cannot count on her alcoholic mother for parental support. Ogden complicates the plot by introducing Anne, Marta's vivacious younger sister, with whom Marta has long had a strained relationship. Because her father has failed to support her financially in college, Marta forges his name on financial application forms she is required to submit to the university. The forgeries are eventually discovered by the college's assistant comptroller, a threatening figure who seems to take pleasure in interrogating Marta. This event triggers Marta's psychotic breakdown, and she is taken to the university health center where, pregnant with her first child, she spends several months in a locked psychiatric ward. Ogden portrays Marta's psychiatrist, Dr. Anders, sympathetically.

> I know that you're feeling so frightened that you're cut off from words, and that you've all but given up on finding your way back to words and people. If you

have any words or any other way of speaking to me, I'd welcome that, but I'll understand if you can't or don't want to. (138)

Marta never does find the words to express her feelings, even after she is released, and she remains consumed by rage, bitterness, and paranoia.

The Parts Left Out is not a feel-good novel celebrating the benefits of mental health treatment. Marta remains beyond help despite a prolonged psychiatric intervention. Moreover, her husband and children all feel guilty over her death. In the novel's final and most shocking act, Warren hangs himself, believing, as he pens his suicide note, that he is not fit for life and that his sister and father will be better off without him. Warren's suicide recalls that of Little Father Time in Thomas Hardy's 1895 novel *Jude the Obscure*, who also hangs himself because of the belief that the world will be better off without him. *The Parts Left Out* ends with Earl looking at his daughter, not knowing what to say.

"The test of a book," Hemingway told Lillian Ross in a 1950 interview published in *The New Yorker*, "is how much good stuff you can throw away." Hemingway created stories like icebergs, with the meaning lurking below the surface of the narrative. Ogden also omits the most salient details of a story because of his conviction of the limits of knowledge—and to implicate readers into the story, where they must form their own judgments. "For me," he told Noya Kohavi, "some of the most important aspects of writing lie in the effects created by the parts left out. They create mystery, suspense, the plausible and yet inexplicable. Leaving out parts shows respect for the reader's ability not only to be affected by what she or he reads, but also to participate in the writing of the novel." But to succeed aesthetically as well as psychologically, *The Parts Left Out* must imply what is omitted from the story. Ogden does this. Although Earl and Anne are attracted to each other, they never consummate their passion. Nevertheless, Marta immediately suspects betrayal when she returns home from the health center. "I smell the smell of sex" (166), she sputters, and Earl withholds the truth of his love for Anne. The deputy sheriff knows that Earl is not telling the truth, but he doesn't know why. Earl never mentions to anyone that Marta has long been unbalanced, perhaps because of the stigma of mental illness. Nor does Earl know how to clarify to his daughter why Marta hates her children. "I wish I could explain it to you, Melody, but I don't know how" (18). Earl claims that he has nothing to hide from the deputy sheriff, but he never attempts to acknowledge his deep ambivalence toward his wife. Ogden conveys Earl's feelings of guilt, anger, bitterness, jealousy, and infidelity before he hurls himself at Marta, yet we still cannot know whether his primary motivation is to protect his son or kill his wife. "I don't know what goes on in Daddy's head" (37) Melody complains, unable to grasp why her father continues to protect her deceased mother. *The Parts Left Out* reads like a psychological detective story, but unlike most stories of this genre, where the unearthing of a clue leads to the villain's arrest and imprisonment, we never learn the outcome of the deputy sheriff's investigation.

Ogden's compassion for and empathic understanding of his characters never waver. His sensitivity to language is palpable, as when Marta, walking into the comptroller's office, reflects on the word. "What kind of word was 'comptroller?' Are there any other words in the English language on which the letters 'mp' are pronounced as if they were an 'n'"? (115). In addition to his insights into character, he captures the farming rhythms of fertilizing, planting, growing, and harvesting. His use of figurative language is striking, as when Melody says about her mother's sister, "It's as if a hummingbird were born to a family of lizards" (189).

Ogden is best known for his concept of the "analytic third," which he defines in a 1994 article as an unconscious intersubjective construction arising in analysis that is a third subject with a life of its own. Such a moment occurs in *The Parts Left Out* when Earl and Marta, reacting to Anne's passionate presence in their lives, feel heightened erotic feelings for each other.

> Without realizing it, they were seeing one another through Anne's eyes, and imagining Anne in one another. Sex, for both Earl and Marta, had been disappointing from the outset, and had gone downhill from there. That summer, for the first time in her life, Marta learned what it was to experience lust. (102)

The Hands of Gravity and Chance

The Hands of Gravity and Chance opens with 13-year-old Catherine Keane tumbling down a staircase in her Midwestern farmhouse as her mother, Rose, and two brothers, Damien and Erin, stare in horror. Did she trip or have a seizure? Was she pushed—and, if so, by whom? The mystery is never solved. The only certainty is that an event has been set into motion that cannot be reversed. She was now, we are told on the second page of the story, "fully in the grip of gravity and chance." As a result of an acute subdural hematoma that requires an emergency craniotomy, Catherine is left with a limp, required to wear orthopedic shoes, and forced to walk with a cane for the rest of her life. The accident adds to the family's woes. Rose's husband was killed in a motorcycle accident when she was pregnant with Catherine, and the widow suffers a mental breakdown and is hospitalized. Rose is never as psychotic as Marta in *The Parts Left Out*, but she cannot parent Damien, screaming at him, when he is a baby, "I wish you'd never been born" (21). She asks her older sister, the career-oriented Margaret, to be Damien's mother. Margaret agrees but with one condition: she will legally adopt the baby and permanently separate him from his mother, siblings, and home. Damien makes the adjustment with the help of a loving live-in Jamaican woman, but after she unexpectedly leaves, three years later, Margaret, unable to raise him by herself, recognizes the mistake of tearing him away from his family. "She had taken Damien out of the natural habitat of a growing child and made a zoo animal out of him—in a zoo in which he was the only animal, a zoo staffed by two zookeepers" (78). Mortified by her actions, Margaret returns Damien to Rose, and the confused boy feels triply abandoned and bereft.

The Parts Left Out and *The Hands of Gravity and Chance* both examine the consequences of parental abuse or neglect on young children, a signature Ogden theme. Rose and Margaret's father has deserted his family, and when he returns, seven years later, he realizes that no apology can undo the damage caused to his daughters. Ogden's interest in fractured families, defective parenting, mental illness, and shameful family secrets is striking. He captures the rage and desperation of mothers and the bewilderment and anguish of damaged children. Damien has no memory of having lived with Catherine and Erin when he returns home. Rose tries to explain why she gave him to Margaret, but he cannot understand. "What's a Mommy?" he poignantly asks her, a question that Ogden explores throughout the story.

In the most curious chapter in *The Hands of Gravity and Chance*, Margaret, seeking the assistance of a mental health professional to help her manage a divorce, visits a psychiatrist who is recommended as the best in Chicago. The meeting does not go well. He constantly interrupts Margaret, claiming that she conceals the real reason for beginning therapy, and then declares, half-jokingly, that he would marry her "but my wife would kill me if I did." When she asks him how he can help her, he replies, "How would I know? You'll have to teach me that," to which she responds, "I thought it was only in cartoons and Woody Allen movies that psychiatrists use couches," adding, "I didn't come here to talk about lying on your couch" (122). The expression "lying on the couch" has a long and fraught history in psychotherapy. In "Lying on the Couch," the penultimate chapter in the irreverently titled 1976 book *Lying, Despair, Jealousy, Envy, Sex, Suicide, Drugs, and the Good Life*, the psychoanalyst Leslie Farber contrasts two types of truths, the first partial and modest, the second revelatory and emotionally charged. Farber is interested only in the first type: "I think that speaking truthfully is a more fitting ambition than speaking the truth" (211). *Lying on the Couch* is also the title of the existential psychiatrist Irvin D. Yalom's 1997 novel, in which he dramatizes the most dangerous act in psychotherapy: sexual boundary violations. For whatever reason, Margaret never returns to therapy. Rose herself visits a psychiatrist for a year or two to diminish her self-loathing, but we never overhear her therapy sessions. Erin also suffers from psychological problems, numbing himself with alcohol, and visits a psychiatrist who prescribes an antidepressant, which helps temporarily but doesn't stop him from feeling like a failure. Counterintuitively, Ogden the novelist denies his fictional characters the benefits of lying on the couch.

After Damien returns home, *The Hands of Gravity and Chance* depicts his awakening desire for Catherine. Because he feels like a foundling, having no biological connection to his sister, it doesn't seem to them that their love is forbidden, at least in the beginning. Rose later tells him that he is illegitimate, the offspring of her brief affair with a stranger when she was experiencing marital troubles—which helps explain why she never treated him lovingly. Years pass, and we next see Damien as a junior in college, a student of Geoffrey Barnes, the Spellman Professor of English who offers his protégé a coveted position as assistant managing editor of the literary journal *Interludes*. "A group of us see you as having one of the finest critical minds that has come along in a long time," Barnes exclaims (189). The problem with this section of the novel is that Ogden tells rather than shows us Damien's brilliant literary mind. For example, Damien interviews Philip Roth—though we do not see insights into the novelist's life or art. Ogden succeeds, however, in hinting that Barnes becomes a father surrogate to his student. By this time, Damien and Catherine have acted on their secret, forbidden love. He begins to experience paralyzing migraines, and the rest of the story anatomizes his growing guilt and paranoia. Damien and Catherine marry, and to ensure that their daughter, Alice, will not suffer any genetic abnormalities, Catherine undergoes artificial insemination with a sperm donor. Alice, however, is a troubled child, as can be seen from her stick drawings. "I'm not a child psychologist," Catherine explains to Damien, "but anyone can see that the family she's drawing lives in a black box—a prison or vault. I may be reading too much into it, but I'm afraid that she already knows we have a secret, and that we live in a world separate from the rest of the world" (237). Damien and Catherine receive a veiled threat from an unknown person who seems ready to expose their skeleton in the closet. *In extremis*, Damien has reached his breaking point. Lost and frightened, and increasingly paranoid, he is pursued by outer and inner demons.

This Will Do...

The most affirmative of the three novels, *This Will Do...* highlights three youths who struggle to break free of their past. The title, with its intriguing ellipsis, is perhaps an allusion to Winnicott's celebrated expression, the "good enough mother," liberating parents from the impossible goal of perfection. As in *The Parts Not Told* and *The Hands of Gravity and Chance*, *This Will Do...* shows how childhood experiences shape character development, albeit not deterministically. Ogden sees the family as the source of his characters' conflicts, and the sins of the parents are revisited on their children. Part I, "Bobby and George," recalls the same theme in *The Hands of Gravity and Chance*: the challenge of being a brother's keeper, a theme we will see in the Jacobs brothers' novels. Bobby Renfro adores his older brother, George, but he watches in dismay as George becomes more and more lost in his inner world. How does a novelist portray a youth who is developing schizophrenia? George begins talking to himself non-stop in bed, oblivious to Bobby's presence. George loves making plastic planes and ships and setting them on fire, entranced with the menace of smoke and flames. The melting plastic singes George's body, and when he tosses the burning plane out of the window, the embers ignite the grass surrounding their home in New York's Hudson Valley. The accident only inflames the father's hatred of George. "His father often acted as if George didn't exist—not talking to him for weeks at a time—or screamed at him that he was a disgrace to the family, dumber than dirt, should never have been born" (22). It is the same curse that Rose shouts in *The Hands of Gravity and Chance*. Like Erin, who promises to protect Damien, Bobby vows to defend George—a promise that he cannot keep.

Part II, "Carol," spotlights a different family crisis: a daughter's effort to care for an alcoholic mother. Literature abounds in characters who have lost their lives to alcohol or drug addiction, but few descriptions are more harrowing than Carol screaming at her mother who is in an alcoholic haze. Carol grows to despise her mother's body, which she must clean everyday as if she were an infant. Nor can Carol rely on her father, another parent who has abdicated his marital and parenting responsibilities. We see no happy families in Ogden's fictional world; his novels confirm Tolstoy's sardonic observation that unhappy families are unhappy in their own ways. After five years, Carol forsakes the demands of caregiving and travels to Buffalo to begin graduate study in English, anxious to sever all ties to her dysfunctional family.

Part III, "Madeline and Robert," limns the developing love between two people who have been carrying the ghosts of the past with them. Carol has reinvented herself as "Madeline," a name she associates with her grandmother, a French storybook character, and Proust's famous cookie. She meets Bobby, now called Robert, who is working as a gas station attendant but is a talented painter, with a college degree in fine arts. Ogden deftly portrays their growing attraction to each other amidst the tumultuous 1960s, when the nation was torn apart by the Vietnam War, racial tensions, and the assassinations of John F. Kennedy, Robert Kennedy, and Martin Luther King, Jr. As Madeline and Robert get to know each other, respecting each other's privacy but yearning to understand the other's secrets, the nightmarish past suddenly appears in Part IV, "The Visitor," the unexpected arrival of George. Ogden's portrait of the Vietnam veteran—unwashed and foul-smelling, living in a Volkswagen van, his memory impaired by shock treatments, tortured by the people who live inside his head—conveys both profound sadness and quiet dignity. George desires nothing more than to protect his younger brother from imaginary dangers. George terrifies Madeline, yet she, too, suffers from thoughts that do not feel her own, though not in a disabling way. Robert feels torn between his loyalty to his brother and his girlfriend.

> All I can tell you [Robert admits to Madeline] is that he's the remainder of a life I wanted to leave behind when I met you. He's like a satellite that revolves around me, invisible to everyone but me. I'm the only thing between him and the gutter or between him and the grave. I love him, but it's complicated. (140)

The power of the novel lies in Ogden's depiction of this complexity. *This Will Do…* closes with Robert reassuring George that he will never abandon him but that he must be free to have his own life with Madeline, conflicting goals that may be mutually exclusive.

An instructive difference may be seen between Ogden and Christopher Bollas, who earned a PhD in English before becoming a psychoanalyst. Bollas's three novellas and collection of plays, like Irvin Yalom's "teaching novels," represent a unique subgenre of literature that has a therapeutic function to illuminate, often satirically, aspects of the talking cure while at the same time entertaining the reader. In his 2004 novel *Dark at the End of the Tunnel*, Bollas propounds several radical ideas that he is not yet ready to advance in his clinical writings, such as "objecthood," a "malignant transformation in which a person's being with the other is destroyed by the other, who replaces one's self-as-other with one's self-only-as-object" (44). By contrast, Ogden's major interest as a novelist lies in the stories themselves rather than in their validation of a particular psychological theory. I suspect that few readers would be able to glean that the novelist is also a psychoanalyst. Nor is there anything overtly autobiographical about Ogden's stories. He does not "apply" psychoanalytic terms to literature or trace his characters' "symptoms" to distant childhood events. Nor does he show how symptoms may be "treated" successfully with verbal therapy. Instead, he brings his characters to life and encourages us to care for them. Ogden's novels may be appreciated by anyone who wishes to learn more about the mystery of character and the power of storytelling to affirm thoughtfulness, compassion, and resilience.

Mental health professionals have found many valuable clinical insights in Ogden's novels. Theodore Jacobs, in his review of *The Parts Left Out*, calls Ogden America's "most original and influential psychoanalyst." Jacobs singles out the novel's extraordinary depiction of an acute psychosis.

> It captures the bewilderment, the increasing anxiety, the outbreak of the psychosis itself with its delusional thinking, with a veracity that only one who has deep knowledge of, and experience with, serious mental illness could achieve. Ogden accomplishes this without recourse to technical language or the vocabulary of the clinician. (397)

Gregory D. Graham praises Ogden for "expanding the horizon of psychoanalytic thought, inquiry, and experience in a way that few others have shown the ability to do" (522). Reading *The Hands of Gravity and Chance* was a "harrowing experience" for Dawn Farber.

> The complex characters are rendered in such depth, in a multigenerational telescoping of trauma, that I was instantly drawn into profound identifications with each one's point of view. I felt traumatized myself, to the point of nausea, while feeling unable to break the spell, escape the illusion by reminding myself that the created world is, after all, a fictional one. (80)

Sara Boffito similarly found herself immersed in the mental flow of Ogden's characters. "Dignity is given to every breath, every jolt, every nuance of thought through a style that reflects a specific aspect of the psychoanalyst's ear, of his compassion" (828).

Ogden's dual interest in psychoanalysis and literature may be seen in *The Analyst's Ear and the Critic's Eye: Rethinking Psychoanalysis and Literature* (2013), coauthored with Benjamin H. Ogden. It is the first volume of literary criticism coauthored by a psychoanalyst and a literary critic—and the first cowritten by a father and his son. (In his review, Stephen Rojcewicz mistakenly refers to the coauthors as brothers.) The book seeks to avoid the reductiveness of what it calls "applied psychoanalysis," but it is not entirely successful, partly because it is only about 100 pages long, and partly because, as Ellen Handler Spitz complains in her review, the language never springs to life. A more successful book demonstrating Thomas Ogden's longstanding interest in literature is *Conversations at the Frontier of Dreaming* (2001), where he points out that poetry and fiction have become increasingly important to him as sources of both pleasure and "disturbance" (14). We see the disturbance mainly in *The Parts Left Out* and *The Hands of Gravity and Chance*. Ogden observes later in *Conversations* that one turns to literature and psychoanalysis "with the hope of reclaiming—or perhaps experiencing for the first time—forms of human aliveness that we have foreclosed for ourselves" (113)—an apt comment on *This Will Do...*

Works Cited

Boffito, Sara. "Review of *The Hands of Gravity and Chance*." *International Journal of Psychoanalysis*, vol. 101, 2020, pp. 828–830.

Bollas, Christopher. *Dark at the End of the Tunnel*. Free Association Books, 2004.

Bollas, Christopher. *The Shadow of the Object: Psychoanalysis of the Unthought Known*. Columbia UP, 1987.

Farber, Dawn. "Review of *The Hands of Gravity and Chance*." *Fort Da*, vol. 23, 2017, pp. 80–87.

Farber, Leslie. *Lying, Despair, Jealousy, Envy, Sex, Suicide, Drugs, and the Good Life*. Basic Books, 1976.

Gougoulis, Nicolas and Katryn Driffield. "Interview with Thomas Ogden." *International Forum of Psychoanalysis*, vol. 30, 2021, pp. 223–233.

Graham, Gregory D. "Review of *The Parts Left Out*." *Psychoanalytic Quarterly*, vol. 84, 2015, pp. 517–523.

Jacobs, Daniel. *The Distance from Home*. International Psychoanalytic Books, 2019.

Jacobs, Theodore. "Review of *The Parts Left Out*." *Journal of the American Psychoanalytic Association*, vol. 63, 2015, pp. 395–397.

Jacobs, Theodore. *The Year of Durocher*. International Psychoanalytic Books, 2013.

Kleiger, James Herman. *The 11th Inkblot*. International Psychoanalytic Books, 2019.

Kluft, Richard P. *A Sinister Subtraction*. International Psychoanalytic Books, 2019.

Kohavi, Noya. "How Psychoanalyst Thomas Ogden Found His True Self in Fiction." *Haaretz*, March 29, 2017. www.haaretz.com/life/books/2017-03-29/ty-article-magazine/.premium/how-psychoanalyst-thomas-ogden-found-his-true-self-in-fiction/0000017f-e36a-d75c-a7ff-ffefeafa0000. Accessed January 15, 2023.

Kohon, Gregorio. *Red Parrot, Wooden Leg*. Karnac, 2007.

Ogden, Benjamin H. and Thomas Ogden. *The Analyst's Ear and the Critic's Eye: Rethinking Psychoanalysis and Literature*. Routledge, 2013.

Ogden, Thomas H. "The Analytic Third—Working with Intersubjective Clinical Facts." *International Journal of Psycho-Analysis*, vol. 75, 1994, pp. 3–20.

Ogden, Thomas H. "Analytic Writing as a Form of Fiction." *Journal of the American Psychoanalytic Association*, vol. 69, 2021, pp. 221–223.

Ogden, Thomas H. *Conversations at the Frontier of Dreaming*. Jason Aronson, 2001.

Ogden, Thomas H. *The Hands of Gravity and Chance*. Karnac, 2014.

Ogden, Thomas H. *The Parts Left Out*. Karnac, 2014.

Ogden, Thomas H. *This Will Do…* Sphinx Books, 2021.

Rojcewicz, Stephen. "Review of *The Analyst's Ear and the Critic's Eye: Rethinking Psychoanalysis and Literature.*" *Journal of Phenomenological Psychology*, vol. 44, 2013, pp. 263–286.

Ross, Lillian. "How Do You Like It Now, Gentlemen?" *The New Yorker*, May 6, 1950. www.newyorker.com/magazine/1950/05/13/how-do-you-like-it-now-gentlemen. Accessed February 27, 2023.

Spitz, Ellen Handler. "Review of *The Analyst's Ear and the Critic's Eye: Rethinking Psychoanalysis and Literature.*" *The Psychoanalytic Quarterly*, vol. 83, 2014, pp. 198–204.

Tarc, Aparna Mishra. "Those Old Familial Feelings: Transference in Reading Thomas Ogden's *The Parts Left Out.*" *Textual Practice*, vol. 34, 2019, pp. 1845–1863.

Yalom, Irvin D. *Lying on the Couch*. Harper Perennial, 1997.

Chapter 9

Arlene Heyman
Scary Old Sex and Artifact

Arlene Heyman has lived a double life as a psychoanalyst and fiction writer, two careers that have much in common, including a "feeling for humanity that underlies both," as she observed to Julia Felsenthal in a 2016 interview published in *Vogue*. Additionally, both psychoanalysts and fiction writers work with vulnerable characters who require empathic understanding.

From the age of five or six, Heyman told Dusty Sklar in a 2022 interview, she wished to be a creative writer. In 1963 Heyman earned her BA at Bennington College, in Vermont, which she attended on a full scholarship. At the time, Bennington was an all-female undergraduate institution. Heyman studied with the celebrated novelist Bernard Malamud, with whom she had a two-year romantic relationship she later fictionalized in a short story. The 25-year friendship continued until Malamud's death. After receiving an MFA at Syracuse University, Heyman taught literature for five years at community colleges. Her short fiction, which she began writing at an early age, has appeared in the influential *New American Review*; *Epoch*, Cornell University's literary magazine; and twice listed in *The Best American Short Stories*. Heyman has received several prestigious awards, including Woodrow Wilson, Fulbright, Rockefeller, and Robert Wood Johnson fellowships. Heyman then switched career direction and earned her medical degree from the University of Pennsylvania. She has spent her life practicing psychiatry and psychoanalysis in New York City while at the same time penning well-wrought fiction. She was also instrumental in the publication of the final volume of the Library of America's edition of Malamud's writings.

Heyman was a septuagenarian when her volume of short stories, *Scary Old Sex*, appeared in 2016. Anyone who has lost a beloved spouse will appreciate her dedication: "For Len, and in memory of Shepard." I've never seen a book dedicated to both a living and a deceased spouse, mainly because, I suspect, the former may be threatened by the latter. ("Dedicatory bias," quipped a friend with whom I discussed this phenomenon.) It is not easy for the living to compete with the dead, especially when the writer idealizes a spouse who has died young. Heyman's dedication alerts readers to the central traumatic loss in her life, one that casts a long shadow over her fiction, particularly over second marriages involving stepchildren.

Heyman was 37 when she married her first husband, the psychiatrist/psychoanalyst Shepard Kantor, who died of acute myelogenous leukemia in 1997 at age 53. Heyman and Kantor were married for 17 years and had two sons. (Kantor had been married previously and had one daughter.) Ten years after his death, Heyman married Leonard Rodberg, who earned a PhD in theoretical physics from MIT and was, until his retirement, professor and chair of the Urban Studies department at Queens College. Rodberg played a leading role, Heyman proudly informed Felsenthal, in the publication of the *Pentagon Papers* in 1971.

Literary critics have lauded Heyman's portrayal of sensual pleasure among elderly lovers in *Scary Old Sex*. In a review published in *The New Yorker*, Alexandra Schwartz noted alliteratively that compared with the

> familiar priapic preening of hunger-for-younger lit, Heyman's frank tales of conjugal relations among the old—the competing desires, the jealousies, and always the particular demands of the "aged flesh" itself, with its "papules, papillomas, skin tags, moles"—feel paradoxically taboo on the page, all the more so for the fierce candor with which they examine the sexuality of older women, a demographic generally assumed to have none to speak of.

The title of Elaine Showalter's review published in the *Guardian* conveys her delight reading Heyman's stories: "lusty, tough and life-affirming." And in his *New York Times* review, Dwight Garner affirms the tales' humor and eroticism: "Ms. Heyman's stories are seriously sexy; they generate a lot of heat. Read them in public and you might be seen blushing." Psychoanalysts have also acclaimed *Scary Old Sex*. "Reading this sort of literary fiction provides sensibility training for us," Fred Griffin enthuses in his review published in the *Journal of the American Psychoanalytic Association*, "a laboratory in which to practice keeping our senses alive as we enter uneasy clinical territory" (915).

Lurking Death in *Scary Old Sex*

What is scary about Heyman's short fiction is not sex, either with hoary or nubile lovers, but the Grim Reaper, who lurks in the background and, in some cases, foreground, of all seven stories. In the first tale, "The Loves of Her Life," Marianne, the 65-year-old ex-social worker who has become a filmmaker, cannot stop thinking about being loved "immoderately" by her first husband, David, an orthopedic surgeon who died suddenly of a heart attack a year earlier at age 52. "Death had come out of nowhere" (10), the narrator remarks. Cleaning out the storage cabinets in the basement of her apartment building, Marianne cannot throw away the income tax forms filed by her deceased husband without looking nostalgically at each one. "She occasionally recognized that she had an eternally summery image of her marriage to David" (19), but only recently has she realized that in extolling the inaccessible, she has deprecated her current husband, Stu.

"In Love with Murray," dedicated to the memory of Bernard Malamud, who died in 1986 at age 71, honors the man who was, as Heyman discloses in the Acknowledgments, "a climate to me—his jokes, his Jewish atheism, his aliveness, his loving-kindness, his feeling for art and me, his total immersion in literature, and, above all, his writing" (228). Malamud's biographer, Philip Davis, points out that Heyman was the inspiration behind the fetching young Fanny Bick in the 1977 novel *Dubin's Lives* (207). (Thomas Mallon, in his introduction to the 2003 paperback edition of *Dubin's Lives*, asserts that Fanny is a "generous gift from the zipless decade of Erica Jong" [x], but that was before the publication of Davis's biography or Heyman's short fiction.) As a result of the 28-year difference in their ages—the same age difference between Malamud and Heyman—the 19-year-old Leda worries that "he'd kill himself fucking her—he was getting so little sleep—and even suggested, as a lifesaving measure, that they cut back" (33–34). The opposite seems true: Leda was an "antidote to middle age" (39). Each seems the other's muse. Murray Blumgarten gives the inchoate Leda excellent counsel for any aspiring painter or writer:

> I know you're not seeking advice, but the thing about painting is, you have to create a rhythm for it. It's rough if you work and quit, work and quit. You have to stay with it almost every day, if only for a little while. The quitting seems to check the flow, and then you have to break through into the rhythm all over again. Having a bad time at the beginning is almost necessary. It's a struggle and a struggle and a struggle, but if you keep at it right, the struggle can become a dance. (36)

It was the same advice, Heyman told Sklar, that Malamud had given to her years earlier. After Blumgarten's romantic relationship with Leda ends—he refuses to leave his wife—he dies unexpectedly during a dinner party, at age 53, Shepard Kantor's age when he died.

Heyman's "deepest literary fame," Elaine Showalter claims in her review of *Scary Old Sex*, relying on information provided by Heyman's publisher, comes from Phillip Roth's *The Ghost Writer*, where she was purported to be the inspiration for Amy Bellette, the beautiful young mistress of the novelist E.I. Lonoff, based on Malamud. The only problem with the Heyman-Malamud-Roth triangle is that it never existed. According to Heyman, Roth did not know about her affair with Malamud: "He just happened to hit on something that happened to have been true" (Felsenthal). Heyman's deepest literary fame rests on her exquisite fictional stories.

Heyman celebrates without sentimentalizing Leda's relationship with Blumgarten. He tells her near the end of the story that he has wasted her "precious time" with him, but she ardently disagrees. "You've made my time precious, made my life precious" (*Scary Old Sex* 55). Malamud's portrait of their relationship is darker, more complicated, but because of Fanny, Dubin "was a different man, had grown new attributes, elements of a new self" (*Dubin's Lives* 241).

Heyman's expression of gratitude to Malamud must have been difficult for his family to appreciate. In *Private Matters* (1997), his daughter, Janna Malamud Smith, a clinical social worker and psychotherapist, admitted the family's anguish over having their privacy invaded. She did not want to hide her father, she wrote after his death, but she did not want to share him with the public. "The undertaker could have his body, but I wanted to ward off the biographer, at the wheel of a different hearse, demanding either his soul or the details of my family life" (4). She knew that *The Fixer* (1966), which won both the National Book Award and the Pulitzer Prize, was a work of fiction, but she could not complete reading the novel when she came to the section where the Jewish handyman, Yakov Bok, flees a sexual encounter after seeing a drop of menstrual blood. One can sympathize with her comment that reading a parent's fiction is eerie, "like a dream where familiar things get jumbled and strange" (5). Smith makes no further reference to her father until the last page of her book, where she ruefully confesses an irony: "one among many reasons for wishing to fend off his biographers was a wish to protect him from my own desire to write and thus invade his privacy" (243). Fiction protects privacy by enabling the novelist to reveal personal truths through imaginative lies.

The 99-year-old Gussie Fernmann Klein is blessed with a long life in "At the Happy Isles," but the first of her three husbands died of cancer at age 25. Gussie's 68-year-old physician-daughter, Marilyn, lost the only man she loved, a Chinese American neurologist, in a car accident. Marilyn was 11 when her mother married for the second time, and the bereft daughter fought back tears at the wedding: "her father had been dead less than a year" (71). Marilyn is a devoted, albeit reluctant caregiver, and she wonders how much longer her mother will live. "For a moment she feels profound grief, and then she is aware of a wish to get Gussie into the ground" (81). The story ends with the daughter's matricidal fantasy, along with the thought that in the future, her adopted daughter may feel the same way about her.

"Dancing" is the most autobiographical tale in *Scary Old Sex*, and the most heartbreaking. The story begins as a teenage boy, Solly, watches in horrified fascination from Stuyvesant High School, in lower Manhattan, as the World Trade Center collapses, a national catastrophe that foreshadows a personal tragedy: Solly's father, Matt, is battling acute myelogenous leukemia. "Talk to me," Matt implores his wife, Ann, a psychiatrist. "It keeps me alive" (98). Heyman's decision to write about her husband years after his death keeps her memory of him alive. With the help of chemotherapy, Matt is fortunate enough to make it into the first 40 percent of patients who go into remission. The story then switches from New York City to Seattle, where Matt undergoes a harrowing bone marrow transplant at the Fred Hutchinson Cancer Research Center. He does well, for a time, until the treatment stops working. As his health declines, he grows "situationally" depressed, though he rejects taking an antidepressant. He has three wishes: "To eat. To have my gut not hurt. To survive" (113). Ann is jealous when one of Matt's former lovers visits him in the hospital; she regards Lucinda as the "green-eyed monster," admitting, "One gets over nothing in this life" (116). When a physician informs Ann and Solly that Matt has run out of treatment options, the boy rises from his chair and hurls a basketball through the wall-size window, evoking Matt's explosive laughter. "It is like the breaking of a summer storm in hideously humid weather and no one much minds getting soaked to the skin just so long as the weather changes" (124). The story ends on New Year's Day, 2003, with Ann's visit to the former site of the Twin Towers, where she gazes at the huge hole, recalling sadly the many times she and her husband went dancing at Windows on the World, the fabled restaurant on the 106th and 107th floors of the doomed North Tower.

Heyman has never published a story about a child's struggle accepting a parent's death, but if she did, she might describe how her protagonist attempts to avoid feelings of protracted grief and the finality of loss. Indeed, this is Martha Wolfenstein's thesis in "Loss, Rage, and Repetition," a paper published in a 1969 issue of the *Psychoanalytic Study of the Child*. "The loss of a parent while the individual is still immature inflicts a massive trauma from which it is very difficult to recover" (444). Wolfenstein was an analyst in Heyman's residency program in the Department of Psychiatry of the Albert Einstein College of Medicine; Heyman was so impressed with the paper that she gave a copy to Malamud, whose mother died, likely by her own hand, when he was 15. Heyman learned while reading Philip Davis's biography that a copy of the paper was on Malamud's desk when he died. After reading Wolfenstein's article, Malamud sent a note to Heyman. "Thank you for letting me read your paper. It was like being allowed to look into a forbidden room. I saw more than I had meant to" (Sklar). Malamud was unhappy when his father later remarried. But losing a parent to divorce may sometimes be as devastating as losing a parent to death, involving many of the same feelings: anger, sadness, confusion, and guilt, especially when children fear they have been responsible for the breakup of their parents' marriage.

"Night Call" opens with Dan Dorenbusch, an OB/GYN physician, receiving a telephone call at two o'clock in the morning from Rosemarie Petrowski: "He's dead. He's dead. Your father's dead" (133). Dan's father, a pediatrician, had been having, unbeknownst to his family, an affair with his nurse, at whose house he suddenly died, perhaps of an embolism, while having sex. Fearful of the compromising circumstances of the death, Dan and Rosemarie transport the body to his office. Dan's father was an absent presence in his son's life, and he is overcome by regret that the two were not closer.

The penultimate story in *Scary Old Sex*, "Artifact," part of a longer novel of the same title that appeared in 2020, focuses on a research scientist, Lottie, who has submitted a paper outlining her discovery of new techniques for examining tiny structures in the cells of a rat's salivary gland. No one knows the function of these cells, though they are implicated in several diseases, one of them fatal. Lottie's paper, submitted for publication in a microscopy journal, has received harsh rejections by anonymous evaluators who demand extensive revisions. Lottie ruminates over the scathing criticisms throughout the story; she types the referees' objections on a separate sheet of paper and tapes them upon her lab walls. The critics maintain that far from describing the salivary gland cells, she is merely limning the distortions created by her use of fixations and buffers. Her paper, to cite one evaluation, "is no more than a collection of artifacts" (157). Lottie disagrees, insisting that morphologists always confront the biological equivalent of the uncertainty principle. Nevertheless, she reruns the experiment again so that the results will appear less artifactual in her critics' eyes.

"Artifact" succeeds in authenticating Lottie's credibility as a scientific researcher. Her struggle with publication may reflect Heyman's difficulty getting her *own* writings published. In the interview with Felsenthal, for example, Heyman acknowledged, albeit "cheerfully," that for decades she endured being "rejected, and rejected, and rejected." Each rejection of a manuscript strengthened her determination to succeed. "Every time I had a rejection, I'd pull it back and work and work and work." In "Meet the Author," an email interview at the Suffolk Libraries in England, Heyman gave future writers the advice she had received from Bernard Malamud: "When you send out a manuscript, have at the ready the cover letter to the next publisher you're sending it to so that when the manuscript comes back, you remove the rejection letter (be sure to remove the rejection letter) and shoot the story out again" ("Suffolk Libraries"). Heyman is, like Lottie, "innovative" and "creative." Although women fiction writers may have more than the two choices faced by women scientists—"bitterness or foolishness" (158)— they nevertheless often confront challenges male fiction writers do not: working while being the main caregiver for their children. It is revealing that Lottie has a copy of Virginia Woolf's *A Room of One's Own* in her lab, along with scientific journals. Woolf's 1929 extended essay argues that women must have both money and their own space if they are to write fiction—or, as in Lottie's case, conduct scientific experiments.

Cancer appears in "Artifact" in three ways: the experimental rats are injected with chemicals that may be carcinogenic; Lottie's present husband, Jake, has lost his father to cancer at age 49; and a black parking attendant's wife died of leukemia in her 50s. Most of the tension in the short story centers on the combative family dynamics arising from divorce. Lottie has two young sons, Simon and Davy, with Jake, and an 18-year-old daughter, Lily, with her divorced husband Charlie. Jake's 14-year-old daughter from his first marriage, Ruth, despises Lottie. "I hate her! I hate her! I hope she drops dead!" Ruth hisses. When Lottie conveys her indignation to Jake, he responds diplomatically, "Well, everybody wishes everybody dead now and then" (174).

Much of the power of "Artifact" lies in Lottie's inability to understand her stepdaughter. Was Ruth hurt by being surrounded by her father's new family, from whom she felt excluded? Did she want her biological mother to remarry and have more children? Is there an Oedipal explanation for Ruth's hatred of Lottie? Did Ruth feel drawn toward her stepmother, which might represent a betrayal of her biological mother? As hard as she tries, Lottie cannot fathom her stepdaughter's inner life, which remains a mystery. Heyman raises these vexing questions, allowing readers to reach their own conclusions about problems that appear in many second marriages. One recalls Chekhov's observation that the artist's role is to ask questions, not answer them.

Lottie is unforgiving of her graduate students who are not meticulous with the storage of the carcinogenic and toxic chemicals used in rat dissection, but a terrible accident occurs when she brings home her experiment and Simon, the two-year-old, despite her warnings, comes into contact with the corrosive reagents. Lottie is flooded with guilt when he is rushed to the ER. Although Simon never displays any ill effects from the accident, news that her revised paper has been accepted for publication brings Lottie vindication but little joy. "Artifact" implies that female scientists and creative writers pay a heavy price for their creativity, regardless of whether it is a scientific discovery or a literary achievement.

The final story in *Scary Old Sex*, "Nothing Human," highlights an unnamed married couple, in their 60s, on a European cruise ship touring romantic castles and medieval towns. The Roman playwright Terence may not have had anal intercourse in mind when he stated two thousand years ago that "nothing human is alien to me," the source of the story's title, but Heyman is never afraid to probe her characters' unruly erotic desires. Not that the story is mainly about sex. "Nothing Human" begins with a humorous argument over the husband's refusal to wash his hands when he wakes up in the middle of the night, sometimes three or four times, to urinate, but their argument becomes increasingly acrimonious, exposing their attitudes toward germs, mortality, and previous spouses. This is the husband's third marriage, the wife's second. She and her first husband, both pediatricians, enjoyed a close marriage. He has been dead for a long time, but she continues to dream about him, fearing she has been "cuckolding" him (204). Her first husband died of lung cancer, and she worries that her present husband, to whom she has been married for over a decade, will succumb to the same disease. He suffers from obstructive sleep apnea, and she is annoyed that he refuses to use the CPAP machine he has brought with him. "Put it on, dear. The CPAP machine. It's bad for you to sleep without it" (204). Without the machine, she warns him, he is 30 percent more likely to have a heart attack or stroke. As their bickering continues over her desire to have anal intercourse—like most of Heyman's female characters, she is the more sexually adventurous of the two—he asks why she's doing a medical workup in the middle of the night. She angrily exclaims that she should have married another physician, one unafraid of germs. "Like your sainted husband," he sarcastically replies, to which she counters: "Don't you even *mention* my husband" (222), using the present tense to describe a past relationship. Amidst their shrill accusations of the other's lack of "emotional intelligence," the wife complains that her husband doesn't realize that he will eventually die—not an earth-shattering revelation—but then, perhaps thinking about her first husband, she shouts, "You figure I want to hang around the apartment taking care of you twenty-four seven? Why don't you just drop dead already, like right now?" (224).

The specter of the Holocaust lurks throughout "Nothing Human." The cruise ship travels through German towns reconstructed after the Second World War, and the local guides are uncomfortable admitting the horrors of the past. When the wife asks the guides what happened to the Jews in these towns, they always turn off their mics before answering the question. This discomfort with the past showed up in an interview Heyman gave to a German interviewer. Asking whether readers noted the importance of the Holocaust in "Nothing Human," she was told that they were interested only in the story's depiction of sex among the elderly. "I was astonished," Heyman told me. "And thought there must be some denial at work here. Some willful blindness." Tellingly, the couple in the story make love only when the ship arrives in Luxembourg.

Heyman's characters largely muddle through life on their own, without the help of psychotherapists, though they are sometimes mentioned in the stories. In "The Loves of Her Life," Marianne refers to her son's wife as a "borderline personality—from the human point of view, an outright bitch" (2). If Heyman's characters have been in analysis, it has been in the distant past. Marianne looks at the "shrink bills" that her deceased husband paid. "She'd gone to Dr. Levinson with the complaint that she was in the wrong profession and that she'd married the wrong man" (19). Ann is a psychiatrist in "Dancing," but despite her professional training, she remains in denial over her husband's imminent death. Ann and David never have the emotionally charged end-of-life discussions Atul Gawande advocates in *Being Mortal* (2014). The wife in "Nothing Human" is not a psychiatrist, but she is "always trying to get to the bottom of things." She urges her husband, overweight and afflicted with high blood pressure due to atherosclerosis, to see a shrink to understand his feelings toward his deceased second wife, who was killed by a hit-and-run driver. But the present husband is not introspective: he is a physicist, uninterested in exploring the inner world of feelings. The "overexamined life is not for him" (208). (One recalls Adam Phillips's provocative question in his 2012 book *Missing Out*: "The unexamined life is surely worth living, but is the unlived life worth examining?" [xi]). By contrast, the present wife thinks she has "deep psychological insights," but when she asks him to visit a therapist, as she herself did after her first husband died, he refuses. "CPAP yes; a psychiatrist, no" (208). Ethical reasons prevent Heyman from writing about her patients: "I never use anything from patients in anything I write," she told Felsenthal, "because they pay to get help, not to get into a story." Apart from this explanation, the idea of dramatizing the talking cure has little interest for her as a creative writer.

The seven stories in *Scary Old Sex* affirm but also go beyond the pleasure principle. Freud first introduced the repetition-compulsion principle in his 1914 essay "Remembering, Repeating, and Working Through," where he argues that a patient's compulsion to repeat traumatic experiences can be overcome through the arduous process of working through. "If there were a single article in Freud's corpus that contained the whole of psychoanalysis," the analyst in Tom Wooldridge's 2019 novel *Ghosts of the Unremembered Past* explains to her patient, "she felt that this would be it" (43). Freud elaborated on this idea in *Beyond the Pleasure Principle* (1920), one of his most speculative works, where he links the repetition-compulsion principle to the death drive, "*a need to restore an earlier state of things*" (*SE*, vol. 18, 57). Much of the drama—and trauma—of Heyman's fiction arises from the interplay between the living and the dead. Her stories return repeatedly to her characters' central losses, not to repeat them, but to make sense of them, to work through them, to learn how to live with them. Love and loss, Eros and Thanatos, remain a central subject in Heyman's stories; her characters brood over death almost as much as they yearn for sex. The dead spring to life at any moment in Heyman's stories: during lovemaking, bitter marital quarrels, or discussions of health. Warren S. Poland's observation in *Intimacy and Separateness in Psychoanalysis* (2018)—"Facing Thanatos stirs the defiant vitality of Eros" (166)—is true of Heyman's characters. They turn to sex not only for pleasure but also to alleviate intense death anxiety. The living and the dead communicate with each other in her stories, not to suggest a final reunion in an afterlife, but to show how the living cannot give up their loved ones. One of the most poignant moments in *Scary Old Sex* occurs on the last page, where the wife imagines making love to her dead husband, who tells her, reassuringly, "I've got the easy part, I'm dying" (226).

Heyman's fiction implicitly rejects Freud's theory of bereavement as outlined in "Mourning and Melancholia" (1917), where he declares that "mourning impels the ego to give up the object by declaring the object to be dead and offering the ego the inducement of continuing to live" (*SE*, vol. 14, 257). "Mourning and Melancholia" remained for nearly a century the most influential pronouncement about bereavement, but a new theory emerged in the 1996 book *Continuing Bonds: New Understandings of Grief*, in which Dennis Klass, Phyllis S. Silverman, and Steven L. Nickman suggest that the bereaved can maintain a relational bond with the deceased while forming new bonds with the living. The coauthors quote a statement by the playwright Robert Anderson, following his wife's death: "death ends a life, but it does not end a relationship, which struggles on in the survivor's mind toward some resolution which it never finds" (17). Continuing bonds are precisely what we see throughout *Scary Old Sex*, beginning with Heyman's dedication to her past and present husbands and ending with her Acknowledgments, where she expresses gratitude for her long friendship with Bernard Malamud. Heyman's stories affirm William Faulkner's insight that the "past is never dead. It's not even past."

Heyman never endorses in any of her stories Freud's notorious concept of "penis envy." I mention this because the only clinical paper I can find written by Heyman, as listed in PEP-Web, the online database of psychoanalytic articles, books, and films, reports on a 1984 meeting of the New York Psychoanalytic Society & Institute in which the problematic concept was discussed by several analysts. Without offering her own position, Heyman agrees with James Nininger's belief that the concept of penis envy is "troubling," one that does not do "justice to the full richness and range of the female character as we know it today" ("Meeting of the New York Psychoanalytic Society" 352).

Artifact

Heyman struggled with *Artifact* for decades. Part of the challenge was compressing the nearly 800-page novel into a reasonable length. She described the uncut version as a "baggy monster," an allusion to Henry James's wry remark that nineteenth-century novels, like those of Tolstoy and Dostoevsky, were "large, loose baggy monsters." "I think you write a book fighting against yourself," Heyman confided to Felsenthal. She was referring to authoring the stories in *Scary Old Sex*, but her comment also applies to *Artifact*, which gave her more difficulty over a longer period of time.

Artifact chronicles the story of a woman's coming of age as a wife, mother, and scientist, though not necessarily in that order. The novel takes place, Heyman observes in the only footnote in the story, from the 1950s through the 1980s, "transitional periods in the lives of women" (3). Lottie Kristin remains uncertain about the possibility of fulfilling herself in both love and work, Freud's definition of psychological health.

> One of the problems in the big, big version [Heyman disclosed in her Suffolk Libraries talk] was that Lottie didn't see how much damage she was doing her daughter as Lottie struggled to become who she wanted to be. In the novel as it stands now, she knows, she worries about it, she feels guilty but she does it anyway. That makes her a much more real, conflicted character.

One may infer from Heyman's interview with Felsenthal that, like Lottie, she also worried about becoming who she wanted to be without hurting her children. "My sons will not read it [*Scary Old Sex*], and that's okay; they're entitled... They just need to be respectful of me." After *Scary Old Sex* received positive reviews, her younger son told her: "It's quite amazing that you can write something that is so distressing to your sons, and yet it's an excellent book." (One is reminded of Janna Malamud Smith's inability to finish reading *The Fixer*.) Heyman must have smiled sardonically over the back-handed compliment.

Artifact is composed of seven parts, plus an intriguing "Loose Part." Part One consists of the events that take place in the short story until the accidental contamination, which occurs, appropriately, at the end of Part Seven. There are a few minor changes between the novel and the short story. "Lily" in the short story becomes "Evelyn" in the novel; the black man in the short story whose *wife* died of leukemia is changed to a man whose *child* died of the blood disease. In the novel, the ages of the two young sons are reversed, and the accident occurs to Davy, not Simon, who loses vision in one eye. More significantly, Ruth is a darker character in the novel. Heyman accentuates in the novel the antagonism between stepmother and stepdaughter. The novelist describes Ruth's visit as comparable to a swarm of mosquitos: Lottie wanted to be "rid of Ruth, swat her away, *smash*" (17), a sentence that does not appear in the short story. Heyman compares Ruth in the short story to a "small high-pressure front" (156), but she corrects the atmospheric simile in the novel: Ruth is like a "small low-pressure front that brings a storm" (4). Jake characterizes Ruth in the novel as "temperamental, very smart," and Lottie finds herself feeling "jealous, as if the girl were a threat to her" (239–240). In both the short story and the novel, Jake's first wife never remarried, and he believes that leaving his daughter was the worst thing he has done in his life. In both versions, Lottie complains to Jake that his daughter is vexed that he is not still married to his ex-wife, adding, "And she knows it's not my fault," to which Jake replies, "She knows and she doesn't know" (*Artifact* 21). It is a shrewd insight about different types of knowledge, one upon which Freud remarks in the *Introductory Lectures on Psycho-Analysis* (1916–1917): "Knowledge is not always the same as knowledge: there are different sorts of knowledge, which are far from equivalent psychologically" (*SE*, vol. 16, 281).

Part Two takes us back in time to Lottie's childhood and adolescence. Lottie's mother, an English teacher with a voracious appetite for reading fiction, has named her daughter after Charlotte Brontë. (In Malamud's novel, Fanny tells Dubin that she was named after a character in Jane Austen's *Mansfield Park*.) Ironically, during key moments in the story, when Lottie desperately needs maternal guidance, her mother is too busy reading literature to give her much-needed advice. Reading is essential in Heyman's world, but it is no substitute for the practical advice necessary for day-to-day living. Even when she is young, Lottie thinks as a scientist, but her creator always thinks as a novelist. *Artifact* contains dozens of references to poets and novelists, all expertly woven into the narrative. When asked the name of the character who becomes pregnant in Thomas Hardy's fiction, Lottie's mother snaps, "They all do." The answer is incorrect, but it comments on Lottie's unwanted pregnancy, like that of the eponymous heroine in Hardy's greatest novel, *Tess of the d'Urbervilles*. The "Romantic poets" do not appeal to Lottie—"too self-dramatizing"—but Keats's ballad "La Belle Dame sans Merci" forms the basis of the sadistic, pornographic poem written about her by Nathaniel Burden. Part Three focuses on Lottie's growing intimacy with her high school sweetheart, Charlie Hart; her miscarriage at age 16; her future husband's career-ending injury, which results in his depression and their eventual divorce; and her graduation from high school as the salutatorian (the sinister Burden is the valedictorian). Part Three ends with lines from T.S. Eliot's *The Waste Land*, conjuring up the grimness of Lottie's situation.

In Parts Four and Five, Charlie and Lottie are in Texas, he pursuing a graduate degree in economics, she working as a lab technician in a hospital. Lottie gives birth to Evelyn, and the baby becomes the focus of the mother's life. Motherhood is life-transforming to Lottie, but nothing clears her mind as working at the lab. As Lottie's marriage deteriorates, she meets an Armenian-American pediatrician resident, George Kenadjian. Readers are soon convinced she will marry George once her contentious divorce is complete. Heyman conveys George's goodness in subtle ways. He cares deeply about Evelyn; buys a car seat to transport her in his Volkswagen; and loves poetry, introducing her to his favorite poet, William Carlos Williams. "He's a physician, you know, from New Jersey, my home state" (142). George is supportive of Lottie's professional needs, recommending that she apply to graduate school for a doctoral degree. George knows, by instinct and training, how to discipline Evelyn who in a fit of anger bites him, eliciting Lottie's furious words to her child. George's calming words soothe mother and daughter:

George knelt down on the floor next to Lottie. "You lost your temper," he said to Evelyn. "Grown-ups lose their tempers, too. When your mother loses it, she slaps you and she screams out things she regrets. When you lose your temper, you cry and wail and, well, you bit me." He tried to grin. (155)

George is a marvelous character, embodying all the qualities for which Lottie is searching: understanding, dependability, and loyalty. Moreover, he is politically progressive (opposed to the Vietnam War), humorous ("You give my life porpoise"), and a punster (upon hearing her name, he calls her "Lotta Heart"). For all these reasons, we are surprised when Lottie leaves him, mainly because, as we discover in the next section, she does not find him sufficiently exciting. Security is vital to Lottie, but it does not substitute for passion.

Part Six spans Lottie's years in graduate school in Wisconsin, where Burden rapes her and forces her to perform fellatio. The worst part of the assault for Lottie is the fear that her young sleeping daughter may have witnessed the traumatic event. Burden, a screenwriter and assistant professor of English at UC Berkeley, informs her about a negative review he received of his new novel. "When you write a book," the reviewer observed, "it tells on you, it tells about your character, and you are the only one who doesn't know what it tells." Asked by Lottie what the reviewer meant, Burden replies, "That I write a mean sentence and am a nasty, unfeeling son of a bitch" (196). Burden agrees with the first part of the sentence and disagrees with the second part, but both criticisms are true. Tellingly, we can apply the first part of the reviewer's sentence to the author of *Artifact*. Many of Heyman's meanest sentences describe Burden, as when he hands Lottie his menacing-looking pipe. "Two entwined snakes made up the stem. On the bowl were two heads of vultures, and between them, composing the circumference of the bowl, were two lizards, one astride the other, and two monkeys who were licking each other's genitals" (195). The sentence deftly conveys the reptilian Burden who is about to entwine himself around his protesting prey. Heyman crafts multiple mean sentences, and we can tell from the novel that she is devoted to her sympathetic heroine, who tries her best to be a good mother and scientist.

Lottie confronts many challenges, including the fear that she puts her own needs first in pursuing a profession, a classic fear of women who long to have both a family and a career. After Lottie moves with her 11-year-old daughter to Philadelphia, where she has received a postdoc fellowship at the University of Pennsylvania, Evelyn complains about not spending enough time with her mother. "Let me proofread this grant application first, and then I'm all yours," Lottie replies, but her words annoy her daughter. "Couldn't you be all mine first and *then* proofread the application?" "Work before pleasure," Lottie says, to which her angry daughter retorts: "Your work *is* your pleasure" (213–214). Heyman does justice to both points of view here and elsewhere. Toward the end of this section, Lottie receives an assistant professorship in a medical school in New York City, but Evelyn is enraged that they are moving again. Heyman develops the relationship between Lottie and the man she eventually marries, Jake Levinson, Evelyn's music teacher. "He's a good guy," Evelyn tells her mother, "A really good guy. Leave him alone" (227). Heyman's dialogue is not only convincing but also artful: she makes every word count.

Part Seven of *Artifact* is largely the ending of the original short story in *Scary Old Sex*, but Heyman adds new material about Lottie's clash with her stepdaughter, Ruth, Jake's daughter from his first marriage. The stepmother–stepdaughter relationship remains fraught in Heyman's fictional world. Lottie sends Ruth a copy of a book she has coauthored with her postdoc professor, *Great Women of Science*, inscribing it *To My Ruth, With Love from Lottie*, but she worries whether her words are genuine. "Was it honest to call the girl *My Ruth*? Lottie didn't have any other Ruth, thank God" (250). Ruth never admits receiving the book, but Lottie notices that her stepdaughter had thrown it out in Lottie's kitchen garbage can. Interestingly, Lottie later sees a paperback copy of the book containing Ruth's copious handwritten comments in the margins. As always, Heyman allows readers to draw their own conclusions about Ruth's feelings about the book. One of the novel's most noteworthy sentences occurs when the narrator admits that Lottie was "ignorant of her stepdaughter's inner life" (249). Malamud observes in *Dubin's Lives* that "[w]hen you write biography you want to write about people who will make you strain to understand them" (303), but the same is true of novelists who struggle to understand their fictional characters, even if they are finally unknowable.

A Loose Part

Heyman closes *Artifact* with "A Loose Part," a radio interview with Lottie, who objects to being called by her first name. "If I were a man," she reproaches the female interviewer, "you'd call me Dr. Levinson." Heyman must have had fun imagining the interview, for Lottie resents all the personal questions and insists on speaking only about her work as a cell biologist. The most revealing moment occurs at the end of the interview when she is asked a leading question: "Wouldn't you say your children come before everything else?" After a long pause, Lottie replies, "I don't care to comment on this." She then narrates the following joke about a transexual man who goes to Johns Hopkins for a sex change operation but is worried about the pain—a joke that turns out to be a satisfying ending to *Artifact*:

> "The procedure's painless," the surgeon tells him.
> "What? You cut off my penis and testicles and there's no pain?"
> "You're under anesthesia. There's no pain."
> "And afterward, Doctor, when I come to, there's still no pain?"
> "Nope, there's no pain."
> "Now how can that be? You mean, there's no pain at all? None whatsoever?"
> "I didn't say *that*. The pain comes later when you return to work and find your pay's been cut in half." (273)

Works Cited

Davis, Philip. *Bernard Malamud: A Writer's Life*. Oxford UP, 2007.
Felsenthal, Julia. "In *Scary Old Sex*, Writer Arlene Heyman Confronts a Timeless Taboo." *Vogue*, March 12, 2016. www.vogue.com/article/scary-old-sex-arlene-heyman-profile. Accessed December 13, 2022.
Freud, Sigmund. *Beyond the Pleasure Principle*. 1920. *The Standard Edition of the Complete Psychological Works of Sigmund Freud*, translated and edited by James Strachey, vol. 18. The Hogarth Press, 1955.
Freud, Sigmund. *Introductory Lectures on Psycho-Analysis*. 1916–1917. *The Standard Edition of the Complete Psychological Works of Sigmund Freud*, translated and edited by James Strachey, vol. 16. The Hogarth Press, 1963.
Freud, Sigmund. "Mourning and Melancholia." 1917. *The Standard Edition of the Complete Psychological Works of Sigmund Freud*, translated and edited by James Strachey, vol. 14. The Hogarth Press, 1957.
Freud, Sigmund. "Remembering, Repeating and Working Through: (Further Recommendations on the Technique of Psycho-Analysis II)." 1914. *The Standard Edition of the Complete Psychological Works of Sigmund Freud*, translated and edited by James Strachey, vol. 12. The Hogarth Press, 1958.
Garner, Dwight. "Review: In *Scary Old Sex*, Arlene Heyman Mines the Details." *New York Times*, March 8, 2016.
Gawande, Atul. *Being Mortal: Medicine and What Matters in the End*. Metropolitan Books, 2014.
Griffin, Fred. "Review of *Scary Old Sex*." *Journal of the American Psychoanalytic Association*, vol. 65, 2017, pp. 911–919.
Heyman, Arlene. *Artifact*. Bloomsbury, 2020.
Heyman, Arlene. "Meeting of the New York Psychoanalytic Society." *The Psychoanalytic Quarterly*, vol. 53, 1984, pp. 351–352.
Heyman, Arlene. *Scary Old Sex*. Bloomsbury, 2016.
Klass, Dennis, Phyllis R. Silverman, and Steven L. Nickman, editors. *Continuing Bonds: New Understandings of Grief*. Taylor and Francis, 1996.
Malamud, Bernard. *Dubin's Lives*. Farrar, Straus and Giroux, 1977; reissued, with an introduction by Thomas Mallon, 2003.
Mallon, Thomas. "Introduction" to *Dubin's Lives*. Farrar, Strauss and Giroux, 2003.
Phillips, Adam. *Missing Out: In Praise of the Unlived Life*. Farrar, Straus and Giroux, 2012.
Poland, Warren S. *Intimacy and Separateness in Psychoanalysis*, edited and introduced by William F. Cornell, with a Preface by Nancy Chodorow. Routledge, 2018.
Schwartz, Alexandra. "The Erotic Truths of *Scary Old Sex*." *The New Yorker*, March 29, 2016.
Showalter, Elaine. "*Scary Old Sex* by Arlene Heyman—Lusty, Tough and Life-Affirming." *Guardian*, February 25, 2016.
Sklar, Dusty. "The Ghost Writer's Mistress." *Table*, May 9, 2022.
Smith, Janna Malamud. *Private Matters: In Defense of the Personal Life*. Addison-Wesley, 1997.
Suffolk Libraries. "Meet the Author: Arlene Heyman." www.suffolklibraries.co.uk/meet-the-author/arlene-heyman
Wolfenstein, Martha. "Loss, Rage, and Repetition." *Psychoanalytic Study of the Child*, vol. 24, 1969, pp. 432–460.
Wooldridge, Tom. *Ghosts of the Unremembered Past*. International Psychoanalytic Books, 2019.

Chapter 10

Austin Ratner

The Jump Artist and *In the Land of the Living*

It's not uncommon for a student with an advanced degree in literature to become a psychoanalyst, usually for economic reasons—many starving English majors—but it's rare for a person with a medical degree to become a full-time creative writer. Such is the case with Austin Ratner. Born in 1971, he graduated from the University of Michigan in 1994, received a medical degree from the Johns Hopkins University School of Medicine in 1998, but gave up a neurology residency and switched direction, winning a fellowship to the famed University of Iowa Writer's Workshop. His first novel, *The Jump Artist*, published in 2009, earned the Sam Rohr Prize for Jewish Literature in Fiction, which came with a $100,000 purse. His second novel, the highly autobiographical *In the Land of the Living*, appeared in 2013. Ratner then wrote *The Psychoanalyst's Aversion to Proof*, published in 2018, a scholarly study of one of the most intractable problems in psychoanalysis, one that if not solved may doom the fate of the talking cure.

Ratner is not a psychoanalyst, but in 2023 he was appointed editor of *The American Psychoanalyst* (*TAP*), the official magazine, which until that year had been a newsletter, of the American Psychoanalytic Association (APsA). The appointment would have been inconceivable a few years earlier, when the professional organization was stubbornly resistant to change. As Ratner wrote in the wryly titled "Unprotected Speech," in his inaugural issue as editor, "I was invited to think of ways *TAP* might evolve. The search committee specifically welcomed change in tandem with APsA's evolution into a more open and public-facing organization" (7). Ironically, an asterisk appeared in the same inaugural issue indicating that APsA's new president had unexpectedly resigned. Soon afterwards, an article in the *Guardian* by J. Oliver Conroy—"Inside the War Tearing Psychoanalysis Apart: 'The Most Hatred I've Ever Seen'"—outlined the bitter controversy in the spring of 2023 that roiled APsA's listserv, in which members accused each other of anti-Semitism, racism, bigotry, and intolerance, belying the organization's ongoing struggle to become more inclusive. In an article titled "Beyond Immolation and Infighting" published in the next issue of *The American Psychoanalyst*, Ratner wrote perceptively and diplomatically about the vituperative emails on the APsA listserv, concluding that people need psychoanalytic wisdom: "They need psychoanalysis to think things out clearly before intense emotions electrify into destructive action" (8).

The key event in Ratner's life, as he spells out on the second page of *The Psychoanalyst's Aversion to Proof*, was the death of his father, the Cleveland hematologist/oncologist Norman Gordon, from a rare form of lymphoma, on December 4, 1974, at age 29. The death occurred 11 days before Austin Ratner turned three, and on the same day of his cousin Jeremy's birth. Ratner thus grew up "beside a ghost" (2), one that would haunt him for decades. His mother, Susan, remarried the Cleveland real estate developer James Ratner, who adopted her two children. (The novelist dedicated *In the Land of the Living* to his stepfather.) Paternal loss lurks throughout Ratner's novels. As a consequence of his father's death, Ratner struggled with depression as a teenager, one of the symptoms of which was his inability to wish his cousin a happy birthday, an example of an anniversary response. While growing up, Ratner told "neurotic, depressing stories" about himself and his relationships with others. "These were ugly daydreams that hid even uglier feelings from myself." Without being specific, Ratner admits that "I would probably be dead without psychoanalysis" (200). Ratner has not written about how psychoanalysis saved his life, but we can infer some of his psychological difficulties from his two novels which, despite their many differences, share one overwhelming similarity: the two central characters are sons who lose their fathers at an early age, one to an unsolved murder, the other to cancer; in both stories, the sons suffer from intense father hunger and dedicate themselves to honoring their fathers' memory.

The Jump Artist

According to an interview with Gemma Kappala-Ramsamy published in *The Guardian*, Ratner discovered the story of Philippe Halsman by googling "psychoanalysis" and "murder." "I find him to be a fascinating bundle of contradictions," Ratner remarked, "in terms of the joyousness of the latter half of his career and the darkness of his early experiences." Born in 1906 in Riga, then part of the Russian empire and now Latvia, Halsman was accused of bludgeoning to death his father while on a hiking trek in the Austrian Tyrol in September 1928. In a highly publicized and controversial trial at Innsbruck in December 1928 and a retrial in 1929, the prosecutor, confronted with the absence of a credible motive, death weapon, or witnesses, sought the help of the Innsbruck Faculty of Medicine, which claimed, outlandishly, that Freud's newly theorized Oedipus complex was the hidden reason for the patricide. Halsman, a secular Jew, was found guilty in a miscarriage of justice that exposed the virulent anti-Semitism rampant in Austria and elsewhere in Eastern Europe. Halsman became a *cause célèbre*, like the infamous Dreyfus Affair in France a quarter of a century earlier. Halsman was sentenced to four years in Innsbruck Prison, but in light of the furor over the trial, he was pardoned by Austria's chancellor in 1930. Josef Hupka, a law professor at the University of Vienna, led a campaign to clear Halsman's name. Hupka enlisted Freud's help, who stated in "The Expert Opinion in the Halsmann Case" (1931) that the court's mention of the Oedipus complex was misleading. "Precisely because it is always present, the Oedipus complex is not suited to provide a decision on the question of guilt" (*SE*, vol. 21, 252). Freud compared the Halsman case to Dimitri Karamazov's situation in Dostoevsky's novel. "This son, Dimitri, makes no secret of his intention to avenge himself on his father by force," Freud wrote. "It is therefore natural that after his father has been murdered and robbed he should be accused as his murderer and, despite all protestations of his innocence, condemned. And yet Dimitri is innocent; another of the brothers has done the deed" (*SE*, vol. 21, 252). Quoting Dostoevsky, Freud added that "psychology is a knife that cuts both ways." Psychology can not only serve both sides of an argument but it also has good and bad effects, as *The Jump Artist* shows.

After being pardoned, Halsman left Austria for France, where he recovered from tuberculosis and became enamored of the new art of photography at which he excelled. During the beginning of the Second World War, he secured a US visa with the intervention of Albert Einstein and arrived in New York City in 1940, where he established himself as one of the world's great portrait photographers. His stunning photographs often graced the covers of *Life* and *Time* magazines. Halsman photographed many famous celebrities in the act of jumping in mid-air, believing that it caused them to drop the "mask" from their faces: "a picture of a jump reveals the soul," he affirms in *The Jump Artist* (248). Hence, the title of Ratner's novel. The title has another meaning, as Ratner explained in an interview with Karen R. Long. "I think of Philippe Halsman as a jump artist in the sense of having the skill and finesse to be able [to] proceed in his life with the weight of memory on his back. That requires a kind of skill, a kind of navigation around these shoals of depression and sadness." Ratner recreates much of the mystery of Halsman, who died in New York City in 1979. Although *The Jump Artist* is shaped by the historical facts of Halsman's existence, the novelist's intention being to capture the photographer's inner life, Ratner also reveals, consciously or not, aspects of his *own* inner life.

"Death plays tricks in the mind" (73), Halsman's defense attorney, Franz Pessler, explains to him. These tricks involve irrational guilt (including survivor guilt), sorrow, anger, and the need for self-punishment. Father and son did not appear to have a close relationship—"I resolve not to lose my temper with him ever again" (92), Halsman pledges in a 1922 diary entry to his sister. The novel's second chapter opens with a sentence containing a literal and metaphorical truth: "In the beginning, on the path through the mountains that was called the Zamserschinder, all he wanted was to get away from his father" (15). Father and son have strikingly different personalities: the former is extroverted, cheerful, and hearty; the latter is introverted, sullen, and withdrawn. Halsman is flooded with guilt after his father's death, thinking about him during the day and dreaming about him at night. There's no evidence he wished for his father's death, but ambivalence is present in all parent–child relationships. Halsman tortures himself for a crime he did not commit; suicidal thoughts besiege him. During the trial the forensic pathologist, Karl Meixner, demands to know why the defendant tried to cut the arteries in his wrists, and when Halsman responds that he cannot live in a world without justice, Meixner icily retorts, "I can tell you that people don't attempt suicide after false accusations... The innocent fight for their honor" (117). Yet the reader can understand Halsman's despair, which continues after his release from prison. Not every suicide or suicide attempt betokens self-hatred, but it seems to be true in Halsman's case.

Agenbite of Inwit: Remorse of Conscience

Ratner conveys Halsman's all-consuming guilt through the mysterious words *agenbite of inwit* (212). The expression, a translation of a thirteenth-century French treatise on Christian morality, literally means the "again-biting of inner wit": remorse of conscience, guilt that turns against the self. James Joyce uses the expression in *Ulysses* to limn Stephen Dedalus's guilt over his mother's death—he refuses to pray for her, as she asks him to do—and Leopold Bloom's guilt over failing to observe Jewish rituals. Sins of the past haunt Joyce's two characters throughout the novel. It's likely that Ratner learned about agenbite of inwit from *Ulysses*; in a 2021 review of Michael Zimmerman's *Tyrants of the Heart*, a psychoanalytic study of mothers in the Irish novelist's writings, Ratner singled out Joyce as the most Freudian of all the great twentieth-century writers. In *The Jump Artist*, Halsman uses the expression agenbite of inwit to characterize a man falsely accused of a crime who, after being released from prison, cannot forgive himself for being alive. In what is perhaps the most emotionally intense moment in *The Jump Artist*, Halsman engages in a singular inner monologue with his father, foreshadowing, as we shall see, a similar revelation of agenbite of inwit near the end of *In the Land of the Living*:

> *I'm sorry I failed to find your killer, Papa. You were right about my loud mouth. I'm sorry I let those Austrians defeat me with my loud mouth. I'm sorry I let Mama hire a Jew the first time and screw it all up. I'm sorry we were all so weak. I'm sorry I failed you. And I'm sorry you dragged me all across the Alps and I'm sorry you left me behind to rot for two years in an Austrian prison. I'm sorry that I hate you, Papa, you stupid corpse.* (212)

Love and hate are inextricably fused in this remarkable passage along with a son's helplessness in saving his father from death. One cannot reasonably feel anger toward a parent who did not want to die, but emotions are not always reasonable. Nothing can defuse Philippe's fury over his father's death: "*The dead betray the living*" (175), he fumes. And the living betray the dead. One can be guilty of an imagined crime, as Freud theorizes in the "omnipotence of thoughts," where the unconscious mind makes no distinction between thought and deed. Ratner's recognition of the ambivalent nature of Halsman's love for his father contributes to the success of *The Jump Artist* as a *psychological* novel. "*You told me to be a doctor*," the son recalls. "*I can't hear you anymore. I can't see you*" (49). But he cannot stop talking to his father, and though he doesn't become a physician—his father was a dentist and hoped the two of them would practice together—he yearns to make his father proud. Ratner includes details in *The Jump Artist* that eerily parallel his own situation. He tells us, for example, that Marilyn Monroe, whom Halsman photographs, had never known her own father, who had abandoned his family and died in a motorcycle accident when she was three, Ratner's age when he lost his own father. Again foreshadowing *In the Land of the Living*, Halsman vows to "rise where his father had fallen and dedicate to his father all the glories he would never witness" (154). Filial love remains central in his life.

Ratner ends *The Jump Artist* with Halsman's meditation on his father. The final chapter, "The Persistence of Memory," quotes a letter Halsman wrote in prison in 1930. "I doubt about my success in life. But I have known one man who always believed in me and my success and that was my poor father" (242). The son's grief-stricken memories of his father slowly become more accepting of the finality of death. The last sentence, recalling a distant idyllic time when Halsman was with his family in a Latvian resort city by the sea, conjures up not only the persistence of memory but also the magical power of the imagination—Halsman's and Ratner's—to recreate past beauty.

> He wished he could go back there now, to the edge of the birch forest where the gnats tumbled in the light of the sunset, back to that place where he'd gotten lost chasing a butterfly in the woods and Papa had come for him, crashing through the weeds in the red shirt with the ox-horn buttons. (252)

"Sidewalk Phantom," published in the *New York Times Magazine* in 2009 and selected in 2017 as one of its 16 all-time best Lives columns, is a nonfictional rehearsal for *In the Land of the Living*. Ratner recalls watching the 2003 film *American Splendor*, a biopic about the underground comic book legend Harvey Pekar (played by Paul Giamatti), Ratner's cousin. "I'd heard that Harvey once dropped my father's name into a comic strip, but my father was unlikely to figure into any condensed story of Harvey's life." To Ratner's surprised delight, late in the film Giamatti speaks his deceased father's name. "He said: 'My cousin Norman died of lymphoma. He was 29. He was a brilliant oncologist.'" After moving to Brooklyn, New York, Ratner saw Giamatti a number of times—they both lived in the same neighborhood—and imagined introducing himself as "Norman's son." But the opportunity never presented itself. Ratner still sees Giamatti walking in his neighborhood, still feels like the actor is a "ghost of my father," a ghost who comes to life in his next novel.

In the Land of the Living

In the Land of the Living is a Bildungsroman, a story about the growth and education of the authorial hero, Leo Auberon. The first third of the novel chronicles the life and death of Leo's father, Isidore Auberon, based largely on Ratner's biological father, Norman Gordon. (Ratner chooses his names carefully: "Isidore" is Greek for "gift of Isis"; Auberon is German for "noble" or "royal bear.") According to Gordon's obituary, he was the son of Hyman Gordon and Leah Gordon, the husband of Susan Ratner, and father of "Private and Private"—indicating, perhaps, that the manager of the obituary website, Susan Ratner, did not wish to disclose the names of their two children to preserve their privacy. If this is true, one can only wonder how Susan Ratner felt about her son's novel. It's unlikely she would have been displeased with her son's loving evocation of their family history. Isidore comes across as immensely talented and kind-hearted—except toward his abusive immigrant father, who is angry at the world over the early death of his wife, from stomach cancer, and who subsequently abandons his parenting responsibilities to their three young sons. The only negative detail about Isidore is that, like his father, he could be unforgiving—though the only person he cannot forgive is his father. "He would let his hatred wrestle his father's hatred in some realm of eternal hatred, some rank of the inferno cold and dark forever" (31).

In the Land of the Living offers biographically accurate portraits of Austin Ratner's prominent maternal grandparents. Isidore's father-in-law, Dr. Leonard Neuwalder, is based on Austin Weisberger, chair of the department of medicine at Case Western Reserve School of Medicine. Weisberger, after whom Ratner was named—just as Leo is named after Neuwalder—died in 1970 of a heart attack at age 56 while driving. Neuwalder had, the novel's third-person narrator states, the "sort of gentle humility about him that only the most powerful people can afford" (40). Neuwalder embodies a "Confucian wisdom," including the knowledge, reminiscent of Philip Roth, whose quick-witted sarcasm resembles Ratner's, that the "key to life is recognizing what you can't control, which is everything" (49). Ratner conveys Neuwalder's death in a single sentence, as startling as it is unsentimental. "Doc went to California and leaned his head on a steering wheel and coasted to a stop in the highway sun and he came back in a wooden box" (72). In lightly fictionalizing Isidore's father-in-law, Ratner observes that Neuwalder's mother died when he was three, a detail that, if true, calls attention to the trauma of early parental loss in both the fictional character and the novelist's lives. Dr. Neuwalder's wife, Evelyn, is based on Ratner's maternal grandmother, Eleanor Weisberger, a child therapist, assistant professor at Case Western Reserve University, and the author of a number of books, including *Your Young Child and You* (1975), which contains an introduction by Benjamin Spock, with whom she taught an undergraduate course. Evelyn Weisberger trained in psychoanalysis and was a member of the first class of trainees at the Hanna Perkins Center for Child Development, a therapeutic nursery school and kindergarten in Cleveland in which Ratner's mother enrolled him following his father's death. Attending Hanna Perkins, Ratner wrote in a 2015 article published in the *Forward*, was his first experience of the world outside his family. "It was an ordered world, an empathic world, a rational, kind, well-lit world of 'home-like warmth,' as one of Hanna Perkins's longtime directors, Robert Furman, put it" ("A Cleveland Son's Debt to Anny Katan and Sigmund Freud"). As an example of this rational, ordered, and empathic world, consider the pragmatic advice about the consequences of losing a close relative or friend

Eleanor Weisberger offers readers in her 1987 book *When Your Child Needs **You**: A Parents' Guide Through the Early Years*:

> If the person who died was very close to you, you may not be able to help your children very much at all. Facing your own feelings may be all that you have the emotional energy for. You will be embarked on a long process of feeling your sorrow over and over. The feelings death brings are complex and varied. You may feel sorrow at one time, remorse at another. You may be irrationally angry at the person who died. (It was his leaving that caused you the pain, wasn't it?) You can feel relief that the person's anguish may be over. Guilt may follow, or depression—a feeling that life isn't worth living without the other person. Sometimes a forced gaiety ensues. (119)

Significantly, Ratner's maternal relatives were, unlike Ratner himself, deeply private about their grief. In the above paragraph, notice that Eleanor Weisberger avoids mentioning her first husband's death; it's likely that she was thinking about herself when she notes that one can be irrationally angry at a person who has died. In the first paragraph of Austin Weisberger's obituary, published in the journal *Blood*, we learn that he "knew that he had heart disease, but he kept it to himself and followed the advice that he had given to his own patients, that one should live a full life" (Ham and Murphy 113). And Susan Gordon Ratner avoids remarking on her first husband's death in a 2021 interview with Alex Krutchik. "If you've suffered—which I've had some tragedy in my life—you really understand what it's like for people to struggle."

Eleanor Weisberger was a guest on many radio and television programs, including "The Mike Douglas Show." After her first husband's death, she remarried David Weintraub, a neonatologist, and died in 2014 at age 94. A jokester, Ratner revels in quips and banter, and he reserves the best jest in the novel for Evelyn Neuwalder, who tells a dirty story abounding in double entendres about a priest, a minister, and a rabbi taking the train to an ecumenical convention in Pittsburgh:

> The woman selling train tickets had big breasts, she said, and wore a low-cut blouse that showed a lot of cleavage and turned the clergymen into stuttering fools: the minister asked for his change in nipples and dimes; the rabbi asked for two pickets to Tittsburgh; but the priest would not be pushed on his heels and wouldn't let the woman's brazen apparel go without comment and declared, "When you get to Heaven, Saint Finger's gonna shake his peter at you!" (*In the Land of the Living* 50).

In the Land of the Living implies that Leo's psychological problems arise from his father's death. Apart from using the word *depression*, Ratner avoids psychiatric terms or diagnoses, but he refers repeatedly to his protagonist's fears, compulsions, and rituals. We never learn when, why, or how Leo's symptoms end—presuming they do end—but the novelist makes clear the seriousness of the illness. "*This must be what it is to lose your mind*" (146), Leo frets, and while it's always problematic to equate a novelist with a single character, it's likely that in his psychological distress, Leo is a portrait of the artist as a young man.

Leo's mental health challenges begin when he is in the sixth or seventh grade and steadily grow worse. His psychological symptoms appear in the middle of the novel, in a chapter curiously titled "Labiaphobia," though anxiety over his or a female body seems to be the least of his problems. In an effort to diagnose and cure himself, Leo reads medical textbooks, but to no avail. To convey his protagonist's distressed state of mind, Ratner lists 15 of Leo's chronic worries, including feeling like a failure and believing he is neither good, brave, nor smart. Leo also fears sexual inadequacy, though we do not see this in any of his relationships with women. While visiting Rome, he fears he will succumb to the Devil. "He would not step on cracks, especially in the church floors, because that superstition seemed to him not at all childish but rather august and ancient" (145). Leo washes his hands compulsively and engages in other rituals to avoid dangerous thoughts. He tries, futilely, to keep his mind blank lest a loved one perish: "he could involuntarily wish for his mother to die and his wish might be granted, or wish for her to live and the opposite might come true" (145–146). Leo's stepfather would make five different restaurant reservations and then cancel them, citing fake medical emergencies. Ratner does not explicitly link Leo's obsessional thinking with Freud's theory of magical thinking, but the self-tortured teenager is terrified that words and symbols are dangerous portals. Writing brings no relief. "He wrote pages and pages of theories on his compulsions, but they were not meant to understand, they were meant to keep the Devil away" (146). Upon returning from Italy, Leo visits a psychologist who tells him that his problems are related to his dead father, an insight that does not help him, at least not then. Later, unable to find relief through reading nor, presumably, speaking or writing, Leo raises a tormenting question: "How was he to escape this trap of self-hate if acknowledging the trap just led to more self-hate?" (242).

Leo's intense idealization of his father and maternal grandfather, both physicians, both heroes, in his eyes, compels him to become a physician himself, mainly, it seems, to win their love and enjoy the prestige of a physician rather than to alleviate suffering. The novel glosses over his education in college (spending a year at Yale and then transferring to the University of Michigan) and medical school. We never see his growing doubts about his medical career or the excitement and challenges of becoming a full-time novelist. Nor do we see his family's reaction to his decision to give up medicine. *In the Land of the Living* is a story about intergenerational relationships, legacies that are passed down from generation to generation, yet it is not a story about the sins of the fathers being visited on the children, mainly because Isidore Auberon and Leonard Neuwalder remained idealized figures. Nor does Ratner describe any of his stepfather's failings. Ratner is circumspect about characterizing Leo's relationship with his stepfather, referring only vaguely to early resentment toward him. Leo calls Philip "father" and "dad," never "daddy," which he reserves for his biological father. Philip's attitude toward Leo is never in doubt. "I love you, boy" (113), he exclaims, a heartfelt feeling that never changes. Had Leo recognized the frailties in his father, maternal grandfather, and stepfather, it might have been easier for him to accept his own imperfections.

Everything is grist for the writer's mill, including, indeed, *especially*, rejection. Vowing to attend Yale College—his father attended Harvard—Leo begins wearing a Yale sweatshirt and then becomes enraged when he is turned down. He stabs a hole in the sweatshirt, tearing off the letters, and the next day wears it to school, with the hole over his heart. In an incident too bizarre to be invented, Leo receives a letter from the Yale dean of admissions who begrudgingly accepts him, because, he says, a member of the Yale alumnus association of Cleveland had inappropriately told Leo he would be accepted; himself enraged, the dean of admissions resigns in protest. Is Leo a narcissist, as one of his rejected girlfriends claimed? Perhaps, but the novelist knows this material is too good not to use.

Adept at different forms of prose, Ratner's language becomes more impassioned, alliterative, and mythic when he writes about Leo's father and maternal grandfather's experiences in the merchant marine and navy, respectively, as in the following sentence:

> Verily, they had winched steel and manned decks, trimmed the glim of the human hearth in the sea to keep it afloat and afire, they had sailed into the mouth of the titan waves that ate bow decks and fly bridges, that gulped freighters and battleships like toys. (214)

In elevating Isidore Auberon's story into a modern myth, Ratner turns to elegiac prose, realizing that the elegy, paradoxically, is an art that will never die. The novel is peppered with Latin, Middle English, and Yiddish expressions. A rabid Cleveland sports fan, he ruefully realizes that loss is inherent not only in his own genes but in those of his native city. "To be a Cleveland sports fan is like being Jewish," Ratner declares drolly in a 2012 article published in the *Forward*. "Cleveland, like the Bible, like the Jews, has had vulnerability burned into its memory, and it's consequently liturgical about pain" ("Cleveland Rocks—Not Really").

No one can explain why one child's early loss of a parent results in a psychological crisis while the same is not true of another child in a similar situation. Nor can one explain why Leo's brother, Mack, is spared this trauma—if indeed, he was spared. (Daniel Ratner, who was born six weeks after their father's death, holds a doctoral degree in clinical psychology and specializes in mind-body disorders.) Much of the second half of the novel elaborates on Leo's complicated relationship with his brother and their road trip from San Francisco to Cleveland in 1999, a bonding experience. But Leo never believes that Mack feels the same devastation over paternal loss as he does. "I have sympathy for you, Mack," Leo says. "But you didn't lose him, because you didn't ever know him to begin with" (247), a hurtful statement he instantly regrets.

Grave Truths

How does a novelist resolve a story about a son's desperate search for his long-deceased father? Ratner's solution, in the penultimate chapter of *In the Land of the Living*, the story's emotional climax, is for the son to verbalize, for the first time, the conjoining of love and hate, revelatory of the gravest truth in his life:

> *All my life, you lie in your hole and drink my love. You drink my blood and your hole repays me nothing but the guilty black humors of the grave. And still my every cell dare not breathe, my very ribosomes dare not read the Book of Life without I honor you.*
>
> *I tell you now, for this grave and silent treatment, I hate you. Not Yale, not my brother or yours, but you. And that's not all. I will be better than you. And my other father and uncles, too. It's not too late. This is only the beginning for me. You'll see. It's a noble thing to hope for, a noble thing to try for! NOT a bad thing! NOT an unloving thing. I go to it.* (296)

Freud describes the mechanism of pathological grief in "Mourning and Melancholia" (1917), in which he writes about anger toward a lost love one turning against the self, resulting in feelings of self-hatred and self-punishment. Offering a different model of love and loss, attachment theorist John Bowlby dispenses with Freudian libido theory and concludes that separation from a loved one inevitably produces anger. Whichever theory of bereavement one embraces, it's striking that the melancholic Leo betrays fierce Oedipal rivalry in this passage: he will be *better* than his father, albeit in the process, honoring his father's memory, like his fictional predecessor, Philippe Halsman.

Tellingly, Leo's vampiric image of a dead father drinking his son's love and blood recalls Sylvia Plath's iconic poem "Daddy," written shortly before her suicide in 1963 at age 30. As with Ratner, the central event in Plath's life was the death of her father, a professor of entomology at Boston University, in 1940, when she was eight. Plath mythologized her father in "Daddy" as a monstrous Nazi despite biographical evidence that he appeared to be a loving albeit authoritarian husband and father to his two children. Upon learning of her father's death, Plath vowed that she would never speak to God again. As I wrote in *The Talking Cure* (1985), "It was as if her father and God were mysteriously fused together and lost forever. The man she could not understand in life she began to mythologize in death" (124). Leo's father in Ratner's novel could not be more different from the one in Plath's poem, yet both are mythologized into larger-than-life figures. The fathers' deaths lead to their children's eternal mourning, awakening keening love. Moreover, both fathers engender fear in their children, though of a different kind. "I have always been scared of *you*," Plath's speaker hisses; by contrast, Ratner's protagonist is terrified of *failing* his father, thereby losing his love and failing himself. Paradoxically, the two fathers are muses for their offspring's creativity.

In the final chapter of *In the Land of the Living*, Leo recalls meeting a woman, Dusty, at a Cleveland wedding. Undeterred by his repeated failures to meet the right woman—earlier he has confessed to his "four years of flaying onanism" while a medical student (252)—he explains to her that he is a physician who writes fiction, including a story about a boy with a dead father. Dusty asks, skeptically, whether somebody died in his life:

"Yes, actually," he said. And he told her about his father.

"I don't remember my mother," she said. "The same thing happened to her."

"We ought to go buy a bottle of 1974 Burgundy," he said, since his father and her mother had died within a month of each other in 1974. "We ought to go out together and take the bottle and throw it off a bridge." (300)

It's not apparent on a first reading of *In the Land of the Living* that Dusty is Ratner's future wife, Kristin Kublak, whom he met in Cleveland at a wedding. Here and elsewhere, one must read between the lines. In a 2009 interview with David B. Green, Ratner said that when revising a novel, he finds himself "cutting out things that explained too directly," an aesthetic technique perfected by Hemingway, master of the art of compression. Ratner uses another literary technique; as Leo explains to Mack, while reading *The Aeneid*, he learned about *aposiopesis*, a device in which characters interrupt themselves before completing their speeches. While searching for his novel's title, Ratner stated in his article "Character, Interrupted (Usefully)" published in *The Wall Street Journal*, he came across an example of aposiopesis from a verse in the Hebrew Bible, evoking a moment of doubt: "Unless I had believed to see the goodness of the Lord in the land of the living."

Compression and aposiopesis are only two of the novel's many aesthetic strengths; others include exuberant language, deft wordplay, crisp dialogue, mordant humor, and sharply drawn characters. *In the Land of the Living* is also tightly structured: midway through the story Ratner quotes the song lyrics from "A Wonderful Day Like Today," written by Leslie Bricusse and Anthony Newley in 1965; the last line of the novel ends with "wonderful." As the story closes, Leo is about to begin a new chapter in his life as a novelist. With the spirit of his father to guide him, and fully immersed in the land of the *living*, Leo is, like Philippe Halsman, a jump artist, ready to capture his characters' faces, and inner lives, with masks on and off. It is no accident that on the wall of Leo's home is a framed Philippe Halsman portrait of Albert Einstein, two figures who, along with his lionized father, inspire his own creativity, imbuing him with a sense of destiny.

Works Cited

Berman, Jeffrey. *The Talking Cure: Literary Representations of Psychoanalysis*. New York UP, 1985.

Conroy, J. Oliver. "Inside the War Tearing Psychoanalysis Apart: 'The Most Hatred I've Ever Witnessed.'" *The Guardian*, June 16, 2023.

Freud, Sigmund. "The Expert Opinion in the Halsmann Case." 1931. *The Standard Edition of the Complete Psychological Works of Sigmund Freud*, translated and edited by James Strachey, vol. 21. The Hogarth Press, 1961.

Freud, Sigmund. "Mourning and Melancholia." 1917. *The Standard Edition of the Complete Psychological Works of Sigmund Freud*, translated and edited by James Strachey, vol. 14. The Hogarth Press, 1957.

Green, David B. "A Conversation with Austin Ratner." *Haaretz*, July 1, 2009.

Ham, Thomas and John R. Murphy. "Obituary of Austin S. Weisberger." *Blood* vol. 37, 1971, pp. 113–114.

Kappala-Ramsamy, Gemma. "Debut Author: Austin Ratner." *The Guardian*, July 14, 2012. www.theguardian.com/books/2012/jul/15/austin-ratner-jump-artist-halsman. Accessed June 22, 2023.

Krutchik, Alex. "Meet the 2021 Class of 18 Difference Makers Series." www.clevelandjewishnews.com/differencemakers2021. Accessed June 23, 2023.

Long, Karen R. "*The Jump Artist*: Austin Ratner's Years in Cleveland Color His Outlook." *Cleveland Plain Dealer*, June 26, 2009.

Plath, Sylia. *Collected Poems*, edited by Ted Hughes. Harper and Row, 1981.

Ratner, Austin. "Beyond Immolation and Infighting." *The American Psychoanalyst* vol. 57, 2023, pp. 7–9.

Ratner, Austin. "Character, Interrupted (Usefully)." *The Wall Street Journal*, April 20, 2013.

Ratner, Austin. "Cleveland Rocks—Not Really." *Forward*, March 7, 2012. forward.com/news/152590/cleveland-rocks-not-really. Accessed June 28, 2023.

Ratner, Austin. "A Cleveland Son's Debt to Anny Katan and Sigmund Freud." *Forward*, February 16, 2015. https://forward.com/culture/214585/a-cleveland-sons-debt-to-anny-katan-and-sigmund-fr. Accessed June 24, 2023.

Ratner, Austin. *In the Land of the Living*. Little, Brown and Company, 2013.

Ratner, Austin. *The Jump Artist*. Bellevue Literary Press, 2009.

Ratner, Austin. "The Maternal in James Joyce." *Journal of the American Psychoanalytic Association*, vol. 69, 2021, pp. 215–220.

Ratner, Austin. *The Psychoanalyst's Aversion to Proof*. International Psychoanalytic Books, 2018.

Ratner, Austin. "Sidewalk Phantom." *New York Times Magazine*, June 17, 2009.

Ratner, Austin. "Unprotected Speech." *The American Psychoanalyst*, vol. 57, 2023, pp. 7–9.

Weisberger, Eleanor. *When Your Child Needs **You**: A Parents' Guide Through the Early Years*. Adler & Adler, 1987.

Chapter 11

Joan Wexler

A Pot from Shards and *Make Me the Sky*

Few psychoanalysts write memoirs, and even fewer craft novels; for an analyst to pen both a memoir and a novel, late in life, is indeed a rarity. (The same is true, as we shall see, for Cliff Wilkerson.) For this reason alone, it is fascinating to read Joan Wexler's memoir, *A Pot from Shards* (2019), and novel, *Make Me the Sky* (2023), both written when she was an octogenarian. But there are other reasons to read these two works, including a theme common to both: they are narrated by daughters who have never known their biological fathers. *A Pot from Shards* focuses on Wexler's search for her biological father, who, apart from a few visits, disappeared from her life when she was two years old. *Make Me the Sky* ends with the revelation that the protagonist has never known her biological father, a truth concealed from her, out of shame, by her dying mother. The mystery of provenance, the enigma of biological paternity, characterizes *A Pot from Shards* and *Make Me the Sky*. Betrayal and abandonment define the memoir and the novel, but despite this, the two daughters survive and flourish, demonstrating that resourceful and resilient women can overcome the sins of the fathers.

A Pot from Shards

Felicitously titled, *A Pot from Shards* is a metaphor for Joan Wexler's life. (Note the importance of the preposition: *from*, not *of*.) What would have shattered many people left her strong in the broken places. Born in New York City in 1938, she was largely raised by her grandmother, her primary caretaker, between the ages of four and ten. She had a conflicted relationship with both her mother, who insisted on being called by her first name, Marion, and her grandmother, Fannie Seigel, whom both mother and daughter called "Mama." History repeated itself three times, Wexler avows ruefully; she, her mother, and her grandmother grew up without their fathers, a pattern she was determined not to repeat when she married Harry Wexler in 1960. It was a long and successful marriage that lasted until his death in 2018 at age 82. He stayed around to parent their two adopted children, thus breaking the paradigm of the absent father.

Before beginning Sarah Lawrence College in 1956, where she majored in literature and psychology, Wexler danced professionally with the Martha Graham

Dance Company in New York City, a transformative experience that enabled her to express repressed emotions she did not yet grasp. In her memoir, she writes about the parallels between the dancer and the psychoanalyst:

> The dancer and the psychoanalyst both train for many years to strive for freedom and honesty. The body, in gesture and expression, reveals the nature of the person. The body can be trained to move in complex ways, but no two people and no two trained dancers move precisely alike. Each dancer, particularly if they will become a soloist, seeks suppleness, power, and their own idiom. The psychoanalyst and patient seek the personal truth behind clichés, illusions, assumptions and distorted beliefs. (*A Pot from Shards* 61)

Many have noted that storytelling links the creative writer to the psychoanalyst, but it is less obvious to point out, as Wexler does in a 2018 article, the aesthetic dimension to therapeutic action. Agreeing with Freud's observation in *The Ego and the Id* (1923) that the ego is first a "body ego" (*SE*, vol. 19, 27), she remarks that both the aesthetic, especially in dance, and the therapeutic originate in the body before they are perceived as emotion or cognitive insight. Dancing helped Wexler express her dark emotions before she began her academic study in college or her professional study as a clinical social worker. Fittingly, her prose is most impassioned when she describes the joy of dancing, jumping, leaping, defying gravity—like Philippe Halsman, Austin Ratner's jump artist.

In 1988, when she was 50, Wexler entered into what turned out to be an eight-year psychoanalysis. She doesn't offer any details about her analysis in *A Pot from Shards*, but she reveals one noteworthy detail in her 2018 article. Growing up without a father, she was terrified that she would lose her mother. She began to fear, when she was nine, that something terrible would happen to her mother when she left work at five o'clock. The daughter developed a daily ritual of sitting in almost complete stillness in the center of her couch, holding a copy of *Life* magazine, until her mother arrived home. "This period of magic and rigid posture was my hopefully time-limited sacrifice to insure my mother's life and my life with her." She never told anyone about the ritual until, 40 years later, she disclosed it to her analyst who was about to go on vacation. (She includes this ritual in *A Pot from Shards* but not her analyst's response.) When she finished telling him, he responded in a calm, steady voice, "If you are exactly in the center you can't be left," to which she responded, with both pleasure and gratitude for being understood, "Right!" (211). After the first year of analysis, she decided to become a psychoanalyst herself and began formal training at the Western New England Institute of Psychoanalysis in New Haven, Connecticut. She later became a member of the clinical faculty of the Yale University School of Medicine Department of Psychiatry. The best advice she received about doing therapeutic work came from her favorite supervisor, the Viennese-born Ernst Prelinger, who said: "Each patient will teach you how to work with them." In her own highly figurative words, "It is like finding the grain in the wood to sculpt or the texture of the paint or the way a poetic metaphor evokes a multilayered image" ("Therapeutic Action and Aesthetic Experience" 208).

Wexler had to overcome intense ambivalence before she was ready to reconnect with her father. Visits from him ended when she was five. She made one effort to call him when she was a senior in college, but the meeting did not go well. In a statement over which she ruminated, he said to her, "You must be in love or you would not have tried to find me" (*A Pot from Shards* 27). It was not until 2008 that Wexler began searching for her long-missing father—and she soon discovered that he had died in California in 1970, at age 61. The death certificate indicated that he died of cirrhosis of the liver caused by chronic alcoholism and heart failure. Visiting San Francisco where he last lived, Wexler was startled when, looking at the photograph she had taken of the building's glass door, she could see her own reflection, an unsettling experience that gave rise to a myriad of psychological and philosophical questions. "Who is inside? Who is outside? Was I ever inside my father's mind? Did he ever think about me? This accidental photo trick catches my fantasy that I am a part of his interior" (6). She cannot resolve any of these questions, but they are the driving force behind her memoir. Her father's name, John Pote, stimulated her imagination—and delight in wordplay. His surname reminded her of a *pot*, fragile and broken, of which she is a shard. In her teens, when she found herself infuriated over his absence, she expressed anger with the word "impotent." She wanted to have an all-powerful father, one who was "Pater OmniPOTEns" (10). Sometimes she thought of him as "the john" or "potty," capturing her mother's need to eliminate him from her life. Transposing the *e* in his name, she imagined him as a *poet*, which seemed appropriate because he was an actor and playwright, though he never completed a play. Punning on her father's name is only one example of the metaphorical richness of *A Pot from Shards*.

Bitterly disappointed she was unable to reconnect with her father, Wexler became intrigued by the idea of an absent presence. "Nothing" is one of the most ambiguous words in the English language, as Lear should have known when, in a fit of rage, he warned his silent daughter Cordelia, "Nothing will come of nothing." Wexler doesn't cite Shakespeare, but she quotes a line from Wallace Stevens's poem "The Snow Man": "Nothing that is not there, and the nothing that is" (*A Pot from Shards* 11). John Pote was himself a snow man, destined to melt, evaporate, and disappear; he became a cautionary tale to his daughter who, stung by abandonment, sought a person who would stand by her side and give her nothing more—and nothing less—than a "normal" life, a word that appears nearly a dozen times throughout her memoir, always with an honorific meaning.

Unable to learn much about her father's life, Wexler must conjure him: "Fiction will have to do" (29), she declares, and then proceeds to create a story about the end of his life in San Francisco. The imagined chapter of the memoir, "Good Morning," is only six pages long, but it displays her gift for characterization, dialogue, setting, and metaphor. She envisions him meeting a male transvestite in a bar in the Tenderloin district of San Francisco, confessing his marital failures. Each comforts the other in her scenario. The only entirely fictional section of *A Pot from Shards*, the poignant chapter may have been a preparation for writing her novel. Wexler had always loved storytelling, which helped her make sense of troubling reality, and many of the tales she told as a child and adult were about missing fathers, a subject that became her muse.

A Pot from Shards is elegantly written and searingly candid. She writes openly about the moments in her life when she thought seriously about suicide, including her mother's desperate words to her, after a failed marriage, "Let's turn on the gas and die" (161). She confesses her passionate hatred for her mother as well as her fierce love for her. She never shrinks from describing her rage, capturing its positive as well as negative meanings, as she observes in her 2002 article "Rage to Order," a study of the writings of Wallace Stevens and the psychoanalyst Hans Loewald: "The word 'rage' suggests instinctual passion, fury, frenzy, and madness. It also suggests fervor or zeal, fervor for an order that is not stripped of instinctual feeling" (462). Wexler acknowledges the rough patch in her marriage that she and her husband were able to work through. The memoir begins with Wexler's search for her deceased father and ends with her husband's decision to stop eating and drinking as a result of suffering from advanced Parkinson's disease, a decision supported by his wife and physicians, but *A Pot from Shards* is mainly a story of three generations of women, all of whom struggle to find meaning in life. Wexler doesn't explain how she felt while writing her memoir, but in her review of Danielle Knafo's 2012 book *Dancing with the Unconscious: The Art of Psychoanalysis and the Psychoanalysis of Art*, she affirms the therapeutic nature of artistic expression. "Making art can, like psychoanalysis, heal the effects of trauma and grief; both embrace the search for a possible future so that the movement of life and the movement of the mind may prevail over trauma and rigid pathology" (174).

As Irene Smith Landsman noted in her laudatory review, the "fractured structure of Joan Wexler's haunting memoir replicates the author's lifelong challenge to make sense of a life that seemed to defy the construction of a coherent narrative" (1237). Landsman points out that the memoir's fragmented and at times nonlinear structure "is almost a character in the narrative—a self that is constantly battling confusion, dissociation, and misdirection to arrive finally at the story of a life" (1239). Wexler continues the story in *Make Me the Sky*, where she imagines what life must have been like for her maternal grandmother, "Mama."

Make Me the Sky

Make Me the Sky highlights Wexler's maternal grandmother, born in the Galicia section of Eastern Europe near the end of the nineteenth century. The fourth of eight children, Fannie was chosen by her mother, when she was 15 or 16, to immigrate to the United States for the purpose of sending money to her impoverished family. Why Fannie's mother singles her out, of all the children, to travel to the United States becomes an urgent question in the story. When she began the novel, Wexler tried to evoke the story of her grandmother who was silent about her background, but the fictional character seemed to take on a life of her own, as if she wrote herself into existence regardless of authorial intentions. The result is a character who is far more sympathetic and engaging in *Make Me the Sky* than in *A Pot from Shards*.

To give only a few examples of the differences between the historical Fannie Seigel (who changed her first name to Stephanie and later called herself Frances Glenn) and the fictional Fannie Liebermann, we learn in *A Pot from Shards* that Fannie's father abandoned her mother and their family in Poland when she was 14. By contrast, Fannie's father in *Make Me the Sky* is not missing, but he dies of tuberculosis in a sanitarium, making it easier for the family to grieve his loss. In the memoir, Fannie changes her name to Stephanie because she thought it sounded less Jewish; in the novel, Fannie is never embarrassed over her religion. Wexler states in the memoir that Fannie despised her husband even before he deserted the family; her hatred deepened when she found him in bed with her best friend. "I suspect Mama renounced sex if she ever embraced it" (*A Pot from Shards* 53). None of these details appears in *Make Me the Sky*. In her memoir, Wexler remembers her grandmother as strict, possessive, unforgiving, and wrathful. The opposite is true of the protagonist in the novel; Fannie has a sunnier disposition though it darkens when she is betrayed or abandoned by others. Fannie remains a shadowy character in *A Pot from Shards*, but she shines in *Make Me the Sky*. Writing the novel helped Wexler understand her grandmother's singularity to her. The novelist sought to imagine her grandmother's life as it might have been had circumstances been less harsh. The novel does not contain as much wordplay as the memoir, but Wexler probably chose her heroine's surname because "Lieber" means "loved one" in German and Yiddish; in *A Pot from Shards*, Wexler's grandmother received letters from her family in Europe beginning with "Liebe Fannie."

Like most poor immigrants arriving at the United States around the turn of the twentieth century, Fannie traveled in steerage, the lowest category of long-distance steamship travel. Wexler captures the crowded conditions in which passengers were packed like cattle, the unbearable stench caused by deplorable sanitary conditions, and the high mortality rate: between 10 and 20 percent of those traveling in steerage died. Life in the teeming Lower East Side of Manhattan is not much of an improvement. Uncomplaining, Fannie sleeps on two chairs in her uncle's cramped tenement. She finds a job working on the 8th floor of a shirtwaist factory; had she worked on the 9th floor, she would have perished in the infamous Triangle Shirtwaist Factory fire in 1911: 146 garment workers, mostly girls and women, lost their lives in the deadliest industrial disaster in New York City's history. Wexler reproduces the horror of this event. "I'll never forget the sound of bodies hitting the pavement," Fannie confides to her diary, "I'll never forget the blood and the tangle of limbs. I'll never forget the smell of burning flesh. I'll never forget the sirens and the screams" (66). Nor will Wexler's readers forget this traumatic incident, which foreshadows a more horrific conflagration in New York City 90 years later.

Make Me the Sky consists of Fanny's diary entries and letters to her family spanning the years from 1910, when she boards a ship that sails from Bremen to

New York, to 1919, when she is married and has her own family. *Make Me the Sky* is an epistolary novel that may remind literary historians of Samuel Richardson's *Pamela; or, Virtue Rewarded*, published in 1740, considered to be the first English novel. *Make Me the Sky* follows in the tradition of *Pamela* and other sentimental novels, celebrating the emotional life of a character, including her distress, tenderness, and joy. I'm not suggesting that Richardson's novel influenced Wexler's, but it is instructive to look briefly at the two novels, separated by nearly three centuries, to see their similarities and differences.

The eponymous heroine of Richardson's novel is a virtuous if naïve 15-year-old maid whose main challenge is to preserve her virginity amidst the unwelcome advances of her licentious employer, Mr. B. Pamela Andrews pens emotionally charged diary entries and letters to her impecunious parents describing her employer's sexual assaults. Richardson's damsel in distress succeeds in helping Mr. B overcome his rakishness; the novel ends with their marriage and her elevation into upper-class society. *Pamela; or, Virtue Rewarded* has an obvious didactic purpose, a "conduct" novel that draws attention to marriage and morality. *Pamela* inspired other novelists, most notably Henry Fielding, to write parodies: *Shamela* (1741) spoofs Richardson's heroine. Fielding had Richardson in mind when he observes in his comic picaresque novel, *Tom Jones* (1749), that

> [t]here are a set of religious or rather moral writers who teach that virtue is the certain road to happiness, and vice to misery, in this world. A very wholesome and comfortable doctrine, and to which we have but one objection, namely, that it is not true. (Book XV, chapter 1)

Despite the novel's didacticism, *Pamela* calls attention to problems that are still with us: domestic violence, predatory men, and the plight of vulnerable women.

Fannie endures the same perils in *Make Me the Sky*. Moreover, Wexler's coming-of-age novel describes a world at war in which Jews were singled out for persecution in both the Old and New Worlds. Ironically, the predatory men in Fannie's life are part of her family, two of her uncles. Before leaving for the United States, she is sold by her uncle Shmuel in Budapest to a brothel. She escapes but not before losing her virginity, a fact she tells no one until near the end of the story. The uncle who sponsors her passage to the United States, Oscar, is another predator, leering at her, trying to "grab my woman parts" (24), and keeping her like a slave. Fannie's closest friend, Hannah, is forced into prostitution and becomes pregnant by her pimp, who tells her that she cannot keep the infant. (Fannie later adopts the baby, Daniel, when Hannah dies). Throughout the novel, Wexler describes sexual victimization using summary rather than scenic narration. Notwithstanding its moral didacticism, *Pamela* provoked the charge of titillation, an accusation Wexler avoids through the lack of concrete details about sexual trauma. Given Fannie's understandable fear of male sexuality, it's remarkable that this does not become problematic when she meets Marek Horvath, a widower with a young child, Adela. When Fannie shares her dark secret with him, he responds with his own secret: he had assaulted and likely killed a man who was trying to rape his mother. Fannie and Marek readily accept the other's troubled past, nonjudgmentally. *Make Me the Sky* would be more convincing, psychologically, if it dramatized the lingering legacy of these traumatic events.

A Bintel Brief

What *is* convincing about Fannie's story, however, is that before she finds fulfillment in marriage, she is tortured by guilt, self-loathing, and suicidal feelings. Before running away from her uncle Oscar, she steals from his pushcart a dress, one that he likely stole himself. She steals the dress as an act of revenge, but she now regards herself as a thief. "I wish I could die" (29), she bewails. Believing that her family would be ashamed of her, she begins to hate herself. Finding nowhere to turn, she writes a letter to the advice column called "A Bintel Brief" (a bundle of letters) appearing in the *Jewish Daily Forward*, founded in 1897 in New York City as a Yiddish-language daily socialist newspaper. According to *Wikipedia*, by 1912, *The Jewish Daily Forward* had a circulation of 120,000 readers. Wexler observes in a footnote to *Make Me the Sky* that the letters appearing in the novel are entirely fictional though they are written in the style of "A Bintel Brief." Foreshadowing "Dear Abby" and "Ask Ann Landers," newspaper columns written by twin sisters who became hated enemies, "A Bintel Brief" offered pragmatic advice to readers who wished to unburden themselves and receive pragmatic answers to their vexing questions. In her first letter, Fannie, signing her name as "Haunted," reveals how two relatives sexually abused her; she feels like "filth" as a result of stealing a dress from one of them. She receives the following reply:

> When you write you feel like "filth," it is a sad state you have come to. Two relatives treated you poorly, and you did something that now invites you to treat yourself poorly. Yes, it is wrong to steal, but in the wrongs that we humans can inflict on each other, this is not irreparable. Since this relative was intent on putting you in danger, I advise you not to return whatever you stole. I suggest you consider giving this stolen article to someone who can make good use of it. While it does not erase your theft, it is an effort to give something good instead of a wrong taking. (*Make Me the Sky* 34)

It would be difficult for anyone, therapist or non-therapist, to improve upon this pithy advice. Fannie follows the recommendation, mails the dress to her mother, and feels better putting the stolen garment to good use.

In another letter, Fannie shares her dilemma of loving a man, Mischa, who wants her to travel with him and her father to Palestine, but if she follows her heart, she will not be able to send money home to her family in Galicia, thus abandoning them. What should she do? The advice from "A Bintel Brief" is insightful and compassionate:

There is no correct answer except the one you think you can live with right now. Inevitably, you will have times when you regret the decision you make. Life will be a harsh desert for a while. I hope before too long you will find some oasis, some soothing spring, some peace. (77)

And in her final letter, Fannie describes losing the man she loves and wondering whether she should allow a friend to arrange a marriage for her. The question elicits a historically accurate and psychologically astute response. "The ability to love another is a great human gift, and the ability to fall deeply in love is G-d's blessing. But to pine forever for what you have lost and not take hold of life and move forward is folly" (166). The advice turns out to be helpful to Fannie, and she agrees to marry Marek. Harry Golden, in his commentary on arranged marriages in *A Bintel Brief*, states that the "percentage of successful marriages as the result of the shadkhan's [matchmaker's] efforts were not any more or less than those marriages outside the shadkhan's domain" (152).

In *A Pot from Shards*, Wexler affirms "real talk," truthtelling, language that strikes to the heart of the matter. "Real talk, with anyone, with patients, friends, or family is as stripped of pretense, illusion, and self-protectiveness as is possible, although never perfect." Real talk, she continues, "has layers of meaning expressed by metaphor, tone, rhythm, and timing that gives it its power and its realness" (190–191). We see real talk throughout *Make Me the Sky*: in Fannie's letters and diaries and in the questions to and responses from "A Bintel Brief."

Apart from the excellent advice received from "A Bintel Brief," Fannie discovers the therapeutic value of expressing her thoughts and feelings through writing. She feels lighter after writing, less oppressed by the problems that compelled her to take up her pen. "Writing keeps my spirits up almost as much as singing and dancing" (26), she observes early in the novel, a comment that assumes greater meaning in light of the novelist's passion for dance. Fannie's twin sister, Esther, feels the same comfort in writing: "Please know I feel great relief and even strength in writing to you honestly about what is happening to me" (23). Reading holds the same pleasure for Fannie. Near the end of the story, she becomes friendly with a librarian who works at the public library. Reading, no less than writing, opens up a new world for Fannie.

Wexler's fictional "A Bintel Brief" combines both traditional and progressive advice to those struggling with daily problems. There is nothing narrow-minded or polemical about the historical or fictional "A Bintel Brief." Nor is the advice outdated. Many contemporary readers are wary of self-help publications, but they have a useful purpose for those in need of help. The hopefulness and optimism of the historical "A Bintel Brief" are visible in *Make Me the Sky*. One can understand the wide popularity of the historical column, which spoke directly and honestly to immigrants' *lived experience*. As Isaac Metzker writes in his introduction to *A Bintel Brief*, "in his answers to the letters, the editor is more than just an advisor who gives perfunctory counsel. He is also the teacher and the preacher, and often his answer to a letter turns into an instructive lecture" (16). The same is true of the answers to letters in *Make Me the Sky*.

Wexler is sympathetic to a wide spectrum of Jewish beliefs, ranging from the Orthodox Judaism of Fannie's cousin Itzak, to the secular freethinking Mischa, to the Reform Judaism of her husband, Marek. When immersing herself in a mikveh, the orthodox ritual of female purification, Fannie does not challenge the advice offered to her by the rabbi's wife: "It is your husband's duty to awaken your womanly sources of pleasure" (188). Wexler conveys this point of view without judgment. Before meeting Mischa, Fannie learns that he is Jewish but not religious. When she expresses her concern in a letter to "A Bintel Brief," she is told that because he lives with his religious father, it's likely that they remain bonded as a family despite their differences. Fannie is startled when she attends Marek's reform synagogue and sees men and women sitting together. "I like these differences," she writes in her diary, "but it takes some getting used to" (195). Additionally, Wexler offers a nuanced and balanced understanding of the troubled history between Arabs and Jews in Palestine at the beginning of the twentieth century.

Despite her inclusiveness, Wexler does not conceal her disapproval of Orthodox Judaism's privileging of sons over daughters. Furious when his wife, Sadie, gives birth to a daughter, Itzak begins muttering "Sodom, Gomorrah," bangs his head against the wall, and claims that he is not the father of the child. A rabbi arrives, announces that Itzak is possessed by a dybbuk, a malicious tormenting spirit, and performs an exorcism. Wexler depicts an event that was not uncommon among orthodox Jews at the turn of the twentieth century. After Itzak's death, from the influenza that was ravaging the planet following the end of the First World War—he refused to wear a mask, asserting it would be God's will if he died—his wife dryly remarks, "He had plenty of knowledge but no wisdom" (228).

Itzak's death conveniently spares his daughter the grief of growing up with a rejecting father. Fannie doesn't speak much about her own father, but in light of *A Pot from Shards*, we are not entirely surprised when she learns, from a sister's letter describing their mother's deathbed confession, that she and Esther were the illegitimate offspring of a brief love affair with a Polish carpenter. "Fannie and Esther were my greatest joy and greatest shame. I loved my twins, but I also feared them" (207). This was the reason Fannie's mother sent her to the United States; Esther was too weak to be sent, and she dies earlier in the story of a weak heart. The news of being illegitimate is not devastating for Fannie because she has always felt loved by her father, a marked contrast to Wexler's feelings about her own absent father. Unlike *A Pot from Shards*, *Make Me the Sky* contains two major characters, Marek and Mischa, who are both devoted fathers to their children.

Some of the most powerful moments in *Make Me the Sky* arise from Wexler's own life. In *A Pot from Shards*, she describes witnessing the birth of her adoptive daughter Sarah's baby in 1999. "Hello, little girl" (20), Sarah greets her daughter, and then she gives Wexler the privilege of cutting the cord. The same event appears in *Make Me the Sky*. "Hello, my little girl!" (110), Sadie shouts to her daughter, and Fannie has the honor of cutting the cord, a striking metaphor of her own struggle for freedom and independence.

By novel's close, Wexler has resolved all the issues in her heroine's life. Fannie has given birth to her own set of twins, whom she names Miriam, after Marek's first wife, and Simon, for the father she has always known. Fannie's siblings have safely arrived in the United States and are doing well. Fannie finally achieves what she has long been searching for, a "predictable life filled with the extraordinary, ordinary pleasures of work and home" (221), or what Wexler calls in *A Pot from Shards* a "normal" life. All the evidence in *Make Me the Sky* points to a long, happy marriage. Fannie has overcome her terror of male desire, and Marek will presumably not be called upon again to use lethal violence to protect a loved one. "We lose people we love," Fannie observes at the end, in perhaps the novel's greatest insight, "but then our new loves often remind us of those we lost" (241). In Adela's words, both her parents have made her the sky, a transcendent image on which the novel ends. Despite the story's tidy resolution that strains belief, the novel shows how a resourceful and courageous woman can overcome loss and find new love. Fannie has done her best as a daughter, sister, wife, mother, and friend. She remains deeply connected to her past while holding on to the present and looking forward to the future. When she first arrives in New York, feeling lonely and scared, she wears her sister Esther's blue shawl as a reminder of her presence; she wears the same shawl to her wedding. Small details like this convince us that sometimes the virtuous are indeed rewarded with a good life.

Works Cited

Fielding, Henry. *Tom Jones*. 1749. The Modern Library, 1931.
Freud, Sigmund. *The Ego and the Id*. 1923. *The Standard Edition of the Complete Psychological Works of Sigmund Freud*, translated and edited by James Strachey, vol. 21. The Hogarth Press, 1961.
Landsman, Irene Smith. "Psychoanalytic Lives: Biography and Memoir." *Journal of the American Psychoanalytic Association*, vol. 69, 2021, pp. 1237–1244.
Metzker, Isaac, editor. *A Bintel Brief: Sixty Years of Letters from the Lower East Side to the Jewish Daily Forward*. Foreword and notes by Harry Golden. Doubleday, 1971.
Richardson, Samuel. *Pamela, or Virtue Rewarded*. 1740. Penguin 2003.
Wexler, Joan. *Make Me the Sky*. International Psychoanalytic Books, 2023.
Wexler, Joan. *A Pot from Shards*. International Psychoanalytic Books, 2019.
Wexler, Joan. "'Rage to Order': Wallace Stevens and Hans Loewald." *Psychoanalytic Study of the Child*, vol. 57, 2002, pp. 458–476.
Wexler, Joan. "Review of *Dancing with the Unconscious: The Art of Psychoanalysis and the Psychoanalysis of Art*." *Journal of the American Psychoanalytic Association*, vol. 62, 2014, pp. 173–179.
Wexler, Joan. "Therapeutic Action and Aesthetic Experience: Resonance and Reorganization." *Journal of Clinical Psychology*, vol. 74, 2018, pp. 208–212.

Chapter 12

Cordelia Schmidt-Hellerau
Memento

"Fiction writing is simultaneously scary and fascinating" (181), Cordelia Schmidt-Hellerau admits in "On My Way" (2023). Only four pages long, "On My Way" is her most exuberant and playful essay. She begins by acknowledging her delight in language, playing with words, and her excitement about approaching a new writing project, which she compares to falling in love, a passion that animates her work. The best part of writing, she proclaims, even better than the thrill of potential discoveries, is the "*striving* itself, this *reaching for*, which is mesmerizing" (180). Although Schmidt-Hellerau has always loved creative writing, having published her first poem in a local newspaper when she was only eight, followed by penning a short (unpublished) novel three years later, she struggled to write fiction in her 20s. Instead, for the next two decades she wrote articles and books on psychoanalytic theory, including *Life Drive & Death Drive, Libido & Lethe* (2001) and *Driven to Survive* (2018), a finalist of the American Board & Academy of Psychoanalysis Book Prize. Writing about psychoanalytic theory seemed easier and safer than crafting fiction. Schmidt-Hellerau is also the chair of the International Psychoanalytic Association's Cultural Committee and the editor of *The Analyst as Storyteller/El Analista Como Narrador* (2021), a collection of stories written by 20 female and 10 male analysts from 17 different countries. As I discuss in a review published in *American Imago* (Berman 2023), the tales reveal intriguing gender differences: the male authors write about the world of ambition, achievement, and individualism, while the female authors write about the attachment bonds of family and friendship.

Schmidt-Hellerau comes from a notable German family. According to *Wikipedia*, her grandfather, Karl Schmidt-Hellerau (1873–1948), was a carpenter, furniture manufacturer, and social reformer who founded Hellerau, Germany's first garden city. Her parents fled from East to West Germany in the 1940s, leaving their homes and possessions. Born in 1951, she grew up in West Germany and Switzerland, studying literature, philosophy, and psychology in Heidelberg and Zürich. As she remarks in "On My Way," she was transported by the beauty of Freud's language, which she read in the original German, her own mother tongue. She received her psychoanalytic training in Switzerland and moved to the United States in 2000, where she became a training and supervising analyst at the Boston Psychoanalytic Society & Institute. She was ready to resume her own fiction writing, authoring *Rousseaus*

Traum (2019), not yet translated into English; *Memory's Eyes: A New York Oedipal Novel* (2020); and *Memento: A Novel in Dreams, Thoughts, and Images* (2023). Her command of English is impressive; one cannot tell from *Memory's Eyes* or *Memento* that English is her second (or third) language.

Tellingly, Schmidt-Hellerau implies in "On My Way" that she had one major anxiety about writing fiction. "The subject I choose (and clearly it must be a topic that engaged me deeply) soon develops a life of its own, which I can steer only as much as its inner dynamics will allow" (182). Anyone who believes in the existence of the unconscious knows that one cannot exert complete control over a text; often a story or poem will reveal more than the author intended. "Never trust the artist," D.H. Lawrence warned his readers. "Trust the tale." Crafting a novel, Schmidt-Hellerau avers in "Intimacy in Writing Fiction," the penultimate chapter in *Driven to Survive*, is anxiety-provoking because she never knows where her ideas will take her. "Only if I dare to totally be where the images place me, only if I can, as it were, fictionalize myself, can I translate this intimate inner dialogue into a narrative" (445). But there are other fears associated with writing fiction and poetry, including one that bedevils the characters in *Memento*: the apprehension that one's writing may not be good enough, may in fact be flawed or inferior. This dread of rejection compels one character to commit suicide in *Memento* and has a devastating impact on two others.

Memento

Reading *Memento* is not for the faint-hearted. The novel is narrated through the eyes (and mind) of Sine, short for Gesine, a woman in her late 50s who accompanies her neuroscientist husband, Sam, to an international conference in Europe, where he presents a paper on a monitor he has invented that he claims to have unique powers. Despite the novel's chronological structure, beginning, appropriately, with "Arrival" and ending with "Departure," we often do not know where we are in time and space. One moment we learn that Sine's mother, Marlene, died three years earlier; the next moment she is alive, planning to marry Sam's enemy, Paul Peacock, who insists that *he* invented the monitor. Sine often asks herself, "Am I dreaming?" Readers ask themselves the same question throughout the story. If she is not dreaming, is she reporting events that are only fantasies? Is she delusional? In short, is she a reliable narrator? Sine's reality testing becomes a major challenge in reading the novel. Other questions confront us. A strange young girl, mute, appears in the story, and both Sine and Marlene vie for her affection. Who has brought the girl to the hotel, which has a no-child policy? Is the girl a younger version of Sine? We never learn the answers to these questions. Containing flashbacks and flashforwards, the novel's spatial and temporal discontinuities represent Schmidt-Hellerau's efforts to interrogate the unconscious, a subterranean inner world unconstrained by space or time. The novel works through associational, not chronological logic, and we must read it like a psychoanalyst, trained to understand the connections among thoughts, words, and images.

Sine's relationship with her mother remains the most highly conflicted and competitive one in the novel. Marlene is restless, manipulative, secretive, and demanding. Feeling neglected by her husband, Marlene has numerous affairs. She is always yearning for someone or something to give her life meaning. The novelist uses the name *Lilli* to describe Marlene's coquettish side and *Lenchen* to evoke her early life as a child. In the presence of her mother, Sine feels infantilized. For five years Sine and her older half-sister, Enna, served as their mother's caregiver, an exhausting experience. "Her calls broke into my sleep," Sine complains, "invaded my dreams. Sometimes I dreamt her call and got up, only to find her fast asleep" (9–10). In her 2006 article "Fighting with Spoons: On Caretaking Rivalry Between Mothers and Daughters," Schmidt-Hellerau discusses the many problems that arise in this relationship, especially control and power issues, the same dynamics that can be seen in Sine's embattled relationship with Marlene. Sine has a less complicated and more fulfilling relationship with her father, Lukas, and her own daughter, Mikki, who, we are told, is doing psychoanalytic research on patients' narratives, a promising inquiry that remains undeveloped.

Schmidt-Hellerau's animated prose, often exuberant and lyrical, conjures a sense of magic realism, a style of literary art that offers a realistic view of the world while at the same time blurring the boundaries between reality and fantasy. Magic realism is usually associated with Latin American fiction, but the expression has its roots in early twentieth-century German and Italian literature and painting. *Memento* abounds in rich sensuous descriptions of the everyday world, but the realms of realism and fantasy are always colliding. Magic realism in *Memento* does not imply, as it does in other novels, the supernatural, science fiction, surrealism, or metafiction, which calls attention to its own fictionality. Rather, magic realism affirms a universe of potentiality: incidents in Sine's "real" life are often indistinguishable from those of her imagined, feared, or desired life. In depicting the inner world of its characters, *Memento* is challenging to understand even upon rereading, but upon completion, we experience a sense of plenitude, a feeling of abundance and completeness.

The novel is set in an isolated European hotel that was originally a castle, one that has a spell cast over it. A wealthy hatter had the castle built to escape from civilization, but he and his family were disturbed by the bucolic sounds of nature: a bird chirp, a tree branch's crackle, a howling coyote. The "a-sleepers," as they called themselves, destroyed the surrounding nature, but when that failed to have the desired effect, the last descendants of the family decided to end their agony by jointly committing suicide. Decades later, the castle was transformed into a conference hotel. The hotel is not exactly haunted, but a sense of foreboding surrounds it. At the end of the story, the hotel appears to be razed, an act that coincides with the end of Sine's journey.

Sine has much in common with the novelist. She is in love with the same literary authors Schmidt-Hellerau has long admired, including Kafka, Beckett, Sartre, and

Camus. Indeed, Sine is a college creative writing teacher, and it's likely that she speaks for the novelist when she expresses to students her literary taste, judgment, and pedagogical style. "My students know that I have a fancy for weird authors, peculiar texts, odd characters, surprising moves, and open endings. But I've emphasized that this is just my personal predilection, and they certainly can focus on more traditional or totally experimental styles" (244). Sine has been happily married for 34 years to a loving and supportive man, as is Schmidt-Hellerau; her husband, Fredric N. Busch, a Weill Cornell Medical College professor of clinical psychiatry and faculty member of the Columbia University Center for Psychoanalytic Training and Research, helped her "tirelessly" refine her English, as she gratefully observes in "On My Way." (The two analysts were featured in Amy Gamerman's article published in *The Wall Street Journal* in 2019 about therapists who see patients at home.) In *Driven to Survive* she reveals that the reason she left Switzerland to move to the United States was to marry the man she loved. Of the many commonalities between Sine and the novelist, the greatest is their early doubt about the ability to write fiction. Schmidt-Hellerau overcame this doubt; Sine doesn't. This remains Sine's lifelong regret: a failure of courage or nerve. But Sine has a deeper regret. Her star student Jules also aspires to be a creative writer, and he is fortunate and talented enough to have his first novel published. But his "epic" second novel, a massive 1328-page tome, is rejected by the four publishers to whom he sends the manuscript, and despite Sine's constant support and encouragement, he kills himself, an act that darkens her life.

Not all creative writing teachers are frustrated writers—one recalls George Bernard Shaw's sardonic observation, "those who can, do; those who can't, teach"—but this seems to be true of Sine. She recalls her mother saying, "You used to write so well. Why did you give it up?" (184), and while she appreciates her mother's rare validation, she broods over her determination to renounce fiction writing. Sine's father, Lukas, also wanted to become a writer; instead, he took over his father's business, running a wallpaper factory, rationalizing, "Writing stories is for idle hands" (32). And Marlene gave up her desire to become a painter, confessing, "I wasn't courageous enough." She wonders whether she had the talent to be a painter. "Did I squander it? Could I still try?" (184). Insofar as parents are usually role models to their children, it's not entirely unexpected that Sine failed to pursue a career in creative writing—though if she taught at most colleges and universities, the expectation for tenure would be extensive creative publications. Perhaps no less surprising is Sine's belief that fiction writing courses smother students' originality. Nevertheless, Sine encourages her students to do their best, takes her teaching seriously, and strives to be constructive in her criticisms of student writings. "It's delicate to give feedback," she realizes; "I want my students to know what I think without discouraging them" (165). Sine doesn't seem overly disturbed by the irony of the words she writes on the blackboard at the beginning of the semester: "**DARE TO WRITE**" (82).

The Legacy of Suicide

The crushed artistic ambitions of mother, father, and daughter are sad but not tragic, unlike Jules's suicide. We see Jules through Sine's eyes, not through his own, nor do we have direct access to his writings, thus preventing us from evaluating his originality as a writer. There is no doubt that he takes his own life, as his distraught girlfriend, Marian, reports to Sine. Nor is there doubt that his suicide has a shattering impact on his teacher's life.

There is a long and troubling history of creative writers who have died by their own hand, including, to name only a few poets and novelists, John Berryman, Richard Brautigan, Paul Celan, Thomas Chatterton, Hart Crane, Ernest Hemingway, Randall Jarrell, Jerzy Kosinski, Vachel Lindsay, Malcolm Lowry, Vladimir Mayakovsky, Yukio Mishima, Cesare Pavese, Sylvia Plath, Anne Sexton, Sara Teasdale, Hunter S. Thompson, John Kennedy Toole, David Foster Wallace, and Virginia Woolf. Many of these writers suffered from depression or manic depression (bipolar disorder), as Kay Redfield Jamison documents in *Touched with Fire: Manic Depressive Illness and the Artistic Temperament* (1993). Countless poets and novelists have written about their own depression and suicidal thinking. Because we have so little information about Jules's life, and because suicide is overdetermined, motivated by several reasons, we don't know what the other factors were, apart from depression over the rejection of his manuscript, that influenced his fateful decision to end his life.

Despite the ambiguity surrounding Jules's life and death, it is evident that he interpreted the rejection of his manuscript as a judgment on his own life, a narcissistic injury he could not endure. Not that he lacked other options. After receiving a master's degree in creative writing, he earned his living by giving private lessons in Greek and Latin, a job, however marginal, he presumably could have continued until a better one came along. He could have set aside his manuscript, as Sine advised, temporarily or permanently, to begin another writing project. He was also young enough to begin another occupation: "it's never too late to change one's career!" (213), Sine muses. Yet when one experiences depression, particularly feelings of worthlessness and hopelessness, one suffers from constricted or dichotomous thinking. Schmidt-Hellerau captures her character's binary thinking. Either my magnum opus will be published, Jules thinks, or it is fatally flawed, like me.

Sine cannot stop thinking about her student's death. The novelist deftly conveys the grim legacy, or illegacy, of suicide, where suicide survivors, those whose lives are changed irrevocably by a loved one's willed death, hold themselves accountable. Yet Sine's behavior toward Jules was exemplary when he was her student. No one can fault the advice she gives to him and her other students. Nor is she guilty of a boundary violation. After his graduation, she finds in her home a package containing his manuscript and wonders how it arrived there. Did he visit her home without her knowledge to drop off the manuscript? If so, she cannot remember the visit. She tortures herself over the unread manuscript. Sine's guilt over her failure to read the manuscript, to "rescue" her former student, is palpable. Nothing that Sam says in her defense can mitigate this guilt. "It's an unreasonable demand on you to read over a thousand pages, he said, and he isn't even your student anymore" (212). Guilt, along with the desire to "apologize, do reparations," compels her to consider editing the manuscript, but when she expresses this wish to Enna, Sine is startled to learn that she had the manuscript shredded, to which she responds: "Shredded!—I forgot, I brought it to a shredder, and now I see it vanish, hear the screeching noise as the machine crushes it, and the ground breaks, I'm falling, try to grab for something but only catch some airy paper shavings" (229).

How do we interpret this confusing moment? How can she have forgotten that she shredded the manuscript? Traumatic amnesia? How much significance should we attach to "shredding" the manuscript? One generally shreds valuable documents, those containing confidential information that others should not see. But Sine could have simply disposed of the unread novel. Does shredding imply her anger toward Jules, especially if suicide is viewed as internalized aggression initially directed toward another person, as Freud maintained, and as we saw in Alan Krohn's *The Mind's Eye*? Was shredding the manuscript an act of aggression or retaliation against the student who, in ending his own life, seemed to end hers, too? Sine recalls Jules looking at her with a "hostile glance" (141), implying his accusation that she has somehow failed him. Sine's language in the above passage suggests that she is experiencing a breakdown, or at least a panic attack, as the next two sentences imply: "I have to get out. I feel imprisoned, and there is no need to confine myself in this room" (229). Two pages earlier she visits her analyst, the only time in the story when Schmidt-Hellerau mentions that her protagonist is in treatment. Sine confesses that she has given up, lost her zest, but her analyst's only response is that she is depressed, which she denies, unconvincingly. The analyst appears to ignore her, playing instead with his new iPhone. The session does not go well, and she is mortified when he falls asleep. She sneaks out of his office, and he remains in repose, as if dead.

Sine's life darkens toward the end of the novel. She announces in her seminar her decision to retire, to which some students respond by chuckling. She encounters Marian, who admits that she cannot talk about Jules's suicide. Afterwards, Sine's heart aches so much that she fears, and possibly desires, that she is having a heart attack and that she will be dead in a moment. She fantasizes jumping out of the balcony of her hotel room, plunging to the ground, landing with a thud, and placed in a coffin. After imagining her own death, she sees Sam, who, giving her a concerned look, asks what's troubling her. "I can't tell him, and I keep my eyes closed, pretending not to have heard his question" (264).

Unlike other novelists, such as Virginia Woolf, who romanticizes suicide in her 1925 novel *Mrs Dalloway*, Schmidt-Hellerau never glorifies the act. Nor does she overidentify with a suicidal character, as Woolf does with Septimus Warren Smith, who jumps to his death in *Mrs Dalloway*, an act of defiance against the psychiatrist who was trying to institutionalize him. Clarissa Dalloway participates vicariously in Septimus's suicide, with Woolf's apparent approval, experiencing cathartic release: "She felt somehow very much like him—the young man who had killed himself. She felt glad that he had done it; thrown it away" (283). Sine fantasizes suicide not as an act of rebellion against repressive psychiatry but as a way to end her paralyzing guilt, grief, and hopelessness.

In the final chapter, Sine imagines being in an assisted-living residence, where she vows to write until her last glimmer. Another fantasy or memory: as she leaves the conference hotel, she sees Jules standing, unsteadily; she cannot tell whether he looks desperate or angry. She asks herself, once again, whether she could have stopped him. "I'll never know, I'll always wonder" (295). The novelist then invokes classical Greek mythology to characterize her protagonist's consciousness. In her 1997 article "Libido and Lethe," Schmidt-Hellerau proposed a new psychoanalytic concept, "lethe," for the energy of the death drive. Lethe was the Greek river in Hades associated with forgetfulness or oblivion. The opposite of a libidinal cathexis, Schmidt-Hellerau contends, is a "lethic cathexis," which she associates with feeling spiritless, apathetic, gloomy, and sad, precisely Sine's state of mind at the end of the novel. Sine envisions her father in a boat steered by Charon, the ferryman who transports dead souls across the river of Acheron to the netherworld. Sine's father, mother, and Jules are dead souls, as is possibly Sam, whom she imagines in an ICU, stricken with sepsis. Amidst these melancholy fantasies, Sine is finally "ready to go home," driven by Mikki, who announces that she is going to have a baby. On the seat next to Sine lies Sam's monitor, which "hums," the last word in the story.

Jules's suicide remains the most shadowy event in *Memento*, even more enigmatic than the mysterious monitor that Sam has described to Sine as a mind reader, a device capable, he hopes, of recording a person's unconscious thoughts and feelings. The monitor may be a symbol of the novelist's ability to capture a person's innermost reflections. If this is true, the humming monitor represents *Memento* itself, with its lively portrayal of one of life's most disturbing events, one which suicide survivors may spend a lifetime trying to understand and exorcise.

"There is but one serious philosophical question," Albert Camus remarks in the opening sentence of *The Myth of Sisyphus* (1942), "and that is suicide. Judging whether life is or not worth living amounts to answering the fundamental question of philosophy." And perhaps psychology. William Styron quotes this passage in *Darkness Visible*, asserting that it is one of the century's most famous intellectual pronouncements on suicide (23). Suicide dominates *Memento*, but it haunts *Memory's Eyes*. Four characters take their own lives, including Joyce, the biological mother of the narrator, Ann, also called Antje, short for Antigone. As the subtitle, *A New York Oedipus Novel*, suggests, *Memory's Eyes* is a contemporary reworking of the Sophocles play, but, no less significant, it is a story about characters who, unable to endure grave truths, judge that life is not worth living. "Joyce was a wound that always bled," Ann's father, Eddie, informs her, "and nothing could stop her life from running out of her. Her wound was an abyss, he then murmured, a voracious abyss that swallowed him too" (*Memory's Eyes* 235). The abyss swallows Joyce's 11-year-old sister, Leslie, who appears to jump to her death when a school bus passes; swallows Janis, Eddie's stepmother; and swallows Chris, who is in love with Ann's brother, Paul. Additionally, the wound almost swallows Ann's sister, Issy, who threatens to kill herself. Ann briefly considers suicide, as a way to end intolerable pain, but she knows she will never do it, mainly because of its shattering impact on relatives and friends. Unlike Jules, who commits suicide because of his perceived failure as a novelist, the characters in *Memory's Eyes* kill themselves largely because of Oedipal transgressions and, in Joyce's case, postpartum depression. Despite the different causes, both novels depict the contagious nature of suicide: one person's suicide increases the risk of suicide in relatives and friends. The sheer number of suicides in *Memory's Eyes* suggests that the subject is close to the novelist's home, something that has deeply affected her own life, an event that compels her to write about it in her two novels. Curiously, if suicide has touched Schmidt-Hellerau's life personally, as her two novels suggest, there is hardly a word about suicide in her two books on psychoanalysis, nor, as far as I can determine, in any of her published articles.

Among the most intriguing characters in *Memory's Eyes* is Teresa, who is noteworthy for *not* thinking about suicide. Like her namesake, Tiresias, the blind prophet in Sophocles's play who accuses Oedipus of murdering King Laius, Teresa is the first to discover that Eddie, Joyce's son, was also her husband. But it is not only her oracular power that makes Teresa singular; she is an octogenarian literary critic who is writing a "virtual autobiography," a story not unlike *Memento*, filled as it is with a "movement of awareness," in Teresa's words, "radiating to all sides" (382). Teresa is interested in writing a story of skipped potentials, a tale of what "*could have* but did *not* happen even though I thought about and wanted it, opportunities I missed, efforts I shunned—that sort of thing" (382). Writing the virtual autobiography is a continuation of Teresa's analysis that ended 12 years earlier, a life-transforming experience. Teresa speaks for Schmidt-Hellerau when she affirms the value of truthtelling, however challenging the process may be. "My whole history taught me it is better to know than not to know the truth" (401). Teresa continues to mourn the death of her analyst, a "wonderful woman, quiet, sensitive, smart or rather wise, with a warm sense of humor" (383). Ann, who is in training to become a psychoanalyst, respects her own analyst, Dr. Shepherd, but she feels uncomfortable when he begins disclosing aspects of his life to her. "I would have preferred a more old-fashioned analyst and be left alone with all his personal sharing" (311). Ann reflects Schmidt-Hellerau's own viewpoint; she has little interest in relational or intersubjective psychoanalysis, as is evident in her 2002 review of Jay Greenberg's work.

Schmidt-Hellerau has not discussed in detail how she felt writing *Memory's Eyes* or *Memento*, two novels about memory and desire, but in *Driven to Survive* she describes returning to Hellerau to bury her elderly father. To her surprise, she found herself deeply at home there, although she had traveled there only a few times for brief visits. "I lost my home, I mourned it, and still sometimes I miss it" (449). She now lives in a place, Boston, far from home, one that she enjoys but regards as, professionally, a "barren land," where Freud "has been marginalized and relegated to the land of the dead" (449). All her writings seek to restore Freud to the land of the living.

Whether we read *Memento* as experimental fiction or as virtual autobiography, a story about events that could have happened but did not, the novel demonstrates the value of storytelling. And truthtelling. Writing fiction, Barbara Stimmel observes in an enthusiastic review of *Memory's Eyes* and Daniel Jacobs's *The Distance from Home*, "is an open-ended, complex, and truth-seeking process. That also describes effective psychoanalytic therapy" ("Seeing the World" 148). Sine imagines writing a novel about writing, but never does, unlike her creator, who, by daring to write, gifts us with *Memento*. Intellectually satisfying and emotionally charged, *Memento* offers insights into why writing is both scary and fascinating. Jules was probably too depressed to appreciate his creative writing teacher's advice that the best part of writing is the striving itself, the reaching for—in short, writing for *pleasure*—but readers of the novel will appreciate the many challenges posed by *Memento*.

Works Cited

Berman, Jeffrey. "Review of Cordelia Schmidt-Hellerau, editor. *The Analyst as Storyteller/El Analista Como Narrador.*" *American Imago*, vol. 80, 2023, pp. 607–614.

Camus, Albert. *The Myth of Sisyphus and Other Essays*. Vintage, 1942; rpt. 1991.

Gamerman, Amy. "The Doctor Is in (the House)." *The Wall Street Journal*, January 31, 2019.

Jamison, Kay Redfield. *Touched with Fire: Manic Depressive Illness and the Artistic Temperament*. Free Press, 1993.

Schmidt-Hellerau, Cordelia, editor. *The Analyst as Storyteller/El Analista Como Narrador*. International Psychoanalytic Books, 2021.

Schmidt-Hellerau, Cordelia. *Driven to Survive: Selected Papers on Psychoanalysis*. International Psychoanalytic Books, 2018.

Schmidt-Hellerau, Cordelia. "Fighting with Spoons: On Caretaking Between Mothers and Daughters." *Psychoanalytic Inquiry*, vol. 26, 2006, pp. 32–55.

Schmidt-Hellerau, Cordelia. "Libido and Lethe: Fundamentals of a Formalised Conception of Metapsychology." *International Journal of Psychoanalysis*, vol. 8, 1997, pp. 683–697.

Schmidt-Hellerau, Cordelia. *Life Drive & Death Drive, Libido & Lethe: A Formalized Consistent Model of Psychoanalytic Drive and Structure Theory*, translated by Philip Slotkin. Other Press, 2001.

Schmidt-Hellerau, Cordelia. *Memento: A Novel in Dreams, Thoughts, and Images*. International Psychoanalytic Books, 2023.

Schmidt-Hellerau, Cordelia. *Memory's Eyes: A New York Oedipus Novel*. International Psychoanalytic Books, 2020.

Schmidt-Hellerau, Cordelia. "On My Way." *Journal of the American Psychoanalytic Association*, vol. 71, 2023, pp. 179–182.

Schmidt-Hellerau, Cordelia. "Schmidt-Hellerau on Greenberg's New Look." *Journal of the American Psychoanalytic Association*, vol. 50, 2002, pp. 642–647.
Stimmel, Barbara. "Seeing the World: Now and Then, Without and Within." *Journal of the American Psychoanalytic Association*, vol. 71, 2023, pp. 141–149.
Styron, William. *Darkness Visible: A Memoir of Madness*. Random House, 1990.
Woolf, Virginia. *Mrs. Dalloway*. Harcourt, Brace and World, 1953.

Chapter 13
Cliff Wilkerson
The Cotton Flower

"I'm just like my dad," nine-year-old Charlie Scarsdale proudly boasts to his mother at the beginning of Cliff Wilkerson's engrossing 2022 novel *The Cotton Flower*, a comment she finds distressing. "*I sure hope you're not just like your dad*, she thought. *There're things about him—I never want you to grow up just like him*" (10). The biographical significance of this passage heightens its meaning. Indeed, Charlie is a portrait of the psychoanalytic fiction writer as a young boy, enthralled by an irresponsible, undependable, and unfaithful parent, Douglas Clifton Wilkerson, who deserted his family, and whose absence created a father hunger that can be seen throughout the author's writings.

Wilkerson began his career as a fiction writer with the publication in 2008 of *Beautiful Brown Eyes and Other Stories*, a collection of 18 tales highlighting early versions of the novelist's parents and stepparents. Henry Messenger in "Summer Grit" prefigures Charlie Scarsdale, a "chip off the old block" of his father who is at war in the South Pacific. Many of the stories reveal broken families with a philandering father who abandons his wife and children. In "Not Like You, Pa," Luke Webster "had always prided himself on being totally unlike his father" (81). Easier said than done. Now 62, the same age as his father when he died, when Luke returns home after an absence of 45 years to visit his stepsister, he is filled with resentment and bitterness. Luke is not as racist as his father was, but he feels uncomfortable shaking the hand of a black man, Lamont Willis, who is dating his divorced stepsister. "I see the old acorn didn't fall far from the tree" (86), Willis tells him. Several stories in *Beautiful Brown Eyes* contain thematic and cultural material that Wilkerson develops in later writings, such as life in the Bible Belt. Before Al Eberhart leaves for college, his mother warns him that a college education will lead to godlessness. "She was of the opinion that 'Much learning doth make thee mad'" (161), an allusion, the narrator reminds us, to Acts of the Apostles.

Moving On and Still Moving On

Most psychoanalysts never write one memoir, but Wilkerson has written two, both late in life, both offering an unusually candid and illuminating glimpse into his life and art. *Moving On* (2012) and *Still Moving On* (2016) chronicle his life from his birth in 1933 on a small farm in rural Oklahoma through medical school at the University of Oklahoma and five-year psychiatric residency. He then received a child psychiatry fellowship at the University of Chicago. He worked with Bruno Bettelheim for three years at the famed University of Chicago Sonia Shankman Orthogenic School (referred to as the O school). *Still Moving On* ends with his professional training at the Chicago Institute for Psychoanalysis. The two memoirs are fascinating, and one is struck immediately by Wilkerson's modesty and self-criticism. The reader encounters several self-deprecatory admissions. "I was not a deep thinker," he confesses in *Moving On* (259) about his understanding of religion. He concedes in *Still Moving On* that his first memoir "did not compare with a scholarly work" (xi), adding two pages later, when discussing a renowned scholar's work, that he learned a long time ago to "accept the fact that I was never to reach anywhere near the intellectual level of such academics" (xiii). These statements are belied by the impressive psychological and literary depth of his writing.

Wilkerson's exploration in *Moving On* of the conflicted father–son relationship is perhaps of greatest interest to readers of *The Cotton Flower*. Named after his father, Wilkerson captures his surface charm, restlessness, recklessness, and unpredictability. Wilkerson yearned to be like his father, who called him, recalling the same metaphor in "Summer Grit," a "chip off the old block" (67), words that the son desperately wanted to be true, though the block turned out to be neither solid nor durable. Douglas Wilkerson disappeared from his son's life, living with another woman with whom he had five more children. Wilkerson's mother, Velma, married at the age of 15, became angry and depressed over her husband's desertion and subsequent divorce, living a hand-to-mouth existence until her remarriage several years later when her son was 15. Wilkerson's stepfather, a butcher, was reliable, supplying the family with much-needed security, but he could never replace Wilkerson's biological father. "My stepfather was a good man but I did not want nor could not use him as someone to identify myself with as a father" (270). After a five-year absence, Douglas Wilkerson suddenly reappeared in his son's life, inviting him to work for him during the summer in his insulation business, but the father never paid him for his work, humiliating him when he asked for his wages. Wilkerson offers a memorable portrait of his debt-ridden irresponsible father, constantly bragging about his sexual exploits, cursing his former wife's family, and disclosing infidelities and betrayals of his son's maternal relatives that the adolescent did not wish to know. "I never became a man in my father's eyes" (166), Wilkerson tells us, simply, allowing us to infer his hurt and disappointment.

Wilkerson counteridentified with his father in many ways. He was (along with his wife) a virgin when he married in 1959 at age 22. A teetotaler, he avoided his carousing father's excesses. Unlike his pugilistic father, he never picked fights. Unable to pay his bills, his father kept on moving to avoid his creditors, unlike his son, who, with his wife's help, paid for medical school and psychoanalytic training without incurring debt. Perhaps most important, he learned from his family's quarrels and his mother's unhappiness to be sensitive to others. "I seemed always to have empathy for children whose parents were callous with their children or any child with troubles" (*Moving On* 39).

The "craving" to be a "good father" unifies Wilkerson's writings. During his interview for admission into psychoanalytic training at the Chicago Institute—he had been rejected twice earlier—he brought with him the Valentine he had received from his ten-year-old son. The card, made from a 15-by-10 inch piece of red construction paper on which he had written a small black heart with the words: "I hate you, Dad, but I love you more than I hate you, so I'm sending you this Valentine card" (*Still Moving On* 182), turned out to be the "deciding factor" in being accepted into psychoanalytic training. Few memoirists would be willing to disclose this detail.

Born to parents with only eighth grade educations, Wilkerson had few academic role models who realized his potential. Moving repeatedly in his childhood and adolescence, he did well in school, though he received a "D" in his sixth grade English course, not a good sign, he admits ruefully, for a person who later aspired to be a writer. Worse, when he was in college, he was told by a psychologist that he had earned a score of only 109 on an intelligence exam. Informed he was not "college material," he was advised that he had an aptitude for work such as upholstery. An observation in his 2020 collection of fictional and nonfictional stories, *Siri Doesn't Tango*, reflects his attitude toward those skeptical of his ability: "Throughout my life when I've been told that I'm not capable of doing something, it has motivated me to work all the harder to do so" (225).

Dejected but undaunted, Wilkerson made it to medical school. His one mentor during his psychiatric residency, C.V. Ramana, a Hindu from India who was the only trained psychoanalyst in the state, made a lasting impression on him. Urging Wilkerson to enter psychoanalysis, Ramana told him, "What you learn from patients, lectures, and books alone is insufficient. You must learn in your own therapy how in so many ways you are not so different from your patients" (*Still Moving On* 47). Despite Ramana's support, Wilkerson struggled to become an analyst, partly because he defied the cultural stereotypes of the profession. Years later, someone connected to the Chicago Institute told him, "You weren't Jewish, and you talked funny. The selection committee had no idea what to do with you" (126). Nor did Wilkerson's fundamentalist Christian background help, though he later rejected his fire-and-brimstone upbringing. Wilkerson defied cultural stereotypes in other ways, as when he tells us that in the same year he received certification in psychoanalysis from the Chicago Institute, 1974, he earned a black belt in judo.

In *Still Moving On* Wilkerson discusses a few of his experiences as a young intern, one of which involved a "Freudian slip" by a typist working in the psychiatry department. She was the daughter of a prominent Oklahoma City psychiatrist who was known mainly for giving shock treatments to his patients. Disliking most psychiatrists, she invariably typed "the rapist" instead of "therapist." Had she read Nabokov's novel *Lolita* which, like all his fictional and nonfictional writings, mocks the "Viennese witch doctor," she would have been in full agreement with Humbert's sardonic pronouncement that the difference between "the rapist" and "therapist" is a matter of spacing (147).

Wilkerson's vivid portrait of Bruno Bettelheim in *Still Moving On* may have helped him hone his skills capturing his ambivalence toward the characters in *The Cotton Flower*. One of the most influential psychoanalysts of his generation, the Viennese-born psychologist (1903–1990) earned his reputation studying emotionally disturbed children. The director of the O school, Bettelheim maintained that children could be treated with psychoanalytic therapy rather than with the use of psychotropic drugs. Bettelheim comes across in *Still Moving On* as a man devoted to the understanding of troubled children but who was abrasive and authoritarian. Wilkerson conveys Bettelheim's thick German accent, caustic sarcasm, piercing blue eyes, and sneering mouth. Bettelheim was one of several people who made Wilkerson feel like a country bumpkin. Bettelheim never called him "Cliff," or even "Clifton," but rather "Clifford"—despite Wilkerson's repeated corrections. Bettelheim seemed unerringly accurate in his perceptions about the children residing in the O school, but Wilkerson felt the sting of his harsh criticisms. When, in 1966, he asked Bettelheim for an expanded role at the O school, one that would give him more opportunities and greater recognition, Bettelheim turned him down, which led Wilkerson, unexpectedly, to resign. The irate Bettelheim gave him less than a week to leave. "Bettelheim did not handle separations very well" (167), someone later told Wilkerson. He ends his account of Bettelheim by noting that after his death, some parents of the O school children claimed that he slapped their children, an allegation that Wilkerson acknowledges while at the same time affirming the importance of Bettelheim's work.

> Very infrequently he would open-handedly swat a child, something I did not like. I once went to him and asked why, since he sometimes physically punished a child, he had not written about it in his books, ones like *Love Is Not Enough*? His answer was something like, "I don't want to give every sadist who sees children license to do so."

Significantly, Wilkerson penned his two memoirs partly to preserve the memories of his life at a time when his beloved wife of 61 years, Carolyn, was losing her own memory to Alzheimer's disease. While watching the slow decimation of her memory, he "developed an unconscious desire to preserve my own by putting them to paper" (*Still Moving On* xiv). Penning a memoir, as I suggest in *Psychoanalytic Memoirs* (2023), is a way to write oneself and others into existence. Wilkerson stopped accepting new patients when he was 78 and retired as he approached his 84th birthday. He ends the memoir with the word "write," a sacred injunction that compelled him to craft his novel.

The Cotton Flower

Write what you know best, the age-old recommendation for authors, is strikingly true of *The Cotton Flower*, which Wilkerson dedicated to his mother's memory. An awareness of *Moving On*, *Still Moving On*, and *Siri Doesn't Tango* allows us to grasp the autobiographical nature of Wilkerson's debut novel, published when he was nearly a nonagenarian. Written over a period of 20 years, with many false starts, the novel was originally narrated from a child's point of view, but Wilkerson revised it, conveying instead the viewpoints of four adults, fictionalized versions of his family: his mother, Ruth, the leading character; his wayward father, Chester; and his maternal grandparents, Ida and Bob Choat. Most of the 45 chapters are about ten pages long. Only one chapter, "Charlie," is based on the young Cliff Wilkerson. The author succeeds in limning the points of view of all five figures, demonstrating his analytic and novelistic gift for understanding his characters' inner lives.

Much of the material about Charlie's life in *The Cotton Flower* accurately reflects Wilkerson's own life growing up in Oklahoma. The novelist records in rich detail the rhythms and rituals of rural life: hoeing cotton, mending fences, butchering pigs, milking cows, digging fence holes, stringing barbed wire, feeding the livestock. Members of a humble farm family shared the same bath water: mother first, father second, then the children. The ground water was so hard that it would not lather, requiring the use of water that drained off the roof and collected in cisterns. The fear of tornados was an everyday reality, demanding everyone to flee to the storm cellar. The Choats' home and barn are flattened to the ground and spread along the pasture, along with all its contents, near the end of the story. Ida and Bob still remember the Great Depression. Distrustful of banks, Bob kept his money under the floorboards of the barn and in the false bottom of his wife's trunk, which proved to be providential when the banks failed in 1929. Bob and Ida recall living through the terrifying Dust Bowl drought of the 1930s. Wilkerson knows that privacy does not exist in a small town, where the local tongue-waggers spread gossip. Reputations are easily ruined in a small town, where dark secrets (of which there are many in the story), mostly about illicit affairs, become public knowledge.

Wilkerson also sketches American life during the Second World War: the "patriotic speed limit" of 30 miles per hour to conserve gas; gasoline rationing cards; the rationing of sugar so that it could be used for military explosives; the selling of war stamps and buying of war bonds; the long lines of military convoys on Route 66. The Choats' two pigs are called "Roosevelt" and "Churchill." Charlie's eyes widen when he is given a bomb-shaped penny bank with the words:

> Fill this bank with your spare change. When full, break it open and purchase a WAR BOND at your nearest post office. This bank will hold $18.75 in pennies, nickels, dimes, quarters and half dollars which is the price of a $25 WAR BOND. Bomb the Japs from your own home. (154–155)

Details like this authenticate the novel's historical accuracy.

At the beginning of the war, Chester, to avoid spending two years in prison for assaulting a man in a bar, enlists in the Seabees, the Navy battalion of engineers who built runways and bridges. Chester is sent to the South Pacific, where he is severely injured, suffering a broken neck and shrapnel wounds in his arm and leg, returning home in 1944 disabled. These are all imagined details: Douglas Wilkerson served in the Seabees in the Pacific but was not injured. Wilkerson never served in the armed forces, but he writes convincingly about the horrors of war.

Art imitates life, but does art sometimes anticipate life? I pondered this question when I read Wilkerson's punningly titled "Breakneck Speed" in *Siri Doesn't Tango*. The story describes how the 84-year-old Wilkerson, racing a ten-year-old boy down a sloping concrete drive in a parking garage, lost his balance and nosedived into the pavement, breaking his nose and two fingers, gashing his forehead and lip, and shattering three cervical vertebrae. An X-ray and CT scan later indicated that there was nothing supporting his spine. Taken by ambulance to Northwestern Hospital to undergo emergency surgery, he spent 36 hours in the ICU. While still conscious before the seven-hour surgery, he agreed to the recommendations made by his physicians. "When they told you that they needed to operate on your neck and stabilize your spine," his son later informed him, "I was reminded, by your response, of a war movie where the soldier is told he must face extraordinary odds and he, locked-and-loaded, says, 'Let's get on with it'" (*Siri Doesn't Tango* 199). Wilkerson's description of his near-paralysis experience closely resembles aspects of Chester's war injury. Like Wilkerson, his fictional character suffers fractured neck vertebrae that could have easily resulted in permanent paralysis or death. Like Wilkerson, Chester emerges from his long drug-induced stupor frantic with anxiety. And again like Wilkerson, Chester must wear a neck brace that produces the same discomfort.

Wilkerson exploits the dark humor of these real and fictional injuries. He "bled like a stuck pig" immediately after the fall, he writes in *Siri Doesn't Tango*. "Unlike Humpty-Dumpty, I was put 'back together again'" (201). While being lifted into the ambulance, he cracked jokes, saying, "I handle my anxiety that way" (199). Growing bored with physical therapy to develop new balance skills, he asked a therapist if they could dance together, to which she amiably agreed. "Thereafter, though each day I had a different therapist, I taught a new dance step, Argentine tango, foxtrot, east coast swing, cha-cha, and rhumba" (205). Chester does not ask his nurse to dance, but he seductively calls her "sweetheart," even when she tells him she dislikes the word. He then calls her "honey." "You really are a flirt," she counters, to which he replies, "It's what I live for" (367).

Perhaps the major difference between Wilkerson's life and art is that the fictional Ruth is a much more sympathetic and complex character than the portrayal of his own mother in *Moving On*. We saw the same phenomenon in Joan Wexler's *Make Me the Sky*, in which her grandmother is a far more engaging character than in her memoir. The developing romantic relationship between Ruth and Joe Williams, based on Wilkerson's stepfather, is one of the novel's triumphs. It's likely that Wilkerson chose her first name to honor the memory of Ruth Addis, his favorite high school teacher. In *Siri Doesn't Tango* Wilkerson recalls how, when he visited her at the 25th high school reunion of the Okeene, Oklahoma Class of '51, she told him, "There was something about the hardships you suffered as a boy that affected you positively" (62).

Ruth Scarsdale is simultaneously in love with two men who could not be more different. Guilt and desire torture her, and until the end, we are not sure whom she will choose, her husband, a "good-time-now, damn-the-future sort of man" (410), or Joe, steady, dependable, but whom she had rejected, nearly 20 years earlier, for not being exciting enough. After his rejection by Ruth, Joe married Theresa, on the rebound. It was a good marriage, but then Theresa died, leaving Joe with their young daughter, Sarah, Charlie's age. Despite Chester's many betrayals, Ruth cannot stop loving him, even when he impregnates another woman, Alice Jenson, who gives birth to an illegitimate child. Wilkerson highlights the double standard that existed for women, both then and now.

Wilkerson never pathologizes his characters, never reduces their conflicts or weaknesses to neuroses or character disorders, never uses psychobabble. He understands that love and loss are inescapable. There are moments in the novel when he deftly conveys in a sentence or two moving insights, as when Joe tells Ruth his wife's dying words to him: "I can tell you what Theresa told me when she was real sick and knew she was dying. She wanted me to find someone else after she was gone. Someone to be a mother to Sarah." Anyone who has lost a spouse at a young age will appreciate Theresa's dying wish, but the novelist complicates the situation with Ruth's rhetorical question: "You think she wanted that someone else to be a married woman?" (249). Joe never answers the question, and readers must decide how they would answer it.

Unbidden Memories

Wilkerson never uses the word *repression* in the novel, but unbidden memories, usually painful if not traumatic, assail his characters, conjuring up losses, disappointments, and failures. Charlie reminds Ida of her son Brian, whose early death hardened her heart. Brian is one of the ghosts who populate the Choat farm. Ida cannot forgive her husband for delaying to take their dying son to a doctor. Wilkerson conveys in a single heartbreaking sentence Ida's feeling over her son's death: "Brian took his last precious death and settled into eternity" (27). Another reason for Ida's dislike of Charlie is that he reminds her of Chester, whom she slept with, partly out of desire, partly to spite her husband, an event that now fills her with shame. Bob hates Joe, mainly because he reminds him of his no-good son-in-law, and because Bob hates Chester, he hates Charlie. Bob also loathes George Buchanan, who saw him making love with Sally Tate. "I'll kill you," Bob threatens, "if you ever say a word about what you just seen" (159). Ruth is absorbed in her own memories, many of which involve her husband's betrayals. She married at 15 partly to escape from her parents and their ghostly home, but fate has cruelly brought her back to the same place, where she feels hopeless and trapped. Wilkerson's characters dwell as much in the past as in the present, recalling the Faulknerian observation that the past is never dead, nor even past. Before Ruth makes her final choice, she thinks about Charlie's favorite animal, pushmi-pullyu, a gazelle/unicorn cross with two heads at opposite ends of its body, in Hugh Lofting's Dr. Doolittle series of children's books. It is an apt literary reference. "She had two minds housed in her head, one drawing her toward Chester and the other drawing her toward Joe" (403). Literature does not solve Ruth's dilemma, but it helps her understand her situation.

Wilkerson has two challenges in creating Charlie Scarsdale: first, imagining a young boy who does not have an adult's awareness of the world; and second, maintaining narrative distance from his younger self. The novelist succeeds in both challenges. Charlie is the only significant character, apart from Joe, to whose inner life we do not have access. We know Charlie mainly from his dialogue, actions, and from what the other characters say about him. Charlie looks like his father, walks like his father, sulks like his father, and adores his father. Moreover, he has his father's quick temper and stubbornness. Yet Charlie is different: he is warm-hearted, generous, and concerned about others' feelings. Charlie spends much of his time purchasing war bonds to help his father and the war effort. "My guess is that at least half the county knows him by now," his teacher tells Ruth. "He's out on the streets of Hobart every weekend with his saving stamps and going up to people to introduce himself. I've heard a lot of good things about him" (135). Unlike his father, Charlie brings out the best in people, as can be seen when he sells stamps to the elderly Buchanan, who had served ten years in prison for cattle rustling. After suffering what proves to be a fatal heart attack, Buchanan gifts Charlie with his watch and 40 dollars, which the boy uses to buy more war stamps. There is only one moment when Wilkerson comes close to sentimentalizing Charlie's impact on others. After getting soaked while selling stamps to the town prostitute, he tells his mother, "She ironed my stamps dry that got wet. Wrapped them in wax paper so they wouldn't get wet again" (198). Apart from this detail, Charlie complains, whines, and behaves like other kids, especially boys, strutting around shooting the enemy with his coveted pop-gun, and disobeying his mother's orders not to defend himself when bullied.

The novel's title offers us a clue into its meaning. The cotton plant, with its deep roots in the soil for water and to bear the weight of cotton, becomes a metaphor of resilience. Wilkerson's characters are firmly rooted in the fertile Oklahoma soil and prove sturdy. When Chester lies wounded, he recalls the time he called Ruth "cotton flower," and the novel ends with Joe plaiting her hair with blood-red cotton flowers. Ruth makes the right marital decision, and the novel ends with the birth of the Williams's daughter, Esther (named after the novelist's maternal grandmother) and another child on the way. Charlie continues to love his father at the end of the story, but he has grown close to his new stepfather and stepsister. Chester remains Chester, unchanged and unrepentant. Oddly enough, losing their home and belongings has improved Bob and Ida's marriage. To invoke the titles of Wilkerson's memoirs, the characters keep moving on, prepared to face life's challenges. In a novel filled with personal and historical strife and uncertainty, readers find the all's-well-that-end's well conclusion of *The Cotton Flower* deeply fulfilling.

Works Cited

Berman, Jeffrey. *Psychoanalytic Memoirs*. Bloomsbury Academic, 2023.
Nabokov, Vladimir. *Lolita*. Weidenfeld and Nicolson, 1959.

Wilkerson, Cliff. *Beautiful Brown Eyes and Other Stories*. Infinity Publishing.Com, 2008.
Wilkerson, Cliff. *The Cotton Flower*. Douglas C. Wilkerson, 2022.
Wilkerson, Cliff. *Moving On*. CreateSpace, 2012.
Wilkerson, Cliff. *Siri Doesn't Tango and Other Stories*. Douglas C. Wilkerson, 2020.
Wilkerson, Cliff. *Still Moving On*. CreateSpace, 2016.

Part IV

The Jacobs Brothers

Chapter 14

Theodore Jacobs
The Year of Durocher and
The Way It Ends

One doesn't expect a psychoanalyst to be a jokester or to have a wry, self-lacerating sense of humor, but witness the following passage from Theodore J. Jacobs's 1991 study of countertransference, *The Use of the Self*, in which his patient, Ms. D, notices a noodle on his shoe, a result of a hasty dinner he had eaten prior to seeing her:

> "I guess it is," I replied. Then out of nowhere a thought came to mind and before I could censor it, it popped out.
>
> "I'm always using my noodle," I added. Ms. D laughed.
>
> "You're being defensive, doctor," she chided. "In situations like this one has to put aside rationalizations and confront the harsh reality. This is a noodle plain and simple; by the looks of it an egg noodle that has fallen from your plate and has clung to your shoe. My parents might try to avoid the issue but I expect more of you. You have to face the unvarnished truth; there is very definitely and palpably a noodle on your shoe." (11–12)

Few psychoanalysts would have the honesty and wit to reveal the unvarnished truth about analytic treatment, but these qualities are striking in Jacobs's professional and fictional writings. He delights in showing how patients like Ms. D turn the tables on him, an instance of what he describes as a moment of low comedy but also a high point in the treatment for both patient and analyst.

Theodore Jacobs is a child and adolescent psychoanalyst as well as an adult analyst. He is clinical professor of psychiatry (emeritus) at the Albert Einstein College of Medicine and a training and supervising analyst at the New York Psychoanalytic Society & Institute. The recipient of the Sigourney Award, his profession's highest honor, Jacobs was the first to introduce the concept of "enactment" in psychoanalysis to describe how the unconscious behaviors of patient and analyst lie at the heart of analytic treatment. "In the US, countertransference has typically been viewed as the analyst's problem," Rosemary Balsam wrote, explaining Jacobs's selection for the Sigourney Award in 2018. "It was not openly acknowledged or discussed until Dr. Jacobs lifted the surrounding curtain of silence." Jacobs's short fiction has appeared in *Harpers Magazine*, *Mutiny Magazine*, and Martha Foley's *Best Short Stories of the Year*. His debut novel, *The Year of Durocher*, was published in 2013, and his second novel, *The Way It Ends*, in 2023.

In a 2010 interview with Gabriele Cassullo and Michele S. Piccolo, Jacobs remarks that he was involved in what Arnold Cooper called the "quiet revolution in American psychoanalysis" (240) that occurred in the last 20 years, a revolution that has seen an increasing number of analysts reject Freud's injunction to remain anonymous, impersonal, and detached—advice that Freud never practiced himself. In both *The Use of the Self* and *The Possible Profession* (2013), the title of which alludes to Freud's description of psychoanalysis as one of the three "impossible professions" (along with education and government), Jacobs has urged the analyst's careful self-disclosure to facilitate analytic treatment. "Nondisclosure and analytic anonymity, especially if rigidly and automatically applied, do not always serve patients' interests" (*The Possible Profession* 148). Jacobs concedes that the analytic community has not embraced his emphasis on selective self-disclosure. "People felt I was violating sound analytic principles and was an exhibitionist and a narcissist" (Cassullo and Piccolo 241). Jacobs was willing to incur this criticism, however, and, as *The Possible Profession* demonstrates, he began disclosing personal information, especially about his conflicted relationship with his father. In her enthusiastic review, Jane S. Hall calls *The Possible Profession* a "mind-stretching book" and refers to Jacobs as "constructing a bridge between classical and contemporary theory, a bridge that permits him to visit both sides of the psychoanalytic river: a bridge over troubled waters" (495).

Writing About His Family

Analysts generally do not write about themselves or their family, but Jacobs is the exception. He first started admitting disappointment with his father in *The Use of the Self*. Unable to "appease" his Kafkaesque father, the adolescent moved away from him in sadness, anger, and pain. Jacobs's father was shy and withdrawn, but he could be a tyrant when threatened:

> I recalled the fear I felt when, at those times, his fury was unleashed and he turned with wrath on those around him. Alone in my room, I would hear him ranting at my mother, his voice on fire and threatening to destroy anyone in his path. Sometimes his rage would be directed at me. At those times I would seek the safety of my room and, shutting the door, hope against hope that he would stay out. (35)

Jacobs expands on the troubled father–son relationship in *The Possible Profession*. Growing up, Jacobs feared his father who, as a struggling businessman, would sometimes yell on the telephone at his unproductive salesmen and then hang up on them. "As I imagine this, I feel the same kind of anxiety that, as a child, I experienced when, lying in bed, I overheard my father flying into a rage. I then recall how, through my analysis, I was able, in large measure, to overcome my fear of him" (38). Because money was a constant problem, Jacobs's father was always a half-step ahead of his creditors. The son may not have dreaded that he and his family would be sent to debtor's prison, as Dickens describes in his most autobiographical novel, *David Copperfield*, but he apprehended imminent disaster. Whether out of denial or grim realism, his father would write his mother "generous" checks for household expenses, but they would be unsigned, one of many autobiographical details that appears in *The Year of Durocher*. But there was a positive side of his father with which the son strongly identified. Describing himself as a quiet, painfully shy boy, he longed to hear his father, who was, like himself, deeply private, unwilling to share his hopes or dreams with others, recount stories about his youth, in the process becoming a comic performer. In this respect, the apple did not fall far from the tree.

Jacobs has less to say about his mother, perhaps because the relationship was less strained. A Latin teacher, book reviewer, and lecturer on women's issues, she stimulated his fascination with psychology and literature. Jacobs does not ignore the mother's role in the child's development, but he grew up in a patriarchal culture where ambition and work were a part of a man's world. Tellingly, there are more than twice as many references to "fathers" than to "mothers" in the index to *The Possible Profession*. Additionally, the index contains three references to "ambivalence" toward fathers; there are no references to "ambivalence" toward mothers. The subcategories under "mother–child relationship" (no such category appears under "father–child relationship") are positive, including "attachment development" and "mother's self-reflective categories." In light of these gender differences, it's not surprising that *The Possible Profession* emphasizes Oedipal over pre-Oedipal conflicts.

Humor and affection characterize Jacob's description of his younger brother, Daniel, who, like him, has become a distinguished psychoanalyst and creative writer. When their mother reprimanded her younger son for procrastinating on an American history assignment, he replied, punningly, "Well I have thought a lot about it… and I have decided to let bygones be bygones" (*The Possible Profession* 78). Jacobs describes his brother as a "star," "bright, funny, inventive, and more socially engaging and popular than I. Although I concealed such feelings from myself, I envied him his success and, no doubt, was quite miserly in offering words of encouragement and support" (102). In a later observation in *The Possible Profession*, Jacobs admits to having acted as a "self-righteous know-it-all with my younger brother, Dan" (295). The author's comments about his brother display far more love than sibling rivalry. He refers briefly, and cryptically, to being an older brother in his 1999 essay "On the Question of Self-Disclosure by the Analyst: Error or Advance in Technique?": "As a younger brother, Mr. L quite readily stimulates competitive feelings in me, as older brother, and I am aware that in employing the technique that I have adopted, I run the risk of enacting old scenarios from my own history" (172). In his writings, Jacobs sees the benefits and risks of the analyst's self-disclosure, and he both invites and implicates his readers in his analytic dilemmas. "Was my interpretation worth the price?" he asks after admitting to a patient that he felt attacked by her. "I am not sure. I leave it to the reader to think about" (174). Such openness and awareness of ambiguity are uncommon in any profession.

Theodore Jacobs has written about the role of unconscious body language in analysis. Looking at the bony defects behind a patient's ears in *The Use of the Self*, suggesting the removal of his mastoid bones, he found himself shifting his body away from the patient. Why? He recalled that his brother had developed a severe case of mastoiditis in his childhood that required immediate surgery which, in the preantibiotic era, was life-threatening. Theodore Jacobs remembers the intense fear of mutilation and death he felt during this time, along with his death wishes toward his younger sibling. Daniel Jacobs writes about the same experience in *The Supervisory Encounter*.

Theodore Jacobs is understandably protective of his wife and daughters' privacy, but twice in *The Possible Profession* he refers, mysteriously, to a "time of personal crisis" when, after he had been out of analysis, he and his family "suffered a sudden and profound loss, one that caused me to become quite depressed for some time" (9). The experience left him unable to concentrate on his work, compelling him to seek additional help. He returns to the same event later in *The Possible Profession*, adding that he and his wife struggled with depression, a situation that his "noodle" patient grasped. "With her keen intuition, Ms. D sensed that she was in the presence of a man who was in pain and her need, in part out of identification with me, to repair her analyst, led her to be consistently warm and responsive to me" (158).

Literary references enliven Jacobs's writings. Remembering a patient's sharp disapproval of his analyst's ill-matched clothes, Jacobs compares himself to one of Samuel Beckett's characters, "fresh out of a dustbin" (*The Use of the Self* 127). Describing how in his youth he was enmeshed in a relationship with a relative who tried to seduce him, awakening his confusion, anger, and guilt, he recalls reading *Crime and Punishment*, in which Raskolnikov has similarly conflicting feelings toward his seductive mother. In *The Possible Profession*, Jacobs thinks about correcting a patient's reference to Emerson but then decides against it, mainly because he worries about showing off, but that doesn't stop him from providing his readers with the accurate quote: "A foolish consistency is the hobgoblin of little minds" (38). The most literary chapter in *The Possible Profession*, "Imaginary Gardens, Real Toads," contains extended discussions of Nabokov's 1951 memoir *Speak, Memory* and Eugene O'Neill's 1956 play *Long Day's Journey into Night*. Jacobs quotes these novelists and playwrights to show how, through the act of literary creation, writers can often work through, partly or fully, tormenting feelings of guilt, self-hatred, and the longing for death. Elsewhere in *The Possible Profession*, Jacobs writes about novelists' understanding of the conflicts that bedevil adolescents, as can be seen in Mark Twain's *Huckleberry Finn* and J.D. Salinger's iconic novel *The Catcher in the Rye*.

In his most recent essay, "Chekhov Was a Doctor" (2021), Jacobs discusses how as a medical student he learned that the Irish writer Frank O'Connor would be teaching a short story course in Harvard's summer session. Jacobs told O'Connor, during an interview to gain admission into the course, that he was a medical student; "Glory to Jesus," the latter lamented, "What 'tis it about the study of medicine that makes you so unhappy that you've got to write?" Jacobs's answer, "Gross anatomy," earned his immediate acceptance, mainly because, O'Connor added, "Chekhov was a doctor" (845–846). Jacobs's love for creative writing, which he acknowledges is a "compulsion," has continued over the years. He took another course with the renowned American novelist and literary critic Robert Penn Warren, who gave him the following harsh advice: "Don't come into it if you can stay out of it" (847)—advice that Jacobs fortunately ignored.

The Year of Durocher

The Year of Durocher is a coming-of-age novel that focuses on the growth of the Bildungsroman hero, Jonathan Manheim, a high school student from what was then the unglamorous upper west side of Manhattan. "I never rose beyond the mediocre" (6), Jonathan ruefully admits, speaking about his athletic skills, but his modesty extends to all aspects of his personality. Jonathan becomes infatuated with Cara Rosenhaus, a smart, feisty, and strong-willed early feminist whose family, from the wealthy east side of Manhattan, owns a home in the prestigious Hamptons. Sexually aggressive, Cara is the kind of girl who, two decades later, would read Philip Roth's *Portnoy's Complaint* and exclaim, "Let's put the id back in yid"—though she never does sleep with Jonathan despite awakening his sexuality. He fears that Cara is out of his league, a belief his friend Mel Schleifer traces to an "inherited inferiority traceable to a fear of the Cossacks" (29). The third member of the novel's triangle is Jonathan's rival-turned-friend, Stan Schneiderman, a triple-threat star athlete whose popularity with young women fills Jonathan with envy.

In Jacobs's view, middle adolescence, ages 14 through 16, can be as noteworthy as childhood in influencing adult personality. Mid-adolescence is a "gateway to later adolescence and to the intense, emotionally deep experiences that often characterize those years," Jacobs writes in *The Possible Profession*. The major task of mid-adolescence "is to make the transition, begun in early adolescence, from home, with all of its psychological meanings, to the outer world" (250). The novel takes place in 1948, the year in which Leo Durocher, the brash, outspoken manager of the Brooklyn Dodgers, committed the unforgivable sin of defecting to the arch-rival New York Giants. *The Year of Durocher* is filled with similar betrayals as Jonathan journeys toward manhood. Durocher's betrayal of the Dodgers is a metaphor of Cara's betrayal of Jonathan, which is likened to the betrayal by Tokyo Rose, the notorious nickname given by American soldiers during the Second World War to all women of Japanese descent who broadcast lies and propaganda in English. Durocher's betrayal is also compared to Jonathan's betrayal of Schneiderman, whom he unconsciously assaults and nearly kills on the basketball court.

Among Jonathan's greatest challenges, the most formidable is coming to terms with his father. There are three noteworthy fathers in the novel, his own, Eli, and those of Cara and Schneiderman. Eli Manheim is the same one Jacobs limns in his professional writings. "Not only was his hardware supply business sinking fast under the weight of his all-thumbs management style," Jonathan confesses at the beginning of the story, "but the IRS was threatening prosecution for an unpaid, and ignored, tax bill" (8). Jonathan distances himself from his father, despite the latter's efforts to remain close to him. Eli Manheim's unsigned checks distress his wife precisely as Jacobs describes in *The Possible Profession*, but now we receive additional information that may be fictionalized: "To such schemes my mother reacted with near psychosis," Jonathan admits.

> Raised in marginal poverty, the daughter of a withdrawn man whose habit it was to sit alone in darkened rooms, she was an anxious woman for whom the fantasy of losing everything, of being dispossessed from her home, and of being cast into the world as a street person, constituted an ever-present threat. (33)

Cara's father is strikingly different from Jonathan's father. Sidney Rosenhaus owns a profitable furniture store in Harlem. Although he fancies himself a political liberal, donating money to Democratic fund-raisers and to the United Jewish Appeal, his business tactics are predatory. He is the type of man, in the words of Mel, liberally sprinkled with derogatory Yiddishisms, who "sells a complete living room to *shvatzers* [Negroes] for five hundred bucks, charges twenty percent interest, and repossesses half the *dreck* [garbage] they sell" (36). "King R," as he is called, embodies the "killer instinct," a quality he believes Jonathan sadly lacks. Jonathan does his best to please Sidney Rosenhaus, partly to win Cara and partly to fulfill his father hunger. In one of the novel's epiphanic moments, Cara says to Jonathan, near the end of the story, that "you wanted Sidney to make up for the father you don't have" (338).

Cara is not alone in giving Jonathan advice about his father. "You know, J, your dad's a big fan of yours" (25), Mel advises him. Upon meeting Schneiderman and learning about his father, Eli Manheim declares, "A man like that has a lot to teach a son" (192), a statement that reveals his desire to teach his *own* son. "You treat your father like shit," Schneiderman later tells Jonathan, and when Jonathan expresses puzzlement, his friend explains: "It's obvious. You look down on him. You and your mother. You think he is a *putz* because he is struggling to stay afloat" (261). Schneiderman also has a conflicted relationship with his father, an assistant district attorney who has a hard time trusting people, but unlike Jonathan, he has learned to accept his own father's human failings. Schneiderman urges Jonathan to tolerate his father's faults. Jonathan slowly sees his father with fresh eyes, and his gradual acceptance of his father's love and support represents his most notable insight in the novel.

The novel's armchair psychologist, Mel Schleifer, is a self-proclaimed "student of science," a shrewd guide to winning a young woman's heart, and, like the novelist himself, a natural jokester. He relishes his role as Jonathan's unofficial shrink, advising him, after being spurned by Cara, "If you want to get back in the game, you've got to jettison that *dybbuk* inside you, the one that does a *mea culpa* whenever someone stubs a toe" (235). An adherent to Freud's libido theory and perhaps to Wilhelm Reich's belief in orgone energy, Mel "regularly linked eccentricities of the cardiovascular system to unreleased genital engorgement" (65). When Jonathan begins imitating Schneiderman's "flying trapeze style" of making basketball layups, missing easy shots, Mel diagnoses the problem as not mechanical but Oedipal: "You are suffering from a bad case of pizzazz envy" (249). Jacobs must have had fun inventing the colorful character, the source of much of the novel's irrepressible wit, Jewish wry. Sidney Rosenhaus also sounds like a Borsht-belt comic, particularly when he comments on Jonathan's name.

> You've got the reform Jews way of adding a bit of goy to a name, not too much, just a sprinkle to give it a little class. Jewish families don't use the name John, right? The Catholics have co-opted that one. There is Saint John, John the Baptist, Pope John, a whole slew of Johns. But Jonathan is perfect. It keeps the gentile John, but gives it a little twist. This makes it kosher. (108)

Who can disagree with this enlightened cultural and linguistic analysis?

Schneiderman's talent of speaking to the "injured part of a person, to make him feel understood" (213), suggests that he is, like Mel, an intuitive psychologist, one who understands Jonathan better than Jonathan understands himself. Despite Schneiderman's failing academic record, which results in his suspension from athletic events and his likely flunking out of Harmon, he is rarely wrong about Jonathan's psychological struggles, and at the end of the story Jonathan states that his friend will always remain a steady presence in his life. Not so with Cara, who dumps Jonathan at the end. "I no longer feel that I know who you are, who the real Jonathan Manheim is" (340).

"Brothers Under the Skin"

Jacobs ends his 1986 review of *Blood Brothers: Siblings as Writers*, edited by Norman Kiell, with the observation that the essays in this volume "provide a window on an aspect of the psychology of the writer that is often neglected: the impact on literary creation of the relation of brother to brother" (170). It's likely that Jacobs was thinking about the relationship with his own brother, Daniel, who, six years after the publication of *The Year of Durocher*, had his own novel published, *The Distance from Home*. Unsurprisingly, Daniel Jacobs is also interested in sibling relationships, as his 2006 article "Blanche, Stella, Tennessee and Rose: The Sibling Relationship in *A Streetcar Named Desire*" reveals. In his article on *A Streetcar Named Desire*, Daniel Jacobs cites with approval M. Leichtman's dictum that older siblings play a key role in shaping younger siblings' identity (332), a statement with which Theodore Jacobs is likely to agree.

Jonathan and Stan Schneiderman are not brothers, but the expression "brothers under the skin" appears *three* times in the novel (86, 93, 227). In the last of the references, after Cara explains that he and Schneiderman are "really into each other," Jonathan responds, "You've got us confused with Cain and Abel" (227). Viewing the two youths as sibling rivals helps explain the extreme competition between the two, on and off the athletic field. Twice Jonathan smashes into Schneiderman. The first time occurs at the beginning of the story, when, fumbling a game-winning football catch, he lands on top of his opponent, diving into him with his helmet, to which Schneiderman groggily responds, "You like to play rough" (22). The second time occurs near the end of the novel when Jonathan collides into him on the basketball court, an "accident" resulting in a life-threatening injury that may spell the end of Schneiderman's athletic career. Contrary to Sidney Rosenhaus's criticism, Jonathan *has* the killer instinct!

Other commonalities suggest that Jonathan and Stan Schneiderman are brothers under the skin. Their mothers have experienced either intense anxiety or severe clinical depression, and their fathers have strained relationships with their employees or supervisors. "I know how your dad feels" (206), Schneiderman says to Jonathan, perhaps because of the similar parental dynamics in his own family. Tragedy has darkened both families. Schneiderman's younger sister, Evelyn, has suffered for two years from meningitis. "She was the liveliest little kid you can imagine. Full of fun. Then, practically overnight she became a rag doll." As soon as Jonathan hears this, he discloses why he is an only child. "The story that I'd heard over the years was that after she had a stillborn child, my mother tried once more to get pregnant when I was three, had a miscarriage, and gave up" (246). One wonders whether the "sudden and profound loss" to which Jacobs twice alludes in *The Possible Profession* involved a child's death or disabling illness.

The Year of Durocher is largely chronological, but there are a few references to Jonathan's future after the novel ends, when he goes into psychoanalysis. He mentions his analyst's belief that he is a good example of suffering from a "Fate neurosis," defined as a person with a talent for "slipping his head into a noose but who blames his troubles on fate; on having been born in the wrong century, in the wrong country or to the wrong set of parents—in short, on an unlucky roll of the dice" (2–3). Fate neurosis is not a term Freud used: the expression does not appear in the index or concordance to the *Standard Edition* of his writings. Nor it is clear how much importance, if any, Jacobs attaches to this diagnosis.

The Age of Durocher is a carefully plotted novel filled with lively characters, engaging dialogue, and sparkling humor. Jacobs establishes a convincing parallel between Leo Durocher's move from the Brooklyn Dodgers to their despised crosstown rivals, the New York Giants, and Stan Schneiderman's move from Brooklyn, where he was known on his high school team as the "Flatbush firebrand," to Riverdale, where he becomes Jonathan's teammate at Harmon, an exclusive private school. Schneiderman is Jonathan's "Durocher," fully accepted at the end. Jonathan learns much about himself, mostly dark knowledge: his driving ambition, his previously unacknowledged aggressiveness, his embarrassment over his family's modest resources, and his willingness to betray a friend to win the girl of his dreams. Jonathan never uses the term *projective identification*, a defense mechanism popularized by Melanie Klein, but he implies this near the end. "It was not Schneiderman whom I was attacking; it was who I saw in him, saw reflected in his eyes and could not bear to see; an image of myself, the small-minded, envious person and disloyal friend that I had become" (357). Jonathan discloses at the end that after college he will probably attend law school, but a better choice, I believe, is to become a psychoanalyst and a creative writer.

Reading *The Year of Durocher* is a trip down memory lane for an octogenarian like me. Unlike Jonathan, I was born in Brooklyn; hence, my identification with Jay Greenberg's assertion in Jill Salberg's edited volume *Psychoanalytic Credos* (2022): "You couldn't grow up in Brooklyn when I did, in the late 1940s and the 1950s, and not turn out to be at least a little bit of a Freudian" (59). It was an age, Jonathan reminds us, when many Jews were proud socialists, when men used Brylcreem in their hair, when a movie ticket cost a dollar and a quarter, and when Cara's desire to become a US Senator seemed impossibly out of reach. A few of the details in *The Age of Durocher* are anachronistic. Mel could not have consulted Freud's *Standard Edition* because the first of the 24 volumes was not published until 1953. Cara's statement that "all politics is local" (126), though originating in 1932, did not become popular until near the end of the twentieth century. But to point out these trivial errors is nitpicking, like reminding Cara's brother, who prides himself on constantly writing and citing poetry, that the title of T.S. Eliot's most famous poem is *The Waste Land*, not *The Wasteland*.

Like many psychoanalysts, Theodore Jacobs and Daniel Jacobs cannot resist speculating on the origins and effects of literary creativity. Theodore Jacobs's experience as a creative writer suggests that the "*psychology of composition*" involves the need to "objectify and disguise highly personal concerns, concerns that, although often current and pressing, in most instances also represent long-standing preoccupations" (*The Possible Profession* 268). For many self-destructive authors, Jacobs adds somberly—such as Dylan Thomas, Anne Sexton, Sylvia Plath, John Berryman, Cesare Pavese, and David Foster Wallace—writing is an effort to master traumatic experiences, an effort that leads to a sad paradox: "the artist's life suffers while his art flourishes" (270). But in Jacobs's case, the creation of fiction was entirely salutary. Had he not written about his father in his short fiction, he would not have been able to overcome much of the pain and disappointment surrounding the father–son relationship. Writing also enables the poet, novelist, or playwright to invent solutions to psychic difficulties; stories can serve "as a stalking horse, experiments in problem solving, a means of exploring conflicts, their potential vicissitudes, and possible strategies for their resolution" (277).

Daniel Jacobs would, no doubt, agree with his brother's conclusions. In his discussion of Tennessee Williams's *A Streetcar Named Desire*, Daniel Jacobs quotes D.H. Lawrence's 1913 letter about his experience creating *Sons and*

Lovers: "One sheds one[']s sicknesses in books, repeats and presents again one[']s emotions, to be master of them" (*Letters*, vol. II, 90; "Blanche, Stella, Tennessee and Rose" 332). Additionally, Daniel Jacobs cites two leading psychoanalytic theorists on the creative impulse: Melanie Klein maintained that writing is an effort to repair a lost or damaged object; and Janine Chasseguet-Smirgel contended that the creation of art represents the artist's effort to restore his or her integrity and sense of self. The artist's life and work are often inseparable, Daniel Jacobs points out, as Tennessee Williams believed: "If the writing is honest, it cannot be separated from the man who wrote it" ("Blanche, Stella, Tennessee and Rose" 320; Williams 120).

In a glowing review published in the *Psychoanalytic Quarterly*, Tara S. Robbins observes that Jacobs's characters "follow us into our consulting rooms, deepening our psychological grasp of adolescent conflict and increasing our humanity as a result" (263). In the *Journal of the American Psychoanalytic Association*, Lawrence N. Levenson lauds Jacobs' depiction of one of the most tumultuous periods in life.

> Jacobs shows us what is so terrific about adolescence—the operatic passion, the charming narcissism, the idealizations, the sense of infinite possibility—and what is so awful about it—the defensiveness, the painful insecurity, the deidealizations, and the fundamental loneliness of this time of life. (362)

Coming-of-age novels are generally written by younger rather than older novelists, but in this case, *The Age of Durocher* was penned by an octogenarian. Anyone who reads this novel will see that the author is at the top of his game, exuberant, hopeful, and wise. Levenson concludes his review with a metaphor that captures the youthful spirit of the psychoanalyst-turned-novelist.

> He has made lasting contributions to our profession and already would be in Cooperstown for psychoanalysts if there were such a place, yet here in *The Year of Durocher* he is making a wonderful debut as a novelist. This Jacobs fellow is forever a boy of summer. He is still stretching, still taking his swings and making good contact, still coming of age. (363)

The Way It Ends

Life can be understood only backwards, the Danish philosopher Søren Kierkegaard states, but it must be lived forward. I could not have predicted that Theodore Jacobs's second novel, *The Way It Ends*, would be a murder mystery about a psychoanalyst turned amateur gumshoe, or that it would focus on the Israeli-Palestinian hostilities and the ongoing threat of terrorism in the United States. Reading *The Way It Ends*, however, one can see how much it has in common with *The Year of Durocher*. Both novels explore fraught father–son and fraternal relationships, including the intense ambivalence that lies at the heart of each bond. The armchair psychologist in *The Year of Durocher*, Mel Schleifer, has become Dr. William Strickman in *The Way*

It Ends. He sets off to discover whether his brother, Leonard, two years his senior, whom he thought he knew, is the victim of suicide or murder: he was found dead in a hotel bathtub with a lamp cord around his neck. Did he hang himself or was he hanged? It is the same ambiguity we have seen in Alan Krohn's *The Mind's Eye*. Bill is aided in his psychological sleuthing by a retired New York City detective, Barney Siegel, who, like Bill, has lost a brother, a high school English teacher who perished in a mysterious plane crash. Barney is the novel's jokester, an *alter kocker* ("old defecator," to use a sanitized translation) whose speech is laced with Borschbelt Yiddishisms. Bill and Barney form a tight friendship, much like Jonathan and Mel in *The Year of Durocher*. Barney counsels Bill to use his professional training to solve his brother's enigmatic death. "Lie down on your couch and do that free association bit. What you know will come back to you" (38). *The Way It Ends* is an ambitious and timely novel that anatomizes the three impossible professions, demonstrating art's ability to instruct while it entertains.

The novel's most fascinating character, the Muslim surgeon Dr. Ahmed Aslam, Bill's former medical school teacher, friend, and longtime adversary, seems the most likely suspect. Bill must use all of his analytical skills to figure out how and why his brother died, and, in the process, prevent the blowing up of a New York City synagogue. Like *The Year of Durocher*, *The Way It Ends* is well plotted and suspenseful, but its major strength lies in its insights into family dynamics.

A New York analyst for over 20 years, Bill is married with two children, one of whom almost died in childhood of ulcerative colitis, once again calling attention to a time of personal tragedy in the novelist's life. Bill loves his brother, an accountant in a large firm, of whom he has always been protective. "Lenny was part of me," Bill laments, grief-stricken, "part of us, a necessity in our lives" (4). It's puzzling that neither Bill nor his wife, Alice, fathoms his brother's dark secret, his hidden life as a gay man; Bill assumed his brother was asexual rather than living a tortured life in the closet. The two brothers could not be more different, temperamentally and philosophically. Bill is liberal in politics and religion, supportive of Israel but critical of its often punitive treatment of Palestinian Arabs, while Lenny is conservative, an Orthodox Jew who maintains that Israel has never wronged the Palestinians. Bill is generally open-minded, tolerant, and progressive, Jacobs's own values, but after Lenny's death, Bill's position on the Israeli-Palestinian conflict hardens, and for a time he sounds as prejudiced and opinionated as his late brother. Like Jonathan, Bill learns much about himself and others by novel's end.

Bill never openly criticizes his brother, but Ahmed does. "Leonard Strickman must have been the most stubborn man in the universe. Once he'd made his mind up about something, a bulldozer couldn't budge him" (51). Is the same true of Ahmed himself? One of the novel's most urgent questions is whether people can change. At the beginning of the story, Bill maintains that people do *not* change, an opinion that seems strange coming from a psychoanalyst. There are multiple ironies here, for both Ahmed and Bill appear to change, becoming more strident, vowing vengeance, though appearances are often deceiving. Readers must wait until the end of the story to learn Jacobs's answer to the question of the possibility of change and growth.

Jacobs has never created a character like Ahmed Aslam. To imagine him, the novelist has done justice to the ways in which his life has been shaped by familial, cultural, and political forces. Ahmed has a tangled relationship with Bill, whom he calls, with a mixture of affection and sarcasm, "Siggie." They were once dear friends, but political and cultural tensions have driven them apart: they have not seen each other in the last six years. Ahmed has had an even more complicated relationship with his father, a psychiatrist, the first in Palestine to establish a study group on Freud's writings. He was also the first to translate Freud's writings into Arabic. A peace-loving man, he devoted his life to promoting Israeli-Palestinian relations. Ahmed and his father had a close relationship; both collaborated writing an article on dreams published in a psychology journal. The senior Dr. Aslam was killed by the Israelis while he was visiting a cousin in a Palestinian village. Believing that Israel is guilty of genocide, Ahmed joins an "activist group" bent on the destruction of the enemies of Allah. "They say a man doesn't come into his own until his father dies," Ahmed explains to Bill, echoing Freud's belief that a man's most poignant loss is his father's death. "For me it was the reverse. When I lost him, I went into a nose dive. He was my anchor and support" (53). The reader discerns how Lenny and Ahmed have both become radicalized, embracing military solutions to intractable political problems. Throughout the novel, Jacobs is scrupulously fair in depicting Jewish-Arab strife. He knows that violence breeds violence and that the lust for revenge is ubiquitous. Five children are slain in a Jewish day school; in retaliation, two youths from the Hasidic community drive an SUV into a group of Arab boys. Significantly, Ahmed treats the victims of both terrorist attacks, Jews and Arabs alike. Marco is radicalized first by Lenny and then by the Jihadists. Neither side, Israeli nor Palestinian, is blameless.

Complicating Ahmed's grief over paternal loss is the conviction that his father was weak for seeking peace. "In my heart I called him a collaborator who wanted peace at any price, a traitor willing to sell out our people" (176). This is the only time that Ahmed fails to idealize his father. He says nothing about his mother, suggesting his (and the novelist's) patricentric world. In time Ahmed learns (or relearns) his father's wisdom, namely, that "Pain is all around" (177)—a statement that reflects the authorial point of view.

Much of the success of *The Way It Ends* lies in Jacobs's ability to imagine relationships built on religious and cultural differences. Ahmed, for example, is in love with a Jewish woman, Laura Holtzman. Bill, despite being happily married, is also in love with Laura, recalling the Oedipal triangle in *The Year of Durocher* among Jonathan, Stan Schneiderman, and Cara Rosenhaus. Laura's adopted son, Marco, has been indoctrinated in a so-called school that is a front for the operation of a radical Islamic cell, preaching anti-Israel, anti-American propaganda. The cell is operated by Ahmed's menacing bodyguards, Mohammed and Abdul, who turn out to be Jihadists. Jacobs has created a fictional world disturbingly similar to our own, where extreme ideologies, zealots, and fanatics make it impossible for people to find the common ground to live peacefully.

How can psychoanalysis help heal these differences? Ahmed pens a letter to his deceased father that provides an answer to this question. "The two of you are very different," Ahmed writes to his father, "but in some ways, he reminds me of you." Ahmed then elaborates on these commonalities:

> Maybe it's because both of you are shrinks and you chose a profession in which you listen and try to understand other people's lives, other worlds and dreams. And the fact that he's into dreams reminds me of you. You taught me about dreams, how they carry our wishes into the daylight. Siggie's also fascinated by dreams. He shares our interest. When he was starting out, I taught him what you taught me. He's not you, Dad. You're still the Master. But in his own way he's carrying on your legacy. (*The Way It Ends* 71)

Ahmed finds it therapeutically helpful to write to his father. Writing enables him to express his feelings, maintain a continuing bond with the deceased, and imagine his father's advice to him. Ahmed's letter to his father is spontaneous, heartfelt, and convincing. "I know you're there for me," he exclaims at the end of his letter. "You always were and you always will be. Just give me the strength to see things clearly and to do the right thing" (73). Had we not known that Ahmed was penning a letter to his father, we might have thought he was writing to God, an idealized father.

Once Again, Brothers Under the Skin

Jacobs deftly uses the Freudian legacy of dream association, near the end of the novel, when Ahmed, held prisoner by Mohammed and Abdul, conveys information, in the guise of an elaborate dream, to alert Bill to an impending terrorist attack. Ahmed writes down a long dream filled with cryptic information, including the letters SE, a reference, Bill realizes, to the *Standard Edition* of Freud's writings. Bill ingeniously interprets the feigned dream and notifies the police, but during the resulting shootout, Ahmed is shot by Mohammed. "You did it, Siggie," Ahmed whispers, in his dying words, "You finally got a dream right" (214). Unable to speak, he then manages to point to the breast pocket of his shirt, which contains a photo of his beloved father. Bill takes the photo and places it in his own shirt pocket, close to his heart. Jacobs hints at the fraternal bond between the two characters, brothers under the skin. "You've lost another brother," Barney says to Bill, adding, "When it came down to it, he had your back. And you were right, Doc... You called it. The man was a mensch" (216). After Ahmed's passing, the secular Bill recites lines from the Kaddish, the Jewish prayer for the dead. Jacobs affirms the fraternal bond between the two men by suggesting that the senior Dr. Aslam is Bill's spiritual father through temperament and professional training.

Jacobs is careful not to make his fictional brothers too similar to his relationship with his own brother. Bill and Lenny are not in the same profession, nor are they fellow novelists. Indeed, they have little in common. Oddly, we learn *nothing* about their parents, apart from the fact that they are both deceased, a conspicuous omission. Nor is it obvious that Bill and Ahmed are brothers under the skin. Bill's remark that he and Ahmed "loved to tease one another and to experience the camaraderie that lay just beneath our jousting" (50) is true of many close relationships, but it is especially true of brothers.

Ahmed, though tempted to violence, remains true to his—and his father's—character. And so does Bill. Despite believing, for most of the novel, that Ahmed murdered Lenny, Bill acknowledges misjudging his old friend. Jacobs knows, both as an analyst and novelist, that some people change while others do not. He urges his readers to be as open-minded as possible. In his suicide note, Lenny spurns the attempt to maintain a balanced perspective of Israel, rejecting a "naïve, willfully blind liberalism" (156), but Jacobs endorses a thoughtful, compassionate liberalism that captures both Israeli and Palestinian points of view.

Jacobs uses the epistolary technique to explain Lenny's death. In a long letter to Bill that functions as a suicide note, Lenny discloses that he has decided to kill himself before Ahmed and his allies could do so. "If there is one important lesson we Jews have learned, it is the importance of standing up for ourselves" (157). Lenny acknowledges, however, that Ahmed could not go through with the murder. After disclosing his life as a gay man, plagued with guilt and self-loathing, feeling like "an all-around loser," and confessing his envy of his brother, Lenny took his own life, a way to emulate but also defeat Mohammed and Abdul. Psychoanalysts will recognize Lenny's action as identification with the aggressor: murder by suicide, and suicide by murder. Tellingly, Lenny's suicide angers Alice, who regards it as selfish and self-indulgent; Bill, on the other hand, the empathic clinician, regards it, nonjudgmentally, as an act committed by a person in overwhelming pain. Bill experiences all the emotions of suicide survivors, including perhaps the worst feeling of all, as he confides to Barney. "We talked until I was talked out, until everything poured out of me—including the shameful feeling that in some part of me I felt relief, that a burden had been lifted from me—that I was no longer responsible for my brother" (162). The relief, ironically, only heightens his guilt.

Lenny's epistolary style differs from Ahmed's. His salutation, "My Dearest Brother William," conveys the stiff formality and distance of their relationship. Nevertheless, Jacobs affirms the deep bond of genuine love between them. Lenny sees the Israeli-Palestinian conflict in black-and-white terms, and he invokes a nonexistent "objectivity" to rationalize his worldview. He uses few Yiddishisms: there is nothing comic or rueful about his speech, nothing to suggest that Yiddish is the language of resilience and stubborn survival.

Jacobs thrusts his two major protagonists out of their comfort zone and situates them in frightening situations where he tests their character. The Jewish-American psychoanalyst and Muslim-American surgeon have each other's backs at the end, two mensches who have courage, insight, compassion, and integrity. *The Way It Ends* can sensitize readers to the racism, anti-Semitism, and Islamophobia that infect contemporary society, which remains more polarized than ever. Contrary to Bill's earlier belief, he feels deeper sympathy for his real and spiritual brothers, and a renewed appreciation of the role of active listening. The senior Dr. Aslam's hope that progress in education, psychoanalysis, and government "can only be made through talk, negotiations, and reason" (56) remains Jacob's theme. Ahmed's death, along with Laura's, prevents a feel-good ending to *The Way It Ends*, but the story, nonetheless, is deeply satisfying, celebrating a legacy of tolerance, patience, and understanding that constitutes the basis of the talking cure and the writing cure, psychoanalysis and literature.

Works Cited

Balsam, Rosemary. "The Sigourney Award: Theodore Jacobs, MD, 2018." www.sigourneyaward.org/recipientlist2019/1/26/theodore-jacobs-md-2018. Accessed March 13, 2023.

Cassullo, Gabrielle and Michele S. Piccolo. "An Interview with Theodore J. Jacobs." *International Forum of Psychoanalysis*, vol. 19, 2010, pp. 240–245.

Greenberg, Jay. "An Autobiographical Fragment." In Salberg, Jill, editor. *Psychoanalytic Credos: Personal and Professional Journeys of Psychoanalysts*. Routledge, 2022, pp. 59–69.

Hall, Jane S. "Review of *The Possible Profession*." *Psychoanalytic Quarterly*, vol. 84, 2015, pp. 495–499.

Jacobs, Daniel. "Blanche, Stella, Tennessee and Rose: The Sibling Relationship in *A Streetcar Named Desire*." *Psychoanalytic Study of the Child*, vol. 61, 2006, pp. 320–333.

Jacobs, Daniel. "Tennessee Williams: The Uses of Declarative Memory in *The Glass Menagerie*." *Journal of the American Psychoanalytic Association*, vol. 50, 2002, pp. 1259–1270.

Jacobs, Daniel, Paul David, and Donald Jay Meyer. *The Supervisory Encounter: A Guide for Teachers of Psychodynamic Psychotherapy and Psychoanalysis*. Yale UP, 1995.

Jacobs, Theodore. "Chekhov Was a Doctor." *Journal of the American Psychoanalytic Association*, vol. 69, 2021, pp. 845–847.

Jacobs, Theodore. "On the Question of Self-Disclosure by the Analyst: Error or Advance in Technique?" *Psychoanalytic Quarterly*, vol. 68, 1999, pp. 159–183.

Jacobs, Theodore. *The Possible Profession: The Analytic Process of Change*. Routledge, 2013.

Jacobs, Theodore. "Review of *Blood Brothers: Siblings as Writers*." *Psychoanalytic Quarterly*, vol. 55, 1986, pp. 168–170.

Jacobs, Theodore. "Review of *The Parts Left Out*." *Journal of the American Psychoanalytic Association*, vol. 63, 2015, pp. 395–397.

Jacobs, Theodore. *The Use of the Self: Countertransference and Communication in the Analytic Situation*. International Universities Press, 1991.

Jacobs, Theodore. *The Way It Ends*. International Psychoanalytic Books, 2023.

Jacobs, Theodore. *The Year of Durocher*. International Psychoanalytic Books, 2013.

Lawrence, D.H. *The Letters of D.H. Lawrence*, vol. 2, edited by George J. Zytaruk and James T. Boulton. Cambridge UP, 1982.

Levenson, Lawrence N. "Review of *The Year of Durocher*." *Journal of the American Psychoanalytic Association*, vol. 62, 2014, pp. 359–363.

Robbins, Tara S. "Review of *The Year of Durocher*." *Psychoanalytic Quarterly*, vol. 84, 2015, pp. 261–263.

Williams, Tennessee. *Selected Letters*, edited by A. Devlin and N. Tischler. New Directions, 2000.

Chapter 15

Daniel Jacobs
The Distance from Home

"You must change your life." Daniel Jacobs, the author of the 2019 novel *The Distance from Home*, does not quote Rainer Maria Rilke's iconic injunction that appears at the end of his 1908 poem "Archaic Torso of Apollo," but it describes precisely the predicament of his protagonist, Hannah Avery. The novel begins in 1994, but most of the story occurs 22 years earlier when Hannah, at age 37, decides to journey to Nepal to seek the happiness and self-fulfillment she cannot find at home in New York. Not that Hannah's life was entirely bad when she accepted George Albright's invitation to join him, his wife Pru, and several other middle-aged friends on a trip to Nepal. Hannah was single, still mourning the death of her mother when she was nine. An art curator at the fictional Musée Baudry, Hannah enjoys her work, but it doesn't prevent her from feeling lonely, restless, and unfulfilled. Past relationships with men have not worked out; her boss has recently disparaged her work, and she feels the biological clock ticking. She is looking for someone or something that will help her change her life. Will trekking through the unforgiving Himalayan mountains provide Hannah with that opportunity?

Daniel Jacobs is well known in the psychoanalytic community. He is a training and supervising analyst at the Boston Psychoanalytic Society & Institute and director of the Hanns Sachs Library. He is also director of the Center for Advanced Psychoanalytic Studies at Princeton and Aspen. A coauthor of the 1995 book *The Supervisory Encounter: A Guide for Teachers of Psychodynamic Psychotherapy and Psychoanalysis*, Jacobs has published many articles on psychoanalysis, but *The Distance from Home* is his first novel—a daunting challenge for an octogenarian. "I can write about fictional characters," he told C. Shardae Jobson in a 2019 interview, "and still explore psychodynamics that aren't dependent on patients."

Jacobs holds a master's degree in English and has coauthored a play, *Enter Hallee*, with his wife, the biographer Susan Quinn, the author of *A Mind of Her Own: The Life of Karen Horney*. He has also published psychoanalytic articles on literature. Tellingly, Daniel Jacobs and Theodore Jacobs have written about different playwrights, the former about Tennessee Williams, the latter about Eugene O'Neill, suggesting that neither brother wishes to intrude on the other's literary domain.

Jacobs is not a self-disclosing analyst, but one of his personal revelations is noteworthy. Jacobs describes in *The Supervisory Encounter* how his resistance to some of Melanie Klein's theories can be explained, in part, by a terrifying early childhood experience. Jacobs had long disagreed with Klein's insistence that the infant, struggling with the death instinct, undergoes what Klein calls the paranoid-schizoid position during the first months of life. Jacobs assumed that his objections to Kleinian theory were based on his identification with his admired psychoanalytic teachers who were not Kleinians, but in continuing to muse over his attitude toward the British psychoanalyst, he went for his weekly massage. Referring to himself in third person, he writes: "That day, the masseuse suddenly put her fingers behind his ears on the spots where, at age two, part of his mastoid bones had been removed because of a life-threatening infection." Jacobs then remembered the "long-repressed affects of sadness, anxiety, and helplessness, as well as anger toward his mother, whom he blamed as a toddler for the pain of the surgery, as well as for the separation from her that was inflicted upon him" (119). Self-reflection helped Jacobs realize that Klein's emphasis on the fantasized dangerous mother had hit too close to home. Self-analysis did not convert Jacobs into a Kleinian—he still objected to her developmental theory—but it made him more open-minded about her contributions to psychoanalysis. We can infer from Jacobs's self-disclosure his willingness to rethink his own theoretical assumptions, express publicly his vulnerability, and demonstrate his sensitivity to the traumas of real and fictional people.

A Fascinating Character

The Distance from Home is partly autobiographical. Paralleling Hannah's journey, Jacobs took a similar trip to Nepal with his then 13-year-old son decades earlier, where they trekked for 30 days. "It was such an amazing experience in a culture so different, so far from home," he enthused to Jobson. Jacobs based Hannah on his deceased mother, who was "very loving but couldn't get fully connected," like his protagonist. "Hannah, in particular, has a fear of connection, and I tried to make clear, without being obvious about it, [that that was] based on the loss of her mother." Theodore Jacobs and Daniel Jacobs had the same mother, and it may be significant that the mothers in the brothers' novels, *The Year of Durocher* and *The Distance from Home*, do not come across as entirely present, either because of intense anxiety or clinical depression, as with Jonathan's mother, in the former novel, or early death, as with Hannah's mother, in the latter. A son may grieve as deeply as a daughter over a deceased or emotionally absent mother, but insofar as a daughter is generally more connected to a mother than a son, it is fitting that Hannah is still trying to figure out her life without her mother's guidance.

Hannah is complex, sympathetic, and believable. Jacobs narrates the story through Hannah's point of view, and we trust her perceptions and value judgments. She realizes, from the moment she agrees to travel to Nepal, that the experience may be life-transforming. An authority on seventeenth-century Dutch garden design, she loves paintings because they never change—unlike people, who do. Jacobs knows the art world as well as his brother knows the sports world, and Hannah's judgments about painting are authoritative without being authoritarian. Unlike other curators, she never believes that she knows more about a painting than the artist who painted it. She understands that you must look at a painting for hours before it reveals itself. The same is true for a novel: you need to reflect on it and read it more than once before it reveals itself—though its revelations may change with each rereading and with each reader: the "meaning" of a work is never stable. Indeed, nearly everything Hannah says about painting is true of literature. She is involved in the restoration of art—and as we ponder the novel, we see that she is involved in nothing less than the restoration of her own life, trying to repair the damaged parts of her existence caused by her mother's early death, her father's self-absorption and alcoholism, and her previous boyfriends' lack of understanding. "Only art clarifies things—for a moment anyway" (30), she tells her former lover, the painter Leon Kaminsky, who is eager to resume their relationship in Nepal. The two characters could not be more different. "Loving is so messy," she laments; he opines that the opposite is true: "Love orders things" (62). Part of Hannah's attraction to art is that it gives her the order and control she lacks in her life. Similarly, part of the pleasure of reading *The Distance from Home* is that we see how Jacobs portrays Hannah's pursuit of love and order while trekking through Nepal. She knows that love is not always enough, but without love and self-esteem, she cannot imagine the possibility of happiness.

Jacobs's depiction of a woman's voice contributes to the novel's success. Hannah is aware of the male gaze, remarking about Leon that she hates men's need to "possess a woman, if only with their eyes" (32). When she complains to the museum's director that she has been groped more than once by a trustee, she receives the dismissive response, "Like to put their hands on more than money sometimes" (125). Of all the characters, Hannah is the best reader of others' lives, the most emotionally attuned, and the most gifted with metaphorical language, as when she observes, "My body in a sleeping bag became a larva enclosed by a chrysalis, hanging somewhere in space, hoping to grow wings" (76). She tries to find the best in others while at the same time she is aware of their worst qualities. In Henry James's words, Hannah is one of the people on whom nothing is lost.

Hannah's mother remains an absent presence throughout the novel. There are more than a dozen references to the woman who wasted away from metastatic cancer while her daughter looked on helplessly. Hannah cannot exorcise the image of her mother's harrowing face. "Her eyes seemed to grow bigger and more frightening," Hannah recalls. "They took over my dreams and my waking" (36). She sees the eyes everywhere, including in the paintings that hang in her museum. Anyone who has been bereft will identify with Hannah's anguish. She recalls her mother's illness when, shortly before the end, the dying woman turned away from everyone and said to her husband, about their only child, "She has to go away. I don't want her to know... I don't want her to remember me this way" (135). But this is how Hannah remembers her mother, and the loss is devastating. Hannah refers repeatedly to her dying mother, never her *living* mother: the daughter has *no* positive memories of the woman who brought her into life. Her mother's death has left her with the need for mothering from others, though she has not found anyone, female or male, who can fulfill this hunger. She is aware of this maternal need but perhaps not the extent to which it dominates her thinking, as when, looking at Grace Butler's garden, Hannah says that it "stretched perhaps fifteen yards in each direction before its arms began circling the house like a mother in a bright dress enfolding her child" (154).

Pru Albright plausibly suggests that Hannah's problem with men reflects her fear that love will inevitably end in premature loss. "We all have ghosts haunting us" (26), Hannah tells Leon. Many psychoanalytic readers will immediately think of Hans Loewald's memorable distinction between ghosts and ancestors. "Those who know ghosts tell us that they long to be released from their ghost life and laid to rest as ancestors" (Loewald 29). Hannah contains the spectral traces of her deceased mother, and her challenge is to find a way to transform her mother's ghostly spirit into an ancestor.

The other characters in *The Distance from Home* are convincing, particularly Leon, who evokes Hannah's acerbic wit. Leon's paintings, she remarks, are far better than his lovemaking, which "had that urgent, grabby quality some men never learn to control" (24). Surprised to discover that Leon has been invited to Nepal, she confesses to feeling awkward when meeting former lovers: "finding myself vertical instead of horizontal, talking because there is nothing else for us to do" (3). Leon insists that he has changed, though she still finds him irritating. The non-Jewish Hannah ends her relationship with Leon when she comes across a letter his father, a Holocaust survivor, had written to him. "*How could you do such a thing to your mother? Living with a shiksa*"—to which his son had replied, "*Papa. Don't worry. It's not serious*" (24).

The psychoanalyst in the story, Paul Levin, is considered to be "promising" at the New York Psychoanalytic Institute. (Discretion may have prevented Jacobs from associating Levin with his own institute, the Boston Psychoanalytic Society & Institute.) Levin's article "The Candidate's Transference to his Supervisor," perhaps a reference to Jacobs's own *The Supervisory Encounter*, has recently been published in *The Psychoanalytic Quarterly*. Jacobs satirizes the subtle affectations of his profession, as when Hannah observes that Paul "had that sad pensive look that psychiatrists learn to cultivate" (69). Hannah is close to Paul's wife, Miriam, who suffered a breakdown after her first husband died. Marrying Miriam, Paul finds himself unable to compete with the dead: "Perpetual strength and beauty preserved like marble in her memory" (73). Nor can Paul bond with his stepson, Bobby, who accompanies him to Nepal while Miriam remains home with her other child, Zoe. Self-pitying and resentful, Paul believes that Miriam's insistence on a closer family life interferes with his career. It's always significant when a psychoanalyst writes a novel that contains a psychoanalyst; the latter usually reveals the former's attitude toward his or her profession. There's something comic about Paul's overreliance on his analyst to help him figure out his marital problems, as when Hannah asks him what his second analyst, Shapiro, thinks about Paul's marital situation:

> He shrugged. "He won't answer. Just keeps mentioning Odysseus. I've read *The Odyssey* three times since my analysis began and I still don't get it. 'What are you trying to tell me?' I ask. You know what he says? 'When you've answered that question, you'll be home.' Everyone says he's the best. My first analyst was nice, a good woman, but limited. I think maybe I married Miriam because I couldn't marry her. But she wasn't rigorous. Gave advice instead of interpretations. I don't know how she got as far as she did." (*The Distance from Home* 73)

When Hannah tries to cheer Paul up, reminding him that psychoanalysis is a profession, not a business, he testily responds, "Tell that to Dr. Shapiro. He just raised his fee. Sixty dollars an hour to hear myself talk. And then he starts again with his Odysseus shit" (78). To make matters worse, Paul is obsessed with his wealthy patient, Martha Klingman, who pursues him, clingingly, with his ambivalent approval, to Nepal to have an affair. Paul becomes a comic figure, swearing each person to secrecy while making a spectacle of himself in the throes of countertransference love. Hannah warns Paul about his boundary violation, reminding him of the dire consequences: "oxygen deprivation was clouding his judgment" (131). Once she arrives in Nepal, Martha sleeps with Leon, to Paul's mortification, and he finally discovers the meaning of Shapiro's veiled analytic statement: "she is my inner Circe" (215).

Hannah sounds like a psychoanalyst herself, working in the tradition of contemporary American ego psychology, when she explains the many infidelities of George Albright, director of cosmetic surgery at Lenox Hill Hospital for 30 years.

> If Pru could have seen his sexual behavior, as I had, as a kind of congenital deformity, a persistent malformation of self-regard, she might have understood that his behavior had nothing to do with whether he loved her or not. That his stunted ego development took the form of a constant need for reassurance that no honest marriage could provide was sad, as was the moral dwarfism that grew from it. (92)

But it's unlikely that any explanation, psychoanalytic or otherwise, would have made Pru less embittered.

Pemba Golu

During the trek, Hannah falls ill from dysentery and must return to Kathmandu with her Sherpa guide, Pemba Golu, a man radically different from anyone she has known. Jacobs succeeds in capturing Pemba's otherness, including his Eastern mysticism;

his devotion to the desperate plight of the Nepalese people, on whose behalf he has become a revolutionary; and his indifference to materialism. Jacobs may have chosen his character's name for its closeness to the word *penumbra*, defined by Merriam-Webster as a "space of partial illumination (as in an eclipse) between the perfect shadow on all sides and the full light" or as a "shaded region surrounding the dark central portion of a sunspot." Pemba is the visionary figure in the novel, recognizing and embodying truths to which the other characters are blind. Running his hands along poppy pods, he instructs Hannah how to set the seeds free: "If lucky, seeds find home and marry ground" (106). Is this a foreshadowing of a future relationship and their child together? Pemba offers wisdom that one cannot find in the novel's psychoanalyst—or in any other character. Pemba knows that Leon "Need balance with self" (125). Attuned to mythology, folklore, and spirituality, he often speaks in parables, as when he explains to Hannah what makes a mountain angry: "Wanting only, no giving" (97), a life lesson she takes to heart. Everyone suffers, he reminds her, suffering caused by wanting. Sometimes he speaks like a philosopher, as when he says, "Easier to climb hundred mountains than know own heart" (128). Pemba's eyes convey warmth found in none of the other men. He accepts the cultural tradition of arranged marriages, which are often more successful than marriages based on romantic passion. "Love not something need to marry. Grow with man and woman when live together, have children, when eat from same plate" (105).

Psychoanalysis and Buddhism do not appear to be a likely marriage, yet the dialogue between them has a long history, as Jeremy D. Safran points out in his 2003 edited volume, *Psychoanalysis and Buddhism*. Safran, a Canadian-born psychoanalyst (1952–2018) who practiced Buddhism, acknowledges, however, that the psychoanalysts interested in this dialogue have been outside the mainstream of analytic thinking. The 19 contributors to *Psychoanalysis and Buddhism* are all psychoanalysts representing diverse theoretical approaches to verbal therapy. Despite Freud's fierce hostility to religion, Safran maintains that psychoanalysis is a "secular form of spirituality," one that functions to "fill the void that was once filled by religion" (2). Buddhism does not demand religious faith, Saffran suggests, and it represents a system of healing, as is psychoanalysis. The goal of Buddhism, Safran adds, is not one of transcending worldly experience but rather "one of finding a wiser way of living within it" (12), like psychoanalysis. Although Buddhism represents a wide variety of different practices and beliefs, like psychoanalysis, the Buddha is generally not seen as a divine figure but as a human who "became enlightened through his own efforts, and who serves as a model for other spiritual seekers" (16)—again, like Freud, who is viewed by psychoanalysts as a man who became enlightened through his self-analysis and who serves as a model for his disciples. *Psychoanalysis and Buddhism* highlights the continuing struggle with mortality, helping its adherents come to terms with suffering, dying, death, and loss, the existential issues that lead Hannah to Pemba.

Pemba represents the Middle Way in Buddhism, a pathway between the extremes of ascetism, on the one hand, and hedonism and sensualism, on the other. He never speaks about the cycle of death and rebirth, reincarnation, or karma, central aspects of Buddhism. He does imply, however, freedom from craving. While many Buddhists practice strict detachment from all earthly concerns, Pemba remains attached to people; hence, his relationship with Hannah. She has an idealizing relationship with Pemba, viewing him as the embodiment of wisdom, selflessness, and humility. He is mystical not in the sense of wanting to transcend reality and merge with a godlike creator, as we saw with Kristeva's Saint Teresa, but in his harmony with the cosmos. Pemba recognizes that the only constant is change, and while Hannah does not return to New York prepared to practice Buddhism, she has learned a new mindset, including mindfulness, that enables her to practice a more authentic way of living.

Learning English from a guidebook, Pemba speaks with Hemingwayesque terseness. In creating Pemba's singular dialogue, Jacobs avoids the use of definite and indefinite articles along with adverbs, adjectives, and contractions. Pemba rarely uses the pronoun "I," suggestive of his lack of ego. His language is highly stylized; no one learns to speak this way from a guidebook. He never uses an extraneous word. The economy of Pemba's speech reveals the limitations of language, the difficulty of expressing the ineffable nature of reality. If style is the person, Pemba's simple speech reveals the absence of contradictions or qualifications in his thinking. The words Hannah reads in a guidebook about Buddha—"*By seeking enlightenment, we rise above what's dark and muddy in our lives*" (88)—represent Pemba's own beliefs. He is a dark enlightener, as was Freud.

In two of the novel's most evocative sentences, Hannah explains her attraction to Pemba, a man who is not particularly handsome. "His rutted face contained the mountains I'd climbed, the rivers, however terrifying, I'd crossed. I saw in him, too, the things I'd missed, that I'd not had the strength to face" (150). Pemba is willing to make sacrifices for his people, including his life, if necessary, and he embodies an awareness of social and political injustice that separates him from the other characters. Pemba inspires Jacobs's most metaphorical language; in no other man or woman in the novel do we see the inseparability of character and setting.

Dark desire never tortures Pemba, as in Julia Kristeva's portrait of Saint Teresa. Nor is he a riven character, as is Teresa; rather, he embodies a conflict-free identity that is difficult for Western readers like me to imagine. Pemba may strike some readers as too good to be true, but Jacobs doesn't minimize the cultural differences that separate the Sherpa's world from Hannah's. How can she live with a man who feels comfortable only when he is trekking? Marriage to Pemba is unrealistic, but when Hannah becomes pregnant with his child, she decides to keep it. "May is the name her father and I agreed upon, though she was born in August" (11). May remains Hannah's miracle child, giving her life meaning and purpose. The story ends in 1994, Hannah fulfilled in work and love, having changed her life. She and May remain connected to Pemba, who has married and has a daughter of his own, who often sees her half-sister. Tellingly, we see Pemba's impact on Hannah but not her impact on him. The influence is not mutual. She has changed; he has not.

The Distance from Home is a travel or quest novel, conjuring up the spirit of *The Odyssey*. As Barbara Stimmel observed in a laudatory review, *The Distance from Home* "carried me to far-flung places, yet is written from a familiar perspective" (144). One of the novel's many surprises is the limited value Jacobs attaches to psychoanalysis. Early in the story Hannah relates a recurrent dream that she has difficulty interpreting:

> *I am a girl of seven or eight running down a long hall. Perhaps in a hospital or school. Doors on either side. Some of them open. I seem to be looking for something or someone, but there is no one about. I push open a door and enter a room where I see a bed with someone lying in it. The body is covered with a sheet as if it were a corpse. I pull back the sheet and Leon smiles up at me. I scream and run away. I look behind and it is not Leon but my father who is chasing me.* (65)

Hannah has narrated the dream to many analysts, and Dr. Grossbart, "the best of them," interprets it as meaning that she is running away from the various men in her life, beginning with her father. The interpretation makes sense to her, but she sees another meaning: she is running away from analytic treatment. Both interpretations may be correct, along with a third: the corpse in the bed is her deceased mother, whom she has been remembering and searching for her entire life, a ghost who can't be replaced by a man. Memory is related to both loss and resilience, as Jacobs remarks in a 2002 essay on Tennessee Williams. Declarative memory, by which Jacobs means the system that provides for the conscious recollection of facts and events, "is paradoxical in that it resurrects and keeps alive in the present what is dead and gone forever." Yet at the same time, Jacobs adds, "we often create the memories we need in order to maintain psychological resilience and mental health" (1264–1265). Hannah's maternal memories affirm love, loss, and recovery.

The Novel's Spiritual Power

The Distance from Home is an absorbing, skillfully crafted novel worth rereading. Jacobs is at home in many different worlds: the high culture of museum studies; the rugged Himalayan mountains that span six countries; the turbulent political history of Nepal; and the teachings of Buddha. The story evokes the essence of Eastern mysticism in ways rarely seen in psychoanalytic fiction. Psychoanalysts do not often write novels with the spiritual power of *The Distance from Home*. Jacobs's language rarely disappoints. Daniel Jacobs is not a jokester, like his brother, but the novel contains moments of droll humor, as when Grace Butler tells Leon, who refuses to release the hand she politely extends to him, "It's the one I count upon for spreading manure" (146). I especially enjoyed Hannah's thoughts upon hearing the museum director's secretary saying on the telephone, "Office of the director. Whom shall I say is calling?" Hannah's correction? "I keep telling her it's 'who,' but it doesn't sink in" (21). Woe is I, the grammar police might respond in agreement with Hannah's correction. But Hannah and Jacobs have mastered more than grammar in this well-wrought novel. Nepal comes alive in the story, and we can see why so many people trek there each year in search of transcendence.

The novel's suggestive title has several meanings. Traveling thousands of miles from home gives one a greater perspective on one's past, present, and future homes. Hannah will always associate home with maternal absence; nevertheless, the distance from home has allowed her to overcome traumatic loss. Hannah knows that home is both a geographical and psychic place, and her odyssey has been life-transforming. Freud connected the uncanny with returning home, metaphorically, to frightening ideas that lead us back to what is long known and familiar. Jacobs shows us that Hannah can return home not sadder but wiser, ready to rebuild her life. There's nothing sentimental about Hannah's discovery that there is no place like home.

Not everything in the story works for me. The novel opens and closes with the suicide of George Albright, the plastic surgeon who has organized the trip. Is Jacobs commenting on the despair of a doctor who attends to the surface details of the body rather than more serious medical problems? Does George kill himself because of depression? We don't know. Another of Hannah's previous lovers, Frank Hobart, is haunted by the suicide of a high school friend. For whatever reason, suicide remains on Hannah's mind. Pemba functions as an idealized parent to Hannah, as when she tells him, "I feel I've known you since I was a child. How can that be?" (150). An aura of saintliness surrounds his character, perhaps because of the absence of doubt in his devotion to ending the suffering of his people. Pemba's commitment to revolutionary political change, through force, if necessary, frightens Hannah—and perhaps readers: "To kill system," he rationalizes, "need kill people sometimes. People are system" (174). Some of Hannah's inner musings during sex seem strained, as when she says about having sex with Leon, "At last, he placed me on him and I rode us where we needed to go" (54). But these are quibbles.

What I found most intriguing about *The Distance from Home* is its insight into the lifelong impact of maternal loss on a daughter. Hannah has always been afraid of becoming a mother, fearful of the ghost haunting her life, but at the end the phantom has been transformed into an ancestor with whom she can live. While reading *The Distance from Home*, I was reminded of Hope Edelman's bestselling 1994 study *Motherless Daughters: The Legacy of Loss*. Edelman was 17 when she lost her mother in 1981, an era she describes as the dark ages of grief, when mourning was not discussed outside of a therapist's office. Citing Adrienne Rich's observation from *Of Woman Born*—"the loss of the daughter to the mother, the mother to the daughter, is the essential female tragedy" (Rich 237)—Edelman interviewed 92 motherless women in person and surveyed 154 by mail. Her conclusions were striking.

> More than three-quarters of the motherless daughters interviewed said they're afraid they'll repeat their mothers' fates, even when the cause of death has no proven relationship to heredity or genes. Ninety-two percent of the women whose mothers died of cancer said they feared the same demise either "somewhat" or "a lot." (Edelman 219)

And yet, more positively, Edelman remarks that throughout history, early mother loss has acted as a catalyst for a daughter's later success. The key, Edelman adds, is the need to work through grief. "Some psychiatrists see mourning and creativity as the perfect marriage, with the thought processes of one neatly complementing the other" (265). Daniel Jacobs is presumably one of these psychiatrists, and he demonstrates in *The Distance from Home* how Hannah's creativity—her devotion to art and to her daughter—enables her to come to terms with maternal loss and find the fulfillment she deserves.

Writing *The Distance from Home* allowed Daniel Jacobs to narrate a story that he longed to tell. To my knowledge, the Jacobs' brothers have not publicly acknowledged each other's help in writing their first novels; nevertheless, *The Year of Durocher* may have been an inspiration behind *The Distance from Home*. Reading *The Distance from Home* in light of Theodore Jacobs's writings, one sees certain biographical similarities. Paul's reference to Hannah about a patient who "forgets to sign the checks she gives me" (71) recalls Theodore Jacobs's similar observation about his father first in *The Possible Profession* and then about Jonathan Manheim's father in *The Year of Durocher*. Is it significant that the protagonists of both novels do not have siblings? If so, perhaps this suggests the novelists' unwillingness to imagine sibling rivalry, a subject that might be too close to home. Both novelists show the collision of past and present in their characters' lives. Both novelists know how their characters take on qualities of their parents, as Hannah says about her mother: "I'm more like her than I knew" (191). Theodore Jacobs would likely agree with Grace Butler's statement, "Wellness is the ability to float" (159). Jonathan finds wellness on and off the basketball court; Hannah finds it by trekking, a metaphor of the creative process. "Writing a novel is like climbing a mountain," Daniel Jacobs told Jobson. "It's a different kind of trek and the fact that one has accomplished it gives great satisfaction." Readers will feel the same way.

Works Cited

Edelman, Hope. *Motherless Daughters: The Legacy of Loss.* Delta, 1994.
Jacobs, Daniel. "Blanche, Stella, Tennessee and Rose: The Sibling Relationship in *A Streetcar Named Desire*." *Psychoanalytic Study of the Child*, vol. 61, 2006, pp. 320–333.
Jacobs, Daniel. *The Distance from Home.* International Psychoanalytic Books, 2019.
Jacobs, Daniel, Paul David, and Donald Jay Meyer. *The Supervisory Encounter: A Guide for Teachers of Psychodynamic Psychotherapy and Psychoanalysis.* Yale UP, 1995.
Jacobs, Theodore. *The Year of Durocher.* International Psychoanalytic Books, 2013.

Jobson, C. Shardae. "Local Author Gets Some 'Distance.'" www.wickedlocal.com/story/brookline-tab/2019/07/01/local-author-gets-some-distance/4789548007/. Accessed May 28, 2023.

Loewald, Hans. "On the Therapeutic Action of Psychoanalysis." *International Journal of Psychoanalysis*, vol. 4, 1960, pp. 16–33.

Quinn, Susan. *A Mind of Her Own: The Life of Karen Horney*. Summit Books, 1987.

Rich, Adrienne. *Of Woman Born*. Norton, 1986.

Rilke, Rainer Maria. "Archaic Torso of Apollo." *Ahead of All Parting: Selected Poetry and Prose of Rainer Maria Rilke*, translated by Stephen Mitchell. Modern Library, 1995.

Safran, Jeremy D., editor. *Psychoanalysis and Buddhism: An Unfolding Dialogue*. Wisdom Publications, 2003.

Stimmel, Barbara. "Seeing the World: Now and Then, Without and Within." *Journal of the American Psychoanalytic Association*, vol. 71, 2023, pp. 141–149.

Part V

Short Fiction

Chapter 16

Merle Molofsky
Necessary Voices

Long interested in the arts, Merle Molofsky was 28 when she wrote *Streets 1970*, her thesis in fulfillment of an MFA in creative writing at Columbia University, where she studied with Hortense Calisher, Anthony Burgess, and Jack Gelber. She then took a playwriting course with Gelber and adapted two chapters from her novel-in-progress for the stage. Gelber produced and directed the play, *Kool-Aid*, in a four-day workshop production at the Forum Theater of Lincoln Center in 1971. Gelber cast a young upcoming actor in a supporting role who had recently made his first feature film, *Mean Streets*. Gelber told Molofsky that the film would launch the career of the greatest film actor of his generation—Robert de Niro. It took 44 years before *Streets 1970* was finally published, in 2015, but during this time Molofsky continued writing, penning two volumes of poetry, *Ladder of Words* and *Mad Crazy Love*, both published in 2011. The following year she received the NAAP (National Association for the Advancement of Psychoanalysis) Gradiva Award for Poetry. Her collection of short fiction, *Necessary Voices*, appeared in 2019.

Our careers intersected in the early 1980s when we were both studying at the NPAP (National Psychological Association for Psychoanalysis) Training Institute, the first non-medical psychoanalytic institute in the country, founded in 1948 by Freud's disciple Theodor Reik, on whose behalf Freud had written *The Question of Lay Analysis* (1926). Like nearly all the students at NPAP, Molofsky was studying to become a clinician, while I was studying to deepen my understanding of psychoanalysis for my teaching and research. Molofsky has been active in New York's psychoanalytic community as both educator and administrator while at the same time being in private practice. She was the former dean of training at NPAP and former director of education at the Institute for Expressive Analysis. She is on the editorial boards of *The Psychoanalytic Review* and *The International Journal of Controversial Discussions*, and she is on the advisory board of the Harlem Family Institute, a multicultural psychoanalytic training institute that provides affordable therapy in neighborhood schools and community centers. Full disclosure requires me to say that Molofsky has reviewed two of my books, *The Talking Cure: Literary Representations of Psychoanalysis* (1985) and *Confidentiality and Its Discontents: Dilemmas of Privacy in Psychotherapy*, coauthored with Paul W. Mosher (2015).

Streets 1970

Streets 1970 is an experimental novel that presciently anticipates the current opioid crisis. The characters are heroin addicts who live in New York City. The structure of the novel is deliberately a-chronological: the main character, Douglas, dies of an overdose in the opening chapter but returns to life in later chapters. Two Zen monks from the thirteenth century appear and, toward the end, Dionysus and Jesus. The language is alternately realistic, gritty, and lyrical. The novel is as philosophical as it is psychoanalytic, raising questions about good and evil, the nature of time, the phenomenon of pain, and the possibility of rebirth. Molofsky observes her leading protagonists without judging or condemning them. Douglas dreams he is Jesus Christ, but Three Fates, "a mad crone, a dusky Madonna, a flippant whore" (130), disabuse him of this illusion. *Streets 1970* is metafiction; she frequently addresses the reader to emphasize the hazards of reading, as Douglas does at the end of the story when he compares himself to Shakespeare's Shylock: "Hath not a fictional character eyes; if you prick him he bleeds. If you prick him with the right stuff, he gets high. Your hands are bloodstained" (175). The novel's "very rawness and refusal to yield a morsel of squishy empathy," Tony Pipolo wrote in *The Psychoanalytic Review*, "is what renders it authentically compassionate" (5–6).

Streets 1970 was written before Roe v. Wade, the landmark decision of the US Supreme Court in 1973 that guaranteed a woman's freedom to have an abortion. Molofsky first began writing about abortion in *Streets 1970*, in which several black women share their harrowing experiences. "When I had that shitty abortion you think I didn't feel something?" asks Gloria petulantly. Although she speaks triumphantly about having had five abortions, beating Doreen, who has had three, Gloria recalls one ghastly story in particular. "When I awoke the doctor was standing over me grinning, waving a tiny mess of blood around in a plastic bag" (32). Gloria continues to have nightmares about the event, the worst part of which occurred when the doctor tossed the fetus into an empty garbage can. Another woman, Mona, mentions a cousin who had an abortion: "they had to take her whole insides out. Eighteen and they took her whole insides out. She's never gonna have kids. And she's like an old lady. Her cunt's all dried up" (20).

Necessary Voices

It may or may not be accidental that Miriam is also 18 when she has an abortion in the first and longest of the seven stories in *Necessary Voices*, "Miriam 1960." It's unlikely that Molofsky suspected, while writing *Necessary Voices*, that the Supreme Court would overturn Roe v. Wade, in 2022, but as a consequence, reading "Miriam 1960" becomes more unsettling.

Molofsky captures in a work of fiction what could not be conveyed in a case study. Born to Jewish parents in 1942, Miriam's greatest ambition is for a man to marry her, a goal characteristic of many young women at the time. Distressed when she realizes she is pregnant, by her boyfriend at the time, Barry, Miriam recognizes the impossibility of giving birth to an illegitimate child. Had she done so, her parents would have been disgraced, deepening her own humiliation. "Abortions also meant horror stories in the newspapers," the third-person narrator tells us, "complete with every gruesome detail" (3). Miriam's abortion is not reported in the newspaper, but Molofsky offers us one gruesome detail after another in an effort to authenticate the story. One senses that she wrote "Miriam 1960" around the time she wrote *Streets 1970* because some of the sentences are similar, such as the following about another woman in "Miriam 1960": "After a bungled abortion, her insides were so mangled that she could never have children" (3).

One of the most chilling aspects of "Miriam 1960" is the response of the men she encounters in her efforts to receive an abortion. They see her not as a young woman *in extremis*, overcome by shame and fear, but as an opportunity for quick sex. The men respond to her as if she is promiscuous, which she is not—though even if that were true, it would not change the situation. Before turning down her request because she is unmarried and under 21, a male physician offers to "teach her" how to have sex without becoming pregnant. Another man, Mr. Todd, offers to have sex with her before driving her to an abortionist. "Well, lots of girls like to make a little love before they go through with this. It'll be your last chance for a couple of weeks. Don't lose out on a good thing now" (13).

After receiving an abortion from a licensed practical nurse who confidently tells her that she has performed five abortions on her own daughter, Miriam, afraid to go home, is driven to her former boyfriend's home, Rob, where she overhears his conversation with a friend, Fred, whom he is helping write an essay on *The Brothers Karamazov*. Rob and Fred quarrel over the meaning of Dostoevsky's story, which Freud believed, as he stated in his 1928 essay "Dostoevsky and Parricide," is the "most magnificent novel ever written" (*SE*, vol. 21, 177). During the conversation, Miriam feels increasingly unwell—and unable to express her sorrow, grief, and anger. The reader is aware of the ironic contrast between the abstract literary discussion of good and evil in the novel and the stark reality of Miriam's situation. Rob's statement that "God created the intellect to be subservient to faith" evokes Miriam's response: "Maybe god [Molofsky's refusal to capitalize the word is significant] created the world so that we could never understand it. Book of Job" (21), suggesting her inability to find religious justification for suffering. It's no accident that Molofsky includes a discussion of *The Brothers Karamazov* in her story. In her 2014 essay "Teaching Professional Ethics in Psychoanalytic Institutes: Engaging the Inner Ethicist," she writes about the Grand Inquisitor chapter of the novel, reminding us of Ivan Karamazov's conclusion that if there is no God, anything is possible. "From a psychoanalytic perspective, we could surmise that his background of childhood abuse and trauma leave him with a powerful desire for revenge" (202). Miriam's trauma similarly elicits her desire for revenge, though she has no way to express it.

Upon returning home, Miriam races to the bathroom and sees herself in the mirror, hardly recognizing the image that stares back at her. The story's pro-choice point of view is never in doubt, but Molofsky doesn't shrink from describing the recognizably human fetus:

> The cracking pain repeated, and she delivered, among a gush of water and blood, a tiny blue fetus, perfectly formed, with miniature fingernails, puckered shut eyelids, tiny nipples on swollen breasts, delicate folds of vulva, strained bow of mouth, frail shoulders and thighs, dimpled clenched fists. (24)

If the reader cannot forget this haunting image, how can Miriam?

During the era of Miriam's abortion, psychoanalysts had written little about the subject. Freud made only one comment about induced abortions, in "The Psychogenesis of a Case of Homosexuality in a Woman" (1920), but it's jaw-dropping: One is "amazed at the unexpected results that may follow an artificial abortion, the killing of an unborn child, which had been decided upon without remorse and without hesitation" (*SE*, vol. 18, 167). Amazed indeed! How could Freud *not* have realized the remorse and hesitation of a pregnant woman's decision to abort her unwanted child, along with the guilt, fear, and anger that often attend such an act?

In a 2001 review of the psychoanalytic literature on abortion, Gina V. Remeikis points out that given the fact that one in five women in the United States has had an abortion—the statistics are now one in four—the minimal discussion of abortion among psychoanalysts is noteworthy. Remeikis, a psychiatrist in Rockville, Maryland, and an instructor at the Washington Psychoanalytic Institute, observes that with the conspicuous exception of Helene Deutsch, who believed that every woman has the right to achieve or renounce motherhood, and who understood the traumatic nature of induced abortions, other psychoanalysts either avoided discussing abortion or contented themselves with analyzing what they believed were the unconscious fantasies, usually Oedipal, surrounding abortion. Additionally, Remeikis reveals the striking contradiction between her observation that abortion has been significant in the lives of many of her patients, on the one hand, and the professional literature that minimizes the psychological consequences, on the other hand. She ends with an honest admission about her countertransference while working with one particular woman. At the time Remeikis maintained what she thought was an attitude of "appropriate neutrality," but she now believes that she "colluded with a patient's denial of what she was actually doing as she contemplated an immanent [sic] abortion; further destructive actions on her part followed" (243).

The countertransference of which Remeikis speaks does not occur in "Miriam 1960," if only because Miriam does not enter therapy, but it can be seen in the hostile physicians, medical students, and nurses who treat her in the gynecological section of the city hospital to which she is taken when she begins to hemorrhage. "Every woman in that room was learning her lesson, that she had done something wrong and she must be punished" (27). Miriam encounters only one compassionate person who treats her, a female Asian intern. "I know how much it must hurt. Your womb is badly infected and must clear up. I really don't want to hurt you" (30). Her kindness stands in marked contrast to the callousness of others in the hospital.

Miriam remembers every detail of her ordeal and places them, mentally, in a file she calls "Later." We are informed, near the end, that despite a botched abortion and a close encounter with death, Miriam marries and, within a span of four years, has three children. The story ends with the narrator—Molofsky herself—speaking in her own voice. "I have told Miriam's story as truthfully as I have been able. I believe that this story is true. I have told this truth as the enduring private holocaust of woman's flesh, the flaming consumption of lives, the purgatory sealed into the meat and hollows of body so that people will know and remember. That is my commitment to story" (34). One can only conclude from this remarkable coda that abortion is a subject close to the author's home. Molofsky writes with testimonial fervor, an example of what Sandra Gilbert calls "writing/righting wrong." Truth telling is the driving force behind the stories in *Necessary Voices*, a moral principle that demands lucidity, veracity, and honesty. Just as the empathic Asian intern warns Miriam of the inevitable pain of treatment, so does Molofsky issue her own injunction to the reader: this story will be difficult to hear. The word *Holocaust* is usually reserved to describe the extermination of 6 million Jews during the Second World War, but Molofsky uses the word to underscore the private horror of her character.

Sometimes art and life converge in eerie ways. While waiting to see the doctor who ultimately refuses to treat her, Miriam glances at magazines in his waiting room that she never dreamed of reading, magazines "of worlds that she did not recognize and of which she knew nothing" (9), including *Vogue*. As I was reading *Necessary Voices*, vacationing with my wife and a friend in an Airbnb in Provincetown, Cape Cod, I saw an issue of *Vogue* in the living room, a magazine I never read. Curious about the coincidence, I opened the magazine, published in November 2022, and, lo and behold, there was an article, "Out of the Dark," by the novelist Mary Gordon, detailing her own abortion story in 1971. Gordon's cautionary tale is uncannily similar to Miriam's. Both stories affirm truth telling, the need to take abortion out of what Gordon calls the scary dark. And Gordon's conclusion is the same one that post-Roe readers experience after completing "Miriam 1960":

> As a mother, mother-in-law, godmother, and retired teacher of beloved students, I am enormously distressed to realize that the dangers I had thought were past are still a present threat. And that it is no easier to "come out" about having had an abortion than it was 50 years ago. Harder, perhaps, because America is a more violent country than it was 50 years ago, and many more Americans are armed with ever more dangerous weapons. (Gordon 132)

The second story in *Necessary Voices*, "Lazarus," imagines what Miriam's life would have been like had she not aborted her child. Wanda is 18 when she became pregnant by a 27-year-old man who wished neither to marry her nor accept the responsibilities of fatherhood. Wanda has the child and names him, over her family's opposition, Lazarus, with its rich biblical meaning. Curiously, Wanda states that she is not Jewish, yet she references the "Christian Bible" rather than the more traditional appellation "New Testament," the term used by Christians, not Jews, suggesting that she is indeed Jewish. But if so, why would Molofsky wish to change this detail? Perhaps to achieve distance from her character? After high school Wanda is forced to work, unable to attend college, yet she is a wordsmith, in love with language. She delights in the provenance of words, including the Old English origins of her name. Her linguistic skills would be the envy of most highly educated people. "I know how to look up words in the dictionary, and I know what definition, and etymology, and derivation, and synonym, and antonym, mean, and I know what root words are" (36). "Lazarus" is under eight pages long and lacks the power of "Miriam 1960," yet both stories, companion pieces, depict similar young women, each sturdy and on her own, each choosing the best solution to a life-transforming dilemma. Despite being penniless and on welfare, Wandy is resourceful and resilient, and like her aptly named baby, she keeps returning from the dead, a secular resurrection that unites her with Miriam.

The next two stories contain young female characters who are in strikingly different situations. "Danila," only five pages long, focuses on a 17-year-old woman who appears to be in a psychiatric hospital or residence, treated by a therapist, Dr. Ernest Wiggins, who worries about whether she is getting better or worse. Danila does not appear to be schizophrenic or autistic, but she lives in a different reality, resulting in being misunderstood by others. She has a pet cat she calls "Shro," short for Schrödinger, one of the fathers of quantum mechanics. Danila is captivated by physics, particularly the idea of quantum entanglement, the mystifying phenomenon in which subatomic particles can be linked to each other even if separated by billions of light-years of space. Danila has read about the Nobel-Prize winning physicist's thought experiment, known as Schrödinger's cat, illustrating how a cat may be simultaneously alive and dead. When Danila's high school physics teacher, Ms. Stanton, has difficulty explaining quantum entanglement to her students, Danila tries to help by offering the example of how her own dual-system cat might be both alive and dead. Ms. Stanton becomes alarmed, concluding that Danila was going to strangle her cat; the teacher's misunderstanding results in Danila being taken out of school and placed in a psychiatric unit. Danila's awareness of quantum entanglement justifies her claim that she lives "in eternity, with all reality, among all the eternalists, and I am just dropping in at this space/time locus point" (47). Whatever Danila's mental health challenges, if any, she is the most spiritual character in *Necessary Voices*, regarding each person as an "emanation of the Divine, and the Divine is that whose center is everywhere and whose circumference is nowhere" (44). Like many of the speakers in *Necessary Voices*, Danila revels in language, suggesting she is a poet. "I will take an image, a metaphor, and intone it, and sing the metaphor song to persons, or to the wind, or to the ocean, or beasts or fowl" (44). She is also a punster, riffing on her therapist's name: "Do you live in a wigwam? Do you wear a toupee? Can you wiggle your ears?" (44).

Significantly, Danila is a voracious reader, referring to Jorge Luis Borges, William Butler Yeats, J.D. Salinger, and Oscar Wilde.

Rosie, in "Reader, I Married Him," is also a bibliophile, as the title's allusion to *Jane Eyre* demonstrates. A middle school art teacher, Rosie is in love with Zen koans, her favorite being, "What was your face before you were born?" (52). Finding herself pregnant by a man named "Ron," she married him, but it turned out to be a mistake; he left her when their child, Roxie, was four, becoming "Do Wrong Ron." Rosie remarries a college teacher and musician, Randy, and the three form a successful musical group, singing folk songs and ballads. "Reader, I Married Him" is the most joyful of the seven stories, and the reader wonders whether Molofsky has modeled her fictional husband on her own husband, the poet, singer/songwriter, conceptual artist, and Taiko drummer Les Von Losberg.

There is no doubt that Molofsky based the unnamed speaker in "I Want to Read, and Write, and Learn" on her own mother, Sima, and maternal grandmother, Mirel. The story opens with the now elderly mother recounting her birth in 1910, in a shtetl in Poland, and then moving to Warsaw shortly before the outbreak of the First World War. The speaker's mother had three more children in Poland, all of whom died of malnutrition. Then, when the speaker was ten, her father immigrated to the United States, "die Goldene Medina," the golden land, where he sent for his pregnant wife and daughter. While traveling by train third class from Vienna to Le Havre, France, where they boarded a ship to the United States, they encountered at one station a group of drunken Polish soldiers who threatened to throw the Jews off the train. "I smell Zhids. That's why it stinks so bad. The dirty Zhids are stinking up the train!" (61). The identical details appear in Molofsky's 2010 extended film review "Trauma, Memory, and Guilt: Ari Folman's *Waltz with Bashir*." After viewing the film, Molofsky recalls a story her mother told her about her Polish childhood, including the frightening details of anti-Semitic incidents on a train. "My mother was terrified that they would be tossed to their deaths" (1033–1034).

Molofsky's statement about Ari Folman's animated 2008 film, describing the 1982 war in Lebanon, is no less true about *Necessary Voices*: "As a work of art, *Waltz with Bashir* serves a therapeutic purpose. It documents the recovery of traumatic memory, the working through of haunting guilt, and the reconciliation of the past with the here and now" (1033). Beginning with Molofsky's depiction of abortion in "Miriam 1960," many of the stories in *Necessary Voices* document the recovery of traumatic memory and the working through of guilt and shame.

Although the speaker in "I Want to Read, and Write, and Learn" states that there are a few stories she does not wish to remember or share with the reader, such as what it was like to urinate or defecate on the ship because of the lack of privacy, or the constant seasickness of those traveling in steerage, the lowest category of passenger accommodation on a steamship, she is remarkably forthcoming. Her new home is a vast improvement over Eastern Europe, but it was not perfect. "I learned about the oppression of Negroes, black people stolen from Africa and brought across the Atlantic Ocean to the New World, where they were sold as slaves, where they didn't have any rights, where they were oppressed" (65).

Writing fiction enables Molofsky to imagine her maternal grandmother's lifelong sadness over her three young children's deaths, a tragedy that darkened the rest of her existence despite having two more children in her adopted country. The speaker's mother never looked happy. "Sometimes, she looked so sad, so lonely, so all alone lonely, and I would hug her, and she would hug me, but she had this strange empty look on her face when she hugged me" (68). Maternal loss hovers over "I Want to Read, and Write, and Learn," as it does, to anticipate a later chapter, in Irene Cairo's stories, and one senses even without looking at the authors' names that they are daughters writing about their own mothers and, in Molofsky's story, grandmother. In her review of Elia Kazan's 1963 film *America America*, Molofsky adds a few details about her maternal and paternal roots, stating that her mother became a "social activist, dedicated to civil rights and to providing for the oppressed everywhere" (135), a characterization that also applies to herself.

"I Want to Read, and Write, and Learn" is a paean to the magical power of language. "Words were originally magic," Freud observes in *Introductory Lectures on Psycho-Analysis* (1915–1916), "and to this day words have retained much of their ancient magical power" (*SE*, vol. 15, 17). Molofsky's magical words conjure up the excitement of holding onto old Yiddish customs while learning new traditions in New York City. At the end of the story, the speaker muses over a paradox: how can one be happy to read if every word is full of pain and makes the reader want to cry? Molofsky's story honors the dead while celebrating the living, showing how tears of grief may be tears of joy. She also knows how the act of suffering evokes the art of suffering.

"Street Songs," the penultimate story in *Necessary Voices*, captures the heartbreaking dignity and fierce indignation of a septuagenarian homeless city dweller, "Lightnin'." Regarding himself as the "mayor" of his street, he sets up housekeeping outdoors, blaring music all day and half the night, drinking, and listening to the speeches of the newly deceased Martin Luther King, Jr. "Street Songs" is the least personal story in the volume, and the only one that focuses on a male protagonist, but it reveals Molofsky's commitment to social justice. She dramatizes the clashing perspectives of Lightnin', who against his will is drawn inexorably toward bloodshed; his frustrated neighbors, who recognize that he is going to hurt someone one day; and the police, who alternately try to placate him but then lead him away after he empties his 16 gauge shotgun load of buckshot into a boy and his dog. The story opens and closes with children singing street songs, the last of which highlights two turning wheels, a big one run by faith, a smaller one run by the grace of God, images representing, perhaps, a vision of history that repeats itself in endless violence.

The final story in *Necessary Voices*, "What Are Patterns For?", is the most imaginative and poetic—and the most enigmatic. Eliann, a woman of the early 1970s, dutifully fulfills her many responsibilities as a wife and mother of three young children, but something is missing from her grim life. Indeed, she is a desperate, affluent suburban housewife who wishes for a different existence. A daydreamer, she becomes entranced first by the patterns on her rug, vibrant and alive, and then by the wallpaper in her modest suburban home. At the center of the wallpaper lies a flower that contains a smaller flower, that of a blushing rose. The image first appears in "Miriam 1960": "Miriam shrank into the wall. She became another rosebud on the baroque vine of fantasy flora within the wallpaper" (9). But what was a minor image in the first story of *Necessary Voices* becomes the major image in the last one. Eliann sustains a double vision throughout the story: the demanding external world, to which she is committed out of obligation, and the enchanting inner world of the imagination, a garden of earthly delights, the realm of the blushing rose, with its circean beauty and mythic figures. "Shimmering within the arch, the first rose of creation, wet with the due of paradise, glowed" (94). The scent of roses leads to a bower and a pathway into a prelapsarian Eden of breathtaking plenitude, one she has always mysteriously known and understood, an uncanny world simultaneously familiar and strange. Passing through the bower, the enraptured Eliann finds herself on an exotic island and spies seven figures, wearing white robes, who speak to her in a foreign language she instinctively fathoms. Only women dwell on this island, and while there Eliann learns all the arts created by women. A Queen grants Eliann a private audience, warning her that soon the gateway will close. "One day you will walk away from us once too many a time, through the rose bower, and you will turn to ash upon the threshold, burned by time" (100). Notwithstanding the warning, Eliann reluctantly commits herself to the external world of home and hearth, a practical decision that will forever destroy the possibility of happiness, as the final sentence hints. "In the bleak grey kitchen, without love or reason or beauty or hope, Eliann waited for the rest of the world to need what she knew about what she had lost" (102).

What does this perplexing story mean? Is the Queen an idealized mother forever lost, as a sentence in the last paragraph suggests: "She knew the Queen whose name is never said as she knew herself, knew her as a mother" (102)? The loss of idealized childhood? A rejection of the pleasure principle? If, as I initially thought, "What Are Patterns For?" is about the mythopoetic nature of the imagination, with its possibility of endless delights, why does the story imply an either/or binary rather than both/and? "What Are Patterns For?" reminds me of Charlotte Perkins Gilman's iconic semi-autobiographical story *The Yellow Wallpaper*, published in 1892, about a distraught young married woman seeking to escape from her menacing physician-husband who threatens to send her to S. Weir Mitchell, the American neurologist who treated Gilman with the notorious "rest cure." The wallpaper in Gilman's story becomes a projection screen or Rorschach test of the narrator's growing madness. Molofsky's protagonist also yearns to escape from her husband and children, retreating into the world of the patterned wallpaper, but she never seems "hysterical," as does Gilman's character. Nor does Eliann seem out of touch with reality. "What Are Patterns For?" is deliberately ambiguous, but the speaker is bereft at the end, forever deprived of a transcendent vision that has given her life splendor. And yet, paradoxically, Molofsky succeeds in conjuring this rapturous beauty in the story, achieved by the deft use of alliteration and musicality in the penultimate paragraph: "A melody golden as the hair of young women hovered around the strings of a harp, lingered in the dark hollows of a flute" (102). Whatever the meaning of Molofsky's mesmerizing tale, one cannot reduce the author to her character.

The characters in *Necessary Voices* search for personal meaning and solutions to vexing problems without the help of a psychoanalyst. (The one exception, "Danila," contains a therapist figure who is largely mute.) Nor can one tell from the stories alone that the author is a psychoanalyst. But readers know that Molofsky is a gifted storyteller, attuned to her characters' unconscious fears and desires, their joys and sorrows, their *lived* experience. She offers us insights into her characters' seen and unseen worlds, their spoken and unspoken realities, their known and unknown selves. The seven stories limn the quotidian world with which we are all familiar, but she defamiliarizes that world, placing ordinary characters in extraordinary situations. Molofsky has a particular affinity to characters who are victims, but she knows that they can victimize others, as Lightnin' shows. *Necessary Voices* displays Molofsky's keen moral vision and her humanity, along with her enduring faith in reading, writing, and learning.

Works Cited

Berman, Jeffrey. *The Talking Cure: Literary Representations of Psychoanalysis*. New York UP, 1985.
Freud, Sigmund. "Dostoevsky and Parricide." 1928. *The Standard Edition of the Complete Psychological Works of Sigmund Freud*, translated and edited by James Strachey, vol. 21. The Hogarth Press, 1961.
Freud, Sigmund. *Introductory Lectures on Psycho-Analysis*. 1916–1917. *The Standard Edition of the Complete Psychological Works of Sigmund Freud*, translated and edited by James Strachey, vol. 16. The Hogarth Press, 1963.
Freud, Sigmund. "The Psychogenesis of a Case of Homosexuality in a Woman." 1920. *The Standard Edition of the Complete Psychological Works of Sigmund Freud*, translated and edited by James Strachey, vol. 18. The Hogarth Press, 1955.
Gilbert, Sandra M. *Wrongful Death: A Memoir*. Norton, 1995.
Gilman, Charlotte Perkins. *The Yellow Wallpaper*. The Feminist Press, 1973.
Gordon, Mary. "Out of the Dark." *Vogue*, November 2022.
Molofsky, Merle. *Necessary Voices*. International Psychoanalytic Books, 2019.
Molofsky, Merle. "Review of Elia Kazan's *America America*: A Message for America." *American Journal of Psychoanalysis*, vol. 78, 2018, pp. 126–136.
Molofsky, Merle. *Streets 1970*. International Psychoanalytic Books, 2015.
Molofsky, Merle. "Teaching Professional Ethics in Psychoanalytic Institutes: Engaging the Inner Ethicist." *The Psychoanalytic Review*, vol. 101, 2014, pp. 197–217.
Molofsky, Merle. "Trauma, Memory, and Guilt: Ari Folman's *Waltz with Bashir*." *Psychoanalytic Review*, vol. 97, 2010, pp. 1021–1035.

Mosher, Paul W. and Jeffrey Berman, *Confidentiality and Its Discontents: Dilemmas of Privacy in Psychotherapy*. Fordham UP, 2015.
Pipolo, Tony. "Review of *Mean Streets 1970*." *The Psychoanalytic Review*, vol. 102, 2015, pp. 604–606.
Remeikis, Gionta V. "A Review of the Psychoanalytic Literature on Abortion." *Journal of the American Academy of Psychoanalysis*, vol. 29, 2001, pp. 231–244.

Chapter 17

Richard Reichbart
Curious Stories of Diverse Places

"My experiences play a part in all these stories" (237), Richard Reichbart admits in the afterword to *Curious Stories of Diverse Places*, a collection of short stories, historical fiction, and poems published in 2019. His experiences are indeed varied and fascinating, filled with stunning revelations that do not become apparent until the appearance of his most recent book, *Anatomy of a Psychotic Experience*, published in 2022. Reichbart was born in the Adirondack region of upper New York State in 1943, the only child of secular Jewish parents, both of whom were attorneys. He was close to his maternal grandparents, with whom he lived for the first two years of his life. Growing up in a highly educated family, Reichbart attended Yale College, wishing to become a physician like his grandfather (his grandmother was a dentist), but after graduation, he spent a year at UC Berkeley studying playwriting and acting, cultivating his interest in the arts and humanities. He became involved with Berkeley's Free Speech Movement and was one of 800 students arrested in December 1964 for occupying Sproul Hall to protest the banning of the Congress of Racial Equality from soliciting on campus. Reichbart later enrolled at the University of Minnesota's graduate program in English, again becoming involved in political activity, spending the summer of 1965 as a civil rights worker for the Southern Christian Leadership Council, established in 1957 by Martin Luther King, Jr. The next summer he was Mayor John Lindsay's liaison to Coney Island. Following graduation from Yale Law School in 1968, he worked as a legal services attorney, living on the Navajo and Hopi reservations in Arizona and New Mexico, and representing nine Native Americans in a historic sit-in case at the Office of the Bureau of Indian Affairs (BIA) in Littleton, Denver.

But Reichbart's real passion was psychoanalysis. "As an English major," he writes in *Anatomy of a Psychotic Experience*,

> I had often analyzed character in novels and poetry, and as one who minored in creative writing, I had also created characters in fledgling short stories, short plays, and a novella, but Freudian thought opened up a whole new psychodynamic country for me, as if a scrim had been pulled away on a new (but at the same time familiar) landscape. (52)

He then received his PhD in clinical psychology at the City University of New York. For the past 30 years Reichbart has been a psychoanalyst in private practice in New Jersey. A member of several psychoanalytic associations, he is president of the Institute for Psychoanalytic Training and Research. These unique professional experiences figure into Reichbart's creative writing, as do some of the events in his private life, including the most traumatic event imaginable, the nightmare that terrifies every parent: the loss of a child.

Curious Stories of Diverse Places

That loss, lightly fictionalized in the opening story, "The Cod's Earring," and several of the poems, including, most powerfully, "Poem for Nicole, My Daughter," involved her lifelong disability and eventual death at age 35 from complications of spina bifida, a condition, apparent from birth, that affects the spine and usually results in a drastically shortened life. Only nine pages long, "The Cod's Earring" focuses on ten-year-old Jenny, seated in a wheelchair, who is taken by her unnamed parents to Rocky Harbour located on the west coast of Newfoundland, where they board a small cod fishing boat. As the captain, Gavin, and his mate attempt to lift the wheelchair onto the boat, the father frantically yells, "Don't pick it up by the footrest. It will come off in your hand" (4). The tension in the story is immediately palpable. After the boat returns to shore, Gavin's wife, Mary, asks Jenny why she is in a wheelchair. "I have spina bifida," Jenny explains simply, adding that she has had six operations. "Acchh, it just isn't fair. But you're a beautiful girl, you know, and look at you: such a soulful face" (8). Following the brief conversation, the only time in the story when Jenny speaks, Mary gives her two tiny cod ears to wear as earrings. Jenny appreciates the gift but remains horrified by the way in which Mary has severed and disposed with the cod heads, tails, fins, and scales, images of dismemberment and death that perhaps remind her of her own mortality. As darkness descends, food and beer are served on the beach, and Jenny finds herself feeling alone, wishing to return home to New Jersey.

The most arresting detail in "The Cod's Earring," both for what it reveals and conceals, is that Jenny's father, slightly drunk, has been flirting with another passenger on the boat, a hairdresser named Gazelle. Jenny's mother pretends not to notice, but Jenny is distressed: "she had seen without quite knowing it the flitting shadow of a possible future, in her father's too great attention to the hairdresser. Where she wondered was the solidness she held so dear—what would be rescued from this day?" (11). The implication is that her parents' marriage is in trouble, and this adds to her anxiety over the future. Reading "The Cod's Earring" without knowledge of Reichbart's other writings, one could not infer that he was writing about his *own* family, but in light of four of the poems in *Curious Stories of Diverse Places*—"The Meaning of Cats," about a wheelchair-bound girl who died from her illness, "For Nikki, on Her 19th Birthday," "Let My Hands Be Magical," and "Poem for Nicole, My Daughter," memorializing her death—one sees the biographical connection. By disclosing Jenny's father's seductive behavior in "The Cod's Earring," Reichbart lends himself vulnerable to the reader's criticism while at the same time establishing his honesty and fearlessness as a writer. According to her obituary, Nicole Reichbart died in 2014; like her father, she was a human rights activist.

Truthtelling, however painful or embarrassing, is crucial for Reichbart, as can be seen in the next story, "Dank." One grasps the logic of placing the story after "The Cod's Earring." "Dank" highlights Charlie Kaplan, a balding middle-aged business man living in suburban New Jersey who appears to be in love—or in lust—with an attractive younger woman, Susan, whom he has impulsively invited to join him on a business trip to France. With the insight of a psychoanalyst, Reichbart subtly captures Charlie's ambivalence toward Susan, his wife, Marilyn, and, most important, toward himself. While exploring a cave in Rouffignac, Charlie and Susan had come across a bas-relief of a naked woman, Venus, sculpted onto a wall thousands of years earlier. The nude drawing reminds Charlie of the nude drawings of his mother before she became heavy.

> When he was younger, he had been ambitious for things artistic and intellectual. His mother (he remembered her sometimes with a smoky cigarette smell attached to her like an unseen veil and wet kisses smelling of sickly sweet liquor placed on his childish cheek) had dabbled with one artistic flirtation after another. (17)

What most troubled Charlie was that his mother repeatedly posed nude for various artists; moreover, she often walked around her home in various stages of undress. He recalled his parents often quarreling over her behavior. Charlie sought to please his mother, like the mysterious artists she attracted, but he identifies with his father, a lawyer. The narrator—Reichbart—never uses the word *Oedipal* to describe Charlie's conflicts, but that's what is implied. In marrying his wife, an elementary schoolteacher who gave up her career to raise their two children and now works as a volunteer, Charlie chose a woman, goodhearted but unexciting, who was the opposite of his mother, but he seeks out alluring women like his mother and Susan.

Reichbart sees Charlie more clearly than the latter sees himself. Not that Charlie is entirely blind to his situation. He knows that he married a woman who was the opposite of his mother, but he is only partly aware that his flirtatious behavior with women, behavior presumably linking him to Jenny's father in "The Cod's Earring," represents an Oedipal acting out. Charlie feels wrenching guilt over his many affairs that lead nowhere. He understands that Susan is, in almost every way, temperamentally different from him, but he keeps trying to convince himself that he is in love with her. His feelings wildly fluctuate, and he cannot shake the sense of foreboding that lurks throughout the story. At the end of the tale, the two characters return home, and while Susan's parting words convey hope and optimism—"I love you. Call me"—Charlie is racked by self-hate. "I am so unhappy," he muses. "I have been unhappy for so long" (37), and then bursts into tears.

A therapist can write about a patient like Charlie in a clinical case study, but it is a tribute to Reichbart's storytelling talent that he evokes his riven character in a story replete with evocative images. It is not only the long-neglected castle that Charlie has rented that is dank, along with the cave that he and Susan explore, but also his life, filled as it is with a rotting smell suggestive of a decaying marriage and a dying affair. Charlie can momentarily glimpse himself through Susan's eyes, and what he sees is not reassuring: "his expensive silk tie, his inscribed Rolex watch, his off-putting need to sound like an authority" (16). Significantly, the story's criticisms of Charlie do not extend to Susan; she senses his often insensitive, unkind comments without becoming insensitive or unkind herself. Nor is anything unkind written about Marilyn, whose privacy the author respects. In looking at the profusion of scratches on the cave's wall, Susan says, punningly, "They made their mark," which elicits Charlie's mirthless laugh, wondering whether he will make his own mark. Upon finishing the story, we recognize that Reichbart has made his own mark in penning this disturbing cautionary tale.

Is Charlie's mother a portrait of Reichbart's own mother? Initially, I thought so, especially when I read the paid death notice of Ruth G. Reichbart published in the *New York Times* on March 11, 2007. The 92-year-old woman practiced law with her husband in the firm of Reichbart and Reichbart. There is no mention in "Dank" that Charlie's mother was an attorney, like his father. Nevertheless, what I found most telling about the death notice, almost certainly written by Richard Reichbart, her only child, is the following sentence: "She was a poet, artist, and musician and an outspoken advocate of free speech, environmental concerns and women's rights." She also had her own radio show at Bergen Community College in Paramus, New Jersey. The paid death notice lists Ruth Reichbart's survivors, including her son's companion, Nansie Ross, a clinical psychologist to whom he dedicated *Curious Stories of Diverse Places* and *Anatomy of a Psychotic Experience*. On the basis of this information, I concluded that in many ways, Charlie's mother is a version of Reichbart's own mother: Reichbart went to Yale College as an undergraduate, as did Charlie, but the latter flunked out after a year, which is not true of the former. And yet it is easy for literary critics such as me to jump to wrong conclusions. Mea culpa! Reichbart pointed out to me that he based Charlie's mother on a patient's mother.

> Although my mother was artistic and sometimes less than attentive or practical, she was a rather different character than my patient's mother. It is often strange to weave into stories my personal experiences, yet at the same time to change them: every one of these stories involves just that.

With two parents as attorneys, it's likely that Reichbart felt inclined—or pressured—to become one himself and join (and eventually take over) their law firm. In another story in the volume, "Boxball," the central character, Daniel, is the son of two lawyers who "traveled in intellectual, artistic, and theatrical circles with largely secular Jews such as themselves" (67). And as we shall see, Reichbart writes about his own experience as a lawyer in the longest story in the volume, "The Power of Berry Soup." In *Curious Stories of Diverse Places* he never explains his decision to give up law to begin a second career as a psychoanalyst, but he hints at one reason in his poem "The Lawyer," where he describes how, on the surface, he felt "safe and sane" working in his profession, dressed impeccably (like Charlie in "Dank"), with his "tie coordinated / with his shirt, in pastel shades / of blue or green or mauve; / and silver cuff links understated." His dreams, however, tell another story:

> But when he slept, he loved the cries
> Of enemies, both near and far.
> He knifed, and gauged and bloodied them;
> Cursed fiercely and anatomized. (222)

Reichbart offers a less poetic explanation in *The Paranormal Surrounds Us* (2019): "I increasingly found the actual practice of law intellectually boring and at times ethically tortured" (6).

Fighting for Social Justice

"In Martin's House" records Reichbart's life in the 1960s as a civil right activist. The story is narrated by a black man, Bernard, and it is set in Martin Luther King's home in Atlanta, which he and his family had vacated, either for safety or convenience, in the summer of 1965. The authorial character is a young white man from Manhattan who has traveled to the South to register black voters. He is called "Harry from Minnesota," mainly because he attends college in the North Star state, but the moniker is shortened to "Minnesota." We learn about his life mainly through his italicized inner monologue. Few stories about the civil rights movement interrogate a character's political motivation with the psychological deftness we see in this tale. Analyzing his reasons for traveling to the South, Minnesota reveals that because his mother worked outside the home, he was raised by a black maid, Margaret, who abruptly left his family. "*I had been searching for her eyes in the eyes of the black women I met down South, hoping in some magical unconscious way to find her once again*" (87–88).

Minnesota was in his 20s when he traveled to the South and never mentions having been in psychoanalysis, but his insight into the reasons behind his political activism is impressive. No less remarkable is his candor in acknowledging that as committed as he is to civil rights, he will never fathom what it means to be a black man in the Jim Crow South. Minnesota becomes close with Bernard, almost as if they were brothers, but he knows that when the summer ends, he will return home to his safe, comfortable world. Years later, on a business trip that takes him to the Atlanta airport, Minnesota sees Bernard, and although the meeting is pleasant, each exchanging telephone numbers with the other, they know they will never talk again. Nor will Minnesota see again the black women with whom he has become close, a pattern of abandonment that he traces back to Margaret's sudden departure. *"Had I exacted a terrible revenge,"* Minnesota asks, rhetorically, *"for the loss I had never fully acknowledged, the loss of comfort and connection and love from a black woman?"* (111). Reichbart returns to the question years later in *Anatomy of a Psychotic Experience.*

In a brief note to readers preceding "The Power of Berry Soup," Reichbart states that some of the story is true, including dialogue taken from the transcript of the trial of the Littleton 9, while other parts are fictionalized, albeit true in another way. *"But you be the judge or—perhaps more accurately—be the jury"* (113). The frequent use of the second-person pronoun in the story places us in the jury, forcing us to wonder how we would have judged the defendants. The second-person pronoun also heightens the intimacy between writer and reader. The past comes alive in the story, and Reichbart's vision of American history is haunting; the past repeats itself, returning to the same place, transformed, in ways that are recognizable but heart-wrenching. Reichbart is scrupulously fair to both sides: the white settlers, emblematic of the US government, and the Native Americans, fighting for their land and heritage. Both sides are guilty of atrocities and massacres; many peace treaties, initiated by both sides, resulted in treachery and betrayal, but there is never any doubt where Reichbart's sympathy lies.

"The Power of Berry Soup" opens with a Lakota Sioux creation myth, depicting an old woman cooking wojapi, berry soup, in a large earthen pot. The story then moves backward in time, taking us to Camp Weld in Colorado in 1864, introducing us to two honorable men, Ned Wynkoop and Black Kettle, both of whom desire peace but are betrayed by forces beyond their control. Reichbart chronicles how peace treaties between both sides result in confining Native Americans to smaller and smaller reservations, many of which are not conducive to indigenous life. The story then jumps to 1970 when nine Native Americans are arrested for occupying the building that houses the BIA liaison office in Denver. Reichbart teases out the many ironies and ambiguities of the word *trespass*. "Think of it," writes Reichbart, his voice filled with righteous indignation,

> Native Americans being tried for trespass. Like the fallen dry leaves of autumn, the whites had covered the lands of their ancestors. Occupied them. Built towns. Established boundaries. Made treaties, then each time, after a while, simply broken the treaties they had made in order to get more land, to create homesteads, to build the railroad, to search for gold in the rich earth, to go forth in the manifest destiny of the European races. (132)

The odds of convincing an all-white jury that the Native American defendants were not guilty of trespassing seemed formidable. The key issue was intent, the defendants' motivation in remaining in the building. Mr. Barbarica, the defense attorney, chose a strategy centered around the preparation of berry soup by Nelly

Baker, the mother of a defendant, for the commissioner of the BIA. Insofar as food in Native American culture betokens friendship and respect, Barbarica sought to prove that the intent was welcoming and celebratory, not menacing. But Barbarica then made a lucky rookie mistake, asking a question to which he did not know the answer: the length of time it took to prepare the soup. The prosecutor objected to the question, saying it was irrelevant to the trial, but the judge reluctantly allowed the question. Nelly Baker's answer, five hours, essentially the entire day, moved the jury, which found all nine defendants not guilty, but Reichbart admits that other factors may have affected the trial's outcome, including the number of women, babies, children, and elders who were inside the building earlier in the day. As an attorney and a psychoanalyst, Reichbart knows that motivation is complex and overdetermined. Only in a footnote does Reichbart reveal that he was Barbarica. The story does not end there, however. Reichbart points out that in 2016, Native Americans protested the route of the Dakota Access oil pipeline near their sacred sites. The outgoing American president ordered the construction of the pipeline to cease until the completion of a full review by the Army Corps of Engineers, but the new American president rescinded the order. Reichbart cannot bring himself to name the president, but he sardonically refers to him in the poem "The Populist" as the "flim-flam man with flaxen hair" embraced by voters who "do not know the fate of those / Who choose to hold a monster close" (186). In the notes to "The Power of Berry Soup," Reichbart refers to readers who wish to learn more about the legal aspects of the story, including the larger case, *Morton v. Mancari*, that lay behind the sit-in, to Carole Goldberg's chapter "What's Race Got to Do with It?" in the 2008 case book *Race Law Stories*, edited by Moran and Carbado. Reading the chapter, one sees the constitutional complexities of the case but not the human interest story captured by Reichbart in his notable tale.

Three tales in *Curious Stories of Diverse Places* focus on psychoanalysis. "Praying Mantis" highlights Reichbart's longstanding interest in parapsychology, the subject of *The Paranormal Surrounds Us*, a study of psychic phenomena in literature, culture, and psychoanalysis. Reichbart dramatizes in "Praying Mantis" an analyst's belief in the paranormal and his wife's skepticism. The analyst is writing a book on free associations, which happens to be the title of a four-line poem in *Curious Stories of Diverse Places*. In referring to an exchange between Freud and Romain Rolland, the analyst cites Freud's admission that he has never had an "oceanic experience," that is, a religious-like mystical experience in which the boundary between self and other dissolves. During the heated quarrel, the analyst remarks on the uncanny moments in his life when he has seen a praying mantis, which he interprets as an "omen," but which his wife dismisses as merely a "coincidence," an example of a contradiction within him between his "usually logical self" and his inclination toward "fuzzy, fantastical thinking" (77). Most psychoanalysts have aligned themselves with Freud's secular rationalism rather than with Jung's mystical serendipity or synchronicity, the latter of which Reichbart's analyst endorses. "Maybe we are all connected to the world in ways we do not entirely understand; and our minds and wishes interact with the world or create it in some way" (81). The story ends with the wife giving her husband a framed picture of a grasshopper by Max Ernst that they had seen in a museum, suggesting that although the married couple do not change each other's minds, they can live with their disagreements. "Praying Mantis" is not the only story in the volume that evokes the paranormal. As we saw in "Dank," Charlie and Susan see a pastel of a nude woman in an art gallery that strikingly resembles the bas-relief of a woman who had posed thousands of years earlier in the cave they had recently explored, a "coincidence" over which they repeatedly "marveled" (33). However skeptical readers may be of paranormal phenomena, there is nothing polemical about Reichbart's depiction of "coincidences" in his fictional stories. He asks only that readers remain open to the possibility that, in Hamlet's words to Horatio, there are more things in heaven and earth than are dreamt of in your philosophy.

With its wry humor and nuanced dialogue, "Schnapps" is the volume's most ebullient story. A married couple own a pet Norwegian rat named Schnapps who escapes from his cage and darts into an analyst's office. The young woman, an analyst in training, is listening to a male analysand, a medical research scientist, but the two-year analysis, we are told, seems to be going nowhere. She lets out a muffled scream when she spies Schnapps; the patient jumps off the couch, trying futilely to calm her by saying that the rat is harmless and probably not diseased. But she remains spooked, as the following sentence suggests, perhaps the most inventive one in the volume, fraught with the most ambiguity: "'Out,' she managed, 'Out,' not knowing whom she disliked most at that moment, and not much caring which one left, although as she thought of it, both would have been fine" (161). Amidst the analyst's continued shrieks, the young man opens the door to the waiting room, leaving her alone with Schnapps. "Come back," she cries out plaintively," "Please don't leave me here." Schnapps, unaware of her fright, keeps scurrying around in the office, appearing first between a book on dreams and another on love in the analytic space, and then reappearing between a book on gender and psychoanalytic technique, subjects on which the story comments. Reichbart masterfully captures in the following dialogue the patient's enjoyment of the situation and the analyst's conflict between her rigid professional training and her human instincts. "'I am glad you decided to say more today.' Against all her training advice, she said, 'You, you…' in an accusatory tone, whereupon, after a moment when neither spoke, they both burst into laughter for a long time" (162–163). The next day, her supervisor, a man with a "ponderous authority," reprimands her, claiming she had sabotaged therapy by revealing so much about herself, when the opposite is true. "In fact, it was a turning point and the analysis, which had seemed so bogged down, became infinitely deeper with mutual respect, as if they both recognized that the other was human after all, and ended up being a stunning success" (163). "Schnapps" is a delightful story that should be required reading for all students interested in learning more about the value of self-disclosure in therapy.

The last story in the volume, aptly titled "Termination," has a double meaning: the completion of the character's psychoanalysis, which occurred decades earlier, and the end of his life. Surely it is significant that Reichbart names his dying protagonist "Charles," establishing a link to the self-tormented character in "Dank." The stories are bookends. As in "Dank," "Termination" abounds in images of decay, but it is because of Charles's decomposing body, not because of a wasted life. Much has changed in his life, all of it positive. Charles has led a fulfilling existence, and while lying on his deathbed, he reflects on his devoted wife, Sheila, children, and grandchildren, wondering how they will react to his death. He keeps dreaming about the person who has made his love possible: his analyst. She died more than ten years before the story opens, but she remains an absent presence in his life, the person who saved his life, mainly by listening to him, quietly and patiently, and respecting the analytic process. As close as Charles is with his wife, he cannot share his dreams of analysis with her, which he recognizes, in a single word, as "Strange." We know nothing about her theoretical orientation, but she was no blank screen, silent and detached, as we glean from the following sentence: "his analyst would greet him, just as she always had, with a gentle nod, and he would lie down on her couch again, and he would talk on and on and sometimes he would hear her sensible, warm voice interrupting him—the voice that had seemed to guide him, challenge him, endure him, through all those twists and turns of his tumultuous time with her" (170). Reichbart does not elaborate on this tumultuous time in Charles's life, but he provides us with a few clues about the nature of the analytic sessions. Recalling the time he spent with his grandparents, Charles remembers his mother always reading. "I was so happy to be there with her, even if she seemed to pay no attention to me." "You must be remembering this," his analyst responds, "because you want to remember your mother, even if she was in her own world" (174), a comment that strikes him as exactly correct. The most memorable moment in the story, indeed, in the entire volume, occurs when, in his last therapy session, he expresses his love for her, to which she responds with a heartfelt "Yes":

> Finally, she said, "We've come a long way together." He started to cry. She said nothing.
>
> Then he had difficulty speaking, but, finally, catching his breath, he said, "Thank you, thank you so much. I was so impossible."
>
> "Yes," she said, and she laughed. "And you're welcome."
>
> He waited again. Finally, she said in the same unchanging and kind voice that she always used at the end of a session (even though this was the last one), "And now our time is up." (175)

One cannot imagine a more moving or succinct account, fictional or nonfictional, of the end of a long analysis. Charles realizes that as they gently embrace each other, "in what seemed like a delicate dance," she has become, for a moment, both his mother and wife, a confusion that is part of his complex transference-love for her. Not only has the patient fallen in love with his analyst but she also has fallen in love with him, a non-transgressive analytic love, a phenomenon to which Reichbart calls attention in his admiring review of Sheldon Bach's 2016 book *Chimeras and Other Writings*, where, in Bach's words, "the world becomes enchanted again, just as it was in days of childhood or as we sometimes find in fairy tales" (274–275). Reichbart wisely avoids trying to reproduce this emotionally riveting moment a second time in the brief story, and so when the distraught Sheila returns to the room where her husband has been lying, he is no longer alive. Nevertheless, she bids a silent farewell in the story's last sentence. "'There, there,' she said, patting his silent chest over and over, 'there, there,' as if to reassure him" (175). Charles succeeds in making a "good exit" (171) in life, one that Reichbart, while penning this well-wrought story, must hope will be true in his own life.

Anatomy of a Psychotic Experience

"Don't publish it" (78). Rarely does an author include this unheeded advice at the end of a book, and never, to my knowledge, has a recommendation not to publish appeared at the end of a case study written by a psychoanalyst about *himself*, as we see in *Anatomy of a Psychotic Experience*. To make the recommendation more cogent, it was expressed by an analyst Reichbart greatly admired, Sheldon Bach. But as I suggested at the beginning of this chapter, Richard Reichbart is a fearless writer. Throwing caution to the wind, he has written a book that casts light on his earlier writings, fiction and nonfiction, and in the process, exposes both his vulnerability and resilience.

Anatomy of a Psychotic Experience consists of five sections: an Introduction, in which he refers to a psychotic break and depression he experienced between 1967–1970, when he was between 25 and 27; "The Article," the major section of the book, which contains the original record of this experience, written in 1978 to fulfill a requirement for his master's degree in psychology at the University of Northern Colorado; "Reflections in the Present—50 Years Later," in which he includes aspects of his self-analysis previously omitted; "An Interesting Addendum," further details about omitted information from the 1978 article; and "The Reaction of Psychoanalysts to This Discussion of Psychosis." To give only one example of an omitted detail from the 1978 essay, Reichbart had voluntarily entered an inpatient psychiatric facility for about three weeks in an attempt to remain calm. The main image unifying the book is a gray scrim that is slowly being lifted to reveal a disturbing truth he had not glimpsed earlier.

Unlike most psychotic breaks, Reichbart never experienced hallucinations or delusions, which explains the skepticism of other psychoanalysts who maintain that he suffered from bipolar disorder. But Reichbart stands by his self-diagnosis. During the late 1960s, after his graduation from college, he began struggling with paranoia, intense anxiety, rumination, failure of concentration, and a loss of contact with consensual reality. He later traced these problems to separation trauma experienced in early childhood. His grandfather's death was the precipitating cause of the psychotic break. Incomplete mourning was also the precipitating factor in William Styron's nearly fatal psychological breakdown, as he describes in *Darkness Visible: A Memoir of Madness* (1990); in Styron's case, the early death of his mother created in him, as Reichbart's grandfather's death created in him, a "nearly irreparable emotional havoc" (Styron 79). Styron had no use for psychotherapy or medication; rather, voluntary hospitalization and the passage of time enabled him to regain his health.

One surprise while reading *Anatomy of a Psychotic Experience* was that Reichbart almost failed an important course in college, an organic chemistry lab, necessary for him to attend a top-notch medical school, an event he knew would have disappointed his father. Another surprise was that he did indeed fail a course in law school. He attributes his difficulties in these two courses to his unconscious rebellion against his father's control of his life. It becomes evident that Reichbart identified more closely with Charlie in "Dank" than I had previously realized. Still another surprise was Reichbart's problem of breaking off intimate relationships with women, including a law student to whom he was engaged and a Navajo woman whom he had befriended and then "fairly brutally dropped." He explains this pattern of broken relationships in terms of object relations theory. Instead of a love object leaving him, as with his beloved grandfather's death, he abandoned the love object, thus experiencing the "joy of revenge." He refers in a single sentence to his divorced wife, Paige Hooper-Reichbart, characterizing her as a loving woman whose "humor, warmth and attentiveness" helped him when he was depressed; "unfortunately for both of us years later the relationship did not thrive, but that is another story" (54).

Reichbart does not describe in *Curious Stories of Diverse Places* the nature of his psychotic break he experienced in the 1960s. There are relatively few accounts written by mental health professionals about their own experiences with "madness." In *Mad Muse* (2019), I discuss Elyn Saks's life with schizophrenia in *The Center Cannot Hold: My Journey Through Madness* (2007) and Kay Redfield Jamison's account of living with manic depression in *An Unquiet Mind: A Memoir of Moods and Madness* (1995). Unlike Saks and Jamison, however, who have embraced both medication and psychotherapy for ongoing mental health challenges, Reichbart's crisis slowly ended with psychoanalysis alone. He has no doubt that his two psychoanalysts, both now deceased, saved—and profoundly changed—his life. "You're at the ragged edge" (34), the first analyst told him in 1970, when he was 27. Reichbart came back from that edge as a result of several years of seven-day-a-week therapy. Unlike the "cerebral" and "competitive" first analysis, the second analysis was longer and more emotionally charged. The second analyst was less inclined than the first to make pronouncements, and as a result, "there was more space for the maternal aspect of the transference to develop" (56). Reichbart doesn't name the two analysts in the body of the text, but he acknowledges their help at the end of the book: Jule Eisenbud and Joyce Steingart. Eisenbud (1908–1999) was a classically trained analyst, a member of the New York Psychoanalytic Society & Institute, and a parapsychology researcher who influenced Reichbart's own thinking on the subject. Years after the analysis ended, Eisenbud admitted that he wished he had not been so "hard" on his analysand. Reichbart admired Eisenbud but criticizes him in Appendix A of *The Paranormal Surrounds Us*: "Often Jule ran the risk of seeming to be more interested in acquiring psi data for his own interest than in the patient himself; certainly my own analysis with him suffered from this focus" (211). The second analyst, Joyce Steingart, is the unnamed analyst in "Termination."

One of Reichbart's contributions to psychoanalytic theory, as we have seen in "Praying Mantis," and which he spells out more concretely in *The Paranormal Surrounds Us*, is his belief that "we live and breathe psi phenomena without awareness. It is the sea around us. It is all we know—so integral to how we survive and relate to one another and the world and yet we cannot quite get a hold of it. It is ubiquitous and elusive at the same time" (11). Another contribution, which he learned from his second analysis, is the value of men crying, as can be seen in *Curious Stories of Diverse Places* and in his insightful 2006 essay on *King Lear*, where, in reviewing psychoanalytic studies of men crying, he provides compelling clinical material about two of his patients, "Alan: A Self-Made Man," and "Paul: The Stoic Man." Paul may not be a disguised portrait of Reichbart, but they have much in common. Paul enters psychoanalysis because of severe depression, in part because he was "[a]mbivalently practicing law, a profession he felt his father had forced him to adopt" (1084). Like Reichbart, Paul fears disappointing his father's high ambitions for him; he expresses his anger by "quietly and relentlessly cross-examining the other to show how the person was in the wrong, which inevitably succeeded only in alienating that person rather than extracting an apology, and ultimately provided Paul no emotional release" (1086), traits that recall Charlie in "Dank" and "The Lawyer." Again like Reichbart, Paul "acted in defiance and hatred of his autocratic and financially successful father," trying to please him in an "obsessive internal dialogue" long after his death (1084). In one therapy session, Paul bursts into tears, saying, "I am so unhappy" (1088), the exact words on which "Dank" ends.

In reading Reichbart's stories, poems, and essays, one sees the malleability of character, the extent to which characters can change their lives through insight, determination, and the loving help of others. He has the courage to open himself up and acknowledge his struggles, failures, and eventual successes in love and in work. *Curious Stories of Diverse Places* is so personal and intimate, Luba Kessler laments, that it seems like trespassing to review it. "In fact, knowing that the writer is a colleague psychoanalyst makes reviewing it for readers of a psychoanalytic journal feel like a breach of an unspoken covenant of collegial confidentiality" (237). Yet truthtelling is essential among colleagues and friends, as Kessler realizes, and she was deeply impressed with *Curious Stories of Diverse Places*, as I am. The recurrent theme of his storytelling, she suggests in the concluding sentences of her review, is "Learning, and unlearning in order to learn. What could be more psychoanalytic?" (237). Or as Reichbart writes in his poem

"In Answer to a Yale College Reunion Quest for Information on My Life"—the title is almost as long as the poem itself!—"Protect me still from hale, hearty and well-met; / 'I have so much further to go, to unlearn yet'" (227). Reading *Anatomy of a Psychotic Experience* is even more shocking, as Nancy McWilliams confesses in the foreword. "I would never have guessed, before he wrote about his personal journey, that psychotic demons had tormented him to the degree that this compelling account portrays" (xviii). Reichbart's expansive self-disclosures reveal, in Nietzsche's words, that he is human, all too human, a quality as necessary in a creative writer as in a psychoanalyst.

Works Cited

Berman, Jeffrey. *Mad Muse: The Mental Illness Memoir in a Writer's Life and Work*. Emerald, 2019.

Jamison, Kay Redfield. *An Unquiet Mind: A Memoir of Moods and Madness*. Knopf, 1995.

Kessler, Luba. "Review of *Curious Stories of Diverse Places: The Cod's Earring, the Click of the Reindeer, and Other Adventures and Even Some Poems*." *Psychoanalytic Psychology*, vol. 38, 2021, p. 237.

Reichbart, Richard. *Anatomy of a Psychotic Experience*. Foreword by Nancy McWilliams. International Psychoanalytic Books, 2022.

Reichbart, Richard. *Curious Stories of Diverse Places: The Cod's Herring, The Click of the Reindeer, and Other Adventures and Even Some Poems*. International Psychoanalytic Books, 2019.

Reichbart, Richard. "On Men's Crying: Lear's Agony." *Journal of the American Psychoanalytic Association*, vol. 54, 2006, pp. 1067–1098.

Reichbart, Richard. *The Paranormal Surrounds Us: Psychic Phenomena in Literature, Culture and Psychoanalysis*. McFarland, 2019.

Reichbart, Richard. "Review of *Chimeras and Other Writings: Selected Papers of Sheldon Bach*." *Psychoanalytic Quarterly*, vol. 88, 2019, pp. 641–646.

Saks, Elyn R. *The Center Cannot Hold: My Journey Through Madness*. Hyperion, 2007.

Styron, William. *Darkness Visible: A Memoir of Madness*. Random House, 1990.

Chapter 18

Christopher Gibson
Tales from the Unconscious

"I started writing stories to illustrate psychoanalytic ideas when I became aware that I *thought* about clinical papers more than I *felt* them" (xi). So begins *Tales from the Unconscious*, Christopher Gibson's 2021 collection of fictional vignettes. Before becoming an analyst, Gibson was a headmaster of a school for children and adolescents with emotional problems. After receiving his psychoanalytic training in London, he worked at Kings College and then moved to Gothenburg, Sweden, where he is a psychoanalyst, child analyst, and training analyst of the Swedish Psychoanalytical Association. The dozens of clinical vignettes in *Tales from the Unconscious*, most only a few pages long, highlight the vagaries of our inner lives. Gibson's conviction that stories can reach the heart more effectively than abstract theoretical explanations motivated him to share these vignettes with his readers. He created the didactic stories, evoking the tradition of Irvin Yalom's "teaching novels," to illuminate different aspects of psychoanalysis for beginning students and clinicians.

A brief background of *Tales from the Unconscious* may be helpful. In 1996, Gibson coauthored, with Patricia Hughes, two articles in *Psychoanalytic Psychology* about the need to improve the quality of medical education in the psychotherapy department of a teaching hospital in the NHS, the UK's publicly funded healthcare system. Students had complained bitterly about the poor quality of their psychotherapy education. Gibson and Hughes decided to create a syllabus relevant to students' present and future needs. Believing that psychotherapy becomes more understandable if it gives students a new slant on a familiar subject, the coauthors came up with a stimulating approach. "If the students can identify constructive and destructive interactions between patients and students, or even between teachers and students, and begin to think about why people behave in different ways, they are beginning to think about personality, about anxiety, and about how we defend ourselves when we become anxious" (Hughes and Gibson, 1996, Part I, 6). The articles end with the coauthors' determination to use more active pedagogical techniques to enhance psychotherapy education. Years later, this novel approach to psychotherapy education inspired Gibson to write a collection of fictional stories about patient–therapist interactions.

Tales of the Unconscious is broken into three sections: Expectations, Provocations, and Audacities. Of the three, Audacities is the most compelling. Gibson admits that he wrote this section in response to a "friend and colleague who, in her better moments, would have laughed heartily at these stories but was unable to find her way out of her last depression. For her, mental health was an objective too far removed." Gibson does not explicitly use the word *suicide* to characterize her death, but the next sentence refers to the "culture of silence that surrounds suicide" (272). Gibson enters into the minds of people who are in a suicidal crisis, poised at the abyss. Some turn back, aided through the interventions of "guardian angels," while others leap into the heart of darkness.

The first vignette in Audacities may refer to Gibson's colleague, albeit in highly disguised and sometimes confusing form. "The Interpreter" focuses on a countertransference enactment, a therapist's inability to remain safely detached from a patient's anguish. The story opens with a first-person narrator, George, a psychotherapist who consults for the prison service. George meets Josef, who, along with his mother, was abused by his father. As a child, Josef felt excluded from his parents' bedroom, where he could hear in the middle of the night violent and arousing noises. Josef is now a 35-year-old prisoner who has committed murder out of love. Before the crime, Josef was a "professional interpreter." Imagining himself in a psychotherapy clinic, he sees a young therapist, Charlotte, to whom he is sexually attracted. Charlotte tells him that he will encounter powerful feelings in the psychotherapy clinic and that he must be "strong and hold to the truth" (279), putting aside his own feelings to interpret accurately. Working for social services, Charlotte offers an assessment interview of a young man, Bobby, who admits to abusing his wife and daughters. Is Bobby a version of Josef's father? Josef believes he can rescue Charlotte from Bobby's violence. Gibson offers a classic example of a Freudian rescue fantasy. In a rescue fantasy, Freud writes in "A Special Type of Choice of Object Made by Men" (1910), the son identifies with his father: "All his instincts, those of tenderness, gratitude, lustfulness, defiance and independence, find satisfaction in the single wish *to be his own father*" (*SE*, vol. 11, 173). Or as Josef says, "I wasn't excluded any more from the activities in the bedroom. I thought this was my chance to really do some good. I could save her and put him in his place" (280). The plot then repeats itself with different characters. Josef witnesses another therapist, Julia, who interviews Amira; she and her daughters have been abused by her husband. Amira believes that as a result of her terrible marriage, her heart is locked in a box—and Josef now believes he alone has the key to unlock it. In an effort to save Amira from domestic violence, Josef repeats the behavior of her husband by "mentally possessing her without her agreement" (283). Tortured by his longing for her, Josef stabs to death Amira's husband and then strangles himself.

Are Josef and George the same character, two versions of a psychotherapist who becomes overinvolved with a patient's life? Gibson hints at this in the postscript, observing that the therapist is also an interpreter. Josef and Bobby appear to be doubles: both come from another country, and both lust for Charlotte. The vignette shows how characters search for love in adulthood denied to them in childhood. Moreover, the vignette dramatizes a therapist's rescue fantasy, the belief that the therapist is imbued with a magical power to heal his or her patient. The fantasy reveals the therapist's self-idealization and grandiosity—factors that are often countertherapeutic. Gibson cites Freud's comment in *Civilization and Its Discontents* (1930) that "we are never so defenceless against suffering as when we love, never so helplessly unhappy as when we have lost our loved object or its love" (*SE*, vol. 21, 82; *Tales from the Unconscious* 286). By writing a fictional vignette rather than a clinical case study, Gibson succeeds not only in concealing his colleague's identity but also in urging readers to draw their own conclusions about a disturbing story that reenacts the emotional confusion experienced by therapists. To emphasize the importance of feeling over thinking in the vignette, Gibson uses affective language. Josef sobs, unable to restrain his tears. His heart "swells" when he hears Amira's story. Feeling her humiliation, his desire for her drives him mad.

Gibson knows, as do all suicide survivors—those who have lost a loved one to self-inflicted death—that suicidal pain is passed onto others. "You never get over it" (294) declares Elaine Ratchbull, one of the "suicide spotters." The main question Gibson raises in Audacities is this: how does one dissuade a person from taking his or her own life? Reflections on the audacity of suicide require, he tells us, an audacious approach, which sometimes involves mordant humor. And so in one of his vignettes, "The Bloody Audacity of It," Elaine and another suicide spotter, Janet Crams, both of whom have lost their husbands to suicide, confront a young man, Roger, who is prepared to jump from a bridge. The vignette recalls the 1946 Christmas drama/fantasy *It's a Wonderful Life*, produced and directed by Frank Capra. In the film, George Bailey (played by James Stewart) is prevented from suicide by his guardian angel second class, Clarence (Henry Travers), who shows him how his community would appear had he not been born. In Gibson's story, Elaine tells Roger, sarcastically, what he will look like as he hurtles to death— "Most of the jumpers look up as they fall. Like a baby looking for their mother. It's quite touching"—to which he responds, "That's an unbelievably cruel thing to say at a moment like this" (289). He's right, but the abrasive words unexpectedly have a life-saving effect on him. Sarcasm can sometimes be preferable to sentimentality, though one can imagine Elaine's taunting words having a countertherapeutic impact on others in the same situation. The postscript forces readers to decide whether Freud was right when he argues in "Mourning and Melancholia" that suicide is internalized aggression originally intended to cause pain to others. Another motive behind suicide is the misguided effort to protect a relative or friend from one's rage—misguided in that suicide causes lifelong pain. To evoke the dark legacy of suicide, Gibson quotes in the postscript words from Shakespeare's *Richard II*: "sorrow ends not when it seemeth done."

Gibson devotes five whimsical vignettes to another suicide spotter, Genevieve the Wayward Angel. She is not exactly a fallen angel but a "naughty" one because, disregarding heavenly rules, she has intervened on earth to help people in distress. In one instance, she intervened to save someone from hell who was not supposed to be saved. Like Clarence in *It's a Wonderful Life*, Genevieve seeks to redeem herself, though she is still committed to intervention. Genevieve uses tough words like others use tough love: to jolt people back to their senses. She also conveys Gibson's psychoanalytic experience with suicide survivors, reminding people that dying "takes place in super-slow motion" (343). Freud makes a cameo appearance in Genevieve's tales, appearing as thoughtful and kind. Standing at the back gates of heaven, the Wayward Angel has only one criticism of Freud; referring to his religious disbelief in his 1927 book *The Future of an Illusion*, she asks, "how could he have been so wrong?" (365).

Tales from the Unconscious affirms both the talking cure and the writing cure. In "Miss Playne and Oliver," the first-person narrator, Jonathan Crunchy, recounts a story about a woman, "plain Jane," who, having been bullied by her coworkers, brings to work a hand grenade, her father's wartime souvenir, and pulls the pin, destroying her tormentors and herself. "It hadn't occurred to me until writing this account that perhaps Jane was furious with her father for dying" (324), exclaims Jonathan, an insight gained only though the act of writing. I suspect that Jonathan speaks for Gibson when he says that "writing this was my way of dealing with shock and grief" (325).

In the preface to *Tales from the Unconscious*, the author notes that in all the vignettes "there are secrets that even the writer is unaware of," including Gibson himself. He then makes a puzzling statement. "If I say too much, then a story will continue after I had intended it to end" (xv). But don't all stories continue to exist in the reader's mind indefinitely? The best vignettes in *Tales from the Unconscious* remind us of the value of talking and writing: human connection. Although Gibson never challenges Freud's belief that the Oedipus complex is psychological bedrock, he knows that one's theoretical assumptions shape one's interpretation. "In the world of psychoanalytic psychotherapy, each therapist's preoccupation with their theory is based on their identification with the theorist's way of thinking and feeling" (254). Or as Adam Phillips observes:

> Each psychoanalytic theorist, it could be said, organizes his or her theory around what might be called a core catastrophe; for Freud it was castration, for Klein, the triumph of the Death instinct, and for Winnicott it was the annihilation of the core self by intrusion, a failure of the holding environment. (*Winnicott* 149)

After reading vignettes about patients' destructive rescue fantasies and wayward angels' constructive, albeit problematic interventions, one wonders how this contradiction can be resolved. Gibson does not answer this question, but he cites John Keats's *Negative Capability*: "When man is capable of being in uncertainties, Mysteries, doubts, without any irritable reaching after fact and reason" (Keats 261). Perhaps the best one can do is tolerate the frustration.

One can imagine how *Tales from the Unconscious* would generate lively discussion among medical students learning about psychotherapy. But one doesn't need to be a medical student to appreciate the vignettes. Gibson takes a familiar psychoanalytic theme, the role of childhood sexual experience in shaping adult personality, and he shows how the past repeats itself. Additionally, the vignettes demonstrate the role of projective identification, the "placing of a part of oneself in another and the identification of that part with the other person" (135). Gibson reveals how most people who attempt or complete suicide are deeply ambivalent, wishing, simultaneously, to live and die. Regardless of whether or not I am correct in surmising that "The Interpreter" is about his colleague's suicide, Gibson offers memorable cautionary tales about how humor, when used sensitively, "opens a door through the rage that binds us and inhibits" (274).

Works Cited

Freud, Sigmund. *Civilization and Its Discontents*. 1930. *The Standard Edition of the Complete Psychological Works of Sigmund Freud*, translated and edited by James Strachey, vol. 21. The Hogarth Press, 1961.

Freud, Sigmund. "Mourning and Melancholia." 1917. *The Standard Edition of the Complete Psychological Works of Sigmund Freud*, translated and edited by James Strachey, vol. 14. The Hogarth Press, 1957.

Freud, Sigmund. "A Special Type of Choice of Object Made in Men." 1910. *The Standard Edition of the Complete Psychological Works of Sigmund Freud*, translated and edited by James Strachey, vol. 11. The Hogarth Press, 1957.

Gibson, Christopher. *Tales from the Unconscious*. International Psychoanalytic Books, 2021.

Hughes, Patricia and Christopher Gibson. "Meeting the Challenge: Teaching Psychotherapy to Medical Students. Part I: Students and Syllabus." *Psychoanalytic Psychotherapy*, vol. 10, 1996, pp. 3–9.

Hughes, Patricia and Christopher Gibson. "Meeting the Challenge: Teaching Psychotherapy to Medical Students. Part II: Style and Delivery." *Psychoanalytic Psychotherapy*, vol. 10, 1996, pp. 11–19.

It's a Wonderful Life. Directed by Frank Capra, Paramount, 1946.

Keats, John. *Selected Poems and Letters*. Riverside Press, 1959.

Phillips, Adam. *Winnicott*. Harvard UP, 1988.

Chapter 19

Irene Cairo
Inside Out: Intimate Voices

Like many psychoanalysts, Irene Cairo did not turn to fiction until late in life. After graduating from the University of Buenos Aires Faculty of Medicine in 1964, she moved to the United States and studied at the New York Psychoanalytic Society & Institute, where she is a member of the faculty. She is also a training and supervising analyst at the Contemporary Freudian Society. She has served as the North American Chair of the Ethics Committee of the International Psychoanalytic Association. Cairo is the author of more than two dozen journal articles, chapters, and book reviews, written in English and Spanish, on a wide range of subjects, including shame, envy, and trauma. Her willingness to be self-disclosing, exposing her patients' and her own vulnerability, and to admit her clinical mistakes, sets her apart from other analysts.

Cairo's open-mindedness appears throughout her writings. The heroic, she argues in her book chapter "Voiceless Heroines: Deafened by Theory?", is defined by "courageous acts and nobility of character" (96). The chapter, part of *Changing Notions of the Feminine: Confronting Psychoanalysts' Prejudices*, edited by Margarita Cereijido (2019), explores how Cairo has freed herself from classical psychoanalytic theory, particularly ego psychology, that has limited her understanding of female patients. Growing up in Buenos Aires, Argentina, Cairo recounts how she has "no social or political early memories that do not involve a tyrannical government and a fear of the police." She was cautioned by her mother, "If you get lost, do *not* go to the police" (96). Nor was she allowed to repeat ideas heard at home; even listening to clandestine radio broadcasts was dangerous. Cairo identified with three powerful women: the biblical Judith, the literary Antigone, and the historical Joan of Arc. The adoption of these three women revealed Cairo's early identity theme: "defiance of authority, with achievement of success, but sometimes at a brutal price!" (97). These heroines embodied admirable though risky ideals of bravery and sacrifice. Through her exposure to later psychoanalytic theorists, especially Wilfred Bion, whose concept of container-contained long intrigued her, Cairo began to realize some of her biases, including the overestimation of professional success, which contributed to a countertransference problem that impaired her ability to treat a few patients who were not high achievers like herself. As part of her evolution of thinking, she became a "more patient, less ambitious analyst,

DOI: 10.4324/9781003623908-25

more cautious in my goals for my patients" (96). The three brief clinical vignettes in "Voiceless Heroines" demonstrate Cairo's ability to acknowledge being deafened by theory and adopt a new theoretical approach that has proved more therapeutically effective. Writing "Voiceless Heroines" enabled Cairo to rethink her theoretical views on female development and femininity. She ends the chapter by reaffirming the heroic—and her commitment to psychoanalysis.

Published in 2022, *Inside Out: Intimate Voices* is Cairo's first work of fiction. She writes about traditional subjects, such as love, friendship, marriage, and parenting, but also about the terror of living under brutal dictatorships. Not all of Cairo's fictional characters are courageous and heroic, but many of them are compelling and complex. The seven short stories were written over a period of many years, reflecting different moods and moments, ranging from the playful to the wildly comic to the tragic. The stories reveal her gift for language (she is fluent in Spanish, French, and English), her interest in creating lively characters, and, as Owen Renik remarks in the introduction, her "wonderful ear for internal monologue" (1).

In her clinical and fictional writings, Cairo often refers to poets, novelists, and playwrights, many of them well known to American readers, such as the mid-twentieth-century poet Elizabeth Bishop, but also to other authors, from Europe, who may be obscure, such as the Italian novelist and filmmaker Curzio Malaparte and the Turkish poet and playwright Nazim Hikmet. Cairo puts her literary erudition to good use in her writings, which celebrate intertextuality, a text's interconnection with an earlier one. To give one example, Cairo titled her account of a panel discussion on envy, held by the American Psychoanalytic Association in 2000, "To Have and Have Not," a reference to Hemingway's 1937 novel.

Inside Out

Early maternal loss, particularly from cancer, lurks throughout *Inside Out*. In the opening story, "Waiting for Vermeer," Francine is a 34-year-old "very slightly overweight" anthropologist who now lives in Washington, DC. Francine was 19 when her mother died, and she found herself remembering the nineteenth-century British novels she had read earlier in life, such as *David Copperfield* and *Jane Eyre*, in which orphans endure extreme hardships but are later rewarded with love. Will this also be true of Francine? The question catalyzes the plot. Francine has never married but remains hopeful that her friend Ken, a divorced English professor who is helping her find a nursing home for her dying father, will be the right man for her. The two are waiting on a long line to enter the Vermeer exhibition, but as the story progresses, she reflects on his recent statement to her that they are too alike to marry—it would be incestuous, he declares, to her stinging disappointment. We see a striking disconnect between her composed outer demeanor and her increasingly frantic inner thoughts about her failed history of romantic love: the first of many examples of "inside out" in the volume. "She screamed internally, full of rage now. Rage that she had kept so quietly locked, rage she had not known until now" (11). Near the end of the story, after Ken has departed, Francine meets a new man from

South America who invites her to join him in visiting the Museum of the American Indian. For a moment she fears that he may be a "Pinochet inspired plot" (15), a reference to the notorious Chilean dictator. This is one of the many passages in the short story collection where Cairo's ancient traumas resurface. But "Waiting for Vermeer" concludes hopefully, the only one of the stories with the hint of a traditional happily-ever-after ending.

"Breast Biopsy," Cairo's most inventive story, could not be more different from "Waiting for Vermeer" apart from the specter of early maternal death. Marianne, the first-person narrator, waits anxiously for a needle localization biopsy. Marianne's husband is a surgeon at the same hospital in which she is having a breast biopsy, but he cannot be with her because he is with his dying mother. A catastrophizer, the clinical psychologist finds her imagination running wild with worst-case scenarios. Marianne was a young child when her mother had a mastectomy, and shortly after her mother's death, Marianne's father, holding his wife's diamond ring, promised his daughter that one day it would be hers. The family history of cancer heightens Marianne's dread of the biopsy. It's not surprising that the story abounds in breast images, but what is surprising, indeed startling, is how Marianne focuses on the large breasts of the black woman who takes her personal information in the hospital's admissions office. "Huge boobs," Marianne thinks enviously, "why did this have to happen to me TODAY, I thought, not yet knowing what was to come. Wonderful contralto voice, chocolaty shiny skin, the huge jewelry, BIG pendant between the BIG boobs" (18).

Marianne regards her small white breasts as "dangerous agents of death," in contrast to what she believes is "Miss Rings's" enormous life-sustaining black breasts. Significantly, Marianne's envy of Miss Rings's breasts has nothing to do with their aesthetic or erotic appeal but rather with counterphobic motivation. Miss Rings's breasts become a talisman endowed with death-defying powers. Cairo then complicates the story, radically altering its tone, when Miss Rings discovers that Marianne is a psychologist who treats adolescent children. According to Miss Rings, her foster child, Jesse, has maliciously told a clinical supervisor that Miss Rings ordered him to suck her breasts. Marianne, consumed by her fear of the biopsy, nearly collapses when she hears this, concluding that "A hospital is a CRAZY place full of crazy people who don't even look normal!" (27).

Months after the biopsy, Marianne's youngest daughter has an assignment on Elizabeth Bishop, and suddenly Marianne remembers, in the last paragraph of the story, Bishop's poem "In the Waiting Room." The poem describes the speaker, three days shy of her seventh birthday, accompanying her aunt Consuelo to a dentist's office in February, 1918 in Worcester, Massachusetts. While waiting for her aunt, the speaker looks through an issue of *National Geographic* that contains photographs of naked black women with "awful hanging breasts," an image that horrifies her. She hears a cry of pain from the dentist's office, her aunt's voice. "What took me / completely by surprise," she exclaims, "was that it was *me*: / my voice, in my mouth." She imagines herself "falling, falling," and she instantly realizes, in the poem's central epiphany, that "you are an *I*, / you are an *Elizabeth*, / you are one of *them*" (Bishop 180). Bishop wrote the poem in the mid-1970s, an age when photographs of "native" African women routinely appeared exotic in magazines like *National Geographic*. Bishop's speaker finds herself unmoored by the recognition of her kinship with an alien other. "Breast Biopsy" ends with Marianne remembering how she felt on that day in 1944 when she learned about her mother's death. "I wanted to cry and did not know why. I wanted to cry but only into beautiful black breasts that would shelter me from the world" (33).

Cairo captures in "Breast Biopsy" her narrator's anxiety of dismemberment and fear of succumbing to cancer, like her mother. Cairo does not invoke the theory of "assumptive world," but it is useful in understanding her story. Colin Murray Parkes defines assumptive world as a "strongly held set of assumptions about the world and the self which is confidently maintained and used as a means of recognizing, planning, and acting… Assumptions such as these are learned and confirmed by the experience of many years" (132). Cairo shows how early traumatic loss lies at the center of Marianne's assumptive world, a loss that also becomes, paradoxically, a muse behind Cairo's art—and her wry sense of humor. "Breast Biopsy" abounds in ironies, demonstrating Cairo's delight in surprising the reader with counterintuitive truths. The self-lacerating Marianne worries about her husband's reaction to her possible mastectomy. "Actually, baby," he responds, "I'll like you more, much more… I am a bit afraid of confessing this, you know, I never told you because you would have insisted that I need analysis, but my dream as a kid was to make it with an Amazon… Don't tell your friends the shrinks though, they'll know for sure I'm a pervert" (30–31).

Maternal loss haunts "The Crystal Room," a tender rite of passage story about a father–daughter relationship. Despite feeling overwhelming gratitude for his adolescent daughter, Sheila, the father "felt bitter and full of sorrow for her, for his lovely only daughter, orphaned so early, left with a scar so huge that nothing could really heal her, he believed, nothing would ever be the same for her" (35–36). Or for him. The father is about to remarry, and Sheila seems pleased that Meryl will soon be part of the family. "I love Meryl," Sheila gushes, "she's so much fun!" (37). There is no trace of Sheila's ambivalence toward her father's remarriage; instead, the tension focuses on the daughter's emerging sexuality. She reveals the following Oedipal dream to her father that he will remember until his dying day:

"in the dream I was in bed, just as always, I mean always then, and you were coming in to kiss me good night like you used to, and you came over, and… you leaned over like you always did, and instead, then, you pulled the covers"—she made the gesture, violently, as if yanking her arm "and I was naked! And then I woke up." (40)

The dream evokes in the father a magical crystal room where exquisite flowers grow, his blossoming daughter, the blooming miracle of his life. The story then projects into the future, the father imagining his daughter, with her own children, attending to his death. The thought of Sheila brings him comfort and joy on his death bed. The story ends with the most lyrical sentence in the volume: "And yet, in all the changes of scene he imagined, this invisible path of light would join her to him, through the glittering and the velvet rose petal rain, and her lovely adolescent face reflecting on the crystal" (42).

No such comfort appears in "Hospital Visit," a story about a homophobic narrator, Marcello, who cannot overcome his prejudice to be available to his dear friend, Mario, dying from AIDS. The story implies that Marcello's homophobia may be a defense against unacknowledged homoeroticism. "Vaguely, but quite disturbingly, I felt I could have fallen in love with him, had I been able to cross that barrier even in my mind" (49). Marcello has known Mario for 25 years, having met him at a Communist bookstore in which both reached simultaneously for a book of poetry by Nazim Hikmet, who served a 13-year sentence as a political prisoner in his native Turkey and spent his last 13 years in exile. Cairo may have chosen the Turkish poet because his writings enabled him to survive ordeals that would have crushed another person; "he is one of the twentieth century's strongest voices of the carceral imagination and exilic being," as Carolyn Forché observes in her foreword to his poems (x). When Marcello tells his wife, Renata, that homosexuality is a "monstrosity," she counters with the rhetorical question, "Marriage is not a monstrosity?" and then opines, reflecting the authorial point of view, "Men are strange animals. Life is so much harder for you men, I guess" (63).

"We are all prisoners of our history" (79) broods Mark in "Last Rites," Cairo's darkest story. Reflecting on his failed marriage to the mother of his two children, Giovanna, who lies dying of cancer, Mark wonders how he can make love to his present wife, Muriel, while his past wife lies dying. History is a cyclical nightmare for both Mark and Giovanna; one recalls Santayana's observation that those who do not remember the past are condemned to repeat it. Mark tortures himself throughout the story, not only because of his marital infidelity, which was also true of Giovanna's philandering father, but also because he abandoned his wife and two young children. Mark's explanation of his behavior is that their sex life was miserable: All men should have a happy sex life becomes his new credo. How could he have loved a woman who turned herself into a nun? Notwithstanding his rationalization, he agonizes over her impending death, and when he visits her in the hospital, attempting to reach out to her, the comatose woman seems to withdraw her hand from his, deepening his shame.

Catholicism is a powerful force in "Last Rites," and the story dramatizes the religious differences between Mark and Giovanna. Her mother, the "bulwark of the strict Catholic family," did not approve of her daughter's involvement with a "heretic, a militant socialist" (69). Mark has rejected his own Catholicism; had he not done so, he tries to reassure himself, he would be committing mortal sins repeatedly. "I would end up a suicide, with my faith in God intact but pushing me towards an act I despise" (82). I suspect that Cairo endorses Mark's observation that "Religion demands rigidity to save the soul. Morality demands flexibility, compromise to think of the complex and ever-changing needs of the living" (82–83). This insight brings Mark no relief, however. What does bring Mark temporary solace is a recording of Schubert's Trio in E flat, which he brings to the hospital and gives to Giovanna's present husband. Art in all its forms—painting, poetry, fiction, and classical music—is essential in Cairo's world, sustaining her characters during their most challenging moments. We have art lest we perish from the truth, Nietzsche observed; in Cairo's world, art conveys not only hidden truths but also provides us with beauty and pleasure. Art is, in short, a matter of life and death.

In its tour de force conclusion, Cairo gives us in the last four pages of the story Giovanna's inner thoughts. Though mute, she hopes that Peter will play the Schubert Trio: "*it always makes me feel that life can be beautiful. He will, I'm sure. I think I can hear it now*" (84). As she engages in an imaginary dialogue with her long-dead mother, we learn that in an effort to save her young son Andy from a life-threatening illness, Giovanna, bargaining with God, as Marianne has done in "Breast Biopsy," promised to give up all pleasure, a sacrifice of which her husband was unaware. Giovanna believes that her sacrifice spared her son's life, but it has also doomed her marriage. No clinical case study can capture a dying person's final thoughts; only a creative writer can imagine this. In her delirium, Giovanna, still fearing her mother's disapproval of Mark, cries out for her children, the center of her life, and, in her last words, fantasizes her reunion with her mother in death. "*Please be there. Don't take my children, here I come Mamma*" (85). Giovanna's acceptance of death at the end does not mean that she seeks death. The living are never closer to the dead, the story implies, than when they are dying themselves. Giovanna dies at the end of "Last Rites," but Mark's torment is only beginning.

Shame suffuses Cairo's penultimate story, "Doctor," which opens and closes with references to Curzio Malaparte's Second World War novel *Kaputt* in which he analyzes Italian fascism, to which he was initially attracted. The mother in Malaparte's novel keeps a shameful secret that somehow parallels that of the unnamed narrator, a surgeon, in Cairo's story. Cairo never tells us where her story takes place, though presumably it was in a repressive South American country; the speaker remarks that there is an "obvious connection between different brands or nationalities of fascism" (87). Imprisoned and tortured, the doctor's shameful secret is that he had not denounced, either in court or to the Refugee Commission, a person guilty of a serious crime. "I protected somebody who mothered me in my shame," he confesses, "although protecting him might mean criminals would go unpunished" (99). The doctor was able to survive the torture, which lasted for 19 days, followed by imprisonment for seven months, by insisting to himself that his torturers were not real people. Later he tried another technique, recalling the comic books of his childhood filled with heroes of extraordinary power. One day while in prison, the doctor, who was forced to wear a hood the entire time, is washed by a man whose young son, Luisito, had his mangled fingers saved by the doctor when he was a surgical resident. "At least you are washed now," Luisito's father says gently to the prisoner. The doctor has never forgotten the man's act of kindness, his "*cleansing hand*." The doctor's gratitude toward Luisito's father, who was a janitor, not a jailor or a torturer, contrasts the hatred he feels for his captors, who had crushed his own hands. As the story closes, the doctor awaits an operation that may allow him to work as a surgeon again, enabling him, he hopes, to overcome his shame. Telling a more truthful account of his dark secret will also help him overcome shame.

After three somber stories, Cairo concludes *Inside Out* with a lighthearted one, "Windows of New York," in which the speaker and her husband, Ted, gaze into a shadeless Manhattan window across the street to watch a couple having sex every night punctually at 7. Soon others in the speaker's family enjoy the nightly spectacle. It's one of the few stories in the volume where a character, the speaker's black friend, Jeanne, refers to something she has learned in analysis: "voyeurism is almost always problematic for most of us... but exhibitionism is acceptable, socially acceptable" (113). ("Voyeur," Cairo declares to her patient in "Babette, Interrupted," is "Such a bad word" [114].) "Windows of New York" is the only story with a clear "moral," expressed pragmatically: "If you want to be nice to your neighbors, DO pull the shades closed when you are having sex!" (113).

Maternal Loss

Four of Cairo's characters—Francine, Marianne, the speaker in "Doctor," and Jeanne—refer to being in "therapy" or "analysis": she uses the words interchangeably. Most of the references are positive, but the talking cure is not a subject she writes about in her fiction, perhaps because she has explored verbal therapy extensively in her professional articles and book reviews. Based only on *Inside Out*, I doubt many readers would know that the author was a psychoanalyst. Like many analysts, she keeps her two careers separate and distinct from each other.

Tellingly, the first three stories in *Inside Out*—"Waiting for Vermeer," "Breast Biopsy," and "The Crystal Room"—involve female characters who have lost their mothers at an early age. Another story, "Last Rites," involves a dying mother who will leave her young children orphans—just as that dying mother lost her *own* mother at an early age. These motherless daughters are *in extremis* because of traumatic loss. The two most emotionally intense characters in the volume are Marianne and Giovanna, both of whom are the most connected to their deceased mothers. Giovanna experiences a fusion-like merger with her mother, dissolving the boundaries between self and (m)other. Cairo has never written a journal article about the trauma of early maternal loss, but, based on these four stories in *Inside Out*, one can speculate that she, too, lost her mother at an early age. If so, it's noteworthy that she chose to explore this theme through the veil of fiction, a genre that may be characterized as true lies. Many support groups now exist for motherless daughters, but little was known about early maternal loss half a century ago. The legacy of maternal loss pervades *Inside Out*, just as the theme of spousal loss dominates Arlene Heyman's stories.

"The power of words can sometimes be brutal" (91), the speaker in "Doctor" proclaims, but the fiction writer's words are also haunting, evocative, and enchanting. Cairo's short stories conjure up a myriad of emotions and moods, as Nancy Chodorow reveals in her blurb: "I found myself sometimes unable to stop laughing and sometimes unable to breathe, at descriptions of politics and people during the dark days of dictatorship, and, throughout, noticing Cairo's sustained commitment, across time and space, to parenthood, marriage, friendship, and family." Cairo succeeds in showing her characters' rich inner lives, their unique subjectivity, their alterity, without reducing them to clinical case studies. She is interested in character for its own sake, not to illustrate a particular psychological theory. Her female characters are never, in Freud's bemused words, a dark continent. Cairo's characters are not completely knowable—no character is—but we glimpse their complexity, and some of them approach the heroic in their daily lives. Cairo listens to her characters as they dialogue with others and themselves. She is one of the psychoanalytic fiction writers who listens to listening. "I wish I could dialogue with each of you readers," she writes on the book jacket. "I invite you to dialogue with me in the imagination." As she notes in her 2002 review of Warren Poland's *Melting the Darkness*: "True openness to dialogue is, of course, the prerogative of very secure minds, and it is a rare exercise" (1464). As the stories in *Inside Out* reveal, Irene Cairo also has a secure mind.

Works Cited

Bishop, Elizabeth. *Poems*. Farrar, Straus and Giroux, 2011.
Cairo, Irene. "Babette, Interrupted." *Finding Unconscious Fantasy in Narrative, Trauma, and Body Pain: A Clinical Guide*, edited by Paula L. Ellman and Nancy R. Goodman. Routledge, 2017, pp. 104–116.
Cairo, Irene. *Inside Out: Intimate Voices*. International Psychoanalytic Books, 2022.
Cairo, Irene. "Review of *Melting the Darkness* by Warren Poland." *International Journal of Psychoanalysis*, vol. 83, 2002, pp. 1463–1467.
Cairo, Irene. "To Have and Have Not: Clinical Uses of Envy." *Journal of the American Psychoanalytic Association*, vol. 49, 2001, pp. 1391–1404.
Cairo, Irene. "Voiceless Heroines: Deafened by Theory?" *Changing Notions of the Feminine: Confronting Psychoanalysts Prejudice*, edited by Margarita Cerejido. Routledge, 2019, pp. 95–104.
Forché, Carolyn. "Foreword," *Poems of Nazim Hikmet*, translated from the Turkish by Randy Blessing and Mutlu Konuk. Persea Books, 2002.
Heyman, Arlene. *Scary Old Sex*. Bloomsbury, 2016.
Malaparte, Curzio. *Kaputt*. 1944. Marlboro Press, 1991.
Parkes, Colin Murray. "What Becomes of Redundant World Models? A Contribution to the Study of Adaptation to Change." *British Journal of Medical Psychology*, vol. 48, 1975, pp. 131–137.
Poland, Warren S. *Intimacy and Separateness in Psychoanalysis*, edited and introduced by William F. Cornell, with a preface by Nancy Chodorow. Routledge, 2018.

Chapter 20

Luke Hadge
Psychoanalytic Stories

"How ironic," Luke Hadge's third-person narrator observes ruefully in "A Portrait of the Analyst as a Young Man," one of the eight short tales in *Psychoanalytic Stories* (2019), "how an endeavor that gives unparalleled license to the patient to say the unsayable has been organized to often muffle the voice of the young practitioner" (45). It is a poignant irony, for while a myriad of books depict a patient's experience in psychoanalysis—H.D.'s *Tribute to Freud* (1956), Joseph Wortis's *Fragments of an Analysis with Freud* (1975), Lou Andreas-Salomé's *The Freud Journal* (1964), A. Kardiner's *My Analysis with Freud* (1977), and Tilmann Moser's *Years of Apprenticeship on the Couch* (1977), to name the best known examples—few if any accounts exist of inexperienced practitioners of the talking cure. For this reason alone, Luke Hadge's collection of short stories is worth reading. But there are other reasons to read this stimulating volume.

Hadge is a graduate of the Columbia University Center for Psychoanalytic Training and Research, where in 2014 he received the Alexander Beller Award for scholarly study in psychoanalysis. After working in Boston and New York City for over two decades, Hadge then moved to Hawaii where he is associate clinical professor of psychiatry at the University of Hawaii School of Medicine. He is also the founder of the Hawaii Psychoanalytic Society.

Most psychoanalytic fiction writers have authored scholarly publications, but Hadge is unique in that when he began psychoanalytic training in 2008, he joined a research project studying the career development of the institute's graduates (Cherry et al.). He later wrote about his engagement in the project in "A Candidate's Experience Doing Research During Training" (2012). Writing about his experience of being in psychoanalytic training had many benefits, including creating an "additional level of self-reflection and expression to the already complex, introspective, and self-exposing process inherent in candidacy" (996). Yet in an earlier essay, "Candidate Writing and Its Discontents" (2010), he acknowledged the difficulty of such writing: "exposing myself to fantasized analytic speculation or critical evaluation by my classmates, teachers, supervisors, or my own analyst, who might read it" (41).

Psychoanalytic Stories

Psychoanalytic Stories is a mix of fiction and nonfiction/memoir. Three of the stories were published, in earlier versions, in *The Bulletin of the Association for Psychoanalytic Medicine* and *The American Psychoanalyst*. The volume is only 72 pages, short enough to read in a couple of hours, but the stories are delicious morsels, leaving the reader hungry for more.

Hadge's love for literature appears in every story, unifying the volume. The allusions seem effortless, suggesting an author who has grown up with books. Some of the literary references are obvious, others not, but all are central to the stories rather than simply window dressing. In the opening and, for me, most intriguing story, "The Graduate and the Analyst," Hadge conjures up his foreboding while treating an eminent senior analyst near the end of his life. Hadge's anxiety reminds him of Henry James's masterpiece "The Beast in the Jungle," a story his father had given him as a child—sophisticated reading for any young person! Hadge's renowned analyst, whom he never names, often quoted from T.S. Eliot's "The Love Story of J. Alfred Prufrock," lines that appear throughout *Psychoanalytic Stories*. The second and fourth tales, "Jacob Arlow's Office" and "The Salman Rushdie Bird," enable Hadge to discuss how the author of *The Satanic Verses* lived under a death threat as a result of a fatwa issued against him in 1989 by the Iranian government. In the third story, "Two Charlies on the Subway," Hadge paraphrases a line from John Donne's iconic seventeenth-century sermon, "No Man Is an Island" (the source of the title of Hemingway's 1940 novel, *For Whom the Bell Tolls*), to highlight how Charles Brenner's *Elementary Textbook of Psychoanalysis* (1955) is still relevant. In the fifth story, "The Day a Billionaire Walked into My Office," Hadge shows how his patient, a cofounder of a social media platform, became disillusioned with his monstrous creation, recalling Mary Shelley's *Frankenstein*. The title of the next story, "A Portrait of the Analyst as a Young Man," owes its existence to James Joyce's first novel, but there are more than a dozen references to literature and film in the tale, including poems by Robert Frost, William Butler Yeats, T.S. Eliot, and Allen Ginsburg. Additionally, Hadge cites Flaubert's injunction, "Be regular and orderly in your life, so that you may be violent and original in your work." Hadge's own writing may not be violent, but it is original. The penultimate story, "Subway Odyssey in Trump Town," contains lines from Yeats's apocalyptic poem "The Second Coming," which is frighteningly appropriate to contemporary American politics, where raging narcissism and cruelty trump reason. And the last story, "The Night an Analyst Couldn't Sleep," abounds in references to Freud, Sandor Ferenczi's *Clinical Diary*, contemporary analysts, such as Sheldon Bach, and Elizabeth Hardwick's novel *Sleepless Nights*. Hadge also cites lines that he does not identify: "We died a whimper, not a bang," a paraphrase of the ending of "Prufrock," and "To sleep, perchance to dream," from Hamlet's soliloquy on death.

Hadge admits in "A Portrait of the Analyst as a Young Man" that he reads more poetry than psychology. I suspect that he would agree with Adam Phillips's provocation in *Promises, Promises* (2001): "Literature is probably a better preparation for the practice of psychoanalysis than the reading of anything else" (xvi). He might also agree with Phillips's even more iconoclastic remark: "For me—for all sorts of reasons—there has always been only one category, *literature*, of which psychoanalysis became a part" (364).

The main challenge of writing a story like "The Graduate and the Analyst," about a distinguished analyst, "Dr. Z.," in the twilight of his career, with whom Hadge had taken a seminar during the early part of his training, is preserving confidentiality. We learn nothing about why Dr. Z. chose the unseasoned Hadge as his analyst nor what each man learned about himself and the other during treatment. Hadge is a master of raising intriguing questions and allowing readers to reach their own conclusions:

> I wondered: Was he having a crisis, at this time in his life, in his faith in psychoanalysis? Was he afraid he had gotten something terribly wrong in one of his analytic ideas? Was there some old neurotic ghost visiting him again? Was he terrified of his mortality? Did he desperately not want to be deprived of practicing—and *experiencing*—more analysis? (3)

It would be inaccurate to say that Hadge reveals nothing about Dr. Z., but he remains phantasmal, like the story itself, tantalizing in arousing and frustrating our desire for something unobtainable. Hadge wonders, while sitting in his office during their fateful first meeting, whether he was making a "Faustian bargain" (3). We wonder too.

Other questions come to mind. While treating his former instructor, was Hadge aware of Nietzsche's droll dictum that one repays a teacher poorly by remaining a student? Hadge would agree with this statement, for in a later story, he quotes a philosophy instructor saying that "professors are there to learn from the students" (41). If Dr. Z. experienced a crisis in his faith in psychoanalysis, did this affect Hadge's own confidence in his new profession? What misgivings or resistances did Hadge overcome when writing about Dr. Z.? Hadge understandably interprets the beast in James's 1903 novella as an awareness of impending mortality, but John Marcher's terror that a catastrophe will befall him turns out to be, ironically, fear of the unlived life. Was this also true of Dr. Z.? The take-home lesson from Hadge's story lies in the last sentence, when Dr. Z. reminds him, "Everything is interesting if you look deeply enough" (7).

Treating Dr. Z. was presumably not a Faustian bargain—otherwise, why write about the experience? "The Graduate and the Analyst" is not a cautionary tale but a rite (write) of passage in which a young, untested analyst passes a life-changing test. "I cannot forget his expression of gratitude to me when we decided to end the treatment with his reported satisfaction" (2). Satisfaction notwithstanding, Dr. Z. had imposed one condition on Hadge: the elderly analyst entrusted the new graduate with his unpublished papers but ordered them burned after his death. Hadge felt like he was forced into the position of Max Brod, Kafka's friend and first biographer, ordered to destroy his writings. "I think he left it purposely up to me," Hadge acknowledges, "so that I would have to use my own judgment and honor his legacy, as I saw fit" (4). Hadge thus found himself in a Kafkaesque (or Catch-22) situation, for by writing "The Graduate and the Analyst," he made it impossible later to edit and publish Dr. Z.'s writings. Had he not written "The Graduate and the Analyst," he could have published Dr. Z.'s papers without anyone knowing that the latter was the former's analysand. Did Hadge destroy Dr. Z.'s writings, as he was asked to do? We probably will never know the answer to this question.

"The Graduate and the Analyst" contains Hadge's most metaphorical writing, as when he says, about Dr. Z.'s mind, that it was a "vast place, with nooks and crannies, hidden corners, expansive vistas, even culs de sac" (5). The reader strongly identifies with Hadge, especially when he grants, humbly, "Heaven knows how little I really understood about psychoanalysis at that time" (3). Two of Hadge's strengths are his modesty and self-effacing wit. He could not help being impressed, and perhaps intimidated by, the illustrious figures with whom he came into contact. This is apparent in "Jacob Arlow's Office." He had rented an office in a suite in which Jacob Arlow (1912–2004), the former president of the American Psychoanalytic Association and the New York Psychoanalytic Society & and Institute, had worked. After his death, he continued receiving mail that Hadge occasionally came across. The young analyst imagines that Arlow had written some of his most influential papers in the suite that Hadge himself now occupied. "Arlow's interest in art and creativity apparently extended beyond the grave" (11), Hadge muses, hoping that his predecessor's spirit would ignite his own creativity. The story then explores insightfully how writers and painters as diverse as Virginia Woolf, James Baldwin, Truman Capote, Vincent van Gogh, and E.M. Forster have been inspired by workspaces—including Freud, whose Viennese consulting room, Berggasse 19, is "perhaps the most famous office in history" (13). Near Hadge's office was the elegant townhouse in which Salman Rushdie worked, an author living, and writing, under a death sentence. A meditation on the writer's legacy, that which is transmitted by or received from an ancestor, "Jacob Arlow's Office" ends with the consolation that "like Arlow, we all may well continue to receive mail long after we're gone" (14).

I use the word *reading* (or *rereading*) nearly 100 times in this book, but Hadge is the only psychoanalytic fiction writer who concedes, in "The Salman Rushdie Bird," how his taste for literature may have disclosed something objectionable about himself of which he was unaware at the time. Hadge's former girlfriend, whom he knew in graduate school, suggested that they give each other their favorite short story. She chose Rushdie's "The Courter," and he chose Chekhov's "The Bet," a tale about a man who, on a wager, voluntarily locks himself up for ten years, in complete isolation from the world, to devote himself entirely to reading. She was, like Rushdie, of Indian descent, and he was her favorite author, albeit not Hadge's. He was disappointed when he read "The Courter," though years later, upon rereading, he came to admire it. Rethinking why he loved "The Bet" so much, Hadge suspected that it might have revealed the "antisocial or schizoid side of me that would like to be shut away from humanity for years with only books to keep me company" (29). Was this the reason his girlfriend broke up with him? "The Salman Rushdie Bird" is an ode to reading, as are all the stories in Hadge's volume. I recall Sophie Freud, Sigmund Freud's granddaughter, telling my students in 2002 that books were her closest friends, an admission upon which she elaborated in an article published in *American Imago* in 2004. "Books are my best, my most faithful, my most reliable friends. People have to meet rather high standards to match my books in terms of being good company" (77). I agree with Sophie Freud, and my bet is that Hadge does too. I also believe, as Hadge does, in bibliotherapy, the healing power of reading. As a teenager, Hadge suffered a sports injury that kept him in bed for months. "Deprived of playing the game he loved, to stave off depression and loneliness, he started to read, this time with purpose. He became the boy who couldn't stop reading. Literature was his balm" (41).

"A Portrait of the Analyst as a Young Man"

The only story in which Hadge writes about himself in third person, to achieve greater narrative distance, "A Portrait of the Analyst as a Young Man" is the most biographically revealing, a self-deprecating Bildungsroman. Hadge discloses that his mother was also an analyst, though he doesn't convey anything about their relationship. In *Children of Psychiatrists and Other Psychotherapists* (1989), Thomas Maeder contends that children of mental health professionals feel different from other people. Maeder, whose father was a psychoanalyst and mother a clinical social worker—a double whammy, in his view—argues that these children believe they suffer from a variety of personal problems they attribute to their parents, such as the belief that their parents can read their minds, violate their privacy, and overanalyze innocent remarks. Does Hadge also believe this?

Hadge's mother died during the COVID-19 pandemic, as he indicates in his 2021 article "Psychoanalysis Underwater." The brief essay, an account of how he spent much of his time during the pandemic swimming and snorkeling in the Pacific Ocean off the coast of Hawaii where he and his family live, contains his most lyrical, elegiac writing. "Like an 'oceanic feeling,' floating lubricates my mind." He doesn't mention his mother's name, but there can be no doubt of her identity: "I lost a family member last year to the virus, and I still grieve the loss. Much of the time I have spent in the ocean these past months has been floating around thinking about my loved one—also an analyst—reflecting on her life and what she meant to me" (32).

Throughout *Psychoanalytic Stories* Hadge is careful to disguise his training and supervising analysts' identities, but in "A Portrait of the Analyst as a Young Man" he refers to a senior analyst who, in interviewing him for possible acceptance into psychoanalytic training, bluntly warned, "I'm here to find out what your neurosis is" (43). It is a daunting statement, one that was perhaps deliberately intended to be anxiety-provoking. Hadge adds, almost in passing, that the analyst had asked, on the cover of a book, "Is there life without mother?" (43). This is indeed the title of Leonard Shengold's 2000 book, *Is There Life Without Mother? Psychoanalysis, Biography, Creativity*. Shengold (1925–2020) was a clinical professor of psychiatry at the New York University School of Medicine and the author of many books, including, most famously, *Soul Murder: The Effects of Childhood Abuse and Deprivation*. Shengold treated the neurologist Oliver Sacks, who dedicated *The Man Who Mistook His Wife for a Hat* to him. It's likely that Hadge would agree with Shengold's conclusion in *Is There Life Without Mother?* that although creativity is "inevitably related to psychopathology since we are all, being human, at least neurotic if not, one hopes, temporarily even sicker," it makes "no sense to base the sources of our talents and creative powers principally on pathology" (Shengold 187). Hadge seems to be the perfect candidate for psychoanalytic training, a healthy neurotic who uses his fears as a catalyst for creativity.

The only puzzling criticism Hadge makes in *Psychoanalytic Stories* appears in "A Portrait of the Analyst as a Young Man," where he asserts his lack of enthusiasm for theoretical pluralism. "The popular view of multiplicity of perspectives was overvalued, he thought, and without real critical analysis for fear of appearing authoritarian or overly conservative" (45). Does he mean that he is opposed to relational and intersubjective approaches, the conviction, increasingly accepted in the profession, that meaning is co-created by both analysand and analyst? "It seemed pretty clear to him how the creator of psychoanalysis had defined psychoanalysis. And it looked to him how that pluralism had unfortunately begotten tribalism in the discipline." Hadge then quotes a Janis Joplin lyric: "*Freedom's just another word for nothing left to lose*" (45).

Yet Freud's writings, as indispensable and revolutionary as they are, constitute only a small fraction of contemporary psychoanalytic theory and practice; moreover, key aspects of Freudian doctrine have been eliminated or revised, such as penis envy and the belief that the analyst should remain a blank screen. Hadge's willingness to be self-disclosing may itself be seen as an analytic "deviation." Without rehearsing the long and depressing history of self-destructive splits and schisms that have bedeviled psychoanalysis from its inception, I'll simply point out, as John Frosch and many others have, that the Columbia University Center for Psychoanalytic Training and Research broke away from the conservative New York Psychoanalytic Society & Institute for personal, theoretical, and ideological reasons. As early as 1953, during the "golden age" of psychoanalysis, Robert Knight complained that "Perhaps we are still standing too much in the shadow of that giant Sigmund Freud to permit ourselves to view psychoanalysis as a science of the mind rather than as the doctrine of its founder" (Frosch 1060). Nearly all psychoanalysts, past and present, would be horrified by Dr. Z.'s subversive suggestion that "Maybe every graduate should analyze a senior analyst" (6), but this tongue-in-cheek assertion bears serious thought.

The other stories in Hadge's volume are lively and candid. In "Two Charlies on the Subway," Hadge reveals his unglamorous life, after graduating from college as a psychology major, as a "utilization reviewer," reading patient charts, day after day, one of the "nameless authorial villains" who worked in a community-oriented setting. Treating the fabulously wealthy may elicit the analyst's countertransference, in the form of envy, as Hadge admits in "The Day a Billionaire Walked into My Office." Hadge never comes across as enamored of money, but he is honest enough to admit that he was not indifferent to his patient's "ungodly wealth." To Hadge's disappointment, the patient wanted only a consultation, not analysis, leading to this ironic conclusion: "The fact that I did not have the opportunity, in working with him, to make my unconscious envy more conscious and deal with it in the service of understanding him, remains for me the unanalyzed billion-dollar dynamic" (36). In "Subway Odyssey in Trump Town," the most political tale in the volume, Hadge confesses his struggle not to allow his outrage over the 45th president of the United States to interfere with his treatment of a Trump supporter. And in the last story, "The Night an Analyst Couldn't Sleep," Hadge casually mentions his family's background in the performing arts, a detail that may explain his talent for the humanistic arts, including writing. Asking himself why people write, Hadge cites a person who said, "I write to know what I think" (66). That person was E.M. Forster, who famously asked in *Aspects of the Novel* (1927), "How can I tell what I think till I see what I say?" (97). After defining himself as a "good ego psychologist," Hadge then discloses a bout of insomnia that seemed to arise, counterintuitively, from psychoanalysis. Once he realized that his sleeplessness was caused by his fear of not dreaming, and that he could not analyze his patients' dreams without having his own, he drifted off to sleep, ending *Psychoanalytic Stories* with the delightful sentence, "I thought of what my children like to say to me as they fall to sleep, 'See you in dreamland, Daddy,' and I was no longer afraid too" (72).

Psychoanalytic Stories is a joy to read, and I hope that it presages Hadge's future fiction. He may be, in his own words, a "dinosaur," almost extinct, or, worse, a "Luddite," opposed to progress, but he is a superb prose stylist. One can only agree with his wish for more personal writing about psychoanalysis. *Psychoanalytic Stories* will appeal to not only candidates-in-training and junior analysts but to anyone interested in reading good stories. Early in the volume he quotes Orson Welles's pronouncement that middle age is death for artists and that the period of greatest creativity is in youth and old age. Middle-aged when he wrote *Psychoanalytic Stories*, Hadge belies that statement.

Works Cited

Brenner, Charles. *An Elementary Textbook of Psychoanalysis*. Knopf, 1955.

Cherry, Sabrina, Juliette Meyer, Luke Hadge, Madeline Terry, and Steven P. Roose. "A Prospective Study of Psychoanalytic Practice and Professional Development: Early Career Interviews." *Journal of the American Psychoanalytic Association*, vol. 60, 2012, pp. 969–994.

Forster, E.M. *Aspects of the Novel*. Edward Arnold, 1927.
Freud, Sophie. "The Reading Cure: Books as Lifetime Companions." *American Imago*, vol. 61, 2004, pp. 77–87.
Frosch, John. "The New York Psychoanalytic Civil War." *Journal of the American Psychoanalytic Association*, vol. 39, 1991, pp. 1037–1064.
Hadge, Luke. "Candidate Writing and Its Discontents." *Association for Psychoanalytic Medicine*, vol. 44, 2010, pp. 37–44.
Hadge, Luke. "A Candidate's Experience Doing Research During Training." *Journal of the American Psychoanalytic Association*, vol. 60, 2012, pp. 995–1013.
Hadge, Luke. "Psychoanalysis Underwater." *The American Psychoanalyst*, vol. 55, 2021, pp. 32–33.
Hadge, Luke. *Psychoanalytic Stories*. International Psychoanalytic Books, 2019.
H.D. [Hilda Doolittle]. *Tribute to Freud: Writing on the Wall*. Pantheon, 1956.
Kardiner, A. *My Analysis with Freud: Reminiscences*. Norton, 1977.
Maeder, Thomas. *Children of Psychiatrists and Other Psychotherapists*. HarperCollins, 1989.
Moser, Tillmann, *Years of Apprenticeship on the Couch: Fragment of My Training Analysis*. Introduction by Heinz Kohut, translated by Anselm Hollo. Urizen Books, 1977.
Phillips, Adam. *Promises, Promises*. Basic Books, 2001.
Salomé, Lou-Andreas. *The Freud Journal of Lou Andreas-Salomé*, translated with an introduction by Stanley A. Leavy. Basic Books, 1964.
Shengold, Leonard. *Is There Life Without Mother? Psychoanalysis, Biography, Creativity*. The Analytic Press, 2000.
Wortis, Joseph. *Fragments of an Analysis with Freud*. McGraw-Hill, 1975.

Chapter 21

Other Psychoanalytic Fiction Worth Reading

My discussion of psychoanalytic fiction writers is comprehensive but not exhaustive. Space prevents me from writing in depth about other worthwhile psychoanalytic fiction, but I want to note briefly the following lively and illuminating stories.

Paul Buttenwieser: *Free Association*

I came across Paul Buttenwieser's name in a most unusual way—from reading the program guide to the August 13, 2023 concert at Tanglewood, in western Massachusetts, the summer home of the Boston Symphony Orchestra.

> Sunday afternoon's performance is supported by a generous gift from Great Benefactors Catherine and Paul Buttenwieser. Elected a BSO Advisor in 1998 and Trustee in 2000, Paul was elevated to Life Trustee in 2017. He served as President of the Board of Trustees from 2014 to 2017 and a Vice-Chair of the Board of Trustees from 2010 to 2013.

The program guide notes, additionally, that Buttenwieser had the honor of performing as pianist in Beethoven's Cello Sonata No. 3 in A, Opus 69, at the Institute of Contemporary Art, in Boston, with Yo-Yo Ma. In his other life, Buttenwieser earned a bachelor's degree in history and literature at Harvard College and his MD at Harvard Medical School. He teaches psychiatry and psychoanalysis at Harvard and the Boston Psychoanalytic Society & Institute. He is also the author of two novels, *Free Association* (1981) and *Their Pride and Joy* (1987).

Roger Liebman, the besieged protagonist in *Free Association*, is a 32-year-old psychiatrist on the verge of graduating from the Manhattan Institute for Psychoanalysis. In light of his creator's musical talent, one might expect Roger to enjoy classical music. He does, but he is tone-deaf, a noteworthy detail suggesting that, despite Buttenwieser's intimate understanding of his self-absorbed analyst, it would be misleading to conflate novelist and character. Roger worries that his analytic work is becoming like the piano music performed by a woman he had once dated years earlier: "facile, correct, and soulless" (36). Roger's rocky journey toward psychological health, fulfillment in work and love, becomes the focus of this darkly satirical novel that could be called "Psychoanalysis and Its Discontents."

Roger's overwhelming dread is that he is "mediocre" and will never accomplish anything meaningful in life. The fear of mediocrity also appears in *Their Pride and Joy*, a study of the Gutheims, a privileged New York City family. "You know how it is in this family," the youngest son, Carl, a gifted pianist, complains. "If you're a lawyer, you make the Supreme Court. If you're a tennis player, you win the Davis Cup. If you're a pianist, you play in Carnegie Hall. If not, forget it" (295). Like Carl Gutheim, Roger lives in perpetual doubt about his personal and professional life. One would think that his six-year analysis helped him grasp the origins of this fear and gave him a more positive view of himself, but he remains self-lacerating and insecure. Pointing out his analysands' self-defeating thoughts and behavior, Paul feels like a hypocrite. But his vulnerability makes him an engaging character, one with whom the reader sympathizes.

First novels sometimes reveal insufficient narrative distance, resulting in the novelist's overidentification with the Bildungsroman protagonist. Buttenwieser avoids this problem by maintaining a caustic view of his characters. The novelist uses satire to mock every aspect of the insular psychoanalytic world, beginning with his flawed protagonist. An ironist, Buttenwieser shows how Roger's words lead to unintended consequences. An early example of this is Roger's patient Ellen Hirsch, a 27-year-old woman who has lost her passion for work. She loved to write poetry but, fearing she could not support herself through writing, became a teacher of poetry instead (like Sine in Cordelia Schmidt-Hellerau's *Memento*), thus dooming her dream. Doing more speaking than listening, which is the opposite of the advice given to him by his analytic supervisor, Roger urges his patient to get more out of life, including having an affair, if that's what she desires. Around the same time, Roger, who is desperate for a sexual affair, decides to answer an ad placed in the *Village Voice* by "SJF"—Single Jewish Female—who seeks a "SM" in his 30s. Roger's epistolary exchange with SJF leads him to the Metropolitan Museum of Art where he discovers, to his horror, that SJF is Ellen Hirsch. During the next session, Ellen bursts into tears, unable to understand why they cannot have an affair if they are both attracted to each other. Mortified by the situation, Roger, to his credit, explains how a romantic relationship would sabotage therapy. Ellen leaves, concluding that analysis is not what she needs at this time. Roger recoils from bringing this up with his own analyst who will say, as he always did, "It's all grist for the mill" (61).

Buttenwieser sees Roger more clearly than Roger sees himself, but both share the same attitude toward homosexuality, one reflective of the late 1970s, when the novel takes place. Freud did not pathologize homosexuality, as did many others of his time; he regarded homosexuality not as an illness but as a developmental arrest, a fixation at an earlier state of psychosexual development. The American Psychoanalytic Association (APsA) supported the American

Psychiatric Association (APA) in its decision to include homosexuality as a "sexual deviance" in the 1968 edition of the *Diagnostic and Statistical Manual of Mental Disorders* (*DSM-III*); but whereas the APA decided in 1973 to eliminate the homosexuality diagnosis from the *DSM*, APsA refused to endorse this decision. It was not until 1991, when confronted with an anti-discrimination lawsuit by the American Psychological Association, that APsA allowed for the training of gay and lesbian analysts. *Free Association* betrays the slowness of this change. Hendricks has recently come out of the closet, yet Roger believes that he is not gay but going through a prolonged adolescent rebellion. Hendricks disagrees. "Even the great American Psychiatric Association cleared our name and everything" (18), he laments to Roger, who counters by claiming that his patient uses the word "gay" to try to convince himself of something he does not fully believe. Although Roger does not think that being gay is sinful, he does not believe that it is healthy. Visiting Cape Cod during August, the month most analysts take their vacation, Roger meets a person who recommends that he visit nearby Provincetown, long associated with the gay community. "That's not really my scene" (124), he sputters. With Roger's encouragement, Hendricks begins dating a woman, albeit reluctantly. The novel implies that Hendricks is now heading in the right direction, toward heterosexuality, a detail that reveals subtle rather than blatant homophobia.

Although some readers of *Free Association* may conclude the novel believing, with the early twentieth-century Viennese satirist Karl Kraus, that psychoanalysis is the disease it purports to cure, Roger remains committed to his profession. He reflects Buttenwieser's belief, and my own, that psychoanalysis is "still the great intellectual movement of this century" (217). Roger is rewarded for his patience and diligence by meeting the woman of his dreams, Peggy Wilmot, who stands by him, nurturing his growth as a character. Peggy is a breath of fresh air in the stifling world of psychoanalysis. Roger is drawn toward her because she is "so amazingly unconflicted"; he attributes this to the "lack of so much as a drop of Jewish blood in her veins" (175), a curious statement about his Jewish heritage that the novel does not explore. With Peggy's help, Roger changes, embracing life more fully. Debussy wrote that music is not in the notes but in the spaces between them; toward the novel's end, Roger heeds his supervisor's advice and learns to read his patients' silences. He also proves to be a peacemaker, enabling his splintering psychoanalytic institute to remain whole. Adding icing to the cake, his former patient, Ellen Hirsch, sends him a letter indicating that, thanks to his efforts, she is writing poetry again, making her dream come true. All's well that ends well.

David Hellerstein: *Loving Touches*

David Hellerstein's 1987 novel *Loving Touches* and Buttenwieser's *Free Association* both focus on young male psychiatrists who have much to learn, personally and professionally, about themselves. Both novels reveal the hierarchical structure and complicated politics of psychiatric hospitals and psychoanalytic institutes. And both novels contain a mixture of sympathy, sarcasm, and black humor. Hellerstein's protagonist, Harvard-trained Dr. Pete Roth, married to an ambitious lawyer, whom he calls a "phallic woman," works at a private psychiatric hospital on Manhattan's Upper West Side. According to the gossip of those who work there, "No resident ever left Curtiss Psychiatric without suffering" (4). Pete is less self-absorbed than Roger Liebman, less self-conscious, less self-doubting. Indeed, he is regarded as the star psychiatric resident. Pride cometh before fall, the reader predicts. Juxtaposing past and present, *Loving Touches* shows how Pete, while a fourth-year medical student in Cambridge, Massachusetts, had a summer affair with a young woman, Celine Walter, with a history of suicide attempts. Fast forward: now a resident in New York City, Pete is told to interview a patient at Curtiss. He does not recognize her at first, but she recognizes him: "You are a bastard," she curses, humiliating him in front of his peers and teachers, "an uncaring *fuck* like I've never seen before" (11). Until this moment, Hellerstein's psychiatrist has not transgressed professional boundaries—Celine was not his patient two years earlier—but he becomes hopelessly involved with her treatment and progress, thus generating the novel's plot.

Hellerstein is a psychiatrist, not a psychoanalyst, but there is little difference in a novel that skewers the mental health community. Hellerstein attended Harvard College (like Paul Buttenwieser) and received his medical training at Stanford University. Medicine was in his genes: in his 1994 memoir *A Family of Doctors*, he chronicles his family's links with medicine through five generations. In "How to Become a Doctor-Writer," Hellerstein reveals that he became passionate about writing when he was in college, rebelling against his "apparent destiny" by taking a year off to study creative writing. He could not permanently defy destiny, but he has combined his twin passions. His short stories have earned him several prestigious literary prizes and fellowships, and his second novel, *Stone Babies*, a detective mystery about an OB/GYN physician who blows the whistle on a corrupt fertility center, to his own peril, appeared in 2001. His other books include *Battles of Life and Death* (1986) and *The Couch, the Clinic, and the Scanner: Stories from Three Revolutionary Eras of the Mind* (2023). Hellerstein is a professor of psychiatry at Columbia University Medical Center and a research psychiatrist at the New York State Psychiatric Institute.

Hellerstein's ambivalence toward psychoanalysis is evident in *The Couch, the Clinic, and the Scanner*. His residency training took place in Manhattan's Payne Whitney Clinic, considered to be the most desirable psychiatric training program in the country. "We residents gossiped that the Payne Whitney educational method entailed a deliberate attempt to *induce* deep psychological crisis (and then a referral for psychoanalysis) among those of us in training, its aim being to make us anew. Certainly, that's what happened for me" (57). Hellerstein was startled when his clinical supervisor accused him of being a "flirt" (10), though he later came to acknowledge the countertransference problem. He learned much about himself during his training analysis, yet he still finds psychoanalysis "peculiar, quaint, scientifically questionable," wondering at the same time whether his doubts are "just another form that my ever-mutating resistance is taking" (17). He remains "a bit of an outcast and rebel" (58), a description that also characterizes Pete Roth.

Celine is drawn toward Pete partly because he resembles her father. "I mean, knowing you're a surgeon—like my father, of course, but entirely different—and my analyst is about to go on vacation, which usually completely unhinges me" (*Loving Touches* 53). We learn little about Pete's own father except one salient detail: he wanted his son to become a surgeon. "I wasn't sure if I wanted to be a surgeon because *I* liked surgery or because everybody else wanted me to," he informs his wife. "My father, you" (213–214). Hellerstein discloses the same conflict in *A Family of Doctors*. "Dad made us want to be doctors—that is, when he wasn't driving us crazy" (13). Hellerstein's decision not to become a cardiac surgeon, like his father, and to choose psychiatry, "a field that to many doctors hardly seemed to be a part of medicine," was greeted "unenthusiastically" by his father (216). This biographical detail helps explain one of the most curious moments in *Loving Touches*: Pete's decision, upon meeting Celine, to abandon surgery for psychiatry. We rarely see in *Loving Touches* Pete's fascination with psychiatry, a passion Hellerstein fully conveys in his nonfictional books.

The most traumatic moment in Celine's adolescence is not her mother's suicide, as we might expect, but her father's seductive behavior. While she was walking along the beach with her drunken father, he *touched* her, an act that she felt was her own fault, one she has been talking about with her analyst for the last year. Celine then refers to Freud's seduction theory, a turning point in the early history of psychoanalysis, or perhaps the *beginning* of psychoanalysis, when Freud realized the distinction between reality and fantasy: some stories about early sexual abuse were imagined, not real. "You must know all the controversy that's going on in psychoanalysis about the seduction theory?" Celine asks Pete. "Well, some people would say that I've just imagined the whole thing, that I'm just getting myself all screwed up for some fantasy. I bet you don't even believe me" (162). He does. But shouldn't. She confesses near the end of the novel that *she* attempted to seduce her sodden father—and then became hysterical.

Why did Hellerstein imagine this conclusion? In offering a counterintuitive ending, the novelist startles his readers. Oedipal fantasies may be ubiquitous, but most cases of parent–child incest are initiated by the father or stepfather. *Loving Touches* conjures up the "Daddy's Girl" theme in F. Scott Fitzgerald's last completed novel, *Tender Is the Night* (1934), in which the charismatic psychiatrist-hero, Dr. Dick Diver, succumbs to the advances of his beguiling patient, Nicole Warren, whose incestuous relationship with her father, following her mother's death, triggers a psychotic breakdown. Like Dick Diver, Hellerstein's protagonist learns little about himself as a result of his sexual misadventure, apart from one singular insight: "he was in love with an illusion she created" (*Loving Touches* 133), a revelation contradicted by many self-justifying statements. It is hard to imagine any mental health professional, even those emotionally or romantically involved with a patient, saying, as Pete does to Celine, "you *stink* of innocence. Everywhere you go you're a poor little victim" (228). Unchastened at the end, Pete "sauntered" toward the hospital's elevators and tries to persuade himself, in the story's last sentence, that his life will be fine if he can break his obsession with Celine. "If only he could stop trembling, everything would be great" (233)—a detail confirming the truth that no one leaves Curtiss without suffering.

Avodah Offit: *Virtual Love*

In the olden days, before the creation of the internet, epistolary friendships were slow to develop, dependent upon the time-consuming transmission of letters and mail carriers, but now snail mail is almost as archaic as telephone booths. Avodah Offit's 1994 novel *Virtual Love* highlights a cyberspace relationship between two psychiatrists separated by 3000 miles. Communication is instant. Aphra Zion and Marc Martell enact the roles of teacher and student, analyst and analysand, so that she can teach him the theory and practice of sex therapy, about which she has written a textbook. They had once met in person, when Marc, who calls himself "E-man" in his virtual correspondence, attended a seminar given by Aphra, "go-dot" (a pun on the pixels that form an image on a computer screen), in New York City. Complicating the situation, Aphra does not send Marc her most self-disclosing emails—though we scrutinize them. As *Virtual Love* progresses, so does their friendship; when they meet in person, at the end of the story, and become intimate, we discover that they have more in common than we imagined.

Born in 1931, Offit was a lifelong New Yorker, graduating from Hunter College and New York University Medical School. She was a pioneer in the emerging field of sex therapy, an approach that began in the late 1960s. Before penning her novel, Offit authored two acclaimed books on sex therapy, *The Sexual Self* (1971) and *Night Thoughts: Reflections of a Sex Therapist* (1981). *The New Republic* hailed her as the "Montaigne of human sexuality," words appearing as a blurb on the novel's dust jacket. Offit was the Coordinator of the Sexual Therapy and Consultation Center of Lenox Hill Hospital in New York City, which she founded, on the staff of the Payne Whitney Psychiatric Clinic, and a faculty member of the Cornell University Medical College. *Virtual Love* was her only novel, but her short stories appeared in national magazines that included *Glamour* and *Vogue*. She died in 2015.

Like Pete Roth in *Loving Touches*, Marc becomes a psychiatrist in opposition to his father's wishes. If Marc's father could have afforded medical school, he would have become a surgeon; years later, he was willing to pay for his son's medical education, but Marc decided he would enter a specialty the furthest from what his father wanted to be: "most shrinks rate body-hacking as their second favorite career choice," he tells Aphra. "When you're really impatient with a disease, you just chop the bugger out, no fuss, no talk, no bother!" (*Virtual Love* 107). Aphra is passionate about psychiatry, offering a compelling reason for being a psychotherapist. "Unless I was somehow entering people's minds rather than the rest of their bodies, I was afraid I'd feel robotic. I'd lose interest. I craved the varietal experience of entering other people's psychic lives, which was spiritually different from the warm connection of love given through manual labor" (120).

Offit and Aphra entered medical school during a time when few women became physicians. Offit describes in *Night Thoughts* how she seemed to "get the bulk of the genital and fecal work," including being forced to perform adult circumcisions (131–132). She attributes this to male physicians hazing female students. She dramatizes the event in *Virtual Love*, remarking that Aphra couldn't sleep the night before she was required to perform the circumcision in the presence of a male surgeon who supervised the procedure. Holding the "ritual blade," she was "terrified" before bestowing a "rite of passage."

Aphra is an excellent therapist, able to listen empathically and offer valuable clinical advice. Her insights into Marc's patient, Toni, are exemplary. Aphra recognizes that when psychiatrists, no matter how well analyzed, begin training as sex therapists, they struggle with submerged fantasies that inevitably surface. She repeatedly speaks for the novelist, as when she instructs Marc that sex is not the real reason patients visit her. "Usually they're depressed, they're angry at each other, they're fighting" (44). Later Aphra reminds him that "[m]ost sex problems turn out to be affectional disorders that we can't touch with easy-does-it therapy!" (244). Additionally, Aphra casts much light on Marc's own problems: his marriage is falling apart, and he's becoming sexually obsessed with Toni. "Something is going on with me," he confides to Aphra, "i really need my own psychiatrist and i really can't afford one right now—it's a miserable irony to be in the shrink business and not to be able to afford a good shrink!" (23). It's ironic that Aphra attributes her need to hear other people's stories to her own mother, who has taught her that men are "beasts" and confessed that she never wanted Aphra to be a girl—a mother with whom her daughter has counteridentified her entire life.

Offit has wisely avoided the temptation to make her protagonist flawless. For years, Aphra's first husband, Harry, was unfaithful. How could she have been so blind, she asks herself, about his infidelities? Given her mother's bitterness, her inclination toward martyrdom and vengeance, and her father's remoteness and miserliness, how was Aphra able to develop the empathy necessary to be a psychiatrist? Unable to obtain warmth, comfort, or guidance from her parents, she appears to have parented herself, learning to deal with terrors on her own. "It is difficult to shock me," she admits. "That is as much a grief and a loss as it is a professional advantage" (*Virtual Love* 240). It is likely that Aphra's attitude toward her parents reflects the novelist's attitude toward her own parents. Aphra's parents owned a hotel in the Catskills in upstate New York, as did Offit's parents. In *Night Thoughts* Offit calls herself a "hotel brat" during summers, where she learned that sex was "recreation"; only later in life did she realize that sex might involve "complicated feelings" (175).

Offit's husband, Sidney Offit, the author of two novels, ten young adult novels, and two memoirs, wrote about his experience working in his in-laws' Borscht Belt hotel, the Aladdin, in his 1959 novel *He Had It Made*, dedicated to his wife. The novel describes Marsha Mandheimer's bitterness toward her parents, owners of the Sesame Hotel, based on the Aladdin. "All I ever heard day and night for twenty years was the hotel, the hotel—should we build a new casino and how much will it cost?" (185). Her parents' biggest worry, she continues, when she developed the measles, was that all the guests would find out and leave, ruining the season. Aphra's father was a civil engineer in New York City, like Offit's father, Abraham Komito, who died in 1972 at age 70. Aphra's mother was not a writer, but the novelist's mother, Carrie Offit, was, authoring when she was nearly a centenarian two memoirs on her life as a Catskill hotelkeeper. Based on these similarities, much of the material about Aphra's parents is autobiographical. A curious sentence appears in the acknowledgments in *The Sexual Self* in which Offit expresses gratitude toward her mother, Carrie Komito, "for suffering my long silence" (8)—silence that appears to indicate estrangement. Offit refers to her mother in *Night Thoughts* as "both the toughest woman in the East and the least depressed person I have ever met" (137), praise that does not appear in *Virtual Love*.

Aphra shares the novelist's commitment to writing and reading. "Writing is my affirmation of life" (36), Aphra tells Marc at the beginning of the novel, a passion he, too, experiences, referring to his "compulsion to write" as "both sickness and salvation" (76). Offit admits in *Night Thoughts* that she became "addicted to writing. Perhaps it came from a need to figure out what I was doing, even as I was doing it" (12). Aphra and Marc sleep together at the end of the novel, and we are shocked that she signs her last letter to him as "Your sister." The ending stunned the two reviewers in *The New York Times*. Nevertheless, both Rosemary L. Bray and Christopher Lehmann-Haupt praised the novel's exploration of boundaries in psychotherapy and its search for mental health. *Virtual Love* was prescient in its depiction of life and love on the internet.

Josh Bazell: *Beat the Reaper*

No psychoanalytic fiction writer has created a narrative voice like the one in Josh Bazell's 2009 novel *Beat the Reaper*. Witness the opening sentence: "So I'm on my way to work and I stop to watch a pigeon fight a rat in the snow, and some fuckhead tries to mug me!" (3). What makes the narrative voice singular is not his profanity-laced language; or his unique way of looking at the world, melding attentiveness to detail and mordant wit; or the copious footnotes, a treasure trove of useful and useless information; or the narrator's disarming candor about his many personality flaws. Rather, the narrator's easy colloquial speech and use of second-person pronoun, conjuring the spirit of *The Catcher in the Rye*—"I'm not sure this is any of your business, but if you really want me to talk about her, here it is" (148)—make the novel a page-turner.

The first-person narrator, Pietro Brnwa, later called Peter Brown, is a former mob hit man turned ER physician now in the Federal Witness Protection Program.

He became a killer to avenge the murders of his beloved grandparents, Stefan Brnwa and Anna Maisel, Polish Jews who survived the horrors of Auschwitz only to be slain by two New Jersey mobsters. After their deaths, Peter is befriended by Mafia lawyer David Locano and his son, Adam, known as "Skinflick," a nickname that refers to the porn film he made with his babysitter when he was 12. Peter loved Skinflick as a brother, but later Skinflick tries to kill him in the shark tank in Brooklyn's Aquarium. Readers encounter many surprises in the criminal/medical thriller, beginning with the provocative epigraph from Camus: "If Nietzsche is correct, that to shame a man is to kill him, then any honest attempt at autobiography will be an act of self-destruction." I was so enamored of the quotation that I planned to use it for a future book—until I read the warning at the end of *Beat the Reaper* that everything in the novel is fiction, including the epigraph.

Bazell earned a BA in English literature from Brown University and began writing *Beat the Reaper* while a medical student at Columbia. He is now an instructor in neuroscience at the William Alanson White Institute and an associate editor of *Contemporary Psychoanalysis*. *Beat the Reaper* garnered many positive evaluations. Matt Ruff admitted in his *New York Times* review that although he struggled to suspend his disbelief, by novel's end "Bazell had more than earned my indulgence as a reader." *Time* magazine's Lev Grossman judged *Beat the Reaper* as one of the top ten novels of the year: "I defy you to put it down." Even the reviewer in the *Journal of the American Medical Association* begrudgingly lauded the novel: "Bazell's thriller is brutal and vulgar but at the same time hilarious and unflinching" (Mitsanek 2278). The novel became a bestseller, and a sequel, *Wild Thing*, appeared in 2012. *Beat the Reaper* darkly satirizes the sickening business side of healthcare in the United States, but it reserves its deepest moral outrage for the Holocaust. There is nothing funny when Peter travels to Poland and discovers the ghoulish contents of the death camps and the ongoing efforts to revise history. In an extended footnote, Bazell offers a brief history of I.G. Farben, the German chemical and pharmaceutical company that ran Auschwitz's death camp. In another footnote, which has a slightly different narrative voice (as do all the footnotes), Bazell reveals his favorite Lech Walesa story, one that occurred shortly before Peter's trip to Poland. "Realizing he was about to lose the presidency, Walesa announced that his opponent was secretly Jewish. He then denied he was a bigot, saying, 'Actually I wish I was Jewish myself. Because then I would have a lot more money.' Funny guy!" (98).

Peter has no qualms killing the two men responsible for his grandparents' deaths, but he learns at the end of the novel that his grandparents had died in Auschwitz, their identities stolen by two Poles who came to the United States after the war. Russian Jews recognized the two imposters and, as a favor to them, David Locano ordered their deaths. Peter never regrets killing them or the other thugs. He has his own code of honor: he never targets women or people whose misdeeds are entirely in the past. In the words of his former medical teacher, Professor Marmoset, he is an "interesting and possibly redeemable individual" (234).

Given the novel's medical authenticity, one can infer that the author is a physician. In one harrowing scene, Peter breaks his own fibula and uses it to stab to death his archnemesis Skinflick. The autofibulectomy so impresses Professor Marmoset that he urges Peter to write an article about it for the *New England Journal of Medicine*. Peter mentions in passing the *Diagnostic and Statistical Manual of Mental Disorders* and in a footnote calls attention to Elisabeth Kübler-Ross's flawed stage theory of dying: "what we avoid thinking about when we think about Kübler-Ross is how she later changed her mind and decided we'll all be reincarnated. I wish I was shitting you" (124). There is only one reference in the novel to psychoanalysis. Inside Auschwitz's gates, Peter sees a group of nuns and skinheads handing out pamphlets stating that "hysterical international Jews" are trying to prevent Catholic services in the deathcamp. "It makes your hands itch," Peter laments, "and you wonder if twisting a skinhead's neck would satisfy Freud's dictum that the only thing that can ever make us happy is the fulfillment of childhood desires" (99–100).

Leslie Schweitzer Miller: *Discovery*

Leslie Schweitzer Miller dedicates her 2018 novel *Discovery* to her husband, Robert H. Miller, whom she calls "my beshert Bob." My non-Yiddish-speaking parents occasionally used this word, but I had no clue what it meant. Reading Miller's dedication, I was too lazy to google the word. But "beshert" reappears several times in the novel, along with its meaning. The fictional David Rettig, a gregarious American archaeologist living in Israel, is instantly smitten by Giselle Gélis, an American-born scholar of early Christianity now teaching at the Institut Catholique de Toulouse in France, when they meet at an annual international conference of biblical scholars held in Amsterdam. Although not Jewish, David invokes the Yiddishism. "In Israel they say 'it's beshert' when something is meant to be; and when someone—say me, for instance—finds the one—you, for instance—who's meant for him, he says she is his 'beshert.'" Giselle immediately exclaims: "soul mates" (107). Maybe not soul mates at the start of their relationship, but amor vincit omnia in this engaging novel.

Miller is a psychiatrist and psychoanalyst in New York City, and her novel reveals impressive historical/biblical scholarship in bringing to life one of the most controversial questions in early Christianity: Jesus's relationship to Mary Magdalene. Giselle points out that Marie-Madeleine, as she is called in France, had been maligned as a fallen woman for over a thousand years, beginning with Pope Gregory I's branding her a sinner in 591. Not until 1969 did the Roman Catholic Church declare the lack of evidence for its previous condemnation. There has long been speculation, strenuously opposed by the Church, that Jesus was alive when he was cut down from the cross and later married Mary Magdalene. This heresy contradicts the two central tenets of Christianity: Jesus's crucifixion and resurrection. Relying on the scholarship of Karen Leigh King, a professor at Harvard Divinity

School, Miller imagines the existence of a newly discovered papyrus, written in Aramaic, that turns out to be a ketubah, a Jewish marriage contract, confirming the union between Miriam, daughter of Cyrus of Magdal, and Yeshua, son of Joseph of Nazareth, in 28 CE. Miller acknowledges that she has taken literary license in her novel. Based on subsequent research, the papyrus King introduced at a scholarly conference in Rome in 2012 proved to have a false provenance (Wangness). No matter: *Discovery* is a novel, not a history lesson, and the well-plotted story seems plausible.

Melding historical fiction, detective fiction, and romance, *Discovery* contains two interrelated stories. Abbé François Bérenger Saunière makes a momentous discovery when he arrives in the mountaintop village of Rennes-le-Château, in southern France, in 1885: he unearths a first century urn containing a rolled papyrus. Convinced of its authenticity, he hides it for safekeeping. But danger and intrigue surround the papyrus, and his mentor, Father Gélis, is bludgeoned to death, a murder that is never solved. The murder happened, historically, exactly as Miller presents it. Saunière and his companion, Marie, were also real people, and the source of his accumulation of vast wealth remains an enigma, one that inspired Miller to write the novel. Giselle and David rediscover the urn, with its priceless papyrus, buried in a cave, and they smuggle it to the United States, where it is authenticated. "It's the most remarkable story I've ever heard" (190), enthuses Giselle's sister. Even if readers of *Discovery* do not entirely share that conviction, the novel is nevertheless compelling, largely because of its two believable characters.

David and Giselle could not be more different. One is a doubter, the other, a believer. An English major in college, which explains his fondness for quoting Shakespeare, poetry, and song lyrics, David is extroverted, smart, and self-confident. Why does Miller make him into a "fallen Methodist" rather than a secular New York Jew? Few non-Jews know what "beshert" means. Most gentiles in his situation would have invoked "kismet," a word that also appears in the story. David refers to the historical Jesus as a "nice Jewish boy" (26); later, he tells a waiter, "In Israel, where I work, we say *l'chaim*, to life" (127)—spoken like a real Jew. But I concede that my minor criticism may reveal more about me than about the novel: my desire to see all secular Jews as heroes! In any event, Giselle is a woman of deep Christian faith who is understandably unnerved by the idea that everything she has learned as a Catholic may be wrong. Having been jilted by her fiancé 20 years earlier, and long resigned to remaining single, she is wary of David's faithful pursuit of his holy grail.

Unlike the rational David, Giselle is mystical, reminding us of Teresa of Avila, whom Giselle cites. *Discovery* does not contain the intense mysticism of Julia Kristeva's *Teresa, My Love*, but it effectively contrasts rationalism and mysticism. Inside a grotto in Sainte Baume, Giselle spies water droplets on stained glass windows and shivers, whispering, "The walls are weeping" (86). She *feels* Mary Magdalene's presence, as if her spirit is reaching out to her, reminding her of suffering. At the same time, Giselle fears that she may be losing her grip on reality. Miller succeeds in conveying her character's apprehension of a deeper, unseen reality of which David is unaware. Miller connects the otherworldly Giselle, troubled by David's efforts to bring the document to the world's attention, to the unearthly ancient papyrus. Despite her powerful faith in the Roman Catholic Church, Giselle objects to its history of misogyny—and both she and David are appalled by the hatred associated with religious intolerance and persecution. Giselle bears a striking physical and perhaps spiritual resemblance to Mary Magdalene, whose face has been portrayed in countless paintings. If Giselle is a modern-day incarnation of Mary Magdalene, who was in love with Jesus, does that make David, who loves Giselle deeply, a Son of God? Perhaps, but that is another story.

Near the end of Miller's story, Giselle abruptly breaks off the relationship, believing that the differences between the two of them are insurmountable. How can a woman who has always been afraid of human entanglements suddenly, or even slowly, live with another person? Miller knows as both a psychoanalyst and a novelist that differences often doom relationships. Differences also generate the tensions that drive a story, for without conflict, there is no art. But Miller knows equally well that people have the ability to change. David gently reminds Giselle that her conflicted relationship with her mother may explain her fear of closeness—a psychoanalytic insight that proves correct. *Discovery* closes with the couple happily married with an adopted baby aptly named Madeleine—proof that they are indeed beshert.

Kerry L. Malawista: *Meet the Moon*

"I'm not sure if it's worse remembering or forgetting her." Fourteen-year-old Jody Moran raises this agonizing question about her newly deceased mother, expressing a fear to which an adult friend responds sympathetically: "Remember her and miss her a little more, until one day we can remember her without all the sad feelings" (102). Love and loss lie at the heart of Kerry L. Malawista's 2022 coming-of-age novel, *Meet the Moon*. Written mainly for young adults, *Meet the Moon* contains psychological truths that will appeal to older readers as well, especially to those who continue to grieve a lost loved one.

Malawista is a psychoanalyst in private practice in Potamic, Maryland and McLean, Virginia. A board member of the Washington Baltimore Center for Psychoanalysis, she is co-chair of New Directions in Writing, a three-year postgraduate training program that encourages clinicians, academics, and authors to use writing for personal and professional growth. Malawista co-edited with Robert Winer *Who's Behind the Couch* (2017), interviews with 17 psychoanalysts that span a wide variety of clinical and theoretical approaches. She is also the editor of *The Things They Wrote: A Writing/Healing Project*, a collection of stories by doctors, nurses, and other frontline workers about surviving the COVID-19 pandemic.

Malawista leaps to fiction in *Meeting the Moon*, showing how literature and psychoanalysis complement each other in a poignant novel.

Jody Moran is an endearing and relatable protagonist, smart, funny, kind, and articulate. A budding wordsmith, she learns each day a new word from the *Oxford English Dictionary* (*OED*), a weighty tome she keeps near her bed that expands her universe. Young adult fiction usually displays simple prose, reflective of a teenager's language, but Jody's *OED* words add richness to the story. Scores of advanced words abound. She is, as she proudly notes, a sesquipedalian, a lover of polysyllabic words. Am I the only English professor who did not know the meaning of *longevous* despite being ancient myself?

Jody's mother dies in a car crash on April 20, 1970, at age 36, shattering her family's happiness. Jody's three-year-old brother, Billy, is seriously injured, though he recovers. Without sentimentalizing the turbulent 1970s, Malawista has carefully researched the novel to capture the spirit of the decade. A favorite expression is "What the Sputnik," a reference to the first artificial Earth satellite launched by the Soviet Union in 1957. Jody and her classmates anxiously watch the Apollo 13 splashdown, aware of the three American astronauts who lost their lives three years earlier. Jody enjoys hearing the Beatles albums *Abbey Road* and *Yellow Submarine*. It was a decade in which stores were closed on Sunday and when a gallon of milk cost one dollar. The Irish-American Morans identify with another Irish-American family beset by tragedy. "I liked to think we were like the Kennedys—Catholic, lots of kids, just without the cash" (114). Jody talks about the challenge of learning the metric system, one of the few anachronisms in the novel: Congress passed the voluntary Metric Conversion Act in 1975, an event that still has not occurred.

Jody is a voracious reader, and of all the books she reads, the one that is most helpful is Elisabeth Kübler-Ross's *On Death and Dying*, published in 1969. Jody sees the book in a library, begins reading it, and encounters the sentence: "*We cannot look at the sun all the time, we cannot face death all the time*," words used by Kübler-Ross originally expressed by the seventeenth-century French writer La Rouchefoucauld (*Meet the Moon* 77; *On Death and Dying* 39). It's not surprising that Jody's library had a copy of this newly published book; Kübler-Ross, known famously and infamously as the "death and dying lady," was the most influential thanatologist of the second half of the twentieth century. Believing the book will help her grieve her mother's death, Jody steals it from the library—and then worries that she has committed a mortal sin. Jody is especially impressed with Kübler-Ross's Freudian insight that "we cannot distinguish between a wish and a deed" (*Meet the Moon* 78; *On Death and Dying* 3).

Reading *On Death and Dying* allows Jody to grasp that despite her occasional anger toward her mother and statements like "I don't care if you die," she was not responsible for her death. This is a fraught concept for anyone to grasp, especially a young teenager. Another insight is the realization that the dead do not return to life regardless of our deepest wishes. And still another revelation, as Kübler-Ross observes, is that we cannot imagine our own death, to which Jody ruefully adds,

"We can't imagine anyone being dead" (82). *Meet the Moon* demonstrates all of Kübler-Ross's responses to the approach of death. The problem with Kübler-Ross's stage theory of death, as clinicians and researchers have concluded, is that it greatly oversimplifies a process that is different for each person. Robert Buckman points out that the stage theory ignores emotions like guilt, hope, and despair. David Wendall Moller likens Kübler-Ross and those who agree with her ideal of a good death to "travel agents for the dying, offering therapeutic intervention to a singular destination: tranquil, peaceful death" (51). Jody could not have known that late in her life Kübler-Ross became increasingly mystical, writing about out-of-body experiences and speaking with Jesus. As I remark in *Dying in Character*, contrary to the advice Kübler-Ross had given earlier in her career, when she was vehemently opposed to physician-assisted suicide, after a massive stroke in 1995 left her paralyzed, she asked a friend to hasten her death. "She fought with God until the very end," Carolyn Myss writes in her foreword to the 2008 edition of *On Life After Death*, "angry that she could not determine her time of death" (vii).

Criticisms of Kübler-Ross do not mar *Meet the Moon*. It's true that the story offers a tidy resolution to the family's grief, but this is understandable in a young adult novel, which usually ends on a hopeful note, even if it is only a happy-for-now conclusion. Contrary to the advice given by Jody's adult friend, it may be impossible for most people to recall a lost loved one without any sad feelings. "Oh, it's too hard to remember," Jody's maternal grandmother confesses; "We need to all of us move on" (187). Using one of the most powerful metaphors in the story, Jody worries that she may forget her mother. "Was memory like a puddle of water in the sun that evaporates?" (58). The novel is authentic in a myriad of ways. *Meet the Moon* presents a variety of points of view with respect to religious faith, ranging from Jody's devoutly Catholic maternal grandmother to Jody's "agnostic" father, an *OED* word. The novel allows readers to reach their own conclusions about the existence of an afterlife. To an adult's consoling remark that her mother is in a "better place," Jody sarcastically muses, "A better place! What did that say about us?" (42). Jody's father represents what is almost certainly the authorial point of view: "Remember, Jody," he says, "heaven is what you make it on earth" (16–17).

Malawista conveys children's fears of death that adults may not remember. "Did the funeral guys see her *naked*?" Jody asks her father; later, she wonders whether her mother would suffocate under all that dirt. Near the end of the story, she silently notices a faint white stripe where her father's wedding ring had once been. Jody remains an endearing guide in a convincing story of love, loss, and *recovery*. It's refreshing to see a father who is committed to his family's well-being and hopeful about the future. *Meet the Moon* celebrates literature. The title of the novel comes from a line in Robert Frost's poem "Going for Water" in his 1913 volume *A Boy's Will*: "We ran as if to meet the moon." The moon in Malawista's novel is associated with Jody's mother, who reveled in looking at it, proclaiming, "*I love you to the moon and back*" (68). Jody's favorite novel is *Pride and Prejudice*, which enables her to find a suitable wife for her father. Reading remains Jody's lifeline, her way of working through grief. If we can imagine Malawista's protagonist, with her *prodigious* (another *OED* word) appetite for literature, growing up, she will likely become a writer, like her creator.

Works Cited

Bazell, Josh. *Beat the Reaper*. Little, Brown, 2009.
Bazell, Josh. *Wild Thing*. Little, Brown, 2012.
Berman, Jeffrey. *Dying in Character: Memoirs on the End of Life*. U of Massachusetts P, 2012.
Bray, Rosemary L. "Please Mr. E-Man." *New York Times*, August 7, 1994.
Buckman, Robert. "Communication in Palliative Care: A Practical Guide." *The Oxford Textbook of Palliative Medicine*. 2nd ed. Edited by Derek Doyle, Geoffrey W.C. Hanks, and Nell MacDonald. Oxford UP, 1998, pp. 141–156.
Buttenwieser, Paul. *Free Association*. Little, Brown and Company, 1981.
Buttenwieser, Paul. *Their Pride and Joy*. Dell, 1987.
Fitzgerald, F. Scott. *Tender Is the Night*. Scribner's, 1934.
Frost, Robert. *A Boy's World*. Henry Holt, 1915.
Grossman, Lev. "The Top 10 Everything of 2009." *Time*, December 8, 2009.
Hellerstein, David. *Battles of Life and Death: The Discoveries of a Young Doctor During His Medical Education*. Houghton Mifflin Harcourt, 1986.
Hellerstein, David. *The Couch, the Clinic, and the Scanner: Stories from Three Revolutionary Eras*. Columbia UP, 2023.
Hellerstein, David. *A Family of Doctors*. Hill and Wang, 1994.
Hellerstein, David. "Keeping Secrets, Telling Tales: The Psychiatrist as Writer." *Journal of Medical Humanities*, vol. 18, 1997, pp. 127–139.
Hellerstein, David. *Loving Touches*. Houghton Mifflin, 1987.
Hellerstein, David. *Stone Babies*. Xlibris, 2001.
Kübler-Ross, Elisabeth. *On Death and Dying*. Macmillan, 1969.
Lehmann-Haupt, Christopher. "Books of the Times: Plumbing the Recesses of Psyche and Cyberspace." *New York Times*, April 14, 1994.
Malawista, Kerry L. *Meet the Moon*. Fitzroy Books, 2022.
Malawista, Kerry L., editor. *The Things They Wrote: A Writing/Healing Project*. Room: A Sketchbook for Analytic Action, 2023.
Miller, Leslie Schweitzer. *Discovery*. Notramour Press, 2018.
Moller, David Wendell. *Confronting Death: Values, Institutions, and Human Mortality*. Oxford UP, 1996.
Myss, Carolyn. New foreword to *On Life After Death*, by Elisabeth Kübler-Ross. Celestial Arts, 2008.
Offit, Avodah. *Night Thoughts: Reflections of a Sex Therapist*. Congdon & Lattès, 1981.
Offit, Avodah. *The Sexual Self*. Lippincott, 1977.
Offit, Avodah. *Virtual Reality*. Simon & Schuster, 1994.
Offit, Sidney. *He Had It Made*. Crown, 1959.
Ruff, Matt. "Brown's Anatomy." *New York Times*, January 9, 2009.
Wangsness, Lisa. "'Jesus' Wife' Papyrus Likely Fake, Scholar Says." *Boston Globe*, June 17, 2016.
Winer, Robert and Kerry L. Malawista, editors. *Who's Behind the Couch: The Heart and Mind of the Psychoanalyst*. Routledge, 2017.

Conclusion

Psychoanalysts and fiction writers are fascinated with characters' inner lives, particularly with what Christopher Bollas calls in *The Shadow of the Object* (1987) the "unthought known," the part of the unconscious that a person has not been able to process mentally. The union between the analyst and fiction writer is thus obvious. Both the analyst and the fiction writer dwell in the outer and inner worlds of human existence. Both are concerned with storytelling—and story listening: what is said and left unsaid. And both explore how "memory and desire," as T.S. Eliot wrote in *The Waste Land* (1922), the twentieth-century's most influential poem, combine to regenerate new life.

The marriage between psychoanalysis and literature is as old as psychoanalysis itself. Psychoanalytic literary criticism was conceived when Freud, reflecting on his tempestuous self-analysis, made a connection to two plays, *Oedipus Rex* and *Hamlet*, and gave us a radically new approach to reading literature. In the beginning, the marriage was one-sided, with Freud and his followers looking to literature mainly to confirm the truth of psychoanalysis, but now it is more equal, neither attempting to dominate the other. Vera J. Camden, the editor of *The Cambridge Companion to Literature and Psychoanalysis* (2022), calls the union, using a Puritan term, a "companionate" marriage, "not between two minds, but between two mentalities, two languages of human meaning. Literature and psychoanalysis draw from the heart of each other and in doing so foster new creations" (3). Several psychoanalytic fiction writers began their training as literature students. Christopher Bollas earned a PhD in English at the University of Buffalo before becoming a psychoanalyst and a creative writer. Thomas Ogden was a literature and premed undergraduate at Amherst College. Arlene Heyman and Merle Molofsky earned MFA degrees in creative writing at Syracuse University and Columbia University, respectively.

Surprises

I was surprised by the popularity of detective fiction among psychoanalytic fiction writers, nearly all of whom are, to judge from my research, male. (An exception is Judith L. Mitrani's 2021 novel *Couched in Blood*.) The cognitive psychologist and bestselling author Frank Tallis remarks in his murder mystery *A Death in Vienna* (2005) that just as Freud influenced the course of detective fiction, so did detective fiction influence Freud, but he doesn't discuss why this genre of literature appeals to male but not female psychoanalytic writers. Is it because of the violence inherent in murder mysteries, violence particularly against women, the usual victims of these stories? (Tallis describes in graphic detail a pathologist cutting open a female body, exposing all of its organs.) Is it because most serial killers are men and most detectives men, suggesting male-dominated fiction? Is it because women are more interested in the attachment bonds of family and friends? For whatever reasons, murder mysteries attract male psychoanalytic writers.

Another surprise was that psychoanalytic fiction writers pursue a wide variety of stories, including historical fiction, detective fiction, coming-of-age fiction, and quest fiction. Some writers situate their stories in psychoanalytic settings and dramatize the talking cure; reading these stories, one rarely forgets that the authors are mental health professionals: Julia Kristeva, James Herman Kleiger, Jonathan Kellerman, Alan Krohn, Richard Kluft, Bruce Fink, Cordelia Schmidt-Hellerau, Christopher Gibson, Paul Buttenwieser, and David Hellerstein. But other writers, drawing a sharp distinction between their identities as psychoanalysts and fiction writers, privilege the latter over the former: Gregorio Kohon, Thomas Ogden, Arlene Heyman, Austin Ratner, Joan Wexler, Cliff Wilkerson, Theodore Jacobs, Daniel Jacobs, Merle Molofsky, Richard Reichbart, Irene Cairo, Luke Hadge, and Leslie Schweitzer Miller.

Another surprise is the number of psychoanalytic fiction writers in my study who are Jewish. According to a 2007 University of Chicago Medicine study, psychiatrists are the least religious of all physicians. Twenty-nine percent of psychiatrists are Jewish, compared to 13 percent of all physicians. Nearly *three-quarters* of the psychoanalytic fiction writers in my study are Jewish, mainly secular Jews. Why? It was not selection bias on my part: I wrote about nearly all the authors I came across or who were suggested to me. I have no convincing explanation apart from the fact that Jews have long been called, appropriating a term that originates from Islam, the "people of the book," revering the written word. According to Jewish tradition, God is a writer, inspiring the creation of written texts. Jews were among the first to use the printing press when it was invented in the mid-fifteenth century. Written texts became turning points in Jewish history, Adam Kirsch suggests in *The People and the Books* (2016), adding that for a people who lived much of their history in diaspora, books replaced temples.

Another surprise, though it perhaps should not have been, is the number of analysts who write about traumatic loss: the death of a parent (Austin Ratner, Joan Wexler, Irene Cairo), spouse (Arlene Heyman), or child (Richard Reichbart and possibly Theodore Jacobs). The list expands if we include the loss of one's country due to political repression (Gregorio Kohon) or the loss of a patient due to suicide (Christopher Gibson). A reader might not infer that these fictional traumas were disguised *personal* traumas, but in many instances, the authors referred to these losses, if only briefly, in their nonfictional writings or in their responses to my chapters. An observation made by Chaim E. Bromberg and Lewis Aron in "Disguised Autobiography as Clinical Case Study" (2019)—"Our best theorists and contributors have mined their own minds in the creation of their theories" (707)—is no less true of disguised autobiography in fiction. Psychoanalytic novelists and short story writers recognize the many commonalities between the talking cure and the writing cure. "Rewriting personal experience as fiction," A.O. Scott observes in the *New York Times*, "can be a way of processing trauma, exacting revenge or asserting control over emotional chaos."

Still another surprise was that all of the psychoanalytic stories were written in the late twentieth or early twenty-first centuries, long after Freud created psychoanalysis. This leads to my greatest surprise: the number of analysts who began publishing fiction when they were sexagenarians, septuagenarians, or octogenarians. (One must distinguish between writing and publishing fiction: Merle Molofsky penned *Streets 1970* when she was in her 30s, but it wasn't published until more than four decades later.) Arlene Heyman, Austin Ratner, and Luke Hadge were in their 30s when their stories appeared. Julia Kristeva, Bruce Fink, and Gregorio Kohon were older, in their 50s. Thomas Ogden was in his 60s when he began his career as a novelist, as were Alan Krohn and James Herman Kleiger. Others were older: Richard Kluft, Cliff Wilkerson, Richard Reichbart, Theodore Jacobs, and Daniel Jacobs were in their 70s. Joan Wexler and Irene Cairo were octogenarians when their fiction appeared. Who knew that the expression "life begins at 80" applies to so many psychoanalytic fiction writers?

Why did most of these analysts wait so long before they began publishing novels and short stories? As I noted in the Introduction, Muriel Gardiner believed that analysts' need to preserve the privacy of their patients accounts for the scarcity of novels and memoirs, but I suspect there are other explanations. Was it because they needed lengthy life experience to write fiction? Jonathan Kellerman never would have become a novelist without first working as a psychologist; clinical training gave him a "great education in human nature," as he reported to Kristen Masters. Was it because, as they were winding down their clinical careers, they needed something to do that they hadn't done earlier in their lives? Was it because, now that they are older, they can afford to experiment with a new hobby? Was it to fulfill a dream long deferred? Was it because fiction thrives on intimations of mortality? Or was it because of the rise in self-publishing, which makes it easier to produce a book? Regardless of the reasons, psychoanalytic fiction writers are older rather than younger than most clinicians, in many cases much older, and some, such as Cliff Wilkerson, continue to write in their 90s.

Showing Authors How You Write About Them

One of the pleasures of writing about living authors is sending them a copy of the chapter about their fictional stories and inviting them to share their impressions with me. As I observe in *Psychoanalysis: An Interdisciplinary Retrospective* (2023), there are advantages and disadvantages of showing people in advance how you write about them. "The advantages include their willingness to correct factual errors, point out interpretive differences, remark on authorial intentions, and sometimes offer additional information about their work that leads to new insights." (6–7). The main disadvantage is the unconscious tendency to write puff pieces about living authors, something I have tried to avoid in this book.

Some authors did not respond to my email queries, but most did. Bruce Fink wrote that "you see things in my novels I myself do not see (the unconscious functions in all of us!)." He added, tantalizingly, "There is certainly plenty to criticize about French analytic institutes. Perhaps in the next Inspector Canal installment!" Gregorio Kohon was pleased when I wrote that, after reading *Red Parrot, Wooden Leg*, I never would have suspected he was a psychoanalyst. After writing *The Mind's Eye*, Alan Krohn did not realize until reading my discussion that the complementarity of Ivan's and Jake's personalities, when combined, leads to real psychoanalytic insight and therapeutic power. "I thought about the contrasts between them but not the idea of them complementing each other to make a whole." Arlene Heyman was surprised to discover that she had Murray Blumgarten die in her story "In Love with Murray" at age 53. "Good pick up on your part! I didn't realize I killed him off at the same age that Shepard died." Irene Cairo found it useful, as I did, to read Hope Edelman's *Motherless Daughters: The Legacy of Loss*. Until reading my discussion of *Inside Out*, she was not entirely aware of how many of the stories highlighted maternal loss. Jim Kleiger said that like others who had read *The 11th Inkblot*, I had made observations about the novel of which he was unaware.

> For example, your play on the concept of time and its metaphorical richness went beyond my conscious design. Sure, there were plenty of plump metaphors, but I appreciate how you added to the significance of time in Anton's story. I guess that's what art strives to do.

Christopher Gibson, author of *Tales from the Unconscious*, was struck by the parallels between the suicide spotters and guardian angels in "Audacities" and the iconic Frank Capra film. "I liked your creative connection with 'It's a Wonderful Life.' I had forgotten about this movie from my childhood; no doubt my unconscious has had some use for it, and you have made the connection. Thanks." The friend and colleague to whom Gibson had referred in "Audacities" was a combined figure. "My first therapist died of natural causes during the therapy; my second therapist committed suicide, thus ending the therapy; and my long analysis ended when the analyst tried to end her life." But Gibson was not yet ready to include these details in *Tales from the Unconscious*. He is now writing a new story, "The Stoned Wizard," that fictionalizes these events. Gibson added that the analyst's suicide in "The Interpreter" may be viewed as a "grave form of countertransference acting out: the suicidal therapist murders the therapy, as if to take the patient down with the analyst." I recommended that Gibson read *Who's Behind the Couch*, edited by Robert Winer and Kerry Malawista, in which analysts write about *patients'* suicides. "It's a terrible, terrible experience," admits Rosemary Balsam; "I've had students to whom it has happened" (Winer and Malawista 80). Suicide is an occupational hazard for mental health professionals. "Physicians have the highest suicide rate of any professionals," according to a 2023 survey, "and among all specialties, psychiatrists were among the second-most likely to have suicidal thoughts" (Haeffele). Of those surveyed, 12 percent reported having had suicidal thoughts, and 1 percent had attempted suicide. Perhaps most ominously, 25 percent reported that they would not seek professional help because of the fear of being reported to a medical board.

Reading my discussion of *Curious Stories of Diverse Places* was emotionally intense for Richard Reichbart, an experience for which he was not prepared. "No one else has done this, not even those who are closest to me, where the details of my writing and life are assumed without being formally articulated. I found it both containing and curative to read your discussion (even though of course it is not an analytic session). To realize that you have entered into my writings and my life to the extent you have and particularly to have framed it so clearly is a revelation."

Another writer told me, after reading my chapter, that he thought I understood him "as a person and author" better than his former analyst; even if this is an exaggeration, I appreciate the compliment. I don't believe that literary critics are "smarter" than creative writers. I've never had the courage or the talent to write fiction or poetry. I also lack the gift of metaphorical language, a talent I would kill for. I believe that it's harder to create something out of nothing, except from one's imagination, than to examine something already written.

Using richly figurative language, Jim Kleiger agreed with my conjectures about why psychoanalysts write fiction late in life:

> I am more passionate about writing fiction at this age (71) than I ever was about writing professional books, chapters, and papers. But I couldn't have done any of that without the drive and deep interest in the topics I pursued. However, missing from my professional writing was the element of joy. Writing about quirky, often damaged characters with complex inner lives full of contradictions is to nonfiction what crème brulee is to a pot roast (or vegetable stew if you're veg or vegan). They both offer sustenance, but the former is more fun to eat.

Jim Kleiger expressed another reason psychoanalysts turn to fiction late in their careers, an idea offered by Ishak Ramsy, a pioneer in child analysis at the Menninger Foundation in Topeka and the translator of Freud's writings into Arabic: "analysis is what the analyst does." At the time, Jim didn't understand what Ramsy was trying to say, but now he sees wisdom in his words.

I know I continue to practice analysis in how I write about patients in my psychological testing reports and now through creative writing. There is something deeply satisfying in thinking about characters' inner lives and struggles and then imagining the analytic exchanges between my fictional therapists and their damaged patients. I wonder if this might be true of others who no longer practice clinical analysis or therapy—to be able to continue doing "what the analyst does" through their creative writing.

A Cyberspace Friendship

As a result of his response to my query on the American Psychoanalytic Association's listserv soliciting the names of psychoanalytic fiction writers, Cliff Wilkerson and I developed a valuable email friendship. We sent each other copies of our books and shared information about our current and future writing projects along with our thoughts about old age. It is not death of the body that scares Cliff, he revealed in an email, but death of the mind—my fear, too. He had recently received a cortisone shot into both of his knees to diminish the pain of walking and decided, playfully, to title his next memoir *Now Limping Along* or perhaps *Barely Wheeling Along*. Sometimes I found myself disagreeing with his email revelations, such as his conviction that the only people interested in reading his fiction and creative nonfiction are relatives and friends. The opposite is true, in my opinion: his writings deserve a wide audience. The primary goal of his memoirs and fiction, he added, was to entertain his readers, but I believe that his writings also educate, recalling Horace's axiom about art's power to instruct and delight.

I had sent Cliff a copy of my 2012 book *Dying in Character: Memoirs on the End of Life*, and he was struck by a comment made by Lisl Marburg Goodman in her 1981 book *Death and the Creative Life: Conversations with Prominent Artists and Scientists*. Goodman concluded, based on her interviews with more than 300 people, that those who felt fulfilled in life were more accepting of death than those who felt unfulfilled. Cliff approaches death much as Goodman writes:

> to know that one is doing all that one is equipped to do, to experience life as meaningful while one is still in the midst of it, may well take the sting out of death and liberate us from the fear that inhibits most people to strive toward self-actualization in the first place. (Goodman 157)

Cliff also identified with D.W. Winnicott's wish: "Oh God! May I be alive when I die." He pointed out to me that Susan Sontag, one of the authors I discuss in *Dying in Character*, was born only 28 days before him and Philip Roth 19 days after him. After reading my discussion of Elisabeth Kübler-Ross, best remembered for her famous albeit flawed stage theory of dying, Cliff recalled that while he was working as a counselor at the Orthogenic School and finishing up his second-year training as a child and adolescent psychiatrist at the University of Chicago Medical

Center, she was one floor above him in the adult psychiatry department. "Reading about her life was interesting but upsetting. I'd not realized the distance she had taken from reality as I know it and become convinced of things like channeling, talking to Jesus, the beauty of dying, and life after death."

Reading *Dying in Character* kept "stirring up feelings and realizations" in Cliff about the end of his own life. "I don't expect you respond to all these emails," he wrote—though I did, happily—"but they may keep coming. You have only yourself to blame. You stir me up!" Continuing to revise his novel *A Bird in Flight*, written from the point of view of an aging ballerina whose granddaughter Leah has encouraged her to write a memoir, Cliff realized that he was conveying his own approach to death. He sent me the last page of *A Bird in Flight* in which the ballerina ponders how to end her story—whether it should end when she was at the height of her career or now, when she is in her 90s:

"What do I do? Stop now? Leave out everything after that first performance of *A Bird in Flight*?"

"Oh gosh, no. I don't want you to leave out a thing. You've finished this journey. Now you can embark on a new one."

"I'm afraid my next journey will be into the hereafter. No chance of writing about that."

Leah's pretty face cratered with lines of displeasure, and she said, "Don't talk like that, Grandmother. As far as I'm concerned, you'll live to be a hundred."

"Even that isn't such a long time away, Leah."

"I know. But I don't like to think about it. I will miss you so."

"And if there is an afterlife, I'll miss you until you get there. Now go—and take these pages I've written since you were here last and do your editing wonders with them."

Leah gave me a kiss on the cheek and stuck the pages I hand her into her oversized knitted purse. "Goodbye till next time, Grandmother," she said.

*

Finished writing about Leah's visit. I'm tired but happy. And relieved. I've composed a memoir to my granddaughter's satisfaction. And, to mine as well.

I'm sitting on a comfortable easy chair with my eyes closed while I enjoy imagining that this ancient Bird in Flight has settled down upon a summer's beach after having traveled far. Placing my feet on a low ottoman, soft and warm as sand, I feel satisfied.

I have finished writing of my dance through a long life.

I am content.

Now I can rest.

Reading *Dying in Character* stirred up other feelings in Cliff, including the following dream:

> Hi Jeff,
>
> I would apologize for this onslaught of words if you and *Dying in Character* weren't greatly responsible. Somewhat after my bedtime I was reading the book of death last night before retiring. I then dreamed of impending death. The part that's not your responsibility for this is that three days ago, I, in some mysterious way, blew out both knees and am hobbling around like some old man ninety.
>
> I dreamed last night that I and a companion were in this town somewhere in the mountains walking the streets together—until she disappeared. And I couldn't find her. I began to ask around for her only to find out that she was not the first to disappear. "They go in that facility up the hill there and never return," a man on the street tells me.
>
> "Never return? What is that place anyway?"
>
> "Some kind of restricted area that takes in people who get too close, and they never come out. That or they don't want to come out."
>
> The dream changes and I am prowling the outside of easily accessible grounds though they are surrounded by high walls. I don't want to get too close for fear of being taken inside. *I'm not ready to chance leaving town never to return*, I think, and start back down the hill. And awaken before I get back to town. Only sleep again and finish ten hours of sleep. Tromping up that hill to investigate a place of endless residence, assessing that strange facility and then marching back down toward town must have been exhausting.
>
> Talk about facing death!
>
> But not really being ready for it.
>
> Wary of the possibility.
>
> But not terrified.

Cliff's dream, arising from *Dying in Character*, demonstrates the hazards of reading, a phenomenon we have seen earlier. Leo, in Austen Ratner's *In the Land of the Living*, regards words and symbols as dangerous portals. For one analyst, Dawn Farber, reading Ogden's *The Hands of Gravity and Chance* was a "harrowing" experience. Reading has its hazards, though my guess is that the authors in my study would agree that *not* reading is more hazardous.

When I told Cliff that I felt bereft after completing my chapter about his memoirs and novel, an example of what might be called *postartum* depression, he thanked me and then added the following comment:

> Thank you for sending it to me. I can only say that what you sent allows me to know myself better than I did before I read it. I like your version of me as a

writer much better than the one I carry around in my head. I also didn't quite realize how transparent the novel was in regard to family history. I thought I had taken the *characteristics* of family members and created a fictional story using those characteristics. But with your eyes, you have seen what lies behind my attempts at subterfuge; I told their story even as I attempted to fictionalize it. I always came to see in my practice of psychoanalysis that the myriad of stories a patient told me I eventually began to see coalesce into one or two themes that were repeated over and over again but dressed up to take place in different places with different people: an example of Freud's idea of repetition compulsion, maybe?

Cliff Wilkerson writes memoirs and novels not only to preserve historical memory but also to imagine new memories that might have happened. The same is true, I believe, for other psychoanalytic fiction writers. Cliff writes for a future in which he will be only a memory to his readers who never had the pleasure of meeting him in person. The last stage of Erik H. Erikson's life cycle is *generativity*, the "concern for establishing and guiding the next generation" (*Identity: Youth and Crisis* 138). What better way to end one's life than inspiring future generations through the power of one's words?

Though retired, Cliff still co-teaches a course on case history writing to second year psychoanalytic candidates and co-teaches with a colleague an evening seminar about an important moment in an analysis. He continues to revise *A Bird in Flight* and *Leaving Texas*, the latter highlighting what his life might have been like if he had not left for Chicago to become a psychoanalyst: "I would have likely gone stark raving mad." I end with the following buoyant paragraph, from his September 25, 2023 email to me describing his present life:

> The warranty on my carcass has expired and I can't get any new parts, so I'm taking as good care of the machinery as I know how. I enjoy our correspondence and hope we maintain some contact until I blow a gasket, strip my gears, break my fanbelt, or freeze up my engine block. But I am still dancing and writing. These days my family, socializing, writing, and dancing are all large parts of what defines my character. So when the engine fails completely I hope it is in character with what I'm feeling now.

Works Cited

Berman, Jeffrey. *Dying in Character: Memoirs on the End of Life*. U of Massachusetts P, 2012.

Berman, Jeffrey. *Psychoanalysis: An Interdisciplinary Retrospective*. State U of New York P, 2023.

Bollas, Christopher. *The Shadow of the Object: Psychoanalysis of the Unthought Known*. Columbia UP, 1987.

Bromberg, Chaim E. and Lewis Aron. "Disguised Autobiography as Clinical Case Study." *Psychoanalytic Dialogues*, vol. 29, 2019, pp. 695–710.

Camden, Vera J., editor. *The Cambridge Companion to Literature and Psychoanalysis*. Cambridge UP, 2022.

Edelman, Hope. *Motherless Daughters: The Legacy of Loss*. Delta, 1994.

Eliot, T.S. *The Waste Land*. Boni and Liveright, 1922.

Erikson, Erik H. *Identity: Youth and Crisis*. Norton, 1968.

Farber, Dawn. "Review of *The Hands of Gravity and Chance*." *Fort Da*, vol. 23, 2017, pp. 80–87.

Goodman, Lisl Marburg. *Death and the Creative Life: Conversations with Prominent Artists and Scientists*. Springer, 1981.

Haeffele, Paige. "Psychiatrist Mental Health and Suicidality: 5 Stats to Know." *Becker's Behavioral Health*, April 4, 2023. www.beckersbehavioralhealth.com/behavioral-health-mental-health/psychiatrist-mental-health-and-suicidality-5-stats-to-know.html. Accessed January 9, 2024.

Kirsch, Adam. *The People and the Books*. Norton, 2016.

Masters, Kristin. "Jonathan Kellerman's Journey from Psychologist to Bestselling Author." blog.bookstellyouwhy.com/jonathan-kellerman-journey-from-psychologist-to-bestselling-author. Accessed February 27, 2023.

Mitrani, Judith L. *Couched in Blood*. Judith L. Mitrani, Publisher, 2021.

Scott, A.O. "The Authors Call It Fiction, but in These 2 Novels the Facts Don't Lie." *New York Times*, July 6, 2024.

Tallis, Frank. *A Death in Vienna*. Random House, 2005.

University of Chicago Medical Center. "Psychiatrists Are the Least Religious of All Physicians." September 4, 2007. www.sciencedaily.com/releases/2007/09/070903094243.htm. Accessed January 1, 2024.

Winer, Robert and Kerry L. Malawista, editors. *Who's Behind the Couch: The Heart and Mind of the Psychoanalyst*. Routledge, 2017.

Index

abandonment, pattern 205
Abbey Road (musical album) 246
Abdul (fictional character) 170–171; defeat 172
abjection 14
abortion: having, freedom 190; horror stories 191; inducing 192; receiving 191
Achilles heel, metaphor (extension) 53
Acocella, Joan 60
Adaptations (Kleiger) 36
adolescence, traumatic moment 238
Adventures of Inspector Canal, The (Fink) 69–71
Aeneid, The (reading) 126
Against Understanding (Fink) 72
agenbite of inwit 119–124
aggressor, identification with 42; usage 54–55
AIDS, death sentence 54–55
Akhtar, Salman 2
"Alan: A Self-Made Man" (Reichbart) 211
Albert Einstein College of Medicine 159
Alex Delaware (crime) series 41
Alice's Adventures in Wonderland (Carroll) 34
Allah enemies, destruction 170
alter kocker (old defecator) 169
Altizer, Thomas 22
Amado, Jorge 84
ambivalence 27–28
America America (Kazan) 196
American Psychoanalyst, The 227
American Psychoanalytic Establishment (APE) (fictional organization) 74
American Splendor (film) 120
America's Most Dangerous Psychiatrists and Psychologists (Chaudvent) (fictional publication) 63

Amherst College 92
analysis, practice (continuation) 254
Analyst as Storyteller/El Analista Como Narrador, The (Schmidt-Hellerau editor) 138
analyst office 51–54
Analyst's Ear and the Critic's Eye: Rethinking Psychoanalysis and Literature (Ogden/Ogden) 100
analytic anonymity 160
analytic neutrality 75–76
analytic styles, complementarity 53
analytic third (Ogden) 95
"Analytic Writing as a Form of Fiction" (Ogden) 92
"Anatomy of Adolescent Violence, The" (Krohn) 56
Anatomy of a Psychotic Experience (Reichbart) 200–201, 203, 209–212; surprise 210
Anderson, Robert 110
Andreas-Salomé, Lou 226
"Angry Parrot" (Milner) 87
Anna Karenina (Tolstoy) 74
anti-Freudian revisionism 13–14
Antigone 144, 218
anti-Semitism 117; sensitization 173
anxiety, feeling 160–161
Anxiety of Influence, The (Bloom) 24
aposiopesis 126
"Archaic Torso of Apollo" (Rilke) 175
Arendt, Hannah 12
Arlt, Roberto 84
Aron, Lewis 251
art creation, ruthlessness 85–86
"Article, The" (Reichbart) 209
"Artifact" (Heyman) 106–107, 110–114
artists, questions (asking role) 108

Art of the Deal, The (Trump) 66
ascetism, extremes (pathway) 180–181
"Ask Ann Landers," foreshadowing 134
Aslam, Ahmed (fictional character) 169; Jacobs creation 170; letter to deceased father 171; Mohammed shooting 171
a-sleepers 140
Aspects of the Novel (Forster) 232
Assessing Psychosis: A Clinician's Guide (Kleiger) 28
attachment development 161
Auberon, Isidore (fictional character) 120–121; idealized figure 123
Auberon, Leo (fictional character) 120–121; chronic worries 123; father/maternal grandfather idealization 123–124; Yale College attendance, desire 124
"Audacities" (Gibson) 252
Auschwitz, horrors 242
Austen, Jane 112
authority, defiance 218
Avery, Hannah (fictional character) 175–177; men problems 178; mother, absent presence 177–178

Bach, Sheldon 209
Badiou, Alain 69
Bailey, George (film character) 215
Bakan, David 17
Baldwin, James 229
Balsam, Rosemary 159–160, 253
Barbara, Dominick A. 58
Barbarica (fictional character), defense attorney strategy 205–206
Barth, Karl 22
Baruch, Marianne (fictional character) 14–15, 24
Battles of Life and Death (Hellerstein) 237
Baudelaire, Charles 19
Bauer, Carlene 24
Bazell, Josh 241–243
"Beast in the Jungle, The" (James) 227
beating fantasies 18–19
Beat the Reaper (Bazell) 241–243
Beautiful Brown Eyes and Other Stories (Wilkerson) 148
Beckett, Samuel 140
bereavement, theory 125
Bergman, Stephen 1, 3
Bernard (fictional character) 204–205; Minnesota, travels 204–205

Berryman, John 142, 167
Best Short Stories of the Year (Foley) 160
Betrayal Trauma (Freyd) 59
Bettelheim, Bruno 149, 151; work, importance 151
"Bet, The" (Chekhov) 229–230
Between Hours: A Collection of Poetry and Psychoanalysis (Akhtar) 2
Beyond Madness: Mystery and Meaning in Reflex Hallucinations (Zellinsky) 35–36
Beyond the Pleasure Principle (Freud) 18
Bhagavad Gita 22
Bick, Fanny (fictional character) 104–105
Bildungsroman 82, 120; hero 163; protagonist, overidentification 235
Bill (fictional character) 169; "Siggie" (Aslam naming) 170–171
"Bintel Brief, A" (advice column) 134–137; traditional/progressive advice, combination 135–136
Bion, Wilfred 218–219
Bird in Flight, A (Wilkerson) 255, 257
Bishop, Elizabeth 219–221
Black Sun: Depression and Melancholia (Kristeva) 12, 14, 17, 20
Blanchard, Tammy 58
"Blanche, Stella, Tennessee and Rose: The Sibling Relationship in *A Streetcar Named Desire*" (T. Jacobs) 165
Blanchot, Maurice 85
blank screen, remaining (Freud recommendation) 52
Bleuler, Eugen 27–28, 33
"Blood Audacity of It, The" (Gibson) 215
Blood Brothers: Siblings as Writers (Kiell, editor) 165
Bloom, Harold 24
Bloom, Leopold (fictional character) (guilt) 119
Bloom, Molly (fictional character) 21
Blumgarten, Murray (fictional character) 252
Boffito, Sasra 99
Bollas, Christopher 3, 98–99, 249
Bond, James (fictional character) 65
bon vivant (love of life) 71
borderline personality 109
Borromean knot 72
"both at once" 19
Bovè, Carol Mastrangelo 12–13
Bowlby, John (attachment theory) 125
Bowlby, Tessa Ann (fictional character) 44; father, interview 47; suicide attempt 47–48

Index   261

"Boxball" (Reichbart) 204
Brautigan, Richard 142
Bray, Rosemary L. 241
breakaway psychoanalytic institutes, history 76
"Breakneck Speed" (Wilkerson) 153
"Breast Biopsy" (Cairo) 220–221, 223
Breger, Louis 18
Brenner, Charles 227
Breuer, Josef 11, 28–29
Bricusse, Leslie 126
Brisbane Centre for Psychoanalytic Studies, founding 81–82
Brnwa, Pietro (fictional character) (Peter Brown) 241–243
Bromberg, Chaim E. 251
Bronfman, Earl 93; ambivalence 94; Anne, attraction 94
Brontë, Charlotte 112
Brooks, Peter 3
Brothers Karamazov, The (Dostoevsky) 191
"brothers under the skin" 166, 171–173
Bublekopf, Diane (fictional character) 61–62; credibility 62–63
Buchanan, George (fictional character) 154–155
Buddha, self-belief 20
Buddhism, goal 180
Bulletin of the Association for Psychoanalytic Medicine 227
Burden (fictional character) 113
Burgess, Anthony 189
Busch, Fredric N. 141
Butler, Grace (fictional character) 178, 184; droll humor 182–183
Buttenwieser, Paul 234, 236, 250
"By the Book" 41–42

Cairo, Irene 6, 250–252; open-mindedness 218–219
Calisher, Hortense 189
Cambridge Companion to Literature and Psychoanalysis, The (Camden) 249
Camden, Vera J. 249
Camus, Albert 141, 144
Canal, Quesjac (fictional character) 69; blackmail 73; geniality 70–71; hypotheses, generation (ability) 70; Lovett, interaction 75; neologism, enjoyment 72; pontifications 72
"Candidate's Experience Doing Research During Training, A" (Hadge) 226

"Candidate's Transference to his Supervisor, The" (fictional Levin article) 178
"Candidate Writing and Its Discontents" (Hadge) 226
Capote, Truman 229
Capra, Frank 215, 252
carceral imagination, voices 222
Carroll, Lewis 34
Casaubon, Edward 6–7
Cassullo, Gabriele 160
catastrophizer, role 220
Catcher in the Rye, The (Salinger) 162, 241
Catherine (fictional character) 96; Damien desire, awakening 96–97; Damien, marriage 97
Celan, Paul 142
Center Cannot Hold: My Journey Through Madness (Saks) 210
cerebral first analysis 210–211
Changing Notions of the Feminine: Confronting Psychoanalysts' Prejudices (Cairo) 218
"Character, Interrupted (Usefully)" (Ratner) 126
Charlie (fictional character: *Cotton Flower*) 152
Chasseguet-Smirgel, Janine 168
Chatterton, Thomas 142
Chekhov, Anton 108, 229–230
"Chekhov Was a Doctor" (T. Jacobs) 162–163
Chester (fictional character) 152–154; betrayal 154
childhood sexual abuse, repressed memory (appearance) 59
childhood sexual experience, role 217
childhood trauma, restaging 51
"Child Is Being Beaten, A" (Freud), Kristeva reinterpretation 18
Children of Psychiatrists and Other Psychotherapists (Maeder) 230
Chimeras and Other Writings (Bach) 209
Choat, Ida/Bob (fictional characters) 152
"Christian Bible" (reference) 194
Christianity, tenets (contradictions) 243–244
Christie, Agatha 66
Civilization and Its Discontents (Freud) 11, 74, 215
Cixous, Hèlene 12
Clanians: appearance 74–77; Calanians (ideological warfare) 4

Clarence (film character) 215, 216
Cleckley, Hervey M. 58
"Cleveland Son's Debt to Anny Katan and Sigmund Freud, A" (Furman) 121
Clinical Diary (Ferenczi) 229
Clinical Perspectives on Multiple Personality Disorder (Kluft) 61
Clinic, The (Kellerman) 41; childhood trauma, restaging 51; Lindquist criticism 49; revenger 47–49
clockmaking, metaphor 30
cocoon, theme 87–88
Code Name "Mary" (Gardiner) 1
"Cod's Earring, The" (Reichbart) 201–203
Colette 12
Collected Papers: Through Paediatrics to Psycho- Analysis (Winnicott) 85
collegial confidentiality, covenant 211–212
colloquial speech, usage 241–242
coming-of-age story 82
companionate marriage, term (usage) 249
competitive first analysis 210–211
Complete Letters of Sigmund Freud to Wilhelm Fliess, The 87
composition, psychology of 167
Concerning the Nature of Psychoanalysis (Kohon) 81
Confidentiality and Its Discontents: Dilemmas of Privacy in Psychotherapy (Berman) 189
Confucian wisdom, embodiment 121
Congress of Racial Equality, banning 200
Conrad, Joseph 4, 24, 43, 59
Conroy, J. Oliver 116
conscience, remorse 119–124
container-contained concept 218–219
Contemporary Freudian Society 218
Continuing Bonds: New Understandings of Grief (Klass/Silverman/Nickman) 110
Conversations at the Frontier of Dreaming (Ogden) 100
Cooper, Arnold 160
Cordelia (Shakespeare character) 130
cosmic narcissism, religio-ethical goal 23
Cotton Flower, The (Wilkerson) 5, 148, 151–154
cotton plant, roots 155
Couch, the Clinic, and the Scanner: Stories from Three Revolutionary Eras of the Mind (Hellerstein) 237
counterphobic motivation 64
Counter-Reformation, Saint Teresa (relationship) 11–12

countertransference: action 252–253; discussion (Remeikis) 192–193; problem, acknowledgement 237–238; study (T. Jacobs) 159
"Courter, The" (Rushdie) 229–230
COVID-19 pandemic: death 230; stories 245–246
Crane, Hart 142
Creating Hysteria (Acocella) 60
creative gesture 85
creative writing, love 138
Crews, Frederick 62
crime, guilt 223–224
cross-examination, usage 211
"Crystal Room, The" (Cairo), maternal loss 221–222, 224
curare, poisoning 73
Curious Stories of Diverse Places (Reichbart) 5–6, 200, 201, 203–204, 211, 253
Curtiss Psychiatric, suffering 237
Curtis, Tony 65
cyberspace, friendship 254–257
Cyrus of Magdal 244

Dakota Access oil pipeline, protest 206
Dalloway, Clarissa (fictional character) 143–144
"Dancing" (Heyman) 105, 109
Dancing with the Unconscious: The Art of Psychoanalysis and the Psychoanalysis of Art (Knafo) 131
"Danila" (Molofsky) 194–195
"Dank" (Reichbart) 202, 204, 208, 210, 211
Dark at the End of the Tunnel (Bollas) 99
dark humor, exploitation 153
Darkness Visible: A Memoir of Madness (Styron) 144, 210
David Copperfield (Dickens) 161, 219
da Vinci Staircase: Love and Turbulence in the Loire Valley (Fink) 69–71, 74
Davis, Philip 104
"Day a Billionaire Walked into My Office, The" (Hadge) 227
"Dear Abby," foreshadowing 134
death: child fears 247–248; cycle 181; defiance, powers 220; drive, energy 144; Hamlet, soliloquy 227; instinct, triumph 216; memorialization 201–202
Death and the Creative Life: Conversations with Prominent Artists and Scientists (Goodman) 254
Death by Analysis (Fink) 4, 69, 73–76

Index 263

Death in a Delphi Seminar: A Postmodern Thriller (Holland) 76
Death in Vienna, A (Tallis) 250
Death of a Salesman (Miller) 54
Decalced Carmelites, prayer (life commitment/founding) 16
declarative memory, paradox 182
Delaware, Alex (fictional character) 42–46; Weiss (fictional character), contrast 50
delusions, experience (absence) 209–210
de Niro, Robert 189
depression: impact 183; post-partum depression 145; term, usage 122
derogatory Yiddishisms 164
Derrida, Jacques 75
Descartes, René 18
Desire in Language (Kristeva) 16
desires, role 62
Desnos, Robert 84
detective fiction, popularity 249–250
Deutsch, Helene 192
Devane, Hope (fictional character) 4, 43; murder 48; personal/professional self-control, emphasis 46; perversion, definition (application) 46; prisoner-guardian transformation 46
Devil, succumbing 123
Diagnostic and Statistical Manual of Mental Disorders 60, 243
Diagnostic and Statistical Manual of Mental Disorders (DSM-III), homosexuality (inclusion) 236
Dickens, Charles 161
Dickinson, Emily 3
Diderot, Denis 12
"die Goldene Medina" 195
Discovery (Schweitzer Miller) 243–245
"Disguised Autobiography as Clinical Case Study" (Bromberg/Aron) 251
Disordered Thinking and the Rorschach (Kleiger) 28
disordered thinking, psychosis (distinction) 31
dissociative disorder, commonness 67
dissociative identity disorder 61
Distance from Home, The (D. Jacobs) 5, 92, 146, 175; autobiography 176; publication 165; spiritual power 182–184; travel/quest novel 182
Diver, Dick (fictional character) 238–239
Divided Self, The (Laing) 81
"Doctor" (Cairo) 223–224
"Doctor of the Universal Church" (Teresa Ávila), canonization/proclamation 16

dodo bird effect 34–36
domestic violence, problem 133
Donaldson, Nate (fictional character) 65
Donne, John 227
Doolittle, Hilda 226
Dora (Freud patient) 76–77
"Dostoevsky and Parricide" (Freud) 191
Dostoevsky, Fyodor 13, 16–17, 111, 191
Doyle, Conan 4
Dr. Doolittle series (Lofting) 154–155
dread 235
dream association, Freudian legacy 171
Drew, Nancy (fictional character) 65
Dreyfus Affair 117–118
Driffield, Katryn 91–92
Driven to Survive (Schmidt-Hellerau) 1–2, 138, 139
drive theory 13
Dr. Ruth 72
Dr. Z (fictional character): conditions 228–229; subversive suggestion 231
"Dr. Z." (Hadge) 228
Dubin's Lives (Malamud) 104
Dupin, Auguste (fictional character) 70
Duras, Marguerite 14
Durocher, Leo (Dodgers baseball player) 163
dybbuk: jettisoning 165; possession 136
Dying in Character: Memoirs on the End of Life (Berman) 254–256
dying, travel agents (role) 247

early trauma, restaging 45–46
Edelman, Hope 183
ego, absence 181
Ego and the Id, The (Freud) 129
Einstein, Albert (intervention) 117
Eisenbud, Jule 210–211
Elementary Textbook of Psychoanalysis (Brenner) 227
11th Inkblot, The (Kleiger) 3, 27–29, 56, 92, 252; breadth/depth 28–29; qualities, appearance 28; time, metaphor 30–31
Eliann (fictional character) 196–197; enrapture 197
Eliot, George 7, 11
Eliot, T.S. 112, 227, 249
Eluard, Paul 84
emotional life, description 20
emotional volatility 20
Enchanted Clock, The (Kristeva) 12
"Encountering the Singularities of Multiplicity: Meeting and Treating the Unique Person" (Kluft) 67

English (language), learning 181
Enigma of the Oceanic Feeling: Revisioning the Psychoanalytic Theory of Mysticism (Parsons) 22
enlightenment, seeking 181
Enter Hallee (D. Jacobs) 175
epistolary 71–72; style, difference 172; technique 82
Erikson, Erik H. 23, 257
Eros, vitality (stirring) 110
Eternity Sunrises (Milner) 87
"Even After Debunking, *Sybil* Hasn't Gone Away" (A. Jacobs) 60
excitement, creation 46
exhibitionism, acceptability 224
exilic being, voices 222
exorcism, performing 136
"Expert Opinion in the Halsman Case, The" (Freud) 118

face-to-face verbal intercourse 71–72
Fairbanks, Veronica (fictional character) 63–64; suicide attempt 63
Faith, defender 13–14
Faith of a Heretic, The (Kaufmann) 17–18
"fallen Methodist" 244
False Memory Syndrome Foundation (FMSF): Fredy/Fredy creation 59; reference 62
family members, characteristics 257
Family of Doctors, A (Hellerstein) 237, 238
Farber, Dawn 99, 256
father: alcoholism 177; counteridentification 149–150; death/loss, impact (Freud belief) 170; good father, craving 150; Halsman meditation 120; self-absorption 177; substitute 32–33
"Father Is Beaten to Death, A" (Kristeva) 18
father-son relationship, conflict 149
fears: feeling 160; role 62
Federal Witness Protection Program 241–242
Felsenthal, Julia 102–104
Female Genius (Kristeva) 12
female *jouissance*, embodiment 16
female tragedy 183
Ferenczi, Sandor 227
fiction: personal experience, rewriting 251; writing, act of resistance 83–84; writing, passion 253

fictional characters (Kristeva) 14–18
Fiction as Resistance: Samuel Shem's Writings (Berman) 3
Fielding, Henry 133
Field, Sally 58
"Fighting with Spoons: On Caretaking Rivalry Between Mothers and Daughters" (Schmidt-Hellerau) 140
Fink, Bruce 4, 69, 250, 251; Inspector Canal, narrative distance 71–72; Lacanian psychoanalysis 69; third-person narration, usage 72; wordplay, delight 74
Fires in the Dark: Healing the Unquiet Mind (Jamison) 34
first-person narrator, usage 241–242
Fitzgerald, F. Scott 238
Fixer, The (Malamud) 105
Flaherty, Alice W. 19–21
Flaubert, Gustave (injunction) 227
Fleischl-Marxow, Ernst von (Freud communication) 87
Fleiss, Wilhelm 87
Foley, Martha 160
foliot 30
Forché, Carolyn 222
"For Nikki, on Her 19th Birthday" (Reichbart) 201
Forster, E.M. 229, 232
For Whom the Bell Tolls (Hemingway) 227
Fox, Lorna Scott 12
Fragment of an Analysis of a Case of Hysteria (Freud) 76
Fragments of an Analysis with Freud (Wortis) 226
Francine (fictional character) 219, 224; rage 219–220
Frank, Arthur W. 53
Frankenstein (Shelley) 56
Free Association (Buttenwieser) 234–236
freedom, meaning 231
Free Speech Movement (Berkeley) 200
"French fried Freud" 77
Freud, Anna 54, 76
"Freudian slip" 150
Freudian thinking 13
Freud Journal, The (Andreas-Salomé) 226
Freud, Sigmund 7, 74, 76; bemusement 225; *Bhagavad Gita* immersion, warning 22; creativity, Teresa creativity (contrast) 19; Fleischl-Marxow, communication 87; Fliess communication 87;

homosexuality, pathologization (absence) 235–236; Leclercq dialogue 18–19; readers, benevolent skeptics 67; Rolland, interaction 206–207; Stekel conversation 1; thoughts, omnipotence 33–34; writings, study group (establishment) 170
Freyd, Jennifer 59
Freyd, Pamela/Peter 59
Frosch, John 231
Frost, Robert 227, 247
Furman, Robert 121
Future of an Illusion, The (Freud) 25, 216

Gamerman, Amy 141
Gardiner, Muriel 1, 251
Garner, Dwight 103
gay community, association 236
gay/lesbian analysts, training 236
Gaze of Orpheus and Other Literary Essays (Blanchot) 85
Gelber, Jack 189
Gélis, Father (murder) 244
Gélis, Giselle (fictional character) 243–245
generativity 257
Genevieve the Wayward Angel 215–216
George (fictional character) 214–215
Geschwind syndrome 20
ghosts, haunting 178
Ghosts of the Unremembered Past (Wooldridge) 109
Ghost Writer, The (Roth) 104
Giamatti, Paul 120
Gibson, Christopher 6, 213, 250, 252, 253
Gilbert, Sandra M. 35; psychiatrist, motivations 64; writing/righting wrong 193
Gilchrist, Linda (fictional character) 62; creation 65–66
Gilman, Charlotte Perkins 197
Ginsberg, Allen 88, 227
Giovanna (fictional character) 222–223; mother, merger (description) 224
Gissing, George 6
"Glory to Jesus" 163
God: alone with, ability 17; checkmating 12; communication, writing (usage) 171; divine will, facilitation 24; eye, seeing 29; love 25; mystical unity 19; transference relationship 23
Goetz, Bruno 22
"Going for Water" (Frost) 247

Goldberg, Carole 206
Golden, Harry 135
Goldstein, Daniel (fictional character) 81–82; future 88–89; language, love 84; poet identity, conflict 86
González Tuñón, Raúl 84
good father, craving 150
Goodman, Lisl Marburg 254
"Good Morning" (imagined memoir) 130–131
Good Shrink/Bad Shrink (Kluft) 64–65, 66
Google doodle 27
Gordon, Hyman 121
Gordon, Leah 121
Gordon, Norman 120–121
Gougoulis, Nicolas 91–92
"Graduate and the Analyst, The" (Hadge) 227–229
Graham, Gregory D. 1, 98
graphomania 19–21
graphorrhea 20–21
Great Psychotherapy Debate, The (Wampold/Imel) 34
Greaves, George B. 65
Greek mythology, invocation 144
Green, André 82, 85
Greenberg, Jay 145, 167
Greenson, Ralph (psychoanalyst) 65
Griffin, Fred 103
Grim Reaper, presence 103
Grossman, Lev 242
grown-ups, temper (losing) 113
guilt: feeling, torture 134; motivation 143
Gutheim, Carl 235
gynocentrism, theorizing 14

Hadge, Luke 6, 226, 250, 251; literature, love 227
Hall, Jane S. 160
hallucinations, experience (absence) 209–210
Halsman, Philippe 126; fury, defusing (impossibility) 119–120; inner monologue 119; meditation 120; sentencing/pardoning 117–118; suicidal thoughts 118–119; US arrival 117
Hamlet (Shakespeare) 249
Hamlet, soliloquy 227
Hands of Gravity and Chance, The (Ogden) 4, 92–93, 95–97, 256; parental abuse/neglect, consequences 96; reading, harrowing experience 99

Hanna Perkins Center for Child Development 121–122
Hans Loewald Award for Psychanalytic Education 91
Hanson, Jake (fictional character) 50; no-nonsense character 53; Weiss, theoretical difference (absence) 53–54
happiness, seeking 175
Hardwick, Elizabeth 227
Hardy, Thomas 11, 94, 112
"Harry from Minnesota" 204
Haskell Norman prize 91
Hassler, Patricia (fictional character) 76–77; murder 77
Hatred and Forgiveness (Kristeva) 12, 13, 14, 25
hedonism 180–181
He Had It Made (Offit) 241
Hellerstein, David 2, 3, 236, 250
Helping the Fearful Child (Kellerman) 41, 42
Hemingway, Ernest 94, 142, 227; terseness 181
heroes, power 223–224
"he said, she-said" cases 44
Heyman, Arlene 5, 102, 249–251; awards 102; fiction, drama/trauma 109; mean sentences 113; "Meet the Author" email interview 107; residency program 106; spousal loss, theme 224
Hikmet, Nazim 219, 222
"History of Multiple Personality Disorder, A" (Greaves) 65
holding environment, failure 216
Holland, Norman N. 76–77
Holmes, Sherlock (fictional character) 3–4, 70
Holocaust: specter 108–109; term, usage 193
Holtzman, Laura (fictional character), Aslam love 170–171
homoeroticism, acknowledgement (absence) 222
homophobia 236
homosexuality: pathologization, absence 235–236; sexual deviance, APA inclusion 236
Hooper-Reichbart, Paige (characterization) 210
hostility, motivation 46
"How to Become a Doctor-Writer" (Hellerstein) 237

Huang, Patrick Allan 44
Huckleberry Finn (Twain) 162
Hughes, Patricia 213
human life, timepieces (commonalities) 30
Humbert Humbert (fictional character) 150
humbition 17–18
Humboldt, Alexander von 87
Humpty-Dumpty 153
Hupka, Josef 117–118
hypergraphia 20–21
Hysteria: The Elusive Neurosis (Krohn) 50–51

iconoclastic remark 228
id (realm), darkness 17
Idövel Jobban Leszeck (song) 30, 36
I.G. Farben, history (presentation) 242
"Imaginary Gardens, Real Toads" (T. Jacobs) 162
Imel, Zac E. 34
"In Answer to a Yale College Reunion Quest for Information on My Life" (Reichbart) 212
Incredible Need to Believe, The (Kristeva) 24
"In Love with Murray" 104, 252
inner monologue, italicization 204
inner voices, communication 31–32
Inside Out: Intimate Voices (Cairo) 6, 216, 252; conclusion 224; maternal loss 219; publication 219
"Inside the War Tearing Psychoanalysis Apart: 'The Most Hatred I've Ever Seen'" (Conroy) 116
Inspector Canal novels (Fink) 69, 252
inspiratrice, role 83
Institute for Expressive Analysis 189
Institute of Psychoanalytic Training and Research 201
"Interesting Addendum, An" (Reichbart) 209
Interior Castle, The (Saint Teresa) 21
International Journal of Psychoanalysis award 91
International Society for the Study of Multiple Personality and Dissociative Disorders: guidelines, following 61–62; report 60
Interpretation of Dreams, The (Freud) 88
"Interpreter, The" (Gibson) 214, 217, 252–253
intersubjective psychoanalysis 145

In the Beginning Was Love: Psychoanalysis and Faith (Kristeva) 13
In the Land of the Living (Ratner) 5, 116, 120–124, 256; agenbit of inwit 119; foreshadowing 119–120; nonfictional rehearsal 120
"In the Waiting Room" (Bishop) 220–221
Intimacy and Separateness in Psychoanalysis (Poland) 110
"Intimacy in Writing Fiction" (Schmidt-Hellerau) 139
Intimate Revolt: The Powers and Limits of Psychoanalysis (Kristeva) 13–14
Introductory Lectures on Psycho-Analysis (Freud) 112, 196
Irigaray, Luce 12
Islamophobia, sensitization 173
Israeli-Palestinian hostilities/conflict 168, 172
Israeli-Palestinian relations, promotion 170
Is There Life Without Mother? Psychoanalysis, Biography, Creativity (Shengold) 231
It's a Wonderful Life (film) 215, 216, 252
"I Want to Read, and Write, and Learn" (Molofsky) 195–196; maternal loss 196

Jacobs, Alexandra 60
"Jacob Arlow's Office" (Hadge) 227, 229
Jacobs, Daniel 5, 92, 146, 175, 250, 251; family, writing 160–163; language, impact 182–183; mother, relationship 161; personal revelations 176; writings, literary references (impact) 162
Jacobs, Theodore 5, 92, 98, 159, 175, 184, 250, 251
James, Henry 111, 227
Jamison, Kay Redfield 34, 142, 210
Jane Eyre (Brontë) 219
Jardine, Alice 12, 14, 22
Jarrell, Randall 142
Jarrett, Melody (fictional character): deposition 63; fragility 64; Travers molestation 61
Jenny (fictional character) 201; father, seductive behavior 202
Jesus: identification 16; Mary Magdalene, relationship 243–244
Jewish beliefs, Wexler sympathy 136
Jewish Daily Forward 134
Jim Crow South, black man (existence/meaning) 204–205

Joacaria (fictional character) 87; death 88
Joan of Arc 218
Jobson, Shardae 175, 176
John Jay College of Criminal Justice 60
John of the Cross 16
joie de vivre, embodiment 70–71
Jong, Erica 104
Joplin, Janis 231
Joseph of Nazareth 244
jouissance: experience 21; Nothingness, relationship 17; pleasure principle, difference 16; sublimatory *jouissance* 19
Joyce, James 21, 119
Jude the Obscure (Hardy) 94
Judith (Biblical character) 218
Jules (fictional character), life/death (ambiguity) 142
Jump Artist, The (Ratner) 5, 116, 117–119; psychology, good/bad effects 117
Jung, Carl 3, 11, 27–28; characterization, absence 32–33; fictional Jung, magical thinking (attribution) 33; interview, description 32; message, conveyance 32; wounded healer term, formulation 53

Kaddish, lines (Bill recital) 171–172
Kafka, Franz 86, 87, 140, 160
Kantor, Shepard 5; death 103
Kaplan, Charlie (fictional character) 202, 204; ambivalence 202; death 208; embracing, delicate dance 208–209; time, tumult 208
Kappala-Ramsamy, Gemma 117
Kaputt (Malaparte) 223
Karamazov, Dimitri (fictional character) 117
Kardiner, Abram 226
karma, cycle 181
Katarina ("Kata") (fictional character) 31–32
Kaufmann, Walter 17, 33
Kazan, Elia 196
Keats, John 112, 216
keening love, awakening 125
Kellerman, Jonathan 41, 250, 251
Keloskovich, Nicolai (incarnation) 35
Kenadjian, George (fictional reader) 112
Kennedy, John F. (assassination) 98
Kennedy, Robert (assassination) 98
Kerr, John 32
Kessler, Luba 211–212
Ketcham, Katherine 60

kicsi ("small love") 31
Kiell, Norman 165
Kierkegaard, Søren 168
King, Jr., Martin Luther 200, 205; assassination 98
King, Karen Leigh 243–244
King Lear (Shakespeare) 20, 130, 211
Kings College 213
Kirkus Reviews endorsement 36
Klass, Dennis 110
kleckographia, teaching (promise) 29
Kleiger, James Herman 3, 27–28, 56, 92, 250–252; disordered thinking, psychosis (distinction) 31; epigraphs, creation 35; human life, timepieces (commonalities) 30
Kleiger, Katie 36
Kleiger, Nanette 36
Kleiger, Ralph Richard 36
Klein, Melanie 12, 76, 167, 216; theories, explanation 176; writing, effort 168
Klex (inkblot) 27
Kluchin, Abby 24
Kluft, Richard P. 4, 58, 92, 250; humiliation, approach 65; psychiatric expertise, evidence 66
Knafo, Danielle 131
Knight, Robert 231
Kohavi, Noya 91, 92, 94
Kohon, Gregorio 4, 81, 92, 250–252
Kohon, Valli Shaio 81–82
Kohut, Heinz 23; influence 34
Kosinski, Jerzy 142
Kristeva, Julia 3, 11, 181, 250, 251; disbeliever 15–16; fictional characters 14–18
Kristin, Lottie (fictional character) 106–107, 111; Burden rape 113; Levinson marriage 113–114; pregnancy 112; Ruth hatred 107–108; stepdaughter, relationship 107–108
Krohn, Alan 4, 50, 86, 143, 169, 250, 251
Kübler-Ross, Elisabeth 246–247, 254–255

"La Belle Dame sans Merci" (Keats) 112
"Labiaphobia" (Ratner) 123
Lacanian Subject, The (Fink) 70, 76
Lacan, Jacques 16, 70
Lacan to the Letter (Fink) 75
Ladder of Words (Molofsky) 189
Laing, R.D. 81

Lamour, Loral (fictional character) 73; murderous intent 73–74; psychotic break 75–76
Landers, Ann 72
Lange, Jessica 58
La Rouchefoucauld, François de 246
"Last Rites" (Cairo) 222–223, 224
latter-day multiples 60
Lawrence, D.H. 139, 167
"Lawyering 101" 66
"Lawyer, The" 211
"Lazarus" (Molofsky) 193–194
Leaving Texas (Wilkerson) 257
Leclercq, Sylvia (fictional character) 3; disbeliever 15–16; existence, independence 14; female *jouissance*, embodiment 16
Lehmann-Haupt, Christopher 241
Leigh, Vivien 65
Lenny (fictional character) 169; Aslam (fictional character) criticism 169–170; death 172; epistolary style, difference 172
lethic cathexis 144
"Let My Hands Be Magical" (Reichbart) 201
Letters of Sigmund Freud (Freud) 11
Levenson, Lawrence N. 168
Levin, Miriam (fictional character) 178–179; ambition 190–191
Levin, Paul (fictional character) 178–179
Levinson, Jake (fictional character), Lottie marriage 113–114
libidinal cathexis 144
libidinal charge 18
libido theory (Freud) 125
Lieberman, Fannie (fictional character) 132; "Bintel Brief, A" (advice column), letter (sending) 134–137; diary entries/letters 132–133; fear 133–134; feelings, torture 134; "Haunted" (name), signing 134; Marek (fictional character), marriage 135; sale 133
Liebman, Roger (fictional character) 234–235; self-absorption 237
Life Drive & Death Drive, Libido & Lethe (Schmidt-Hellerau) 138
life, miracle 221–222
Life of Teresa of Jesus, The (Saint Teresa) 21
Lile-King, Phyllis 67
"Lily" (Heyman) 111

Lindquist, Mark (*The Clinic* criticism) 49
Lindsay, John 200
Lindsay, Vachel 142
linguistic skills 69–70
Listening with the Third Ear (Reik) 31
literary erudition 69–70
literary references, impact 162
living, dead (betrayal) 119–120
Lofting, Hugh 154–155
Loftus, Elizabeth 60–62
Lolita (Nabokov) 150
Lomas de Zamora 82
Long Day's Journey into Night (O'Neill) 162
Long, Karen R. 117
"Loose Part, A" (Heyman) 114
Lord Jim (Conrad) 24, 43
"Loss, Rage, and Repetition" (Heyman) 106
"Lotta Heart" (Lottie's nickname) 113
"Loves of Her Life, The" (Heyman) 103, 109
"Love Story of J. Alfred Prufrock, The" (Eliot) 227
Lovett, Jack (fictional character) 70, 73–74; Canal, interaction 75
Loving Touches (Hellerstein) 3, 236–239
Lowry, Malcolm 142
Luis Borges, Jorge 195
lurking death 103–110
Luther, Martin 23
Lying, Despair, Jealousy, Envy, Sex, Suicide, Drugs, and the Good Life (Farber) 96
"lying on the couch" (expression) 96

Machado, Antonio 84
Mad Crazy Love (Molofsky) 189
Mad Muse (Berman) 210
Maeder, Thomas 230
magical power 215
magical thinking: fictional Jung attribution 33–34; theory (Freud) 123
magic realism 140
Make Me the Sky (Wexler) 5, 128, 131–134; coming-of-age novel 133–134
Malamud, Bernard 102, 104; Heyman friendship 110
Malaparte, Curzio 219, 223
Malawista, Kerry L. 245–248, 253
male sexuality, fear 133–134
Mallon, Thomas 104

Manchurian Candidate, The (film) 64
Manheim, Eli (fictional character) 163–164
Manheim, Jonathan (fictional character) 163; "brothers under the skin" 166; identification 165
Man, Paul de 75
Mansfield Park (Austen) 112
manuscript, shredding 143
Man Who Mistook His Wife for a Hat, The (Sacks) 231
Many Faces of Shame, The (Nathanson) 65
Martha Graham Dance Company 128–129
Mary Magdalene (Marie-Madeleine): incarnation 245; Jesus, relationship 243–244; presence, feeling 244–245
masochism, case study 19
Mason, Shirley Ardell 59; fraud, perpetuation 60
Masters, Kristin 41, 251
maternal loss 196, 219, 221–222, 224–225
Matin, Paul (fictional character) 51; appearance 54–57; Nazi memorabilia, fascination 52–53; past, conveyance 55; suicide 56
Mayakovsky, Vladimir 142
McHugh, Paul R. 60
McWilliams, Nancy 212
"Meaning of Cats, The" (Reichbart) 201
Mean Streets (film) 189
Medeiros, Hildon 84
mediocrity, dread 235
"Meeting of the New York Psychoanalytic Society" 110
Meet the Moon (Malawista) 245–248
Meixner, Karl 118–119
Melting the Darkness (Poland) 225
Memento (Schmidt-Hellerau) 5, 138, 139–141, 235; magic realism, presence 140; suicide, impact 144
Memoirs (Wolf-Man) 3–4
memories: childhood sexual abuse, repressed memory (appearance) 59; declarative memory, paradox 182; description 247; discovery 59
Memory's Eyes: A New York Oedipal Novel (Schmidt-Hellerau) 139, 144–145
memory wars: account, accuracy 63; controversies/ambiguities 61–62
men, crying (value) 211
mental illness, explanation 32–33
metafiction 140
metaphor: impossibility 84; richness 252

metaphorical language, gift (absence) 253
metaphors-metamorphoses, cascade 23–24
Metric Conversion Act 246
Metzker, Isaac 135–136
Meyer, Bernard 4
Meyer, Nicholas 4
Middlemarch (Eliot) 7, 11
Middleton, Warwick 65
Middle Way, Pemba representation 180–181
Midnight Disease: The Drive to Write, Writer's Block, and the Creative Brain (Flaherty) 19
Miller, Arthur 54
Miller, Jacques-Alain 69
Miller, Robert H. 243
Milner, Marion 4, 87–88
mind-body disorders, specialization 124
mind, death (trick playing) 117–118
Mind of Her Own: The Life of Karen Horney (Quinn) 175
Mind's Eye, The (Krohn) 4, 50, 86, 143, 169, 252; childhood trauma, restaging 51
Minnesota Multiphasic Personality Inventory (MMPI) 28
Miriam (daughter of Cyrus of Magdal) 244
"Miriam 1960" (Molofsky) 191, 193, 195, 197
Mishima, Yukio 142
misogyny, Catholic Church history 245
Missing Out (Phillips) 109
"Miss Playne and Oliver" (Gibson) 216
"Miss Rings's" (Cairo) 220
Mitchell, S. Weir 197
Molofsky, Merle 5, 189, 249–251; fiction, writing 196
Monroe, Marilyn 65
Montaigne, Michel de 239
Moralist, The (Wheelis) 2
morality, flexibility (demand) 223
Moran, Jody (fictional character) 246–247
Morton v. Mancari 206
Moser, Tilmann 226
Mosher, Paul W. 59, 189
Most Dangerous Method: The Story of Jung, Freud, and Sabina Spielrein (Kerr) 32
mother-child relationship 161
motherhood, transformation 112
motherless daughters: fear 184; traumatic loss, impact 224
Motherless Daughters: The Legacy of Loss (Edelman) 183, 252

mothers: absent presence 177–178; ambivalence 161
"Mourning and Melancholia" (Freud) 125, 215
Moving On (Wilkerson) 5, 148–151
Mrs. Dalloway (Woolf) 143–144
multiple personalities 58–61
multiple personality disorder: DSM appearance/disappearance 60; psychiatric diagnosis, proliferation 59
Murder in Byzantium (Kristeva) 12
murder mystery fans, plot (reading) 48–49
Muscadine, Reed (fictional character) 44; revenge, avowal 47; victim, self-perception 48
My Analysis with Freud (Kardiner) 226
Mystery Fiction (Rodell) 43
mysticism 3; metapsychology 17; religio-ethical goal 23
Myth of Repressed Memory, The (Loftus/Ketcham) 60
Myth of Sisyphus, The (Camus) 144

Nabokov, Vladimir 150, 162
Nagera, Humberto 54
"nameless authorial villains" 232 correct spelling of villains
narrative distance 71–72
Nathan, Debbie 60
Nathanson, Donald 65
National Psychological Association for Psychoanalysis (NPAP) 189
Native American defendants, all-white jury (impact) 205–206
Nazi memorabilia, fascination 52–53
Necessary Voices (Molofsky) 5, 189, 190–198; characters, search 198; reading 193
Negative Capability (Keats) 216
Negroes, oppression 195–196
neologism, enjoyment 72
Neuwalder, Evelyn (fictional character) 121; dirty story/double entendres 122
Neuwalder, Leonard (fictional character): death, depiction 121; idealized figure 123–124
"New Cryptics" 76
New Directions in Writing 245
New England Journal of Medicine 243
New Institute for Psychoanalytic Psychoanalysis on the Lower East Side (NIPPLES) (fictional association) 74–75

Newley, Anthony 126
New Maladies of the Soul (Kristeva) 12
New York Psychoanalytic Society & Institute 70, 210
Nickman, Steven L. 110
Nietzsche, Friedrich 2, 212, 242
"Night an Analyst Couldn't Sleep, The" (Hadge) 227, 232
"Night Call" (Heyman) 106
Night Thoughts: Reflections of a Sex Therapist (Offit) 239
Nike of Samothrace 35
Nininger, James 110
No Lost Certainties to Be Recovered (Kohon) 84, 85
"No Man Is an Island" (Donne) 227
non-Aryans: magical thinking, attribution 33
non-Aryans, readiness 33–34
nondisclosure 160
"Nothing Human" (Heyman) 108–109
"Not Like You, Pa" (Wilkerson) 148
novels: baggy monsters, metaphor 111; crafting 139

Obituary to Die For, An (Kluft) 66
Observing the Erotic Imagination (Stoller) 46
Obsession (Kellerman) 42
"oceanic experience" 206–207
O'Connor, Frank 162–163
Odetta in Babylon and the Canada Express (Kohon) 82
Odor di Murderer, Scent of a Killer (Fink) 69, 70
Odyssey, The (reading) 179
Oedipal conflicts 51, 161
Oedipal explanation, presence 107–108
Oedipal fantasies 238
Oedipal rivalry 125
Oedipal, term (avoidance) 202
Oedipal transgressions 145
Oedipal triangle 170–171
Oedipus complex (Freud) 71, 117; mentioning, mistake 118; psychological bedrock 216
Oedipus Rex (Sophocles) 249
Office of the Bureau of Indian Affairs (BIA): liaison office, occupation/arrests 205; sit-in 200
Offit, Avodah 239–241; "hotel brat" (self-naming) 240

Offit, Carrie 241
Offit, Sidney 240–241
Off the Tracks: The Derailing of Mental Health Care (Berman/Mosher) 59
Of Woman Born (Rich) 183
Ogden, Benjamin H. 100
Ogden, Thomas 4–5, 82, 91, 249–251, 256; characters, mental flow 99
Old Man and the Wolves, The (Kristeva) 12
"omnipotence of thoughts" (Freud) 119–120
On Death and Dying (Kübler-Ross) 246
O'Neill, Eugene 162, 175
On Kindness (Philips/Taylor) 19
"On My Way" (Schmidt-Hellerau) 138–139
On Not Being Able to Paint (Milner) 4, 87–88
On Private Madness (Green) 85
On Reflex Hallucinations and Related Phenomena (Rorschach) 35
"On the Question of Self-Disclosure by the Analyst: Error or Advance in Technique?" (Jacobs) 161–162
O school 151
Other-Being 19
out-of-body experiences 247
overinclusiveness 20
Oxford English Dictionary (OED), usage 246–248

pain (cause), suicide (impact) 215
Pamela or, Virtue Rewarded (Richardson) 133
paranormal, analyst belief 206–207
Paranormal Surrounds Us, The (Reichbart) 206
parental abuse/neglect, consequences 96
parents: knowledge, absence 172; loss, child psychological crisis 124
Parkes, Colin Murray 221
Parkinson's disease 131
Parsons, William B. 22–23
partial illumination, space 180
Parts Left Out, The (Ogden) 4, 92–95; parental abuse/neglect, consequences 96; psychiatric intervention 94
past: reliving, necessity 51–52; sins, haunting 119
pathological grief mechanism, description (Freud) 125
patients: boundaries, maintenance 52–53; dialogue (Reichbart) 207; memories,

discovery 59; privacy, preservation 251; students, constructive/destructive interactions (student identification) 213; therapists, interaction 213
"patriotic speed limit" 152
"Paul: The Stoic Man" (Reichbart) 211
Pavese, Cesare 84, 142, 167
Pekar, Harvey 120
Pemba Golu (fictional character) 179–182; marriage, realism (absence) 181; speech, economy 181
Pentagon Papers, publication 103
penumbra, definition 180
PEP-Web 110
Perelberg, Rosine J. 82
père- vers ("toward the father") (perverse) 15
"Persistence of Memory, The" (Ratner) 120
personal experience, rewriting 251
personal meaning, character search 198
perspectives, multiplicity 231
perversion: hostility, presence 46; Stoller definition 46
Perversion: The Erotic Form of Hatred (Stoller) 45–46
"phallic woman" 237
phallocentrism, theorizing 14
Philips, Adam 19, 82, 109, 216, 228–229
Phillips, Jay (fictional character) 64, 65
physician-assisted suicide 247
Piccolo, Michele S. 160
Picture of Dorian Gray, The (Wilde) 56
Pipolo, Tony 190
Plath, Sylvia 125, 142, 167
Playing and Reality (Winnicott) 85
pleasure principle, *jouissance* (difference) 16
plot, reading 48–49
pluralism, impact 231
Poe, Edgar Allan 76–77
poem, crafting 88
"Poem for Nicole, My Daughter" (Reichbart) 201–202
Poirot, Hercule 65, 70
Poland, Warren S. 110, 225
political motivation, interrogation 204
polysyllabic words, love 246
"Populist, The" (Reichbart) 206
Portnoy's Complaint (Roth) 163
"Portrait of the Analyst as a Young Man, A" (Hadge) 226–228, 230–232
Possessions (Kristeva) 12

Possible Profession, The (T. Jacobs) 160–162, 184
post-partum depression 145, 256–257
Pot from Shards, A (Wexler) 5, 128; candidness 131; fictional section 131
"Power of Berry Soup, The" (Reichbart) 203, 205
Powers of Horror: An Essay on Abjection (Kristeva) 12
Prabuddha Bharata ("Awakened India") 25
"Praying Mantis" (Reichbart) 206, 211
predatory men, problem 133
Prelinger, Ernst 129–130
pre-Oedipal conflicts 161
Pride and Prejudice (Austen) 247–248
Private Matters (Smith) 105
projective identification, usage 54–55, 167
Promises, Promises (Phillips) 228
Proust, Marcel 98
psychiatric diagnosis, proliferation 59
"Psychiatry and Literature: A Relational Perspective" (Shem) 1
Psychoanalysis and Buddhism (Safran) 180
"Psychoanalysis and Its Discontents" 235
Psychoanalysis and Storytelling (Brooks) 3
Psychoanalysis: An Interdisciplinary Retrospective (Berman) 3, 252
psychoanalyst/creative writer (link), storytelling (usage) 128
Psychoanalyst's Aversion to Proof, The (Ratner) 117
Psychoanalytic Credos (Salberg, editor) 167
Psychoanalytic Memoirs (Berman) 87–88, 151
Psychoanalytic Stories (Hadge) 6, 226, 227–230
psychoanalytic therapy, effectiveness 146
Psychodiagnostik (Rorschach) 28, 35
"Psychogenesis of a Case of Homosexuality in a Woman, The" (Freud) 192
Psychological Aspects of Childhood Cancer (Kellerman) 41
psychological crisis 124; inducing 237–238
"Psychological Struggles of Children in Alternate Care Setting" (Krohn) 57
psychology: good/bad effects 117; religio-ethical goal 23; self psychology, creation 34
psychology of composition 167
psychotherapy education, approach 213

"*Pucano u leda. Ne front*" 31, 33
Purloined Love, The (Fink) 69, 70, 74

quantum entanglement, awareness 194–195
Quasimodo, Salvatore 84
Question of Lay Analysis, The (Reik) 189
Quinn, Susan 175

Rabelais, François 84
Race Law Stories (Goldberg) 206
racism, sensitization 173
"Rage to Order" (Wexler) 131
Ramakrishna Order 25
Ramsy, Ishak 253
Rashomon-like family tragedy 59
Ratchbull, Elaine 215
Ratner, Austin 2, 5, 116, 250, 251, 256; father, death (impact) 117; grandparents, portrayal 121; grave truths 125–126; maternal relatives, privacy 122; prose forms, adeptness 124; stepfather failings, description (absence) 123–124
Ratner, Daniel 124
Ratner, Susan 121
"Reaction of Psychoanalysts to This Discussion of Psychosis" (Reichbart) 209
"Reader, I Married Him" (Molofsky) 195
Reading for the Plot (Brooks) 3
reading, term (usage) 229–230
reality: principle, writing (connection) 85; transcendence, desire 181
rebirth, cycle 181
Red Cross disaster 57
Red Parrot, Wooden Leg (Kohon) 4, 81, 252; conclusion 88; publication 82; reviews 89; writer dread 86; writing, vicissitudes 83
"Reflections in the Present— 50 Years Later" (Reichbart) 209
Reflections on the Aesthetic Experience (Kohon) 81, 84, 85, 87
Reformation 23
Refugee Commission 223–224
Reichbart, Richard 5, 200, 250, 251; mother, portrait 203; self-diagnosis 209–210
Reichbart, Ruth G. (death notice) 203
Reik, Theodor 31, 189
reincarnation, cycle 181
relational psychoanalysis 145
Remeikis, Gina V. 192; countertransference, discussion 192–193

"Remembering, Repeating, and Working Through" (Freud) 109
Renik, Owen 219
repetition compulsion (Freud) 257
re-reading, term (usage) 229–230
"rest cure" 197–198
revelation, absence (relationship) 17
revenge 47–49
Rheshevsky ("Shev") (fictional character) 31
Ribeiro, Wanda (fictional character) ("black goddess") 83
Rich, Adrienne 183
Richard II (Shakespeare) 215
Richardson, Samuel 133
Rilke, Rainer Maria 175
Rimbaud, Arthur 77
risk-taking, act 46
Riviere, Joan 7
Robbins, Tara S. 168
Rodberg, Leonard 103
Rodell, Marie 43
Roe v. Wade 5–6, 190
Rolland, Romain 11; Freud, interaction 206–207
Room of One's Own, A (Woolf) 107
Rorschach Assessment of Psychotic Phenomena (Kleiger) 28, 31
Rorschach, Hermann 3, 27–28; inkblot test, administering (avoidance) 35; kindness 33; psychological test 32
Rorschachiana 27
Rorschach's Inkblot Experiment and the Disturbances of the Mind (Zellinsky) 35–36
Rorschach test 27
Rosenhaus, Cara (fictional character) 163–164, 170; father, impact 163–164
Ross, Lillian 94
Roth, Philip 6, 104, 163; interview 97
Rousseaus Trauma (Schmidt-Hellerau) 138–139
Rubaiyat of Omar Khayyam, The 35
Rushdie, Salman 229
Ruth (fictional character): feelings 114; "small high-pressure front" 111

Sacks, Oliver 231
sacred texts, interpreter (Kristeva) 25
sadism, case study 19
Safran, Jeremy D. 180
Saint Teresa of Ávila: canonization (Pope Gregory XV) 16; creativity, Freud

creativity (contrast) 19; "Doctor of the Universal Church" (Pope Paul VI proclamation) 16; flesh, mortification 16–17; humbition 17–18; Kristeva passion, depth (expression) 23–24; Leclercq dialogue 18–19; mysticism 3; reality, transcendence (desire) 181; self-flagellation 16–17
Saks, Elyn 210
Salberg, Jill 167
Salinas, Pedros 84
Salinger, J.D. 162, 195
"Salman Rushdie Bird, The" (Hadge) 227
Samurai, The (Kristeva) 12
San Francisco Psychoanalytic Institute 91
Sartre, Jean-Paul 85–86, 140
satire, usage 73
Savage Spawn: Reflections on Violent Children (Kellerman) 41, 42, 44
Scarsdale, Charlie (fictional character) 148, 154–155; creation, challenges 155
Scarsdale, Ruth (fictional character) 152, 154
Scary Old Sex (Heyman) 5, 102; appearance 102–103; lurking death 103–110; moments, poignancy 110; reviews 111; sensual pleasure, portrayal 103
scenic narration, usage 133–134
Schadenfreudian 62
schizophrenia 27–28; suggestiveness 32–33
Schleifer, Mel (fictional character) 163, 168–169; "student of science" 164–165
Schmidt-Hellerau, Cordelia 1–2, 5, 138, 235, 250; prose 140
Schmidt-Hellerau, Karl 138
"Schnapps" (Reichbart) 207
Schneiderman, Stan (fictional character) 170–171; betrayal 163; "brothers under the skin" 166; father, impact 163–164; "flying trapeze style" 165
Schreiber, Flora Rheta 58; fraud, perpetuation 60
Schwartz, Alexandra 103
Schweitzer Miller, Leslie 243–245, 250
Scott, A.O. 251
Seacrest, Philip (fictional character) 43, 44
Searls, Damion 28
second-person pronoun, usage 241–242
Second World War, German town reconstruction 108–109

Secret Services, private life discussion (avoidance) 70
self-absorbed analyst, understanding 234–235
self-defeating thoughts/behavior 235
self-deprecatory admissions 149
self-destructive splits/schisms 231
self-disclosing, willingness 231
self-disclosure, value 207
self-fulfillment, seeking 175
self-hatred, feelings (result) 125
self-justifying statements, contradictions 238–239
self-loathing, feeling (torture) 134
self psychology, creation 34
self-punishment, feelings (result) 125
self-reflection, capacity 91
sensualism 180–181
sensual pleasure, portrayal 103
Sesame Hotel 241
Seven-Per-Cent Solution, The (Meyer) 4
Sexton, Anne 142, 167
sexual activity, decrease 20
Sexual Excitement (Stoller) 47
Sexual Self, The (Offit) 239, 241
sexual trauma, details (absence) 133–134
sexual victimization (description), summary (usage) 133–134
Shadow of the Object, The (Bollas) 249
Shakespeare, William (poetry, reciting) 244
Shame and Pride: Affect, Sex, and the Birth of the Self (Nathanson) 65
Shamela (Fielding) 133
Shankman, Sonia 149
Shaw, George Bernard 141
Sheherazade (fictional character) 32
Shelley, Mary 56
Shem, Samuel 1
Shengold, Leonard 231
Showalter, Elaine 103, 104
"Sidewalk Phantom" (Ratner) 120
Siegel, Fannie (Stephanie) (Frances Glenn) 132
Sigmund Freud and the Jewish Mystical Tradition (Bakan) 17
Sigourney Award 91, 159
Silberman, Phyllis S. 110
silence, examination 159–160
Sinatra, Frank 65
Sine (Gesine) (fictional character) 139–141, 235; student death 142–143; suicide fantasization 144

Index   275

Sinister Subtraction, A (Kluft) 4, 58, 83, 92; surprises 62–67
Siri Doesn't Tango (Wilkerson) 150; dark humor, exploitation 153
skipped potentials, story (writing) 145
Sklar, Dusty 102, 104
Sleepless Nights (Hardwick) 227
Smith, Irene Landsman 131
Smith, Janna Malamud 105
social justice, search/fight 204–209
social media, impact 71–72
Sollers, Philippe 12
solutions, character search 198
Sons and Lovers (Lawrence) 167–168
sons (Orthodox Judaism privileging), Wexler disapproval 136
Sontag, Susan 254
Sophocles 145
Soul Murder: The Effects of Childhood Abuse and Deprivation (Shengold) 231
Southern Christian Leadership Council, establishment 200
Speak, Memory (Nabokov) 162
"Special Type of Choice of Object Made by Men, A" (Freud) 214
Spiegel, David 61
Spiegel, Herbert 59, 61
Spinoza, Baruch 6
spousal loss, theme 224
Standard Edition (SE) (Freud) 51, 166–167, 171
status quo (destruction), art (impact) 85–86
Steinberger, Julia (fictional character) 44–45
Steingart, Joyce 210–211
Stekel, Wilhelm (Freud conversation) 1
Stempelin, Olga 27
Stevens, Wallace 131
Stewart, James 215
Still Moving On (Wilkerson) 5, 148–151
Stimmel, Barbara 146, 182
Stoller, Robert 4
Storm, Jr., Kenneth 44
storytelling, usage 129
Streetcar Named Desire, A (Williams) 167–168
Streeter, Nick (fictional character) 51
Streets 1970 (Molofsky) 189, 190, 251
"Street Songs" (Molofsky) 196
Strickman, William (fictional character) 168–169
Studies on Hysteria (Breuer) 1, 11–12

Sturges, Milo (fictional character) 42–45
Styron, William 144, 210
sublimatory *jouissance* 19
"Subway Odyssey in Trump Town" (Hadge) 227, 232
suicide 183; attempts 47–48, 63; fantasization 144; feeling (torture) 134; impact 144, 215; legacy 142–146; physician-assisted suicide 247; risk, increase 145; romanticization (Woolf) 143–144; setup, homicide (appearance) 55; spotters 215–216; survivors, emotions (experience) 172; survivors, knowledge 215; term, usage 214; types 54
summary (technique), usage 133–134
"Summer Grit" (Wilkerson) 148
Supervisory Encounter: A Guide for Teachers of Psychodynamic Psychotherapy and Psychoanalysis (T. Jacobs, et al.) 162, 175, 178
surrealism 140
Swedish Psychoanalytic Association 213
Sybil (film) 58
Sybil (Schreiber) 58
Sybil Exposed (Nathan) 60
Szilágyi, Anikó 24–25

Tales from the Unconscious (Gibson) 6, 213, 252; Audacities section 214; background 213; clinical vignettes 213; Expectations section 214; preface 216; Provocations section 214; sections 214; talking/writing cures, affirmation 216; vignettes 215–216
talkativeness 20
talking cure, affirmation 216
Talking Cure: Literary Representations of Psychoanalysis (Berman) 59, 125, 189
Tallis, Frank 250
TAP: The American Psychoanalyst (Ratner, editor) 2
Tate, Sally (fictional character) 154–155
Tavistock Clinic 91
Taylor, Barbara 19
"Teaching Professional Ethics in Psychoanalytic Institutes: Engaging the Inner Ethicist" (Molofsky) 191
Teasdale, Sara 142
Tel Quel, founding 12
Tender Is the Night (Fitzgerald) 238
Terence (Roman playwright) 108

Teresa (fictional character) 145
Teresa, My Love: An Imagined Life of the Saint of Avila (Kristeva) 3, 11, 55, 244; self-reflexiveness 12; success, limitations 24; *Young Man Luther,* theoretical/ methodological differences 23
"Termination" (Reichbart) 208, 211
Tess of the d'Urbevilles (Hardy) 11, 122
Thanatos, facing 110
Thario, L. (fictional character) 74
Their Pride and Joy (Buttenwieser) 234, 235
therapist: interpreter role 214–215; writing 203
therapy, self-disclosure (value) 207
Thigpen, Corbett H. 58
Things They Wrote: A Writing/Healing Project (Malawista, editor) 245–246
Third Girl (Christie) 66
third-person narration, usage 72
This Will Do... (Ogden) 4, 92–93, 97–100; commentary 100; complexity, depiction 98–99
Thomas, Dylan 84, 167
Thompson, Hunter S. 142
thoughts, omnipotence 33–34
Three Faces of Eve, The (Thigpen/ Cleckley) 58
time: concept, manipulation 252; metaphor 30–31
Tiresias (blind prophet) 145
titillation, charge (provocation) 133–134
Tokyo Rose (betrayal) 163
Tolstoy, Leo 111
Toole, John Kennedy 142
Totem and Taboo (Freud) 33–34
Touched with Fire: Manic Depressive Illness and the Artistic Temperament (Jamison) 142
traditional/progressive advice, combination 135–136
training analysis (conflict resolution), absence (reasons) 53
Translation and Literature 24–25
trauma-based disorders, study 60
"Trauma, Memory, and Guilt: Ari Folman's *Waltz with Bashir*" (Molofsky) 195
trauma, multigenerational telescoping 99
traumatic loss: impact 224; overcoming 183; writing, presence 250–251
Travers, Henry 215
Treblinka (Nazi death camp), reliving 52
tribalism, pluralism (impact) 231
Tribute to Freud (Doolittle) 226
Tristan, Jérôme (fictional character) 14–15
Trump, Donald 66
Try to Remember (McHugh) 60
Twain, Mark 162
"Two Charlies on the Subway" (Hadge) 227, 232
Tyrants of the Heart (Zimmerman) 119

Ulysses (Joyce) 21, 119
"Uncanny, The" (Freud) 86
uncertainties 216
unconscious body language, analysis role 162
unconscious fantasies, role 62
Understanding the Bully and Bullying: A Study of Narcissistic/Sadistic Compensation for Personal Inadequacy (Donaldson) (fictional publication) 65
Underwood, Joan (fictional character) 61; counterphobic motivation 64; new name 63–64; past, problems 63
Universidad de La Plata 81
University of Iowa Writer's Workshop 116
"Unprotected Speech" (Ratner) 116
Use of the Self, The (T. Jacobs) 159, 160, 162
"utilization reviewer," role 232

van Gogh, Vincent 229
verbal therapy, value 3
Vercelletto, Pierre 16
Vietnam War: opposition 113; veteran, portrait (Ogden) 98
Virgin Mary, identification 16
Virtual Love (Offit) 239–241
Vodomer, Marina (fictional character) 29, 36; "gypsy-witch," reference 29; marriage 32
"Voiceless Heroines: Deafened by Theory?" (Cairo) 218
vulnerable women, plight (problem) 133

"Waiting for Vermeer" (Cairo) 219–220, 224
Walesa, Lech 242
Wallace, David Foster 142, 167
Walter, Celine (fictional character): adolescence, traumatic moment 238; affair 237; obsession 239
Wambaugh, Joseph 42
Wampold, Bruce E. 34

Wanda (fictional character), pregnancy 193–194
Warren, Robert Penn 163
Waste Land, The (Eliot) 112, 249
watchmaking complications ("*le grandes complications*") 30
Way It Ends, The (T. Jacobs) 5, 92, 159–160, 168–171; *Year of Durocher*, commonality 168–169
Way of Perfection, The (Saint Teresa) 21
Wayward Angel (Genevieve) 215–216
Webster, Luke 148
Weintraub, David 122
Weisberger, Austin 121; obituary 122
Weisberger, Eleanor 121–122; radio/television guest appearances 122
Weiss, Ivan (fictional character): Achilles heel, metaphor (extension) 53; challenge 57; Delaware (fictional character), contrast 50; Hanson, theoretical difference (absence) 53–54; past, reliving (necessity) 51–52; patient boundaries, maintenance 52–53; training analysis (conflict resolution), absence (reasons) 53; wounded healer, role 53
Welles, Orson 232
Western New England Institute of Psychoanalysis, Wexler attendance 129
West, Mae (joke attribution) 72
Wexler, Joan 5, 126, 250, 251; ambivalence, overcoming 130; formal training 129–130; psychoanalysis, usage 129–130; sons (Orthodox Judaism privileging) disapproval 136
"What Are Patterns For?" (Molofsky) 196–198
"What's Race Got to Do with It?" (Goldberg) 206
Wheelis, Allen 2, 3
When Nietzsche Wept (Yalom) 28–29
*When Your Child Needs **You**: A Parents' Guide Through the Early Years* (Weisberger) 122
Who's Behind the Couch (Malawista/Winer) 245, 253
Wieseltier, Leon 20
Wilbur, Cornelia B. 58–59; fraud, perpetuation 60
Wilde, Oscar 6, 56, 195
Wilkerson, Cliff 5, 6, 128, 148, 250, 251, 253; characters, pathologization (avoidance) 154; death, approach (conveyance) 255–256; father counteridentification 149–150; father, recollection 149; unbidden memories 154–155
Wilkerson, Douglas 149
Williams, Tennessee 167, 175, 182
"Windows of New York" (Cairo) 224
Winer, Robert 245, 253
Winnicott, D.W. 85, 216, 254
wisdom, absence 136
Wolfenstein, Martha 106
Wolf-Man 3–4
Wolf-Man by the Wolf-Man, The (Freud) 4
Wolves and Sheep: Why Men Inevitably Hurt Women and What Women Can Do to Avoid It (Devane) 43
women: power, Cairo identification 218–219; voices (Jacob depiction) 177
"Wonderful Day Like Today, A" (Bricusse/Newley) 126
Woodward, Joanne 58
Wooldridge, Tom 109
Woolf, Virginia 107, 142, 229; suicide romanticization 143–144
word: diarrhea 20–21; salad 32–33
wordplay, delight 74
words, power (brutality) 225
work, meaning 177
worst-case scenarios 220
Wortis, Joseph 226
wounded healer: role 53; term, Jung formulation 53
Wounded Storyteller, The (Frank) 53
Wright, Mandy (fictional character) 44, 45
writing: celebration 21–23; cure, affirmation 216; reality principle, connection 85
writing/righting wrong 193
Writing the Talking Cure: Irvin D. Yalom and the Literature of Psychotherapy (Berman) 3
Wrongful Death (Gilbert) 35

Yalom, Irvin 3, 28–29
Year of Durocher, The (T.Jacobs) 5, 92, 159–161, 163–165, 184; chronological approach 166; debut 168; plot, care 166–167; publication 165; *Way It Ends*, commonality 168–169
Years of Apprenticeship on the Couch (Moser) 226
Yeats, William Butler 195, 227
Yellow Submarine (musical album) 246

Yellow Wallpaper, The (Perkins Gilman) 197–198
Yevtushenko, Yevgeny 84
Yiddishisms: derogatory Yiddishisms 164; usage 36, 72, 172
Young Man Luther (Erikson) 23; *Teresa, My Love* (theoretical/methodological differences) 23
Your Young Child and You (Weisberger) 121

Zamserschinder 117–118
Zellinsky, Anton (fictional character) 29–30; Aryan race, outsider status 32; illness (diagnosis/treatment), inkblot technique (avoidance) 34–35; inner voices, communication 31–32; psychiatric publications 35–36
Zimmerman, Michael 119

For Product Safety Concerns and Information please contact our EU
representative GPSR@taylorandfrancis.com
Taylor & Francis Verlag GmbH, Kaufingerstraße 24, 80331 München, Germany

www.ingramcontent.com/pod-product-compliance
Lightning Source LLC
Chambersburg PA
CBHW050530300426
44113CB00012B/2022